Twentieth-Century Chamber Music

ROUTLEDGE STUDIES IN MUSICAL GENRES
R. Larry Todd, General Editor

Keyboard Music before 1700, 2nd edition
Alexander Silbiger, Editor

Eighteenth-Century Keyboard Music, 2nd edition
Robert L. Marshall, Editor

Nineteenth-Century Piano Music, 2nd edition
R. Larry Todd, Editor

Nineteenth-Century Chamber Music
Stephen E. Hefling, Editor

Twentieth-Century Chamber Music, 2nd edition
James McCalla

Twentieth-Century Chamber Music

ROUTLEDGE STUDIES
IN MUSICAL GENRES

James McCalla

Routledge
New York and London

Published in 2003 by
Routledge
29 West 35th Street
New York, NY 10001
www.routledge-ny.com

Published in Great Britain by
Routledge
11 New Fetter Lane
London EC4P 4EE   •
www.routledge.co.uk

Routledge is an imprint of the Taylor & Francis Group.

Printed in the United States of America on acid-free paper.

10 9 8 7 6 5 4 3 2 1

Library of Congress Cataloging-in-Publication Data

McCalla, James, 1946–
    Twentieth-century chamber music / James McCalla.
      p. cm. — (Studies in musical genres and repertories)
    Includes bibliographical references (p.) and index.
    ISBN 0-4159-6695-7 (pbk)
    1. Chamber music—20th century—History and criticism. I. Title. II. Series.
ML1106.M33 2003
785'.009'04—dc20

                                                                95-39109
                                                                CIP
                                                                MN

Photo on cover of Kronos Quartet by Jay Blakesberg © 2003.
Musicians left to right: David Harrington, John Sherba, Hank Dutt, Jennifer Culp.

Contents

Preface

Even at the end of the turbulent twentieth century, the usual definition of *chamber music* seems constant and secure: music performed by a small group of players, normally numbering between two and nine, one on a part, usually without a conductor (to encourage individuality as an essential part of its collectiveness), and emphasizing subtlety and intimacy over a grandeur better realized in the symphony hall or opera house. It is impossible to posit as a requisite of chamber music either "transcendence" (over the supposed obviousness of orchestral music or opera) or "lyricism" (reflecting a love of expressive individuality). Trying to make such distinctions among Mozart's C-Major Quintet, his "Jupiter" Symphony, and virtually any of his operas, between Beethoven's Op. 131 String Quartet and his Ninth Symphony, or between Bartók's Sonata for Solo Violin and Stravinsky's *Symphony of Psalms* will leave the writer facing mind-numbing generalizations or niceties of distinction. With all that is new in the chamber music of this century, the traditional criteria still hold.

What I have attempted in this book is a synoptic study of the principal genres, techniques, and ideas (both traditional and new) of the chamber music of the twentieth century that falls into the European-American tradition usually called "Classical." I have arranged the study by topic, not by chronology, since it is these "topics"—genres, formats, general concerns, implied aesthetics—that make twentieth-century chamber music most distinctive from earlier works. Simple chronology, which is less important in the musical developments and trends of our century, would provide only an artificial and constraining structure for the works I want to discuss. A topical organization, on the other hand, allows a discussion of not just the notes but what lies behind them as well.

Thus the first chapter, an introduction to the chamber music of this century, takes up four quite different compositions: Arnold Schoenberg's *Verklarte Nacht* (*Transfigured Night*) of 1899, the First and Fourth Sonatas for Violin and Piano by Charles Ives (1902–8 and 1906–16), respectively, and Pierre Boulez's *Le marteau sans maître* of 1957. These four works introduce some of the overriding themes of this study: the use of literary narrative in what had earlier been an overwhelmingly "absolute" or "pure music" genre; the conceptions of temporality that are new with modernism; the new ensembles heard in this century, with their result-ing new timbres and timbrai combinations; and the concomitant new musical ideas.

These various threads are picked up and spun forth in the ensuing five chapters. Chapter 2 is concerned with "programmatic" chamber music, that is, chamber music that in some fashion involves an extra-musical narrative. Inherent in narrative is, again, temporality, the musi-cal creation of time (passing, past, present, or perhaps not passing, not linear). Chapter 3 continues the inquiry into music and the extramusical with a consideration of vocal chamber music. I am interested here, as with Boulez's *Marteau* in chapter 1, in the variety of relationships between musical and extramusical, between text, music, and the visual elements that come into play. How does the extramusical indeed become musical?

Chapter 4, "New Ensembles, New Works," offers a potpourri of works, for one of the central characteristics of twentieth-century cham-ber music is its refusal to privilege any single ensemble (e.g., the string quartet) as the central musical genre. In this chapter, too, I begin the process of "looping back": picking up again, from a slightly different per-spective, pieces treated in earlier chapters. Chapter 4 begins with Schoen-berg's *Pierrot lunaire* (1912), already discussed at some length in chapter 3. In that chapter, I look at *Pierrot* from its text; in chapter 4, I am more interested in its instrumental ensemble, which indeed became a modern standard as the *"Pierrot* quintet." Chapter 4 also devotes attention to two instrumental additions to chamber music in this century, percussion instruments and electronic music for "live" acoustic performers and tape. Finally, the last third of chapter 4 constitutes the beginning of a chrono-logical treatment of twentieth-century chamber music. This section takes up a number of chamber works for unique ensembles ranging from Stravinsky's 1923 Octet through the 1987 *Dream of Innocent 111* by Lee Hyla. This chronological approach is pursued further in chapters 5 and 6.

These last chapters turn to twentieth-century treatments of the two most standard chamber music genres since the late eighteenth century, the sonata and the string quartet. My thesis in chapter 5, "The Modern Sonata," is that the twentieth-century sonata is of three types, the modern "Baroque" sonata (e.g., Bartók's Sonata for Solo Violin of 1944), the modern "Classical" sonata (Prokofiev, Ravel, and Stravinsky), and the "modern" sonata (Debussy, Bartók, Poulenc, and Carter). Chapter 6 treats the string quartet, which is still central to our era, even if no longer the locus classicus that it was for chamber music from Haydn through Schoenberg. This final chapter begins with the string quartet of Maurice Ravel (1903), as an example of French "neoclassicism," and Schoenberg's

Second String Quartet (1908). It ends with recent examples by American composers and with what seems to be a sort of contemporary apotheosis brought about by a performing ensemble, the Kronos Quartet.

The initial impetus for this book I owe to William B. Goodman and Joseph Kerman. I am very grateful for their encouragement. More recent encouragement has come from Jonathan Wiener at Schirmer Books and R. Larry Todd, the general editor of Schirmer's Studies in Musical Genres and Repertories series. Their advice and assistance have been invaluable.

I owe thanks to the Music Library of SUNY Stony Brook and its former music librarian, Judith Kaufman, for essential guidance. I would also like to thank Paula Gabbard for her help. Tony Hess of the Bixler Library at Colby College and Sydnae Steinhart of the Robert K. Beckwith Music Library at Bowdoin College helped me track down a crucial bibliographical reference.

Greg Miller did yeoman's service in bibliographical research during one summer. José Ayerve did most of the work in preparing the musical examples and has generally made himself valuable during the final preparation of the manuscript; his efforts have been very welcome.

Other important comments, queries, and observations have come from Mary Thombs; the spring 1992 senior seminar at Bates College and their professor, Ann B. Scott; my colleague Elliott Schwartz; Vera Micznik; and Paul Attinello.

There came a time when I could not have gone on with this book but for the efforts and support of my erstwhile colleagues Professors Gayle Pemberton and Barbara Kaster. They have my deepest gratitude.

Finally, I must mention another former colleague, Professor Robert K. Beckwith of Bowdoin College. Bob was a particular connoisseur of both chamber music and opera of all eras. For several years before his death, our many conversations were of enormous value to me, and they afforded me great pleasure. I wish that he could have seen this book, and I miss him.

For permission to use copyrighted material for my musical examples, I am grateful to Belmont Music Publishers; Boosey & Hawkes, Inc.; the Librairie José Corti; European American Music; Lee Hyla; Peer-Southern Organization; C. E. Peters Corporation; Theodore Presser Co.; and G. Schirmer, Inc.

A Historical Introduction

One of the most accessible paths to the music of the last century is that of *chamber music*, music for small ensembles. One of the seminal developments of the new music was the move into atonality, and many composers took this step first in their chamber music. A major genre of the twentieth century, music for voice and chamber ensemble, was not unknown in earlier eras. But Arnold Schoenberg's *Pierrot lunaire* of 1912 had repercussions across Europe both in its immediate wake and for decades thereafter; indeed an important new ensemble with a great deal of repertory is the so-called "*Pierrot* quintet" or "*Pierrot* ensemble," consisting of flute, clarinet, violin, cello, and piano. In similar fashion, the neoclassic movements between World Wars I and II, the nationalist strains in musical modernism, the so-called "experimental" music of the 1950s and beyond, and recent boundary-crossing or multicultural works all are strongly represented in the chamber music of the twentieth century.

The following chapters of this study deal with these repertories synchronically—that is, across time, considering works by genre, conceptual approach, and so on, rather than diachronically, or in chronological order. Only chapter 6, on the string quartet, treats its subject chronologically. This first chapter, then, is a chronological introduction to modern chamber music, briefly treating issues, techniques, ensembles, aesthetics, and extramusical developments as they arise, and pointing to the fuller discussions later in the book.

Before World War I

Nineteenth-century Romanticism had, in music, a very long and self-conscious death. Death, indeed, had been one of the genre's central themes—not to say obsessions—since the *Lieder* of Franz Schubert (1797–1828), the lyrics of the English Romantic poets (Keats's "half in love with easeful Death," *Ode to a Nightingale*), Goethe's *Sorrows of Young Werther* (1776), and the whole repertory of Romantic tragic opera, especially Richard Wagner's *Tristan und Isolde* (1859). At the end of the nineteenth century and into the twentieth, the horrified or sardonic contemplations of death and of humanity's place in the scheme of existence were most obvious in the symphonies and songs of Gustav Mahler (1860–1911). But a new generation of composers was developing during those same years, and these younger composers—while they admired Mahler tremendously—were less interested in death than in life, especially the inner life of human beings and the emotional life of the artist.

This last trait is of course another theme central to Romanticism, which since Beethoven had seen the creative artist as an intensified and magnified example of the human species and as a martyr figure, suffering deeply as he (and the artist was almost invariably male) shows the rest of us the way to a life that is richer and more real than we otherwise could lead. Those who are unsympathetic to the Romantic attitude to life find this to be a combination of delusions of grandeur and childish self-pity. But for others, the concentrated focus on the inner life opened new vistas. And given that the years from the 1890s to the First World War were also those of Sigmund Freud's rise to prominence, the equation of emotion and meaning in life is not surprising.

Arnold Schoenberg was the first great Viennese example of this. Although death figures in some of his works, his themes in the years before 1918 were the inner emotional life of humans—often dark, haunted, twisted—and at the same time, transcendence and the achievement of rapture through love, whether spiritual, romantic, or sexual. We shall see this attainment of transcendence in his 1899 string sextet *Verklärte Nacht* (*Transfigured Night*; chapter 1) and the Second String Quartet (1908; chapters 3 and 6), which very unusually incorporates a soprano in its last two movements.

A third epoch-defining work of Schoenberg's is his *Pierrot lunaire* of 1912 (chapters 3, 4). The subject of the work, 21 poems set in three groups of 7 (Schoenberg, fascinated by numerology, also ensured that it would be published as his opus 21), is "moonstruck" Pierrot, dizzy in his raptures and terrified by his nightmares. At the same time, a number of the songs are concerned not with this erratic *commedia dell' arte* buffoon, but with "the Poet," a counterfigure to Pierrot who sometimes suffers the same raptures and tortures but who is more immediately the tormented artist and a paradigm of the modern human being.

Pierrot is a perfect example of all the characteristics that come together under the rubric of German Expressionism, an aesthetic (a less constricting word than "school") that lasted from the earliest years of the twentieth century to the First World War in music and the visual arts, and into the 1920s and beyond in film and opera (Alban Berg's *Wozzeck*, 1925, and *Lulu*, left in an incomplete state at Berg's death in 1935 and finished only forty years later by the composer Friedrich Cerha). German Expressionism includes those traits already mentioned: obsession with emotion and the ever-changing unstable flux of the individual's inner life; an often sardonic opinion of humanity in general and of our place in the universe; at the same time, a real love of people and sincere pity for their suffering in a hostile world; and a belief that the horrors can be exorcised and inner peace achieved (at least sometimes). In music, German Expressionism is marked by a move from the extreme chromaticism and tonal instability (reflecting the emotional instability) of Romantic music into atonality, sometimes referred to as contextual tonality. Works are often very brief, as with Anton Webern's op. 9 *Bagatelles* for string quartet (1913; chapter 6) or, if of greater proportions, built up of small units (*Pierrot lunaire* or Schoenberg's *5 Pieces for Orchestra* of 1909). The range of instrumental and vocal colors can be extreme, as in *Pierrot* and Webern's *Bagatelles*. As the emotions expressed are fleeting and irregular, so meter and phrases are also evanescent or unbalanced. Connections from one musical idea to the next can seem tenuous; but connections are often there, nonetheless. It is a musical style that intensifies the *moment*, not the passing of time or the creation of "architectural" works that define their own time-world. Gestures may be striking or may just glance off. Nothing seems predetermined. Much is turbulent. But often, as in Schoenberg's Second String Quartet and *Pierrot*, the music reaches transcendence or at the least a peaceful harbor.

Despite the *wagnérisme* of the late nineteenth century, the cult of Wagner's operas and aesthetic theories among many avant-garde Parisian artists, intellectuals, writers, and connoisseurs, French music did not follow the same paths as German Expressionism. Rather, French composers remained faithful to ideals of clarity, elegance, and a classicist concern for expressing communal emotions more than exploring individual psychologies. By the end of the twentieth century, musicians and writers had rejected the label "Impressionism" for the music of Debussy, Ravel, and others, since the term borrowed from painting is inexact both historically and artistically. Any traits common to Impressionist painting and Debussy's music—for example, the primacy of color, or seemingly improvisatory structures—are superficial attributes, and at this superficial level can be found in German Romanticism and Expressionism as well. Moreover, it is quite clear that Debussy's artistic tastes did not run to the Impressionists and that his principal extramusical influences came from literature, not the visual arts. For this reason, Debussy's music has recently been generally described as "Symbolist," after the contemporary movement in literature, drama, and painting. But this label also remains unsatisfactory, for late-nineteenth-century Symbolism covered a variety of works and approaches, and even at the time was not regarded as a coherent school or set of artists.

What we hear, then, in French music—especially the chamber music—of the early twentieth century is a classicizing approach, or perhaps more than one kind of classicism. There was a great vogue for subjects from ancient Greece, to include Greek-dominated areas around the

Mediterranean. This vogue gave rise to novels and poems (Flaubert, Louÿs, Mallarmé et al.), paintings (Puvis de Chavannes, lightly regarded now but esteemed as a major figure then), and music (Debussy's *Prélude à "l'Après-midi d'un Faune,"* a number of his piano preludes, *Chansons de Bilitis,* or the famous *Syrinx* for solo flute which we shall consider in chapter 2). At the same time, another principal strain in the music is the continuation of recent French classicism in the mold of Gabriel Fauré (1845–1924), "classicism" now referring to the more general aesthetic of the traditional genres and forms, clarity of thought and expression, and avoidance of German Expressionism's hothouse of individualistic emotions. The most straightforward example of this is Maurice Ravel's 1903 String Quartet (chapter 6), with a first-movement sonata form, second-movement scherzo, then slow movement and a fast, tempestuous finale. Other such absolute, classicizing works are Ravel's 1914 piano trio (chapter 5), which also includes a scherzo influenced by the Malayan *pantun,* one of many Orientalisms in French arts from the 1850s to the First World War; and Debussy's *En blanc et noir* (1915; chapter 2) and three late sonatas, for flute, viola, and harp (1915; chapter 4), cello and piano (1915), and violin and piano (1916; chapter 5).

Finally, despite what I have said about French avoidance of German Expressionist developments, they were not deaf to the novel beauties of *Pierrot lunaire.* Ravel's *3 Poèmes de Stéphane Mallarmé* and Igor Stravinsky's *3 Japanese Lyrics* (both 1913; chapter 3) are direct responses to *Pierrot,* albeit in these composers' individual languages. (Stravinsky was of course Russian. But from his arrival in France with Diaghilev's Ballet Russe through his emigration to the United States just before World War II, he was a major figure in France and greatly influenced both French and American music either directly or—like Fauré and Ravel—through the teaching, coaching, and performances of Nadia Boulanger.)

It is thus easy, but not entirely correct, to set up Germany and Austria as the locus of Expressionism and the most turbulent of new artistic developments, and France as the haven of Apollonian clarity and reserve. But such an overgeneralization denies the wide varieties of both German and French musics of the era, as it also ignores the rest of Europe and the United States. In the years preceding the First World War, Béla Bartók and Zóltan Kodály were working in Hungary, moving into new musical realms such as atonality and the opening of classical music to more pervasive and realistic elements from the folk musics of central and eastern Europe. Bartók composed the first of his epoch-defining string quartets in 1908 and the second in 1917 (both discussed in chapter 6). Both these pieces exhibit the expansion of tonality found throughout Europe and the general move toward atonality, realized differently by different composers in different countries. And both quartets exemplify also Bartók's idiosyncratic voice. Kodály's Duo for Violin and Violoncello (1914; chapter 4) is perhaps in some ways more conventional than the contemporary music of Bartók. But its very medium, the instrumentation, is very unusual; and its melodies and harmonies, certainly tonal and on the surface perhaps more immediately accessible than Schoenberg's or Webern's, are still as individual and expressive as any work of the era.

What is now called "classical" music was in the United States almost entirely European, and a very conservative and incurious Europeanism mostly in the tradition of Mendelssohn, until the last years of the nineteenth century. This was due in part to American insecurity in artistic matters, to the fact that a large number of professionals were European immigrants naturally passing on the methods and beliefs that they had learned, and to interest in such "high" art being a sign of cultural status rather than real artistic propensities. (This last characteristic is also, of course, a result of art's being primarily a private endeavor in this country, rather than receiving the substantial patronage that it had from governments, the nobility, and the church in Europe.) This situation began to change with a group of composers centered in Boston and New England: Horatio Parker, Arthur Foote, Edward MacDowell, Mrs. H. H. A. Beach (also known as Amy Marcy Beach), and others. Here was music with energy and imagination, often secure and sure of itself, if not yet with the signal "American-ness"—whatever that proves to be—that later generations have heard in the music of Charles Ives (1874–1954). The music of this generation is only now beginning to make its way into regular performances; our view of "American" music may thus change significantly in coming years.

Part of the "American-ness" in Ives's music is his use of native or folk tunes as basic material, for example in his Second String Quartet (1913; chapters 3 and 6) or the First and Fourth Violin Sonatas (1908, 1916; chapter 1). Unlike his predecessors and contemporaries, though, Ives did not straitjacket this material—or the Native American or black melodies often used by others—into a regularized European metrical and tonal framework. Ives was all for letting his materials speak for themselves, or pushing them up one against another for extramusical reasons or just to see what would happen. Very different from another figure bridging elements from the nineteenth and twentieth centuries, Walt Whitman, Ives also "contained multitudes" and had no qualms about expressing that multivocality as he saw fit. It appears not just in his use of material from other sources, but in polytonality and atonality, polymetrical passages and works, polyphony far beyond any European model because of the radical differences among the juxtaposed voices. This expansion of boundaries, or even the refusal to accept the notion of boundaries, was in his mind the mark and the mission of the artist, not the continuation of tradition for tradition's sake or simply doing things "correctly."

The catch here is that Ives was not heard at all widely until the 1950s and especially from the mid-1960s onward, when the exuberance and inclusiveness (in all senses—mixing traditions, materials, unusual instrumental combinations or uses, seeming freedom of meter and tonality, and so on) seemed to speak directly and vividly to the listeners of the time. During his own life, Ives was very generous with his work, sending out free copies of his *114 Songs*, Second Piano Sonata ("Concord, Mass., 1840–1860"; 1910–15), and its accompanying commentary *Essays before a Sonata*. But his mark on American music did not come until later, when the number of performances seemed to grow exponentially every year and when younger composers began to show signs of his influence. For many listeners and musicians of the early twentieth century, American music was not Ives, but the generation of composers who studied in Europe in the 1920s and whose work then re-emigrated to the United States as a thoroughly modern neoclassicism with distinctively "American" coloration, especially in terms of rhythm and the handling of dissonance, and in some cases (notably Aaron Copland) of texture as well. We now turn to a consideration of the varieties of neoclassicism in the interwar years.

The Inter-War Years

The years between the two world wars were seen at the time, and for some decades thereafter, as a period of bitter, unrelenting struggle between the forces of serialism, with Schoenberg as the figurehead, and neoclassicism, championed by Stravinsky. It is more useful, however, to see both these schools as variations on a single theme, the reestablishment of traditionalism and compositional control. In his magisterial *Music in the 20th Century*, William W. Austin writes of the "abyss of freedom"—the term is Stravinsky's—faced by composers loosed from the guiding framework of tonality, conventional forms, and ensembles, even from the sense of societal cohesion which music has traditionally expressed.[1] The seemingly apocalyptic bloodshed of World War I only increased the desire for the reestablishment of security and norms. In purely musical terms, the onus of unlimited choices yielded to the idea of freedom within common guidelines and procedures.

Serialists and so-called neoclassicists differed, violently and continually, on which guidelines and procedures they preferred and on the provenance they claimed for their work. Schoenberg's development of the twelve-tone method (perhaps a more fitting and less mechanistic term than "system") was a direct outgrowth of the vast expansion of chromaticism in German and Austrian tonal music and the ensuing atonality of the years prior to 1914. Serialism retains that all-inclusiveness, the theoretical equality of all twelve notes of the chromatic scale rather than the hierarchy of pitches in tonal music (tonic, dominant and leading tone, other diatonic members, non-diatonic notes). Yet this all-inclusiveness does not mean composition by random intuition: the twelve tones are organized not in another hierarchy by function but into ordered sets and subsets with which, as Schoenberg said, the artist composes with fully as much freedom as in tonal music. Moreover, Schoenberg returned to the most traditional genres and forms of tonal music, the sonata, the suite, the string quartet, the wind quintet, large-scale orchestral works, opera. We will see this in his 1936 Fourth Quartet (chapter 6).

Schoenberg's groundbreaking work was carried even further by his two closest disciples, Alban Berg and Anton Webern. For whatever reasons or mix of reasons, Berg and Webern have proved much more popular with performers and audiences; at the very least, people seem to be less afraid of their names on a program. This may in part have to do with Berg's compositional eclecticism, with sections that sound tonal or which refer directly to tonality in a very post-modern way, and to an emotional directness and openness that can be overwhelming. His *Lyric Suite* (1926; chapter 2) is an example of that, a work with a hidden personal program that is undeniably effective even for those unaware of the program's existence. For his part, Webern's music has also continued to attract musicians and listeners for his colors and the interplay of instruments and especially for his ability to convey the sense of vast landscapes with the seemingly most reduced means, William Blake's "world in a grain of sand." Webern's music is at its constructive level highly controlled, and sounds it; but when played in accordance with his indications of tempo fluctuations and dynamic range, the sense of freedom and the vibrancy are irresistible. Like Schoenberg, Berg and Webern returned to traditional forms and genres with the use of the serial method. Their uses of these traditions were, however, freer and more rhapsodic than Schoenberg's and *as forms* sound more modern than his.

Vienna, the first home of the serialists, was of course a major European cultural center, but it was Paris which was the locus of a modernism less tied to historical tradition. Before we reach Paris, however, we must note Stravinsky's *l'Histoire du soldat* (*The Soldier's Tale*, 1918; chapter 4), a music-theater piece of a particularly modern type. The work is not in any direct way a response to *Pierrot lunaire* of six years earlier, although it also features a small ensemble—clarinet, bassoon, cornet, trombone, violin, double bass, percussion—with speakers rather than *Sprechstimme* and also a story of a protagonist's frightening journey. Whereas *Pierrot* exemplifies the intense and sometimes exaggerated colors and shapes of the pre-war years, *l'Histoire* is in every way a bleaker testament to the hardships and despair of wartime. Its colors are both purer and flatter than *Pierrot*'s, its rhythms and shapes generally rawer. As in earlier works, Stravinsky appeals to folk traditions, including popular dances, rather than to the high classical tradition in which he had been trained. (In later years, Stravinsky would use such classical models for similar reworkings in his composition.) This use of folk or popular material becomes, in hands other than Stravinsky's, one of the reinvigorating strains of neoclassicism that prevented it from sinking into a slough of redundancy or failing to address its own era.

But Paris, as I have said, became the center of a continuing tradition very different in sound and approach from the classicizing works of serialism in Vienna. This French neoclassicism follows the lines laid out by Debussy and Ravel and their contemporaries, and Fauré in the preceding generation. There was also a new interest in the sounds of African-American popular music, including ragtime, blues, and such performers as the clarinet and soprano saxophone virtuoso Sidney Bechet. Darius Milhaud's sojourn in Brazil as a diplomat resulted in such works as the ballet *La Création du monde* (*The Creation of the World*, 1923). The Brazilian Heitor Villa-Lobos's series of *Bachianas Brasileiras* sought to combine the counterpoint and structures of J. S. Bach with the New World materials of Brazil. His *Bachianas Brasileiras #6* of 1938 is discussed in chapter 4. Ravel included a "blues" movement in his 1928 violin sonata, and Stravinsky wrote both a *Piano-Rag-Music* (1919) and *Rag-Time for Eleven Instruments* (1918). Yet for all their new infusions, the music retains the sounds and qualities almost invariably labeled "quintessentially French": clarity of timbre, texture, and form; wit, elegance, and charm; awareness of the darker emotions but more interest in the pleasurable ones; sensuality, whether robust, delicate, or both; an understanding that surface beauty and what the French call *décoration* (for which there is no English equivalent) do not imply shallowness of feeling or a lack of seriousness of purpose. We will see these qualities in Stravinsky's 1923 Octet (chapter 4) and his 1935 Concerto for 2 Solo Pianofortes (chapter 5). We can also find them in the work of an American composer who spent the interwar years in Paris and whose music is also full of vernacular American sounds, Virgil Thomson. His *Sonata da chiesa* (1926; chapter 4) for E-flat clarinet, D trumpet, viola, French horn, and trombone encapsulates all these traits.

The last trait of neoclassicism, and the one most commonly opposed to Viennese serialism, is one we have not yet broached, tonality. Serialism, to repeat, is a method of organizing the twelve chromatic tones both melodically and harmonically in such a way that the composer can create a coherent structure audible to the listener. The so-called neoclassicists—"so-called" because I wish here to distinguish them from the serialists in their method, not their goal—also wanted to reestablish a systemic framework which would help remove them from Stravinsky's "abyss of freedom." For this they turned to triadic tonality. (It was not a return, for triadic tonality in France and the United States had never been superseded to the degree that it had in Austria and Germany.) The catch here is that these tonal works, such as those of Stravinsky and Thomson, are still not tonal in the way that earlier music had been. The circle of fifths, for example, no longer dominates tonal hierarchies. Tonal syntax can still be fresh and new with each individual work. Theoretical analysis based on the Bach chorales and masterworks of 1750–1900, as taught in most music schools then and today, at least at the introductory and undergraduate levels, will not serve. As with the serialist approach, any sort of synthesizing analysis and theory must begin with single pieces; for the new ways of building and relating triadic harmonies are as various as composers' minds and ears. Furthermore, new means of tonal organization, neither triad-based nor serialist, gain increased importance in the years between the two world wars. We shall see this in the music of Edgard Varèse, Ruth Crawford Seeger, and Béla Bartók.

Of these three, the farthest from any earlier or contemporary tradition is Varèse. His move to the United States in 1915 was concomitant with a decision to be original, as Haydn and Ives had been before him, and few others. Varèse wrote comparatively few pieces, but each of his individual works, for *sui generis* small or large ensembles, seems a new rethinking even of the very essence of music. His piece for solo flute, *Density 21.5* (1936), was intended as a response, or even riposte, to Debussy's *Syrinx*, more suited to a modern world without Arcadian longings. *Ionisation* (1929–31), for a large percussion ensemble (13 players, 41 instruments) is a masterful and exciting use of rhythms, timbre, sound masses, and contrasts of pitched and non-pitched instruments, neither mechanistic nor minimalist, that helped begin the twentieth-century development of percussion works as virtuoso and expressive art music. We will see examples of this in John Cage's *Third Construction* (1941, chapter 4) and *Amores* (1943, also chapter 4), Elliott Carter's *8 Pieces for Solo Timpani* (1950/66, chapter 4) and, in a perhaps surprisingly more traditional work, Bartók's Sonata for Two Pianos and Percussion (1937, chapter 4). Varèse's *Octandre* (1923) is treated in chapter 4. Its unusual instrumentation—flute, clarinet, oboe, bassoon, French horn, trumpet, trombone, and double bass (eight instruments, hence the title)—and original, quasi-organic forms are worlds away from the contemporary neoclassic traditions. Both serialism and the Stravinskyan or French-dominated neoclassicism were, as we have seen, interested in the composer's control of musical materials and in reestablishing their work in a centuries-old tradition. Varèse's music, by contrast, seems self-generated, although of course the gestures and forms are finely calibrated by the composer. But the ear must be recalibrated as well. Varèse is not heard as often as the impact and the worth of his music warrant. The unusual instrumentation is one factor in this—no ready-made ensemble exists for his work, as does for the string quartet, the standard orchestra, even the new standard "*Pierrot* quintet." But the music's adamant refusal to be subsumed into any common tradition is another factor; for it requires an openness to listen and respond to it. The lack of conventional guideposts and the insistence on a message that is new have worked against its moving into the musical mainstream.

Much the same could be said of Ruth Crawford Seeger's music, if for somewhat different reasons. Her best-known composition by far is the 1931 String Quartet (chapter 6), a piece that could be seen as part of an Ives-Copland-Carter tradition (if in fact that could even be thought of as a "tradition") but which is still fiercely independent and original. In this quartet, the four instruments move from radical individualism based on distinguishing musical characterizations and dissonant polyphony to unified anguished clusters and finally a sort of call-and-response duet between the first violin and the three lower strings. Because of its concentrated intensity and brevity, the Quartet stands in stark contrast to others in the genre, with their closer adhesion to historical traditions and their quasi-Beethovenian control of detail within an expansive time span. The Quartet also stands apart among American works of the period precisely because of its individualist voice, vastly different from the self-consciously nationalistic or folk tonalities of, say, Copland, Gershwin, Thomson, or other contemporaries. But the work has achieved real standing among twentieth-century string quartets, if not the repertory status of the Bartók and Shostakovich quartets, as Crawford's other works have not.

Finally, the music of Béla Bartók. His six string quartets (1908, 1917, 1927, 1928, 1934, 1939) are the most noted cycle of the twentieth century, approached in this distinction only by those of Shostakovich. The quartets are treated as a group in some detail in chapter 6. In addition, Bartók's First Violin Sonata (1921, chapter 5), Sonata for Two Pianos and Percussion (1937, chapter 4), *Contrasts* for violin, clarinet, and piano, commissioned by the American clarinetist Benny Goodman (1938, chapter 4), and the Sonata for Solo Violin (1944, chapter 5) round out both the overview of chamber music between the two world wars and Bartók's own compositional development.

The earlier among these works—the violin and piano sonata of 1921 and the first three quartets—testify to the variety, intensity, and individuality of works composed from the beginning of the century's second decade into the 1920s. There is no fear of dissonance or percussiveness, nor of idiosyncratic formal procedures. Moreover, the works begin to absorb characteristics from local ethnic or folk traditions, as had Ives's works, Stravinsky's *l'Histoire*, or French music using African-American elements. Beginning with the Fourth Quartet, though, the widely varying elements begin to fuse into Bartók's own final language. As with the other music of his time, clarity in at least one musical parameter (e.g., formal construction) allows wide freedom elsewhere (e.g., tonality or the treatment of dissonance). Newer sounds inhabit their surroundings with more ease, so that—for example in the Fourth and Fifth Quartets and the Sonata for Two Pianos and Percussion—we hear distinctly untraditional melodies, modes, and/or rhythms developing in structures which would have been immediately comprehensible to Haydn or Beethoven. This version of neo-classicism bears a family resemblance—the formal profile—to such serialist works as Schoenberg's Third and Fourth Quartets or Webern's compositions, and more superficially to Stravinsky's music or—very distantly—such a self-consciously "modernist" piece as Prokofiev's flute sonata. But this language, if not without resonance later in the century, for example in the music of George Crumb, and like the languages of the other great composers, died with Bartók in 1945. Except for a conservative strain, especially in the United States, the music which arose after World War II was vastly different from almost all that had preceded it in the twentieth century.

From 1945 to the 1960s

A striking change in new music after 1945 was its move into the academy. As one of the four elements of the medieval quadrivium, the study of music theory and then history had long been one of the university's liberal arts. Musicology became a rigorous academic discipline in the nineteenth century, first in German-speaking Europe and then elsewhere, and of course composition had always been part of every conservatory's program. There were composers on the faculties of such universities as Harvard, Yale, and the University of California at Berkeley early on. But these last programs were not necessarily intended to train professional musicians, but rather still to include the study of music in a more general liberal-arts program.

After 1945, however, an energetic new generation of young composers such as Elliott Carter and Roger Sessions moved into music departments of the best American research universities, and in this highly charged environment began to develop compositional methods and modes of musical understanding that moved beyond traditional theory into what has been called "post-Webernian" ways, concentrating on motivic manipulation and development and transferring such approaches to musical elements (or parameters) other than pitch. Similar developments occurred simultaneously in Europe, less in universities than through government subsidies to musical organizations (e.g., radio stations or orchestras) and to individual composers.

Discussion of the theoretical researches in such think-tank atmospheres lies outside the scope of this study. What need to be remarked upon, though, are the common beliefs that new music is no longer music but mathematics, that composers have only contempt for lay audiences, and that modern lovers of classical music have nothing left to listen to. Yet in a fascinating and much-needed study, Joseph N. Straus has demonstrated that in fact these music departments were overwhelmingly staffed and administered by composers of conservative bent, whose own music was often tonal and neoclassical.[2] What seems to have happened is that audiences, often led by hostile critics and writers, have tarred much modern music with the same brush and turned deaf ears to all of it because they dislike or disagree with some of it. There are also composers highly resentful of "the academy"–music departments in universities here likened to a dictatorial and elitist cabal—because their own music is of a different stripe but is still commonly castigated as "modern," in music as in no other art a label of rejection. And as we shall see in chapter 4, composers such as Milton Babbitt have also reacted with some bitterness at such summary and willful incomprehension.

The academic war drums may be fading, although too often audiences (and too many critics) are still ready to dismiss new music without listening to it seriously. And since 1968 there has been a trend usually called the New Romanticism, supposedly a turn away from the perceived hyperintellectualism of "the academy," but at the same time simply a new or more widely noticed resurgence of older traditions. In the last decade or so of the twentieth century, composers and performers have also brought into classical music the fruits of their interest and experience in rock, jazz, and world musics. We shall see examples of this in works by Lee Hyla and Steven Mackey (chapter 4) and those created as part of cellist Yo-Yo Ma's "Silk Road Project" (also chapter 4). But first we need to turn to the new music of the World War II years and the twenty years following—Elliott Carter, Milton Babbitt, and the very unacademic John Cage in the United States; Olivier Messiaen, Pierre Boulez, Luciano Berio, Karlheinz Stockhausen, and others in Europe; and some very late works of Stravinsky and Stefan Wolpe. In many ways much of this music was qualitatively new. But virtually none of it is without direct ties to earlier musics of the twentieth century or before. There is much to hear.

Let us begin with the supposedly academic, or think-tank, composers in the United States. It is certainly true that many of these men—for composition in the mid-twentieth century was undoubtedly dominated by men—were interested in theoretical matters and wrote exploratory, descriptive, and/or prescriptive articles in technical language far beyond the capacities of most non-professionals. This needs no apologies, and it follows in many ways the traditions of music theory back to the Middle Ages and beyond. Nor is their theoretical bent a charge of scholasticism to be leveled at Milton Babbitt, Elliott Carter, George Perle, Roger Sessions et al., for when they turn to compose they (like all good composers) are entirely focused on music, and the manipulation of musical materials to make their statements and to create aesthetically and emotionally satisfying works of art. Carter and Babbitt are in many ways representative of 1950s and 1960s American music, different as they are from each other. Babbitt's music is full of wit and sparkle at the same time as it entails the most intricate and virtuosic demands on his performers. As can be heard in his 1957 *All Set* for alto and tenor saxophones, trumpet, trombone, piano, vibes, bass, and percussion (chapter 4), rhythm at every level is one of the most forceful elements of Babbitt's music, equal to the interplay of voices and lines. Like Brahms, Babbitt's surfaces can be quite dense with the interplay of related motives, and seem forbidding. But like earlier American and some European composers, there is also a directness and charm to Babbitt's music that invite the listener to delve more deeply and hear more broadly.

Elliott Carter's music is also widely noted for its seemingly difficult access, but here again concentration on its technical intricacies can lead one to miss its emotive core. As with Babbitt, Carter is noted for the importance of his rhythmic structures and methods, at every level of the composition. (This attention to rhythm seems, for whatever reasons, to be a principal factor in the music of a great many composers of both North and South America, much more so than composers from Europe or Asia.) And Carter is of course widely known for his technique of metric modulation, a shift in meter and tempo analogous to common-chord modulation to change keys. But we can also hear this seeming preeminence of rhythm as actually just one of the elements that make Carter's music so strongly gestural and almost literally of dramatic characterization. By his own account, Carter began to move in this direction—to find and develop what he believed to be his own true and individual voice—after World War II, and we shall hear this in his 1948 Sonata for Violoncello and Piano (chapters 2 and 5), which has become almost a repertory staple, and the first two of his five (as of this writing) string quartets (1951, 1959; chapters 2 and 6).

We can also mention in passing here the late works of Igor Stravinsky, in many ways very far removed from the first work of his treated in this study, the 1914 *Three Pieces for String Quartet*. From the late 1940s to the end of his life, Stravinsky moved to a quasi-serialist style that still, however, reflects some predilections of his earlier years: a taste for small musical modules that lend themselves to manipulation; a spareness in texture reflecting the sounds of High Modernism, especially in France and the United States; striking rhythmic invention; and idiosyncratic writing for standard instruments. These elements, and others, are evident in his *l'Histoire du soldat*, the Octet, the Concerto for Two Solo Pianofortes, and other works. We shall hear them again in two late vocal works, the 1953 *Three Songs from William Shakespeare* for voice, flute, clarinet, and viola, and the 1954 *In Memoriam Dylan Thomas*, for tenor, four trombones, and string quartet (both in chapter 3).

Staking out his own path even more radically than Carter was John Cage. Cage is a much more diverse composer than he is usually credited as being: he has had a popular reputation as a rather loopy, anything-goes free spirit, when in fact he was a man who thought deeply about music and its relationship to the rest of life, whose philosophy was certainly as nuanced as that of Schoenberg (to choose just one example), and whose music-making was always carefully considered and based on concrete experience. The early works for which Cage is still known are those for extended instruments, especially the prepared piano, percussion ensemble, and works involving recordings or tapes. From the late 1940s on, Cage had become interested in Zen Buddhism and studied with the philosopher and teacher D. T. Suzuki. This led him to consider, as many composers and musicians have done, the relationship of music to the world we (and it) live in. The question is again, if narrowly phrased, one of control. Cage's conclusions were far different from those of other composers: he believed in the primacy of sounds for their own sake over their deliberate, reductive, or architectonic manipulation, and wanted to avoid what he felt was the ego-laden aesthetic of Western composition. Cage thus developed a number of methods which would prevent his own personal predilections from determining the course, even the specific content, of his pieces, for instance the I Ching (the Chinese Book of Changes) or star maps. In some of his works, such as the 1958 *Aria* (chapter 3), the performer follows the score's directions, although some elements of the performance will still be left to his or her choice. In other pieces, for example the *Solo for Voice II*, the performer creates his or her own score using materials such as cellophane overlays to indicate register of sounds, their relative duration, and especially the ratio of sound to silence.

Cage's influence has been enormous, especially in the field of performance art, but also in the visual arts and modern dance. One question that remains unresolved for many musicians, however, is the relation of his pieces to the audience. To perform a Cage work takes as much concentration and often as much preparation as a work by a more traditional composer. It also entails a conscious (but, paradoxically, not a self-conscious) effort to enter into the work's aesthetic, to refrain from imposing one's own personal predilections on this performance of sounds. Yet, Cage's works are meant to be performed, and no performer is expected to extinguish his or her charisma or command of the stage; indeed, the works encourage a kind of joyful participation in their creation that is quite unlike the performance of fully worked and notated music. But many audiences feel alienated because the listeners do not share in the expectations of the music's creators, Cage and his performers. The vast majority of music in the Western art tradition entails a "narrative" arc, a sense of logical coherence and continuity that simply is not a factor in Cage's music; so audiences sometimes wonder what their role in the work is. It is not easily resolved. Apperception and appreciation of sounds and gestures is a first step, as is the pleasure shared with the performer. The harder step seems to be willingness to suspend one's expectations that in music, things must happen—not only that there must be the sounds and immediate usage of sounds (melodies, regular meter, conventional use of instruments, and so on) that we are used to, but moreover that each musical event must imply and be followed by certain other events, and that these will eventually become a sort of space-time edifice which will convey some extramusical meaning to us. The way out of this dilemma is to delete the word "must." In Cage's music, things happen, often a lot of things. But it is not the purpose of music, for him, to make those things, those sounds, into something which they are not. This is not in the least to say that Cage's music means nothing; but one must remember that it is what it is.

During these same post-war years, the new-music culture in Europe was both more conceptually thorough and unified than in the United States; but also from the mid-1950s on, the leading composers were more open to simultaneous use of a wider variety of influences or methods. The basic issues were, as so often in the music of the twentieth century, compositional control and the relationship of composer to performer. Post-serial, or more precisely post-Webern serialist, methods sometimes yield to and sometimes coexist with aleatoric techniques. Some works follow "abstract" or "absolute music" traditions, others address the contemporary situation of a continent devastated by World War II. Despite the different national traditions that one can hear in the music of Berio, Messiaen and Boulez, Stockhausen, Ligeti, and many others, their music still somehow seems to present a more cohesive collective profile than does the music of their American contemporaries.

Chronologically the first in this cavalcade is Olivier Messiaen, whose 1941 *Quartet for the End of Time* (chapters 2 and 4), written in a German POW camp, shows much of its era and much that is to come: a product of Messiaen's deep religious faith, it uses his rhythmic researches and idiosyncratic harmonic language, his melodies imitative of bird calls, and in the first movement ("Crystal Liturgy") a use of simultaneous but non-synchronized pedals in harmony, melody, and rhythm that points forward to the total serialism of the late 1940s and early 1950s. Messiaen continued along this path in his *4 Rhythmic Etudes* for solo piano of 1949–50 and (with many other rhythmic explorations) his 1944 treatise *The Technique of My Musical Language*. He was followed by Boulez, Stockhausen, and others, but these younger composers also found in the music of Webern an organizing principle that seemed to coordinate macrostructure and microstructure and ensure maximum internal motivic coherence—a tendency of Western music since Beethoven, or even J. S. Bach—an approach to music that emphasizes music's absolute identity with its materials (a very Modernist goal) but also seems to guarantee the unquestioned predominance of the composer as music's maker, with no messy loose ends or inconsistent elements.

But this was a path that soon enough proved not very interesting, for a variety of reasons. It was noticed, once European composers began to be aware of the work of John Cage, David Tudor, and others, that a totally organized work of music sounds indistinguishable—in terms of its materials and structuring processes—from an aleatoric one. The music also soon moved beyond the limits of human performance, even in that era of extraordinary virtuosity, and composers realized that they could turn to the electronic studio and gain the complete control not possible with live performance, as well as the new sound universe that tape manipulation opened to them. In addition, from the early to mid-1950s, Boulez and other leading European composers were very much aware of John Cage and his philosophy and techniques, a new path toward freedom that did not recall the sounds of earlier, discarded methods. And it may well be that with the success of the new music over that of pre-World War II composers—the younger composers were supported by European governments to an extent absolutely unimaginable in the United States, and had frequent performances over government-owned radio stations—they were able to relax their search for dominance (of their musical materials and procedures, as well as of the general European musical scene) and allow their various heritages (French, German, Italian, Hungarian, and so on) and individual predilections to inform their music more tellingly again. We will see all this in the pages that follow with Luciano Berio's 1953 *Chamber Music* on poems of James Joyce, for voice, clarinet, cello, and harp (chapter 3), *Circles* for voice, harp, and two percussionists (1960; chapter 3), and *Sequenza III* for solo voice (1965; chapter 3); Pierre Boulez's seminal masterwork *Le marteau sans maître* on poems of René Char (1957; chapter 1); Karlheinz Stockhausen's *Zyklus* (1957; chapter 4) for solo percussion and *Stimmung* (1968; chapter 3) for six amplified and electronically manipulated live singers; György Ligeti's 1962 *Aventures* for three singers and seven instrumentalists (chapter 3); and Stefan Wolpe's 1964 *Piece in Two Parts for Solo Violin* and *Solo Piece for Trumpet* (both in chapter 4).

The Late 20th Century

Music seems to have changed again in the late 1960s and early 1970s, as the post-World War II generation (Carter, Babbitt, Boulez, Stockhausen, and the rest) achieved iconic status in the world of contemporary music, the last of the older generations (e.g., Stravinsky) passed away, and a new group of composers born after World War II came to maturity. In addition, of course, many people thought that not just music, but the entire world was changing in those turbulent years. Trying to sum up the present and recent past is always stepping onto a historical minefield, so there will be few—if any—pronouncements about the ultimate meaning of chamber music in the last 30 years. Instead, we will simply survey what seem to be a few representative trends among the younger generation of composers.

As I have noted above, the era since 1968 has been called one of "the New Romanticism," the label first applied to the present scene by the composer Jacob Druckman. But this seems to me to ignore the strain of "Romantic" music that was ever present in the twentieth century. If "Romantic" is taken to mean melodic, "expressive" in a traditional and personal sense, grateful to both performer and audience, more easily apprehended, then there are many good composers who have written well-crafted and beautiful music: Samuel Barber, Ned Rorem, William Grant Still, John Corigliano, back to such modernist luminaries as Schoenberg and Ives. The label also ignores the deeply expressive works, "difficult" as they might be, of Carter, Babbitt, and George Perle, among many others. The label "New Romanticism" thus does not seem to me to be very useful; but I am not going to suggest any other to take its place.

What we see in "classical" music from the 1970s on appears to be a loosening of expectations which a composer is expected to meet. Few systemic requirements seem to exist, and certainly no overriding style or method of composition. This is not to say that there is no longer any aesthetic standard, for new pieces are still expected to have something to say, as the phrase has it, to communicate with an audience and to do that coherently and engagingly. But there now seem to be many paths to that goal. There is no "International Style" in the music of the late twentieth century, as there had been in architecture, and in music between the wars or, perhaps, in the first decades after World War II.

One of the contemporary-sounding developments of music in the last third of the century has been an openness to non-classical musics. I say "contemporary-sounding" because of course this was also a striking element in Stravinsky's *L'Histoire du soldat*, many of Ives's works, Bartók's use of Eastern European folk rhythms and scales, the French and then American adoptions of certain jazz elements in the 1920s and 1930s, and so on. But one can still not deny the immediacy of such multicultural elements, especially in the truly new contexts in which composers placed them. George Crumb's *Ancient Voices of Children* (1970; chapter 3) uses sounds from his native Appalachia and references to Gustav Mahler in his settings of poems by Federico García Lorca, and his *Black Angels* (also 1970; chapter 6) for amplified string quartet, a work very much in response to the Vietnam War then raging, uses newly composed "old" music and the melody of Schubert's "Death and the Maiden," as well as numbers chanted in various languages.

As with the Schubert in *Black Angels*, many contemporary composers have also mined earlier repertories and "re-set," as it were, older musics in a new context. Our examples here will include Barbara Kolb's 1971 *Solitaire* (chapter 4) for solo piano and recorded piano, a sort of meditation on performance and on music, and Joan Tower's *Petrouchskates* (1980; chapter 4), a lovely piece in which the composer combined her love of Olympic ice skating with music and mood adapted from Stravinsky's 1911 ballet *Petrouchka*. Other composers have incorporated the popular or vernacular musics they grew up with—rock, jazz, blues, funk—into their new classical compositions. Steven Mackey has a solid and highly respected place in academia (in his case, Princeton University) but uses his past as a rock guitarist both in his compositions—although not necessarily directly in his String Quartet of 1983 (chapter 6)—and as a performer, since he has toured with the Kronos Quartet and composed works for himself as guitarist. Lee Hyla has a particularly wide-ranging musical background as listener and pianist, and has combined an extraordinary variety of musics into a cohesive, expressive, and very compelling individual style, as will be seen in his Second String Quartet (1985; chapter 6) and *The Dream of Innocent III* (1987; chapter 4) for amplified cello, piano, and percussion.

Use of electronic amplification will be noted in the examples above, and in the 1970s there was also quite a spate of music for pre-recorded tape and live performance, for example Mario Davidovsky's series of *Synchronisms* (chapter 4). With the development of far more flexible and responsive electronic and computer methodologies, this trend continued in the work of many younger composers, but also in the late works of John Cage.

A last "new" development to be mentioned here is works deeply influenced by Asian musics or philosophies. This, too, has a history going back through the twentieth century and beyond, from French infatuation with Asian sounds after the 1889 Paris Exposition, through the work of Colin McPhee in the 1930s and John Cage and other West Coast composers from the 1930s and 1940s on. But there seems to be a new interest in very recent years, as well as new awareness of Asian composers influenced by Western classical music. One example of this is the "Silk Road Project" initiated by the cellist Yo-Yo Ma, which we will examine briefly in chapter 4.

Thus, if one can make any sort of generalization about the most recent chamber music, it would seem to be an openness to the world, in every sense—geographical, historical, traditional, across genres and decades—and an eagerness to join those worlds, across boundaries. We may be in an era of increasing synthesis, although the mainstream of classical music has not approached the inclusiveness of world beat music, or similar trends in the "popular" musical world. But even with as traditional a genre as the string quartet, when one goes to a concert these days, one cannot be sure what one is going to hear. That is new, and very exciting.

So, given the preceding pages as a historical introduction to and overview of the chamber music of the twentieth century, let us now turn to specifics. We will resume the historical approach to a certain degree in chapter 5 (on the sonata) and chapter 6 (the string quartet). But history becomes very fluid in the twentieth century, and before we return to chronology, there are many other interesting aspects to investigate.

Notes

1. William W. Austin, *Music in the 20th Century* (New York: W. W. Norton, 1966), p. 33 et passim.
2. Joseph N. Straus, "The Myth of Serial 'Tyranny' in the 1950s and 1960s," *The Musical Quarterly* LXXXIII (Fall 1999), pp. 301–43.

CHAPTER ONE

Twentieth-Century Chamber Music: An Introduction

We have, as yet, no descriptive term such as *Romantic* or *Baroque* for the music of this century. As words, *modern* and *postmodern* give us no information beyond rough chronology, and even that depends on the particular speaker or writer. We do have a number of terms describing general currents in the mainstream of twentieth-century music—*neoclassical, neoromantic, nationalistic,* and so on—as well as some that purport to describe more specific compositional or technical characteristics—*serial* and *postserial, aleatoric,* and even *tonal* and *atonal.* None of these is particularly satisfactory, because none adequately represents the complexities of the repertory.

A narrative history of the chamber music of our century along such "stylistic" or technical lines thus seems less likely to afford us appreciation of the music than to reinforce attention to conceptual categories, and I am more interested in the music. At the same time, a strictly chronological account would be similarly flawed, since it might too easily beg the questions of aesthetic and humanist context for specific works, ideas, and trends, and thereby descend to the level of lists of titles.

It has seemed more rewarding, then, to organize a study of twentieth-century chamber music around a small number of genres—first, some that seem to distinguish the music of our day from that of earlier eras, and then two genres that continue older traditions. These genres are programmatic chamber music; vocal chamber music; music for new, often unique ensembles; the sonata; and the string quartet. The last two chapters, on the sonata and especially on the string quartet, are organized chronologically, as a sort of linear reconstitution of a history that has been fragmented in earlier chapters. This organization also permits us to consider various ideas that have gained prominence in chamber music since 1899. For example, the combination of programmatic chamber music with the new ensembles that spring up early in the century—such as Schoenberg's *Pierrot lunaire* of 1912—brings into even purely instrumental chamber music the ambience of theatricality. The new ensembles themselves, and their extraordinary variety, speak to the stunning (or bewildering) profusion of activities and possibilities our century has seen. On a different level, a significant amount of great twentieth-century chamber music invites us to consider temporality— not just the compositional manipulation of rhythm and meter, or the creation of a time world that defines (or is defined by) a specific work, but indeed the nature of time itself.

This first chapter introduces what follows by examining four works that fall into or cross over the rubrics just described. It begins with a discussion of Schoenberg's string sextet of 1899, *Verklärte Nacht* (Transfigured night), Op. 4, a work that anticipates both the second chapter (programmatic chamber music) and the sixth, where we take up Schoenberg's Second String Quartet (1908) and other early twentieth-century string quartets. The next section examines two violin and piano sonatas by Charles Ives, the First and the Fourth, and their creation of two different embodiments of time, both musical and extramusical. This serves as an introduction to chapter 2, again, and to chapter 5 (the sonata), and to works in other chapters that take time as their subject. Chapter 1 closes with Boulez's *Le marteau sans maître* (1957), a work for mezzo-soprano and an ensemble of ingenious instrumental diversity, and a work that combines its composer's ear for and knowledge of earlier twentieth-century music, the twentieth century's love of the "exotic" or non-European (in this case, the Far East), and a concomitant expansion of Western usages, the oft-cited "new virtuosity" of much post–1945 music, and the impetus of an extramusical aesthetic (surrealism), all these coming together in a composition of unquestionable importance for the music of the last forty years.

A Musical Narrative: Arnold Schoenberg's *Verklärte Nacht*

By 1899 program music—music that in some way tells a story or depicts a scene—had been in existence for several centuries. Programmatic chamber music, however, had always been a relatively marginal phenomenon. Romantic composers who were at home in both the chamber music genres and the programmatic ones, from Schumann and Mendelssohn to Dvořák and Saint-Saëns, generally chose not to mix the two. Such a work as Hugo Wolf's *Italienische Serenade* (1887) is so unusual as to be the exception that proves the rule. This, as so much else, changes in the world of Arnold Schoenberg.

Schoenberg's *Verklärte Nacht,* based on a poem of the same name by Richard Dehmel, is a programmatic work in the most traditional ways except in its use of a chamber group, the string sextet, for such a purpose. Dehmel's original poem, in five short parts, alternates between descriptions of nature, functioning in the traditional ways as a setting for human activity and as a metaphorical and external sign of the inner states of the protagonists' souls, and two monologues. The first monologue is an anguished, tortured confession by an unnamed woman to the man with whom she walks: the two are in love, but the woman is pregnant by another man, one she loathed and to whom she turned in self-loathing, before she met her great love, her present companion. Even though she had not met him when she became pregnant, she feels that she has betrayed this man, that she is completely unworthy of him, and that the coming child will always exist as testimony to her sin and an impediment to the couple's union. The second monologue is the man's: it simply transcends, or deflects, hers. They are lovers, he tells her, they are one; the child will be theirs, as he feels it is already a warmth binding them together. And he points out to her the glories of the starlit sky, the transfiguration of the sky, of nature, into the sign of their love and the natural setting for it.

Neither character in *Verklärte Nacht* is named or described, but the reader learns much more about her than about him. She, at least, tells her history, which is readily understandable and readily human. The man tells nothing. He simply states that the child will be theirs, not hers alone. She has brought warmth to him, he tells her, and made him into a child. She has, presumably, transfigured him as well. The woman has asked for forgiveness; the man thinks that unnecessary, irrelevant. In a way, the man is a Christ figure and the woman Mary Magdalene. Nature, in this view, would stand in as a sign of God, or of the holiness of the love between the man and the woman. But the man, it is important to note, is not the agent of the transfiguration; rather, he is one of its objects. His role and the nature of his change are the least clear, as well. He, like the woman, is part of a larger story: they are a couple to whom something has happened.

This is the type of story that music tells well. The structure of the poem is that of the story—setting, her monologue, setting again, his monologue, setting transfigured. The poetic language is uncomplicated, and the poem is most striking in the coincidence of line (most of them in iambic tetrameter) and phrase; only occasionally, and only in the woman's monologue, is there a run-on line or a break in the established meter. The structure of the poem is maintained in the music. An introductory passage depicts the cold, bleak night through which the couple walks; a long turbulent section conveys the anguish of the woman's monologue; a brief interlude recalls the introduction; the second principal section embodies the man's response and the transfiguration of the night, which he describes; and the final section reinforces that transfiguration.

Our interest here is in how a story may be told in musical terms. For music is rarely so simpleminded that its role is merely to relay a verbal or visual picture in their terms. The "narrative" of *Verklärte Nacht* lies in its treatment of musical motives, precisely in the "principle of developing variation" that Schoenberg located and discussed in the music of Brahms,[1] and which is more usually seen as the typical treatment of leitmotivs in Wagner operas. If to Schoenberg's contemporaries *Verklärte Nacht* sounded "as if the score of *Tristan* had been smeared while the ink was still wet,"[2] more recently the work has sounded Brahmsian rather than Wagnerian. The ensemble recalls Brahms' two string sextets, and the textures are more thoroughly polyphonic than most Wagner. This may, of course, be a matter of scale. Wagner's use of texture reflects his dramatic or musically dramatic purposes, and he tends to write polyphonically in those situations that are the most unsettled, homophonically when his characters and their situations are most steadfast. But given the sheer size of Wagner's dramas, an alternation of polyphony and homophony is necessary for any sort of articulation (musical or dramatic) and for the constant revivification of a listener's ear. In a work lasting less than half an hour—a Brahms quartet or Schoenberg's *Verklärte Nacht*—such a need is less vital. Schoenberg, like Brahms, is more willing to spread polyphonic writing throughout all the sections of his works. The effect here is narrative. In works such as Schoenberg's Second String Quartet (see chapters 3 and 6), it is less so.

A third Brahmsian characteristic of *Verklärte Nacht* is that, for the most part, it is much more firmly fixed in specific tonalities than is, say, *Tristan*. Only the first principal section (the woman's monologue), through very rapid harmonic motion and chromatic resolution of chords, seems to "suspend" tonality.[3] Otherwise, *Verklärte Nacht* is strongly tonal, and depends for its effect on the perception of the D minor/D major frameworks of the piece as a whole.

These characteristics—an ensemble of six related instruments, the primarily polyphonic writing, and the firmly based tonal scheme—allow Schoenberg, as they had Brahms, more emphasis on development and the developing variation as a formal procedure. The result is a constant evolution of musical thoughts, an avoidance of repetition, a linear and ever-progressing ontological time. In this instance, Schoenberg's role is that of the omniscient playwright, setting the scene and directing his characters. Let us look in some detail at *Verklärte Nacht*'s musical narrative.

Since Robert Schumann, critics have delighted in pointing out motivic and thematic interrelationships in music, and for many years a large number of German and American critics seemed to believe that the very life of a work—its dynamic shape and formal strength, even its legitimacy as serious music—lay precisely in the all-pervasive development of interconnected ideas. In his 1941 essay "Composition with Twelve Tones," for example, Schoenberg attempts to demonstrate that the second principal theme of his Chamber Symphony, Op. 9, is an inversion of the main notes of the first theme.[4] That this relationship defies aural perception, and that Schoenberg as composer was unaware of it—he writes that he saw this "true relationship" only twenty years after the work was composed[5]—are not important. What matters in Schoenberg's demonstration is its exemplification of the "law of the unity of musical space, best formulated as follows: *the unity of musical space demands an absolute and unitary perception.*"[6]

Although Schoenberg is dealing here with motivic relationships, his conception is qualitatively different from earlier views of the musical process: in the Classic-Romantic era, the conception of musical discourse was of a temporal and nonreversible structure of tension and resolution, anchored most firmly in the system of functional tonality but articulated as well by texture and phraseology, the specific use of motives or themes, the use of register, and other ancillary elements. Schoenberg's positing of an absolutely unified musical space has many implications, some of them problematic. But we must note immediately that the absolute unity of musical space does not mean that the space is undifferentiated. A work of Schoenberg's is not a fluid, amorphous body that one may enter and leave at any point. The most important result of Schoenberg's conception is that, because the essential unity of his musical materials ensures the central integrity of the work, he found himself with a much wider range of possibilities for the articulation of space, or for the shaping of a work. This aesthetic outlook provides a general context for the narrative structure of *Verklärte Nacht*.

Schoenberg's motives, like those of his pupils Webern and Berg, tend toward the dynamic and open-ended, rather than the closed, less malleable motive that we shall later see in Stravinsky. The ideas of the Viennese are marked by general pitch contours—that is, by shapes of ascent and descent that remain constant and recognizable even when smaller units within them are expanded and contracted—and by rather more definite rhythmic patterns. These rhythmic patterns are extremely various, but they very often include beginning on weak beats of the measure or between beats; dotted rhythms; a great variety of note values, from long to very short, within a single idea; and the avoidance of metrical "arrival," of closing on a strong beat and thereby grounding the energy contained in the motive. Such motives lend themselves to the widest range of possibilities for development. Since it is melodic contour that is constant, rather than the specific pitches or intervals, a particular motive may imply any number of different harmonies, either stable or shifting. Similarly, the neat rhythmic outlines do not necessitate a fixed metrical context, since the variety of note values and the avoidance of overriding regular strong beats, especially at the beginnings and ends of the figures, allow them to appear almost anywhere within the temporal unit (from measure to phrase) and to be combined in any number of ways, each figure yet retaining its identity.

These motivic types are, obviously, not without historical precedent; one finds them especially in Wagner, to a degree in Brahms (e.g., the late piano pieces), and at a further remove, in Beethoven (e.g., the Fifth Symphony). Schoenberg himself pointed out these debts in his 1949 essay "My Evolution."[7] There, in an analysis of *Verklärte Nacht,* he says that the thematic connection "is based on Wagnerian 'model and sequence' above a roving harmony on the one hand, and on Brahms' technique of developing variation—as I call it—on the other."[8] A prototype of the "model and sequence" construction is the *Tristan* Prelude, in which the motives are repeated and drawn out over shifting chromatic harmonies. The differences between Schoenberg and Wagner are that Wagner's sequential repetitions for the most part remain closer to the model in their intervals, rhythms, and durations than do Schoenberg's,[9] and Schoenberg's "roving" harmonies, sometimes in even such an early "tonal" work as *Verklärte Nacht,* rove further beyond the pull of any fixed tonal center than do Wagner's.

The Schoenberg/Brahmsian "developing variation" extends the Schoenberg/Wagnerian "model and sequence." Walter Frisch has described the developing variation as a "flexible compositional procedure whereby the different elements of a basic idea or shape—what [Schoenberg] called a *Grundgestalt*—are successively modified."[10] Frisch cites Schoenberg's 1950 essay "Bach":

> . . . [the] variation of the features of a basic unit produces all the thematic formulations which provide for fluency, contrasts, variety, logic and unity, on the one hand, and character, mood, expression, and every needed differentiation, on the other hand—thus elaborating the *idea* of the piece.[11]

We are back in Schoenberg's absolutely unified musical space, but this time we approach it with the composer rather than with the analyst working after the fact. Schoenberg's musical ideas, the basic units of his pieces, are so constituted that their successive variations or modifications will at the same time remain recognizable and yet create a constantly moving musical discourse—contrasts, similarities, far-flung extensions and, ultimately, resolutions—that works in tandem with the harmonic structure and formal conventions.

The motives and thematic materials of *Verklärte Nacht* are given in Example 1.1. These are the forms in which they initially appear in the first two large sections of the piece, the scene-setting introduction (mm. 1–28) and the long, churning section that represents the woman's passionate and despairing monologue (mm. 29–201). The motives exemplify the traits mentioned above—beginning on weak beats or within beats; dotted rhythms; variety of note values; avoidance of strong rhythmic closure; and especially, a high degree of chromaticism. Yet various as these motives are, they show a fair amount of internal consistency: the intervals of the minor second and minor third are everywhere; motive *h* seems made out of motive *f;* the last half of motive *j* is motive *g* in a new rhythm. Both "model and sequence" and "developing variation" begin from the very outset, and this immediacy of movement and development gives the music its extraordinary tension, as it will later its extraordinary sweetness.

EXAMPLE 1.1. Schoenberg, *Verklärte Nacht*. Used by permission of Belmont Music Publishers, Pacific Palisades, CA 90272.

(a) mm. 1–3

(b) mm. 22–24, viola I

(c) m. 29, viola I

(continued)

Example 1.1. (*continued*)

(d) mm. 34–35, violins I and II, viola I

(e) m. 50

(f) mm. 62–63, cello I

(g) mm. 75–76, violins I and II, viola I

(*continued*)

(h) mm. 79–80

(i) mm. 104–6, violin I

(j) mm. 137–38, violin I

(k) mm. 255–56, violin I

(l) mm. 278–80, violin I

To "narrate" the music: the first twenty-eight measures are the "kahlen, kalten Hain," the "barren, cold wood" in which the couple walk, set forth in sounds typical of the nineteenth-century German Romantic style: the *pianissimo* open octaves in the cello and viola, and the descending scalar melody also set in octaves. This melody sits uneasily on the octave pedal, forming on the downbeat an open fifth and on the third beat—notice that the cello and viola play these Ds anew every second beat, and do not just sustain them, equally possible on string instruments—a dissonant major second. The low register, the open intervals and octave doublings, the slowly descending line, and the tempo all evoke a desolate mental image in the mind's ear and eye.[12]

This descending line, set against octave As (the dominant of D minor), and inverted so that the line is below the As, all instruments playing tremolos and a crescendo, becomes the transition to the first principal section. This section, again, is marked by extraordinary turbulence, through the chromaticism and rhythmic malleability of its melodic motives, the constant shifts in texture, the avoidance of metrical regularity, and especially the avoidance of tonal definition, done here principally by avoiding cadences. In a typically Wagnerian gesture, Schoenberg's first big cadence (at mm. 41–45; see Ex. 1.2) is deceptive; it implies a strong arrival in D minor, a so-called structural downbeat that absorbs at least some of the tension built up to this point. The cadence is aborted, first with the "unclassifiable" dissonance (m. 42) that, according to Schoenberg, resulted in the work's initially being refused performance,[13] reasserts the approach to the D-minor cadence (i$^6_4$ V^7, m. 45) and then moves, directly, and with a forte pizzicato, to a diminished-

EXAMPLE 1.2. Schoenberg, *Verklärte Nacht*, mm. 41–45. Used by permission of Belmont Music Publishers, Pacific Palisades, CA 90272.

seventh chord that simply leaves ungrounded the energy of the cadence preparation. This aborted cadence is important: we shall hear it
again, to different effects, at mm. 181ff (the end of this first principal
section), and at mm. 393ff (the final transfiguration), where it resolves
to D major, the parallel major to the opening D minor, and the final key
of the work.

In melodic or motivic terms, the first principal section is largely a
succession of the motives as they appear in Example 1.1. Figure 1.1
gives measure numbers for the succession of motives and indicates
their various juxtapositions. This close succession of differing, if somehow generally related, motives is immediately audible. The succession
itself, as well as the nature of the motives, gives this section its churning
turbulence; and Schoenberg avoids any closure, any sense of relaxation
or détente throughout. The most important motives are *c,* with which
we begin and end; *d,* which we first hear doubled in octaves and in
canon with itself (a beat later in the second violin and first cello), and
which leads to the first big deceptive cadence; and *e,* which underlies
most of the section.

This section does not conclude: it simply stops. The climax is motive *d, fff* and *accelerando,* first in octaves in the violins over furious
tremolos in the other instruments, moving chromatically with each
beat, and then in octaves in all six instruments. Still *fff,* and marked *sehr
langsam* (very slowly), we hear again the approach to the cadence at the
beginning of this section (with motive *c* in the first viola and first cello),
its sliding dissonances still unresolved. The end of this cadential approach is twice repeated, and moves not to resolution but to a diminished-seventh chord, the least stable and least defined chord in the
tonal repertory. Then comes a break and new material.

Measures	*Motives* (as listed in Ex. 1.1)
1–28	a, b
29	c
34	d (in canon, doubled); 1st deceptive cadence
50	e, then e and c
63	f, then e and f
75	g
79	h, then g, h, e (cf. h and f)
91	g
105	i, then h, e, h
124	g and h, e
137–138	j (last half of j = g), some e
175	d (all 6 instruments in octaves, m. 177)
181	c; cadence recalling mm. 41ff
188	break, transition to next principal section (A')

FIGURE 1.1. Motives in Schoenberg's *Verklärte Nacht,* Op. 4.

The middle section is a return to, and recharacterization of, the opening pages of the score. From mm. 202 through 234, we hear the motives from the opening section (*a* and *b*), the first reharmonized *fortissimo* over dissonant chords, the second *pianissimo* but over sliding diminished-seventh chords. Then a change occurs, another striking dramatic gesture, a transformation of the tonality (musical and coloristic) of the piece. We reach a cadence in E♭ minor, *pianissimo*. Suddenly, G♭ becomes F♯ (an enharmonic modulation), the other voices drop a half step, and we are in a warm *forte* D major, the parallel major to our beginning key and the eventual key of the entire work. Now begins the transformation of the first section, the man's transformation of the woman's story and of her grief, through the transformation of the musical motives and their context.

Immediately we hear motive *c*, but in a more sustained and smooth setting, and a much more conventional (if still chromatic) chord succession, with roots moving by fifths. Tension from the first

EXAMPLE 1.3.   Schoenberg, *Verklärte Nacht.* Used by permission of Belmont Music Publishers, Pacific Palisades, CA 90272.

(a) mm. 255–57

(*continued*)

(b) mm. 278–81

large section begins to dissolve. Equally striking is the persistence of the straightforward major tonality, the harmonies hardly moving but energized by rapid sixteenth-note tremolos in the second violin and first viola.[14] There is a "new," if seemingly familiar, melody high in the first violin: given its position, it seems to arise like a new, serene development from motive *c*, its intervals expanded, its durations lengthened, its regularity and register lending it an extraordinary consoling beauty. (This is also true of the ensuing call and response between first violin and first cello, which seems to me to arise from the figure accompanying motive *c*.) Example 1.3 shows this new/old melody, as well as the final new melody of the work, which comes to the fore and, with all the motives from the first principal section, permeates this concluding section. Although this new melody shares some of the general characteristics of earlier motives—wide range, dotted rhythms—it is much smoother in contour and rhythm, and much more diatonic, firmly fixed above stable chords, than anything before. Not only, then, are the motives from the first section heard and reheard in a new tonal and rhythmic context, but a new melody made of those same elements also comes out of the texture and seems to transcend it. This new melody even appears in the work's final approach to a firm cadence in D major, in mm. 392ff. Here, for the third time, we hear the cadential approach from the first section; and here, for the first time, it resolves satisfyingly, to D major. The chord progression, which we have heard before, now moves to a I$^6_4$ in D; the new melody enters *dolcissimo,* the rhythms of its last half drawn out in augmentation, and moves to a V^7, which in turns simply resolves to the tonic D-major triad. Here, for the last time, we hear motive *a,* now completely at peace.

Schoenberg, then, has accomplished much: he has "set" the Dehmel poem so that his string sextet is an aural depiction of a literary story; in fact, he has written a musical analogue to that literary story, since the transfiguration is here made manifest, and the work is perfectly comprehensible on purely musical grounds, without knowledge of the poem; and he has combined crucial elements of the musical procedures of Brahms and Wagner. What he has also done is move toward a new synthesis. Everything about *Verklärte Nacht* is thoroughly nineteenth-century in conception, realization, and result. The only exception is the combination of program music and chamber music; and even this might be viewed as simply a continuation of Romanticism, a logical next step that, for whatever reasons, Mendelssohn, Schumann, and Tchaikovsky never took. Schoenberg's accomplishments in *Verklärte Nacht* infuse his chamber works that are indisputably "modern," the First and Second String Quartets and *Pierrot lunaire.* We will discuss the latter two works in some detail in later chapters.

Time Present and Time Past: Two Sonatas for Violin and Piano by Charles Ives

The First and Fourth Violin Sonatas of Charles Ives are works that deal, not unusually for Ives, with his childhood and reminiscences or evocations of that happy time for the adult composer. The Fourth Sonata, which dates from 1906–16, is entitled *Children's Day at the Camp Meeting.* The First Sonata, from 1902–8, has no subtitle, but a note by Ives tells us that it, too, is an impression of outdoor gatherings and holiday celebrations from the 1880s and 1890s, the years of his boyhood and adolescence. What interests us here about these two related works is their creation of a sense of the past: not just the nostalgia for earlier idyllic times that we often hear in Ives, but the creation of extramusical time or time worlds beyond the experienced musical time of the works. This creation is effected through the formal schemes of the sonatas' movements and especially through Ives's manipulation of old tunes. The results, superficially similar in the two sonatas, are in fact substantially different; indeed, the sonatas produce two distinct representations of past time.

The Fourth Sonata, *Children's Day at the Camp Meeting,* is the simpler of the two in virtually every way. Ives has left us an extended note about the piece:

> The subject matter is a kind of reflection, remembrance, expression, etc. of the children's services at the out-door Summer camp meetings held around Danbury and in many of the farm towns in Connecticut, in the 70's, 80's, and 90's. There was usually only one Children's Day in these Summer meetings, and the children made the most of it—often the best of it. They would at times get stirred up, excited and even boisterous, but underneath there was usually something serious, though Deacon Grey would occasionally have to "Sing a Caution."
>
> The First Movement (which was sometimes played last and the last first)—was suggested by an actual happening at one of these services. The children, especially the boys, liked to get up and join in the marching kind of hymns. And as these meetings were "out-door", the "march" sometimes became a real one. One day Lowell Mason's—"Work for the Night is Coming" got the boys going and keeping on between services, when the boy [Ives himself] who played the melodeon was practicing his "organicks of canonicks, fugaticks, harmonicks and melodicks." In this movement, as is remembered, they—the postlude organ practice (real and improvised, sometimes both)—and the boys' fast march—got to going together, even joining in each other's sounds, and the loudest singers and also those with the best voices, as is often the case, would sing most of the wrong notes. They started this tune on "ME" so the boy organist's father made him play "SOH" hard even if sometimes it had to be in a key that the postlude was not in just then. The boys sometimes got almost as far off from Lowell M. as they did from the melodeon. The organ would be uncovering "covered 5ths" breaking "good resolutions" faster and faster and the boys' march reaching almost a "Main Street Quick-step" when Parson Hubbell would beat the "Gong" on the oaktree for the next service to begin. Or if it is growing dark, the boys' march would die away, as they marched down to their tents, the barn doors or over the "1770 Bridge" between the Stone Pillars to the Station.
>
> The Second Movement is quieter and more serious except when Deacon Stonemason Bell and Farmer John would get up and get the boys excited. But most of the Movement moves around a rather quiet but old favorite Hymn of the

children, while mostly in the accompaniment is heard something trying to reflect the out-door sounds of nature on those Summer days—the west wind in the pines and oaks, the running brook—sometimes quite loudly—and maybe towards evening the distant voices of the farmers across the hill getting in their cows and sheep.

But as usual even in the quiet services, some of the deacon-enthusiasts would get up and sing, roar, pray and shout but always fervently, seriously, reverently—perhaps not "artistically"—(perhaps the better for it).—"We're men of the fields and rocks, not artists," Farmer John would say. At times these "confurorants" would give the boys a chance to run out and throw stones down on the rocks in the brook! (Allegro conslugarocko!)—but this was only momentary and the quiet Children's Hymn is sung again, perhaps some of the evening sounds are with it—and as this Movement ends, sometimes a distant Amen is heard—if the mood of the Day calls for it—though the Methodists and Baptists seldom called for it, at the end of their hymns, yet often, during the sermon, an "Amen" would ring out as a trumpet call from a pew or from an old "Amen-Seat". The Congregationalists sometimes leaned toward one, and the Episcopalians often.

The Third Movement is more of the nature of the First. As the boys get marching again some of the old men would join in and march as fast (sometimes) as the boys and sing what they felt, regardless—and—thanks to Robert Lowry— "Gather at the River."[15]

Thus Ives's search for lost time, which I think is rewarded. He describes the programmatic content of his sonata quite precisely in these notes. The main subject of the first movement is one that the listener of Ives's time and place could not have failed to identify immediately, the hymn "Tell Me the Old, Old Story." The story here is not just the one of "Jesus and His glory," the lyric of the first and most often quoted musical phrase in Ives's movement, but the story of these old-time meetings as well. Ives tells himself and us the story from his youth, and from many years preceding his birth as well; he creates a lost moment from his present perspective.

The first and third movements of the sonata are extremely brief, about two and two and one-half minutes respectively. The first movement, marked *allegro (in a rather fast march time—most of the time)*, is built on the "Old, Old Story" melody (Ex. 1.4), especially its second phrase. This alternates with contrasting episodes that come from a fugue by Ives's father.[16] One can hear this movement as a sort of rondo, or as a through-composed celebration of the old, old tune. When Ives quotes

EXAMPLE 1.4. Doane, "Tell Me the Old, Old Story."

Tell Me the Old, Old Story

OLD, OLD STORY. 7. 6. 7. 6. D. with Refrain

KATHERINE HANKEY, 1834-1911   WILLIAM H. DOANE, 1832-1915

1. Tell me the old, old sto - ry Of un - seen things a - bove,
2. Tell me the sto - ry slow - ly, That I may take it in,
3. Tell me the sto - ry soft - ly, With ear - nest tones, and grave,
4. Tell me the same old sto - ry, When you have cause to fear

Of Je - sus and His glo - ry, Of Je - sus and His love:
That won - der - ful re - demp - tion, God's rem - e - dy for sin!
Re - mem - ber! I'm the sin - ner Whom Je - sus came to save:
That this world's emp - ty glo - ry Is cost - ing me too dear:

Tell me the sto - ry sim - ply, As to a lit - tle child,
Tell me the sto - ry of - ten, For I for - get so soon,
Tell me that sto - ry al - ways, If you would real - ly be,
Yes, and when that world's glo - ry Is dawn - ing on my soul,

For I am weak and wea - ry, And help - less and de - filed.
The ear - ly dew of morn - ing Has passed a - way at noon!
In an - y time of trou - ble, A com - fort - er to me.
Tell me the old, old sto - ry: "Christ Je - sus makes thee whole."

(continued)

EXAMPLE 1.4. (*continued*)

REFRAIN

Tell me the old, old sto - ry, Tell me the old, old sto - ry,

Tell me the old, old sto - ry Of Je - sus and His love.

the first phrase of "Tell Me the Old, Old Story," there are also echoes of "Shall We Gather at the River": at the beginning in the violin, in the piano after the violin's next extended quotation from "Old, Old Story," and just before the first fugal episode. (These echoes, which are built into the original hymn tune itself, anticipate the material of the sonata's last movement.) The climax of the movement comes at its end, after an accelerando, when the violin plays in octaves ad libitum the beginning of the hymn's refrain, its title phrase. This is followed by a coda repeating almost literally the music from the beginning of the sonata, returning to where it had begun.

The second movement, on "Jesus Loves Me" (the "old favorite Hymn of the children" that Ives mentions in his notes), is by far the longest of the sonata, lasting some eight minutes. Like the first movement, and unlike the chorale preludes and chorale fantasies of Bach (which Ives would have known), the music does not explore the original hymn phrase by phrase, but rather concentrates on a single emblematic gesture from it, the melody whose words are "Yes, Jesus loves me." The piano accompaniment, as Ives points out, is impressionistic, trying to recreate the sounds of the surrounding brooks, wind in the trees, and so on. This is done through arpeggiation of widely spaced chords in the lower and middle registers of the piano, and the result is sometimes quite like the "layered" textures of Debussy, a combination of stasis in some registers and timbres with more movement in others. The movement is in ternary form; the A sections are based on "Jesus Loves Me," and the B is Ives's *allegro (conslugarocko!)*, given over entirely to the piano. The final A, coming after this boisterous episode, is even more ecstatic in its recalling of the hymn than the first A had been: the slow-moving bass and the murmuring piano arpeggios are still there, but the melody has moved up to the highest piano registers, filled out into full, bell-like chords, with a new countermelody in the violin. All this is soft, emphasizing its cause and effect as memory, rather than being a present-tense affirmation; it moves from *mezzo piano* to *piano* to *ppp* and finally, in its last two measures, *pppp*. It is a contemplation of the past, in Ives's reliving of it.

The third movement is much like the first, though more dissonant—that is, with more and louder "wrong" notes embellishing the straightforward hymn tune, and less tied to a triadic harmonic scheme than the first movement was. (It is still far more triadic in nature, however, than the second movement, whether that movement's contemplative A or rumbustious B section.) The general scheme is like that of the first movement: the music begins with an immediately recognizable snatch of hymn tune, in this case "Shall We Gather at the River," then expands, spins out, and plays with that melody, ending with a full statement of the hymn's refrain. The movement is the least complicated of the sonata, with no contrasting fugal episodes; basically it is all of a piece from first note to last. The similarity between the finale and the first movement presumably explains why Ives felt their order could be switched in performance. But their order as described here—the order of the movements in the score and in the masterful recording by Paul Zukovsky and Gilbert Kalish—is more satisfying. It saves the simplest for last, which is a time-honored procedure; but, more important, it orders the three basic hymns of the sonata into an invitingly shaped succession.

This succession is, first, programmatic: we begin with the request to hear, once again, an old, old story; out of that story comes a contemplation of God's love for humanity, interrupted, as such contemplations sometimes are in church services, by a boisterous distraction (this interruption also brings us back from any possible intimation of pious sentimentality or maudlin self-celebration, which Ives would have adhorred); and finally we join in a communal celebration, a celebration both of religious beliefs and of the society to which we belong. In telling himself, and us, this story, Ives has recreated the experience of such a religious meeting and realized its purpose: the union of men and women, adults and children, in a common society with a common purpose. (It should go without saying that one need not be a Yankee Protestant to appreciate or to enjoy this sonata.) In this sense, in his having recreated an experience, Ives has recovered a time that he and his society had lost; and in this sense the sonata surpasses simple narrative, simple programmatic description.

In contrast, the First Sonata is more abstract in its design, although it also uses a few hymn tunes extensively, and its effect is one of time's passing, not of its re-creation and reliving. Ives has given us program notes for this sonata as well:

> This Sonata is in part a general impression, a kind of reflection and remembrance, of the people's outdoor gatherings in which men got up and said what they thought, regardless of consequences—of holiday celebrations and camp meetings in the 80's and 90's—suggesting some of the songs, tunes and hymns, together with some of the sounds of nature joining in from the mountains. . . .
>
> The first movement may, in a way, suggest something that nature and human nature would sing out to each other—sometimes. The second movement, a mood when *The Old Oaken Bucket* and *Tramp, Tramp, Tramp, The Boys Are Marching* would come over the hills, trying to relive the sadness of the old Civil War days. And the third movement, the hymns and actions of the farmers' camp meeting, inciting them to "work for the night is coming."[17]

Ives' nostalgia—his belief in an original Eden just before one was born—is unquestionably heartfelt. The world he imaginatively recreates is also the world in which he wished his music would be heard. There is a radical disjunction in Ives, even more than in Schoenberg, between an aesthetic that is backward looking and particular ways of composing that are like nothing ever heard before. The only musical materials Ives mentions in this comment are thematic: three particular songs. The first movement suggests "something" that occurs "sometimes." What is new in Western music with this sonata is the conception of form, not unlike Debussy's *En blanc et noir* (see chapter 2) or his late sonatas (chapter 5); the treatment of the various musical parameters (tonality, meter and rhythm, and texture) in ways that seem unsystematic, functionally unorganized (but not *dis*organized); and a striking instrumental effect in the second movement.

The first movement, *andante—allegro vivace*, resembles the sonata forms of Debussy's chamber sonatas or the First Violin Sonata of Bartók. Ives begins with a slow introduction that sets forth the two principal motives of the movement (see Ex. 1.5a). The first (m. 1, right hand) becomes the "first theme" of the *allegro vivace*, and the second (mm. 7–8) becomes a pervasive spinning-out device, the whole-tone scale. Its syncopated rhythm appears only in this introduction. The first, expository section of the *allegro vivace* continues in a virtually unbroken fashion: both instruments play almost without rest, and contrast is achieved by sounding contrasting materials at the same time. The music in general is also continuous, and continuously changing. There are no sections easily labeled "bridge" or "second theme," and the transition into the

EXAMPLE 1.5. Ives, Sonata No. 1 for Violin and Piano. © Copyright 1953 by Peer International Corporation. International Copyright Secured. All Rights Reserved. Used by Permission.

(a) mm. 1–8

(b) mm. 65–67

development section is unarticulated and unnoticed, owing to the constant motivic development and spinning-out of material in both piano and violin. The central section of the movement introduces a new theme, reminiscent of "Bringing in the Sheaves," which along with the whole-tone figure fills out the middle section. The final section, which begins with an upward-rising perfect fifth, like the introduction and the *allegro vivace* proper, is a recapitulation in that no new motivic material is introduced thereafter, but not in the sense that previous thematic ideas are "recapitulated," reconstituted and reintegrated into a stable whole. The continuous development of the sonata to this point goes on unabated until the coda, a reprise of the opening *adagio*.

The second and third movements are similar to the first in that they resemble conventional musical structures—the slow movement is ternary and the last movement is a kind of reverse theme and variations, in which the theme comes last—but the musical discourse is unbroken, the breaks articulating sections are nowhere overwhelmingly clear, and the result is one of formal stasis, of contemplation. This has also to do with Ives's musical material. The third movement is a meditation on "Watchman, Tell Us of the Night," a hymn that Ives's contemporaries knew in their bones. The second movement refers to "The Old Oaken Bucket" and "Tramp, Tramp, Tramp, the Boys Are Marching (and, to my ears, the "Battle Hymn of the Republic"), tunes already old and familiar in Ives's day. In the second movement, the traditional songs work as a subtext to the piano and violin music: they are never really heard as such, quoted directly in their original guise for any length of time, but always lurk just beneath the surface, evident in melodic figures or turns of phrase. This effect is tremendously heightened by the instrumental sound. The violin plays muted throughout, at every dynamic level, while the piano often almost overpowers it with loud, thick chords. The sound itself is thus one of music half-heard, moving in the background, a part of consciousness but not its object.

In the third movement, the hymn tune becomes clearer and moves more toward the fore; after a long opening section with intimations of the tune, we hear its identifying motive in the violin. We then hear a second version, closer to the original but still rhythmically free and contrasted with a free accompaniment in the piano. As the tune grows stronger, we finally reach a section, *andante cantabile*, in which the melody is set unadorned, over a piano accompaniment in clear homophony, and texted in the violin part. The violinist is not meant to sing here, but to hear the lyrics silently, to understand their import for the present performance. The melody of "Watchman, Tell Us of the Night" then sinks back into the music, and the final section of the movement returns to its beginning.

The result is not programmatic but rather a kind of abstract contemplation of times past. The first movement of the First Sonata is continuous, discursive, and motivically permeated. The second and third movements are not "about" their respective hymns—music or words—but use the hymns evocatively for people who know them, who lived through the times when they were part of the very fabric of life. (That they no longer are—or were even when Ives wrote the sonata—is evident in their very use here, as well as in Ives's comments about the sonata.) Yet this is not romantic nostalgia, for its means—atonality, tremendous rhythmic and metrical freedom, textural opacity, and so on—are those of the twentieth century. The music is not evocative of times past or of distant lands, like the romantically nostalgic music (or literature) of the nineteenth century. The First Violin Sonata keeps the past firmly at a distance, and as an *object* of the music, not its subject. Moreover, the past in this sonata is beyond recovering in the present. The quoted hymns in the second movement, again, lurk beneath the surface of the music heard. In the third movement, we do arrive at a clear statement of "Watchman," but its final melodic note is not resolved into a stable tonic, and the hymn tune itself yields again to a thoroughly twentieth-century conclusion of some length. Wistful as its quotation and references may be, this sonata is a recognition of time's passing. The bygone tunes are heard, but in static forms: they live no longer. If the Fourth Sonata recreates the Children's Day, the burden of the First Sonata is that the past is dead.

Wheels Come Full Circle: Boulez's *Le marteau sans maître*

Pierre Boulez's *Le marteau sans maître* (1954; revised, 1957) is as important to post–1945 European music as Schoenberg's *Pierrot lunaire* has been to the entire century. It is a nine-movement cycle based on three short, dense, and surrealist poems by René Char. Boulez treats each poem separately: two of the poems are given a vocal setting and two or three instrumental treatments; the third poem is set twice. That is to say: the poem "l'artisanat furieux" is set as the third movement of the nine, but the first movement is a purely instrumental "avant [before] 'l'artisanat furieux' " and the seventh is, similarly, "après [after] 'l'artisanat furieux.' " The second, fourth, sixth, and eighth movements are built on "Bourreaux de solitude," the sixth being its vocal setting. The fifth and ninth movements set "Bel édifice et les pressentiments." These three different poetic/musical cycles do not come together until the last movement. One of Boulez's essential compositional trademarks is the love of contrast and juxtaposition, as opposed to realignment and integration. The ninth movement of *Marteau* is by no means a recapitulation, but it does in some ways act to close the cycle, to bring its various elements in upon one another.

The musical language at work here is derived from serialism, a serialism closer to Webern than to Schoenberg. But it is equally derived from the sounds of Far Eastern music (e.g., the gamelan-like sounds of the "Bourreaux" cycle) and from the music of Debussy and Ravel. The peculiar effect of stasis and turning that we shall find in Ravel's 1913 *Trois poèmes de Stéphane Mallarmé* (chapter 3) recurs here as well. At the time of *Marteau*'s composition, Boulez's claimed influences were Webern, Messiaen, Debussy, and Stravinsky, although none of these except Webern was acknowledged without some qualms and qualifications. I am not claiming here any direct "influence" from Ravel to Boulez, or from Ravel's cycle to his, though neither would I strenuously deny it.

The world of *Le marteau sans maître* also derives from surrealism, an artistic movement of great violence; if it was not about violence per se, violence is nonetheless one of its more pervasive themes, and violent passions permeate its works. Violent disjunctions occur everywhere, as images and between language and images, the latter being one of the sources of shock that André Breton sought in the aesthetic. It also uses, to a famous degree, highly ambiguous syntax and vocabulary, as in the poems Boulez chose to set. All this would presumably have appealed to the young Boulez: he was known in the 1950s as an iconoclast who chose with great care the elders or institutions to which he would award a nicely calibrated amount of respect; the actor Jean-Louis Barrault, with whom Boulez worked in the late 1940s and 1950s, described him as "hérissé," bristling like a cat.[18] These are not uncommon characteristics of a young man of enormous talent, even genius. But lest this look like condescension to Boulez, we should also note that the poems of René Char appealed directly to his aesthetic concerns as closely as any personal thematic predilections. The text-music aspect of *Marteau* is a chicken-and-egg question. But while the textual violence of the three poems is only sometimes carried out in Boulez's music, the structural processes of the text always are.

L'artisanat furieux

La roulotte rouge au bord du clou
Et cadavre dans le panier
Et chevaux de labours dans le fer à
   cheval
Je rêve la tête sur la pointe de mon
   couteau le Pérou.

Bourreaux de solitude

Le pas s'est éloigné le marcheur
   s'est tu
Sur le cadran de l'Imitation
Le Balancier lance sa charge de
   granit réflexe.

Furious Artisanry

The red caravan at the edge of the
   nail
And corpse in the basket
And workhorses in the horseshoe
I dream, my head on the point of my
   knife, Peru.

Executioners of Solitude

The step has receded, the walker is
   silent
On the dial of Imitation
The Pendulum hurls its reflex
   charge of granite.

Bel édifice et	*Beautiful Building and*
les pressentiments	*Premonitions*
J'écoute marcher dans mes jambes	I hear walking in my legs
La mer morte vagues par-dessus tête	The dead sea, waves over my head
Enfant la jetée-promenade sauvage	Child the wild jetty-promenade
Homme l'illusion imitée	Man the imitated illusion
Des yeux purs dans les bois	Pure eyes in the woods
Cherchent en pleurant la tête habit- able.	Seek, crying, the head in which to live.

The poems of Char's *Le marteau sans maître* were written in the late 1920s and early 1930s and published as a volume in 1934. Most of the poems resemble the ones Boulez chose to set, albeit these are among the shortest in the book. In 1945, in a short preface to the second edition, Char characterized them as a premonition of the horrors of the war years. He writes of "the hallucinating experience of man entwined in Evil, of man massacred and at the same time victorious." Further, "The key to *Le marteau sans maître* turns in the premonition of the realities of the years 1937–1944. The first ray which that key delivers hesitates between the curse of torture and the magnificence of love."[19]

These ideas are perhaps evident in the texts Boulez chose. The first poem has little in common with the other two, except the dreaming of a distant place, which we find again at the end of "Bel édifice." The second and third poems, however, are precisely about the balancing of torture and love, and of imitation and reality. If these nouns do not reappear in Boulez's music—as they could not, unless some musical figure were specifically associated with particular words, for *violence*, *love*, and *reality* are terms far too astract for musical analogy—the structure of balance, hesitation, and ambiguity is Boulez's working method. Again, the love of contrast and juxtaposition, not necessarily resolved or recombined in a new unitary form, is one of Boulez's essential compositional trademarks, from his earliest works to the present day.

The first way in which disjunction and differentiation remain in the foreground is through the instrumentation of the three cycles in *Marteau* (see the accompanying tables) and the resulting textures. The instruments used in *Le marteau sans maître* range from the voice, the instrument obviously the most human and the "closest" to us, to metallic percussion, that with the greatest degree of overtones, the closest to "noise" in the strict sense. Thus, the voice resembles the alto flute (especially in this case, since the alto voice and flute share much of their range); the flute leads to the viola, also capable of pure tones and long legato phrases, but in *Marteau* playing pizzicato as well. The pizzicato viola resembles the guitar; and the strong attack and quick decay of the guitar's notes are connected aurally with the playing of the xylorimba and the vibraphone. (Boulez instructs the players to use a variety of mallets for tonal variety, and to vary the attacks, but he does not use the vibraphone's sustaining pedal, as he would to a high degree in his next vocal composition, the *Improvisations sur Mallarmé,* which would become the core of *Pli selon pli.*) The woody attack and timbre of these instruments is connected to the woody timbres of some of the percussion used, the hand drums, bongos, maracas, and claves. And these, finally, lead to the metallic percussion, which is introduced only gradually into the timbral collection (in movement 4 and then in 8), and which concludes the work along with the flute, the instrument at the other end of the spectrum.

Yet this timbral spectrum is not arrayed as such in the music: rather, Boulez prizes the differences between the instruments, creating a brightly colored and mosaiclike (or pointillistic) timbral surface, which varies from cycle to cycle within *Marteau* as a whole, and less radically from piece to piece within those three cycles. This is what makes *Marteau* a chamber work and not an orchestral song cycle writ small. Boulez's instrumental schemes are evident from a brief look at Figures 1.2 and 1.3. The "Artisanat" cycle is characterized by the alto flute, vibraphone, and guitar; it uses no unpitched percussion. The vibraphone connects "Artisanat" to the sound of the "Bourreaux" cycle, and the alto flute and guitar connect "Artisanat" to the "Bel édifice" cycle (in movement 5). The "Bourreaux" cycle uses both the xylorimba and vibraphone and a wide array of percussion to mark out broken rhyth-

"Artisanat" cycle	Movement 1, "avant"	alto flute, vibraphone, guitar, viola
	Movement 3, "Artisanat"	alto flute, voice
	Movement 7, "après"	alto flute, vibraphone, guitar
"Bourreaux" cycle	Movement 2, "Commentary 1"	alto flute, xylorimba, hand drum, 2 bongos, viola
	Movement 4, "Commentary 2"	xylorimba, vibraphone, finger cymbals, double chimes, triangle, guitar, viola
	Movement 6, "Bourreaux"	voice, alto flute, xylorimba, vibraphone, maracas, guitar, viola
	Movement 8, "Commentary 3"	alto flute, xylorimba, vibraphone, claves, double chimes, 2 bongos, maracas
"Bel édifice" cycle	Movement 5	voice, alto flute, guitar, viola
	Movement 9	voice, alto flute, xylorimba, vibraphone, high tam-tam, low gong, very deep tam-tam, suspended cymbal, guitar, viola

FIGURE 1.2. Musical/poetic cycles in Boulez's *Le marteau sans maître.*

Instrument	Movements								
	1	*2*	*3*	*4*	*5*	*6*	*7*	*8*	*9*
Voice			x		x	x			x
Alto flute	x	x	x		x	x	x	x	x
Xylorimba			x	x		x		x	x
Vibraphone	x			x		x	x	x	x
Percussion:									
drums or woody sounds			x			x		x	
metallic sounds				x				x	x
Guitar	x			x	x	x	x		x
Viola	x	x		x	x	x			x

FIGURE 1.3. Instrumentation in Boulez's *Le marteau sans maître*.

mic sequences at the center of the texture. The "Bel édifice" movements do not really add up to a cycle as do the other two groupings of
movements: if the texture and general sound of movement 5 differ
from anything we have heard up to that point, the instruments are still
close to those of the "Artisanat" cycle, and movements 5 and 9 do not
resemble each other sufficiently to form a separate entity. Rather than
constituting a real cycle, then, these two movements use the same poem
to different ends. Movement 5 acts as a sort of reminiscence of the
"Artisanat" cycle, through its general sound connecting that text
(which we have heard in movement 3) to the text of "Bel édifice"; at the
same time, movement 5 is a commentary or corrective to the
"Bourreaux" cycle, a retreat from the latter's clangorous sound and irregular, start-and-stop motion, separating movements 4 and 6 as it reminds the listener of movements 1 and 3. Movement 9 is the coda of
Marteau as a whole. It uses all the instruments of the ensemble, the only
movement to do so besides movement 6, the climax of the work. In
movement 9 the mezzo-soprano, after singing her entire text, moves
back into the ensemble, singing through closed lips, and becomes one
instrument among several. The movement and work then close, as I
have noted, by joining the two ends of the instrumental spectrum, the
alto flute and the gongs, cymbals, and tam-tams.

Just as the instrumentation serves to distinguish one cycle from
the others, so does it shape the entire work. Movement 1 introduces
Marteau as a whole as well as the first cycle through its seemingly flat,
undifferentiated texture, its brevity, its through-composed form, and
its melodic and rhythmic gestures. The piece, to paraphrase the poet
and critic Charles O. Hartman in another context, is not yet in the
works, but is pointed at the works.[20] Thereafter we hear shifting textures and timbres, which become cumulative because of the resemblances of movements within a given cycle, because of the continuity of
the basic timbral spectrum, and because of the general and well-formed
coherence of the musical language. This accumulation continues

through movement 6, the vocal setting of "Bourreaux de solitude," which becomes the focus of *Marteau* as a whole. Thereafter, the composition reverses itself much as it had grown, with movement 7 a reprise or reminiscence of movements 1 and 3, movement 8 the coda to its cycle, and movement 9 the coda to the entire work. In this way, as a vocal chamber work cast as a multimovement cycle at whose end all is recapitulated, and whose extremes are mediated, *Le marteau sans maître* is a child of Schoenberg's *Pierrot lunaire*.

Timbres and their deployment are thus central to *Marteau*'s general musical language; in this the work is exemplary of its era. Like Stravinsky's *In Memoriam Dylan Thomas* and *Three Songs from William Shakespeare* and Berio's *Chamber Music* (all to be discussed in chapter 3), its harmonic language falls under the vast rubric of post–Webern serialism. A strictly serialist analysis of *Marteau*, even if it were in the scope of this study, would be imponderable; it is virtually impossible to derive from a score of Boulez his original working materials and methods.[21] Even set-theory analysis such as is common today among theorists is not of much avail. The music of *Marteau* is one of gestures, often simultaneous, sometimes successive. The traditional Western construction of antecedent-consequent phrases is sometimes in force, but most often the "consequent" phrases turn out to be continuations, responses that still avoid closure. Textures are thickened by the rarity of common or simultaneous attacks from more than one instrument, an even stronger element than the polyrhythms that are usually cited in this music. (A live performance, given its separation of sound sources, can clarify the textural complications that one hears on even the most virtuoso recorded version.) Given the constant textural interest of *Marteau*, ranging from heterophony to monophony, and the sensuous beauty of the timbres, one should hear the work as exploiting these elements to shape phrases and rhythms, and using these in turn to "set" the voice, literally to contextualize Char's texts.

The cycle around "L'artisanat furieux" is introductory and somewhat distanced. The qualities of movement 1 that make it an open-ended beginning to its own cycle and to the work in general are reprised in movement 7; but with the more frequent rhythmic unisons among instruments, the *ritardando* and *decrescendo* at its end, the thinning of the texture to guitar alone, Boulez here closes this cycle. He may also simultaneously intimate the closure of the entire piece, but this is yet only an intimation and not the beginning of a long conclusion. The pause between the end of movement 7 and the beginning of movement 8 is an "arrêt très court," so that immediately we are thrown again into the most active and variegated cycle. The vocal movement of this "Artisanat" cycle, movement 3, is a direct homage to Schoenberg in its instrumentation: the duet of voice and flute (in this case, alto flute) is that of "Der kranke Mond," the seventh piece of *Pierrot lunaire* and the one that ends that work's first part. Not surprisingly, the setting of "L'artisanat furieux" is also the simplest movement in *Marteau*. The voice and the flute seem to become one here, for as the movement progresses they not only echo one another but also sound increasingly frequent unisons and thus become entwined.[22] Since this is the first vocal entrance in *Marteau*, we can also perceive here the beginning of the singer's integration into the ensemble of instruments, shaped as carefully as the cycle in general. The voice in *Marteau* is, as it were, called forth by the flute, the instrument she most resembles. In the next vocal movement, no. 5, the texture is primarily heterophonic, the instrumental lines parallel variations of the vocal phrases. In movement 6 the voice predominates as we reach the still center of the cycles. And in movement 9, again, the voice begins as in movement 6, at the forefront of the ensemble, but sinks into the common texture and then yields completely to the alto flute at the conclusion.

If the "Artisanat" cycle is primarily introductory—it introduces the entire work, the voice, even (perhaps) the conclusion—the "Bel édifice et les pressentiments" cycle is initially an interruption and then a final conclusion. The first version, as I have noted, is at least slightly reminiscent of the "Artisanat" cycle, in its instrumentation if not in its gestures and textures. The enormously long instrumental interludes between vocal phrases make this movement the one whose text is hardest to grasp; nevertheless, its final phrase carries a central message of the texts (and therefore of the work) and prepares us to hear movement 6 in a very particular way:

> Des yeux purs dans les bois
> Cherchent en *pleurant la tête habitable.*
>
> (Pure eyes in the woods
> Seek, *crying, the head in which to live.*)

The last four words, here italicized, are sung without accompaniment. This search for "la tête habitable" is one of the complex of themes in *Le marteau sans maître* (a related theme is the physical reality of the body and the illusory nature of life); and the same search creates a context in which to hear the walking, the receding step, of "Bourreaux de solitude" in movement 6. Likewise, in movement 9, at the end of the cycle, the voice rises to a climactic *forte* on a high F♯, on the word "habitable," and then ceases. The listener does not know what to expect at this point; when the voice enters humming some measures later, the gesture is thematic as well as purely structural. The voice joins the instrumental ensemble, beyond (or just apart from) words, and is part of the ensemble's atomization into alto flute and gongs. The "tête habitable" is not found—unless, and I find this possibility very attractive, that head is the listener's, where the music has found refuge.

The "Bourreaux de solitude" cycle is the focus of *Marteau,* and within that cycle movement 6, its vocal movement, is the still center of the entire work. This cycle is the most individual, the most particular and characteristic, of the three in *Marteau.* Its emphatic use of xylorimba, vibraphone, and percussion sets it apart from the others. It is marked by extraordinary rhythmic activity and by a completely unpredictable phrase rhythm, starting and stopping, interrupted by pauses of greatly varying lengths. Yet a principal element of the phrases and their aggregate rhythms is the *almost* regular, *almost* metrical rhythmic ostinati in the percussion instruments at the center of each movement's textures: hand drum, then bongos, then hand drum again in movement 2; finger cymbals, then double chimes, then triangle in movement 4; maracas in the vocal setting, movement 6; and claves, then chimes, then bongos and bongos together with maracas (timbrally a closing gesture) in movement 8. These quasi-ostinati also mark most clearly the structural divisions of each tripartite *abc* movement, combining the through-composition of all nine movements with an unmistakable sectionalism at every level, from the start-and-stop phrases to the most general, peculiar to this cycle.[23]

The regularity of texture and phrase rhythm and the regular occurrence of this music in every second movement make this cycle the central one of the piece. I have called movement 6 the still center of the cycle, and of *Marteau,* because of its combination of the quasi-metrical ostinato with the most sustained durations and sounds of the whole piece, its turn here from reiterated colors and gestures to prolonged ones. The movement seems to turn as well to *Klangfarbenmelodie* (Schoenberg's term, meaning a melody of tone colors rather than of pitches), slowly shifting timbres that halt the tumultuous activity, forward motion constantly interrupted and resumed, of movements 2 and 4. This not only contributes to the literal sense of the text of the movement ("The step has receded, the walker is silent"), but it also becomes a Varèse-like crystallization, slowly expanding by duplication of gestures, and self-reflecting and inward at the same time. The voice is most predominant here, more at the forefront than anywhere else in the piece. (Movement 3 is a duet between voice and alto flute as equal partners. In movement 5, the instrumental lines in the vocal sections are heterophonic variations of the vocal line. Movement 9 begins like movement 6, with the voice predominant, but then the mezzo-soprano becomes one instrument among the others.) This focus on the voice, which is to say here on the text, in combination with the vocal treatment in the last movement, leads us to consider what *Marteau* is about, what we are to take away with us.

We must begin by remembering that Boulez has said that if one wants to know what a text is about, one should read it.[24] A musical setting of a text can be a particular reading of that text,[25] or it can be essentially nonliterary, using the text as one of its constitutive elements. It is the latter case with Boulez. A reading of the three poems he chose for *Le marteau sans maître* is not forbiddingly difficult, but moving from that reading to a verbal interpretation of the resulting piece is perilous indeed. Nevertheless, the two more important poems Boulez uses are, in the most general and trite sense, about the human condition. Char contrasts humanity (as illusion) with the physical reality of existence, always to humanity's loss. In these texts, we are each alone, and trapped in our solitude. We may seek company, the stability of physical existence in the physical universe, but this is impossible: people are illusory, imitations, contingent, deserted. If one of the keys to this ever-suspended situation is love, as Char says in his little preface to the second edition of the poems, that love is absent from the poems that Boulez chooses to set.

Also absent from Boulez's setting is the poems' sentimentality. The toughness of Boulez's music—the clarity of its colors, the density of texture and rhythm, its spiky gestures, its extraordinary variety that gradually creates a coherent, self-contained musical world—is equal to the softness at the center of Char's texts. Furthermore, one of the results of Boulez's settings in *Marteau* is precisely to create a context for the poems, a context that the poems seem to be seeking. Boulez's music establishes a real connection, a precise coincidence between humanity and the present in which we live. If the voice of the poems does not see this, if she remains searching, we listeners may hear the establishment of time, specifically of the present, as the presence that we and she seek. The unpredictable rhythms of the *Bourreaux* cycle relax into sustained spiraling sounds in movement 6. As the search for the "tête habitable" at the end of movement 5 leads us directly into the sustained silence of the text in movement 6, the same words in movement 9 lead to the integration of the voice into her ensemble, as one among many, existing on their plane.

By its end, then, *Le marteau sans maître* constitutes a unitary presence, an absolutely unified musical space such as Schoenberg created for his linear narrative in *Verklärte Nacht,* in literary critical jargon a "plenitude." That plenitude is much more—much greater and much more intricate, subtle, various—than the "theme" I have just adumbrated, the resolution of a search or an escape from essential and existential solitude. The poems in Boulez's *Marteau* serve as what one might call a pretext, an initial starting point for the existing (musical) text, but only superficially its raison d'être or its fertile generating seed. The essence of Boulez's *Marteau* is in its music. That music has many forebears: among them we may count the teaching and compositional example of Messiaen, in the rhythms especially; the gamelan, in texture, timbre, and also rhythm; Debussy, in the emphasis on timbres and textures, and in the building of shapes through phrase rhythms more than harmonies; Webern, in phrase shapes; the Schoenberg of *Pierrot lunaire;* and perhaps Stravinsky, at least Stravinsky's music of the years just before World War I. Yet despite all these musical connections, *Marteau* is a truly original work, the first complete efflorescence of a new music. In this sense, it is a post–World War II parallel to *Pierrot lunaire* and *L'histoire du soldat.* Its compositional techniques use those of the earlier era(s), but their combination is new, and they are extrapolated far beyond anything to date. The aesthetic is also in many ways new, insisting on contrast and disjunction, concealing any radical unity in order to concentrate attention on the surface, ultimately (and as a result) confusing any distinction between surface and subtext. The brittleness that is often attributed to Boulez's music may stem from this confusion between surface and subtext, whose separation is central to Western music of the last 250 years, from the music's seeming denial of "depth" in the spatial sense. For critics unable to escape this perspective, the music of Boulez—like that of Debussy, especially from *La mer* onward—sounds superficial in the derogatory sense of the word, or difficult without "meaningful" reason for being so. For listeners who are more open, the point lies on the surface, in the idea that what you hear is what you get, in the realization that the unitary presence which the music has created is the totality and not just a signpost for further delving. This is by no means to say that when one has heard *Marteau* once, one has heard everything it has to offer; but unlike the music of Beethoven or Bach, in which understanding comes ultimately with repeated hearings, in Boulez one does not necessarily hear more than one has heard before, one hears it *better,* more clearly. The unitary presence that I am positing in *Marteau* is one of immediacy as well; and repeated listening leads to greater clarity and even greater vividness. The most obvious ancestor of this kind of music is Debussy, who was in many ways the first modernist. And if *Marteau* is in some ways analogous to *Pierrot* and *L'histoire,* it also establishes new ground, and since its creation has given rise to many musical progeny.

Thus, four pieces that introduce us to most of the themes we shall follow throughout this study: musical space and its articulation; musical and extramusical time; the relationship of music to the world in which it exists; musical relationships among composers; and stylistic characteristics as embodiments—not simply signposts or signifiers—of their own meaning. We shall develop these motives, and introduce new ones, in the chapters that follow.

Notes

1. Schoenberg, "Brahms the Progressive," in *Style and Idea* (New York, 1975), 398–441. See also Walter Frisch, *Brahms and the Principle of Developing Variation* (Berkeley and Los Angeles, 1984).

2. In Charles Rosen, *Arnold Schoenberg* (New York, 1975), 3. See also Schoenberg, "How One Becomes Lonely," in *Style and Idea*, 31.

3. The word "suspend" is Schoenberg's. See, for example, his *Theory of Harmony*, translated by Roy E. Carter (Berkeley and Los Angeles, 1978), 383–84.

4. Schoenberg, "Composition with Twelve Tones," in *Style and Idea*, 222–23.

5. Ibid., 223.

6. Ibid.; emphasis in original.

7. *Style and Idea*, 79–92.

8. Ibid., 80.

9. Although some, such as the "Day" leitmotif in *Tristan*, appear in greatly differing guises.

10. Walter Frisch, "Brahms, Developing Variation, and the Schoenberg Critical Tradition," *19th Century Music* 5 (Spring 1982): 215–32.

11. Ibid., 215.

12. It is frustrating to many nonmusicians, and to not a few general writers about music as well, that there is no system to musical imagery. A given figure or gesture, for example low open octaves, does not "mean" anything specific by itself. The figures I have just described for the opening of *Verklärte Nacht* do not per se "mean" what I have just attributed to them. Only a very few musical gestures or sounds have acquired a general connotation; two examples are the descending minor or major second as a "musical sigh" and the timbre of woodwinds to evoke a pastoral scene. The vast majority of musical imagings are contextual, as they are here. The essential procedure is not to say, "This music sounds desolate," but to demonstrate, from the music itself, how that nonmusical, or rather *extra*musical, association may arise. In this instance, it is a matter of specific figures in the general German Romantic tradition. Because, in this instance and in most instances throughout this book, the drama of a programmatic work is inherent *in* the music, we can discuss the sequence of musical events, which in turn will tell us what the drama, in fact, is.

13. Schoenberg, "Criteria for the Evaluation of Music," in *Style and Idea*, 131–32. Rosen, *Arnold Schoenberg*, 3.

14. Egon Wellesz wished to tie this to the specific line of the poem "Es ist ein Glanz um Alles her," "There is a glory surrounding all" (Wellesz, *Arnold Schoenberg* [London, 1921; reprint, 1971]), 69.

15. These paragraphs are printed in the back (p. 21) of the score published by Associated Music Publishers, with the note: "The above is mostly from remarks written on the back of some of the old music manuscripts."

16. Paul Echols, liner notes, Paul Zukovsky/Gilbert Kalish recording of the Ives violin sonatas (Nonesuch/Elektra HB-73025).

17. Quoted in ibid.

18. Jean-Louis Barrault, "Pierre Boulez," in *La Musique et ses problèmes contemporains, 1953–1963*, Cahiers de la Compagnie Madeleine Renaud–Jean-Louis Barrault (Paris, 1963), 3–6. See also Boulez's 1952 article "SCHOENBERG EST MORT," included in the collection *Relevés d'apprenti* (Paris, 1966).

19. "Feuillet pour la 2ème édition 1945," René Char, *Le marteau sans maître* (Paris, 1963), 13.

20. Charles O. Hartman, personal communication.

21. For an example of Boulez's compositional and precompositional techniques, and the distance from original materials to finished work, see his *Penser*

la musique aujourd'hui (Paris, 1963) translated by Susan Bradshaw and Richard Rodney Bennet as *Boulez on Music Today* (London, 1971).

22. The pitch usage here is also the closest in *Marteau* to classical—i.e., Schoenbergian—serialism. Cf. the eleven-note vocalise on "du," the twelfth pitch class arriving with the word "clou" ("nail").

23. Although the clear structural demarcations do not occur in the other two cycles, they are obviously an element in the overall rhythm of *Marteau*.

24. Liner notes to *Pli selon pli,* reprinted in Jean-Pierre Derrien, "Pierre Boulez," *Musique en jeu* 1 (November 1970): 116–17.

25. There are many studies of this question. For a valuable—because truly musical—one, see Edward T. Cone, *The Composer's Voice* (Berkeley and Los Angeles, 1974), and his reconsideration of parts of that argument in "Poet's Love or Composer's Love?" in *Music and Text: Critical Inquiries,* ed. Steven Paul Scher (Cambridge, 1991), 177–92.

CHAPTER TWO

Music and Literature I: Program Music

The years from 1899, the year of *Verklärte Nacht,* through the First World War saw an enormous output of programmatic chamber music. This activity largely disappears in the years between the World Wars, the years of so-called neoclassicism,[1] and reappears after 1945. But, as we shall see, there is a fundamental difference between programmatic chamber music composed before World War I and after World War II. The earlier music tells a story or depicts a scene, as we saw in Schoenberg's *Verklärte Nacht* and the two Ives sonatas for violin and piano. The later music, like the earlier, often uses titles; but now those titles more often describe the work itself rather than anything extramusical, or are so general that one cannot find in them a program for the music.[2] In the music of the post–World War II era, though, we will find a concern with contemporary literature, especially with literary techniques, as for example in the conception of a poem as a "scaffolding" (the term is Boulez's) on which the composer may construct his or her music. We also find in these years a widespread interest of various composers in early twentieth-century literature, especially in Joyce. The focus of this chapter is on *how* the music discussed here is more or less specifically programmatic. We are interested here, for example, in who is telling a story and in how that narrator is doing so. We are also interested in matters of time, which will prove to be of some importance for nonprogrammatic music as well.

Narrative and Temporal Programs: Berg and Carter

Some narrative music conveys a story that cannot be told in verbal terms, at least in verbal terms analogous to the musical-poetic narrative in Schoenberg's *Verklärte Nacht*. One example is Alban Berg's *Lyric Suite* (1926). In this string quartet, the tempi of the movements move outward like a wedge from the initial *moderato,* the odd-numbered movements becoming progressively faster and the even-numbered progressively slower. An element of Berg's genius was his ability to make seemingly static formal designs dramatic, to use them for movement, tension and release, and immediate and lasting emotional impact; this ability is evident not only in his operas, *Lulu* and *Wozzeck,* but in his instrumental "absolute" works as well. The *Lyric Suite*'s bifurcation of tempo leaves one with the mental image, when the piece is over, of an unbridgeable chasm. Furthermore, at the end of the last movement is a quotation from *Tristan und Isolde*—its most famous motive, the beginning of the prelude. Berg's listener will not simply register this as an homage to Wagner but will hear, *through* the quotation, an expression of infinite longing. The listener will also realize that the quotation is not fulfilled or resolved, for example with a following quotation from the *Liebestod.* An unbridgeable chasm and unresolved longing: perhaps this is what the *Lyric Suite* is "about"?

For years there were discussions of a possible secret program for the *Lyric Suite*. In the early 1980s the composer George Perle published the results of his extensive research and demonstrated the string quartet's hidden program.[3] In fact, the last movement, *largo desolato,* is a "setting" of Baudelaire's poem "De profundis clamavi" ("From the depths have I cried to you") from *Les fleurs du mal,* with the "vocal" lines—that is, the melodic lines to which Berg subscribed the words of the poem—divided variously among the four instruments. In its private program, which the composer never intended to be made generally known, the *Lyric Suite* is addressed to a woman—not his wife—with whom Berg was in love. Thus the purely musical sense of an unbridgeable chasm and of the unfulfilled longing of the first act of *Tristan und Isolde* are fixed in a specific biographical situation.

In a way, this overlapping of private and public programs parallels Berg's use of conventional musical forms for seemingly unrelated dramatic impact. In such cases, the performers may be aware of the musical structures, but it is not essential that an audience be attentive to them. In the case of the private program of the *Lyric Suite*, it is no doubt helpful for the performers to know the program, the Baudelaire sonnet, and even the instrumental lines underlain with the sonnet text, but the work is not to be performed as a poetic setting, for voice and string quartet accompaniment.[4] Such a performance distorts the quartet textures, obscuring the interplay of the instruments and emphasizing the "sung" lines at the expense of the rest of the music. At most, the Baudelaire might be printed in the program, but even this may be too much, perhaps emphasizing the anecdotal over the work itself.

An exemplary case of real and audible overlapping of private and public narratives comes in the post–World War II music of Elliott Carter. All of Carter's scores after the 1946 Piano Sonata are generally conceived of as dramatic scenarios, more or less specific, realized through characterization of the instruments as well as through the manipulation of musical material and, through them, the manipulation of time. The two works examined here are the "breakthrough" scores, in which Carter first realized thoroughly his own compositional voice and his own formal approach. These are the Sonata for Violoncello and Piano (1948) and the String Quartet No. 1 (1951). Carter describes the immediate intellectual and musical background to his thinking:

> Naturally any serious concern with rhythm, time, and memory must include the shaping of music, and I began to question the familiar methods of presentation and continuation, of so-called "musical logic," based on the statement of themes and their development. Certain older works, particularly those of Debussy, suggested a different direction. In considering change, process, evolution as music's prime factor, I found myself in direct opposition to the static repetitiveness of most early 20th-century music, against the squared-off articulations of the neo-classics and, indeed, against much of what is written today in which "first you do this for a while, then you do that." I wanted to mix up "this" and "that," make them interact in other ways than by linear succession. Too, I questioned the inner shape of "this" and "that"—of musical ideas—as well as their degrees of linking or non-linking. Musical discourse needed as thorough a rethinking as harmony had at the beginning of the century.[5]

Carter's musical discourse is one of continuous change, which, he has said, he finds to be the most evocative.[6] But first there must be something that will undergo change, and that object of change is as new a factor in Carter's music as the formal and temporal aspects just described:

> When I was asked in 1947 to write a work for the American cellist Bernard Greenhouse, I immediately began to consider the relation of the cello and piano, and came to the conclusion that since there were such great differences in expression and sound between them, there was no point in concealing these as had usually been done in works of the sort. Rather it could be meaningful to make these very differences one of the points of the piece. So the opening *Moderato* presents the cello in its warm expressive character,

playing a long melody in rather free style, while the piano percussively marks a regular clock-like ticking. This is interrupted in various ways, probably (I think) to situate it in a musical context that indicates that the extreme disassociation between the two is neither a matter of random [*sic*] nor of indifference, but one to be heard as having an intense, almost fateful character.

The *Vivace*, a breezy treatment of a type of pop music, verges on a parody of some Americanizing colleagues of the time. Actually it makes explicit the undercurrent of jazz technique suggested in the previous movement by the freely performed melody against a strict rhythm. The following *Adagio* is a long, expanding, recitative-like melody for the cello. . . . The finale, *Allegro*, like the second movement based on pop rhythms, is a free rondo with numerous changes of speed that ends up by returning to the beginning of the first movement with the roles of the cello and piano reversed.

. . . The first movement, written last, . . . presents one of the piece's basic ideas: the contrast between psychological time (in the cello) and chronometric time (in the piano), their combination producing musical or "virtual" time. The whole is one large motion in which all the parts are interrelated in speed and often in idea; even the breaks between movements are slurred over. That is: at the end of the second movement, the piano predicts the notes and speed of the cello's opening of the third, while the cello's conclusion of the third predicts in a similar way the piano's opening of the fourth, and this movement concludes with a return to the beginning in a circular way like Joyce's *Finnegans Wake*.[7]

These paragraphs introduce a number of issues, which we must take up more slowly: the basic musical materials of the sonata; the various simultaneous formal procedures at work, both simple sectional forms (ABA' in the first three movements, the "free rondo" of the last) and the ongoing, cumulative discourse, which is also a formal procedure; the question of time; and finally, the question of the analogy to *Finnegans Wake* and to the idea of a nonspecific narrative or drama that enfolds the sonata as an extramusical or supramusical program.

The basic materials of the Cello Sonata, the "this" and "that" which Carter mentions, are essentially motives, musical ideas in the most general sense and way of musical thinking. The preference for motives may be necessitated by Carter's desire for music of continuous change and for his reexamination of musical discourse: although twentieth-century composers do use the traditional sonata form (see chapter 5), that standard framework of exposition with two or more themes, development, and recapitulation, if "filled" with material that is always evolving into something essentially new, would be only artificial and unconvincing. Thus Carter's themes are not recurring melodies. His basic materials in the Cello Sonata are instead treatments, reflective of his interest in time and character, ways of using and hearing rhythm and instrumentation.

The play on the characters of his two instruments is evident principally in the slower movements, the opening *moderato* and the third-movement *adagio,* and especially in the first movement. (A similar case obtains with the differentiation of instruments in his First String Quartet.) Although the pianist often endeavors to conceal the fact, the piano is essentially a percussion instrument, its sound produced by a hammer hitting a string and, equally important, initiated by a key hitting a key bed. (When the "attack" is deleted from a recorded piano note, it is extremely difficult to identify the remaining sound.) Carter chooses to emphasize this percussive nature of the piano not simply for its own sake—as Bartók often does, for example—but to identify the percussive with the mechanistic, the "chronometric." That is to say, even at this basic level of musical conception, he is not using a particular quality or sound for its own sake, but because it leads him to something specifically extramusical.

In contrast to the piano, the cello is capable of endless, seamless legato, which does not have to be "faked." String instruments are also capable of changing the timbres of individual notes through slight manipulations of pitch and especially through the use and degree of vibrato. This possibility of timbral inflection is one of the closest connections between the string (or wind) instruments and the voice, and it is something the listener (and maybe the player) responds to almost subconsciously; but it, too, is impossible on the piano, although a good pianist learns how to imitate it, to make a listener believe that it is happening, through voicing and agogic accent. Thus Carter is exploiting the "natural" capacities of his instrument, and again associating them with something extramusical—in the case of the cello, with the rhapsodic and the psychological. This association is strengthened in the third movement, the *adagio,* in some ways reminiscent of Bartók's slow movements in the way it seems to grow out of the motive from the beginning of the movement, the minor-third oscillation. In the *adagio,* however, the piano is much more responsive to the cello, even more supportive of it, than in the first movement. This is part of the long-range scheme of the sonata, to which we will turn directly.

In the meantime, the second and fourth movements of the sonata emphasize rhythm rather than character. As Carter points out, they are based—at some remove—on the pop rhythms of the 1940s, the so-called "jazzy" syncopations that occur, much watered down, in pop (or "populist") arrangements and compositions. More telling than that, however, is the use of the cello at the beginning of the second movement, after the little introductory exchange with the piano: for the next ten measures, the cello plays pizzicato, the sound associated in jazz and pop charts with the string bass as timekeeper and metrical foundation for the ensemble. The cello seems to have assumed this role from the piano in the first movement, but here in a "breezy," to use Carter's word, even humorous manner. The piano now follows suit, both here and when this material returns (mm. 133ff, marked *quasi pizz.* in the score). Even the cello's coda is a third reprise of this witty pizzicato. This sound, its rhythmic emphasis and associations, dominates the entire scherzo, so that the *arco* or legato sections sound not as a contrast to the pizzicato jauntiness but as a continuation by other means. Similarly the last movement, the "free rondo," is really a perpetuum mobile, its material trading off from one instrument to the other until the very last pages of the score, when the piano reintroduces motivic material from the first movement and the two instruments gradually return to the world of the opening pages of the sonata. But now, as Carter points out, their "characteristic" roles are exchanged: the piano plays sustained *pianissimo* melodies and the cello plays regular, metronomic quarter notes, pizzicato.

This exchange of characteristic manners of playing is at the heart of Carter's sonata: they determine the drama of the piece. In this work, forms as such are not expressive. They are not hierarchically cumulative; their internal sections are not interactive. Rather, the formal devices at work are linear and successive, at every level. The first three movements are all in a simple ternary form, in which the third section represents a continued composition of material, not just a simple return and reiteration of the first. The last movement has precisely the same type of formal succession, but as a free rondo. And, as Carter has pointed out, the end of each movement foreshadows the beginning of the next. Things return in this sonata, yet they don't. As Carter suggests, this is what happens in Debussy. The technique, at least superficially, is comparable to the narrative techniques of *Finnegans Wake* and of Proust's later volumes.

One issue to which Carter's technique leads us is that of musical time; for the Cello Sonata makes us aware not simply of itself, its notes, rhythms, textures, and gestures, but equally of its medium, the element in and through which it occurs. Since Carter's musical events are changed as they recur, and since our ears are drawn to the changes and the constant evolution of the musical writing, we are led not to expect literal repetition and recapitulation as the goal of the musical discourse. We are located in a musical universe of the eternal present, to a linear unfolding of "now," as opposed to the recovery of a past within the present that occurs when musical sections are recapitulated or literally repeated. The latter is musical architecture, the former musical arabesques.[8] Here is precisely the dichotomy signaled by Stravinsky in his Charles Eliot Norton Lectures at Harvard in 1939–40.

Perhaps no one other than Stravinsky in this century has thought as deeply about musical time as Carter. It is helpful to consider what Stravinsky has to say, first in his *Autobiography* (1935):

> Music is the sole domain in which man realizes the present. By the imperfection of his nature, man is doomed to submit to the passage of time—to its categories of past and future—without ever being able to give substance, and therefore stability, to the category of the present.
>
> The phenomenon of music is given to us with the sole purpose of establishing an order in things, including, and particularly, the coordination between *man* and *time*. To be put into practice, its indispensable and single requirement is construction. Construction once completed, this order has been attained, and there is nothing more to be said. It would be futile to look for, or expect anything else from it. It is precisely this construction, this achieved order, which produces in us a unique emotion having nothing in common with our ordinary sensations and our responses to the impressions of daily life. One could not better define the sensation produced by music than by saying that is it identical with that evoked by contemplation of the interplay of architectural forms. Goethe thoroughly understood that when he called architecture petrified music.[9]

This belief that music, and only music, places us squarely in the present is qualified and deepened four years later in the Harvard lectures. For the Stravinsky of the *Autobiography,* substance and stability are located in order. Burdened by memory and desire, we cannot order our quotidian physical lives. The order of musical construction allows us to approach such an order, and its contemplation provides the "unique" aesthetic emotion that we seek to experience. Stravinsky does not stop here (or elsewhere in the *Autobiography*) to discuss what he means by "construction"—there are all sorts of musical constructions—or to demonstrate that the emotion that music arouses is in truth singular and unique. He explains himself more fully in the Harvard lectures, published under the title *Poetics of Music in the Form of Six Lessons.* In the second lesson, "The Phenomenon of Music," Stravinsky posits the dichotomy between ontological time and psychological time and, citing a "Russian philosopher-friend," Pierre Souvtchinsky, identifies two kinds of music:

one which evolves parallel to the process of ontological time, embracing and penetrating it, inducing in the mind of the listener a feeling of euphoria and, so to speak, of "dynamic calm." The other kind runs ahead of, or counter to, this process. It is not self-contained in each momentary tonal unit. It dislocates the centers of attraction and gravity and sets itself up in the unstable; and this fact makes it particularly adaptable to the translation of the composer's emotive impulses. All music in which the will to expression is dominant belongs to the second type. . . .

Music that is based on ontological time is generally dominated by the principle of similarity. The music that adheres to psychological time likes to proceed by contrast. To these two principles which dominate the creative process correspond the fundamental concepts of variety and unity. . . .

. . . For myself, I have always considered that in general it is more satisfactory to proceed by similarity rather than by contrast. Music thus gains strength in the measure that it does not succumb to the seductions of variety. What it loses in questionable riches it gains in true solidity.

Contrast produces an immediate effect. Similarity satisfies us only in the long run. Contrast is an element of variety, but it divides our attention. Similarity is born of a striving for unity. The need to seek variety is perfectly legitimate, but we should not forget that the One precedes the Many. Moreover, the coexistence of both is constantly necessary, and all the problems of art, like all possible problems for that matter, including the problems of knowledge and of Being, revolve ineluctably about this question, with Parmenides on one side denying the possibility of the Many, and Heraclitus on the other denying the existence of the One. Mere common sense, as well as supreme wisdom, invite us to affirm both the one and the other. All the same, the best attitude for a composer in this case will be the attitude of a man who is conscious of the hierarchy of values and who must make a choice. Variety is valid only as a means of attaining similarity. Variety surrounds me on every hand. So I need not fear that I shall be lacking in it, since I am constantly confronted by it. Contrast is everywhere. One has only to take note of it. Similarity is hidden; it must be sought out, and it is found only after the most exhaustive efforts. When variety tempts me, I am uneasy about the facile solutions it offers me. Similarity, on the other hand, poses more difficult problems but also offers results that are more solid and hence more valuable to me.[10]

Stravinsky thus admits the sort of music with a "will to expression," something he does not do in the *Autobiography,* although he then says that he finds the other sort preferable in terms of strength and solidity. (This tallies with his saying in the *Autobiography* that construction is the indispensable and single requirement of music in its role of establishing the relationship of humankind and time.) It is still Stravinsky's preferred music of deep similarity that "evolves parallel to the process of ontological time," something that Carter also seems to be working toward in his Cello Sonata.

Carter has never written a response to Stravinsky's notions of time. But the passages quoted above seem to lead us in the same direction—the "mixing up" of various elements of the musical discourse, the music that evolves rather than proceeds by contrast, and yet the contrast of psychological and ontological time. The difference that springs to notice is Carter's combining the ontological, or chronometric, time of his piano with the psychological time of his cello to produce "virtual" time; Stravinsky does not do this. Carter's "virtual" time establishes the general framework within which the rest of the piece takes place. "Virtual" time—the contrast of ontological time and psychological time—establishes at the outset the characteristic element of the Cello Sonata, the temporal world of music to come. This temporal world is briefly left in the B section of the movement, to be reestablished in the brief A' section, which both closes the first movement and reminds the listener of the general temporal framework within which the rest of the sonata takes place, a framework of great rhythmic malleability set against a regular backdrop, stated or unstated. The final few pages of the sonata are a return to this essential ground, a closing of the book. That the roles of the instruments are reversed is simply a change of character that does not essentially alter the nature of the framework, or our hearing these pages as a perhaps wistful, perhaps yielding return to the world of the Sonata's beginning. In essence, then, this is the sort of structural procedure that has dominated Western classical music for some centuries: establishing a framework, either working within it or modifying it, and returning to it, reestablishing it as a closing gesture. Carter does write music of constant evolution—not, therefore, an analogue to Goethe's and Stravinsky's architecture as petrified music—but at the same time music that is ultimately a search for and establishment of unity.[11]

All of this has very little to do with *Finnegans Wake.* That book is many, many things, and only one of its aspects is the fact that its first sentence turns out to be the last portion of its last sentence. At the end of *Finnegans Wake,* one is forced to return to its beginning; not so with the Carter. In the Cello Sonata, the return to opening material sounds like a standard musical structural gesture, a gesture that is in fact impossible in narrative literature: the point of most literary narratives is

precisely that situations cannot be maintained, and that initial innocence cannot be regained. We will turn in a moment to a more poetic
sort of narrative closer to Carter's. We must note first, however, that the
circular temporal scheme that establishes the overall plan of Joyce's
book also permeates the novel in all its aspects and all its levels. This is
possible only because *Finnegans Wake,* like all literature, is a physical object that itself does not move through time. Carter's Cello Sonata, like
all works of music, must transpire through time; it exists only while
time passes.

But we may compare a more poetic kind of narrative with Carter's
Cello Sonata, a kind that we shall encounter in chapter 3 in Schoenberg's *Pierrot lunaire,* and a structure quite common in the first-person
lyric that narrates stories from the past. In *Pierrot* we begin with randy
exuberance, move through terror and chastisement, and return to our
physical point of departure changed psychologically by what we have
been through. This is also possible in first-person narratives in the past
tense, in which the narrator knows the outcome before beginning the
story, and in which the lyrical impulse chronicles the emotional impact
of the story's events on the narrator. This is the effect of Carter's Cello
Sonata, a fairly straightforward narrative (or sequence of events, one
modulating and evolving into the next) in a single temporal channel, in
which the final incarnation is an immediately recognizable version of
the first. The "narrative" model is simply an analogy for the one preferred by most musicians: establishing a framework, embellishing or
modifying it, and finally reestablishing it as a gesture of closure and a
return to stability.

Within this traditional framework—which Carter abandons in
later works—the internal discourse of Carter's music is indeed innovative. He in fact mixes up the "this" and "that" of traditional musical discourse, and he explores the deep similarities of different gestures in
the same way that Stravinsky described. We have seen this at work in
the Cello Sonata, and we will reinforce it here with a brief exposition of
the scheme for the First String Quartet (1951), a piece that we will take
up again in chapter 6.

In the most general sense, the First Quartet moves from absolute
diversity to absolute unity, all within a compressed temporal universe.
At the beginning, the four instruments move in four completely different rhythmic schemes (see Ex. 2.1). The cello, after a characteristic
metrical modulation, proceeds (from m. 22) in steady quarter notes;
the second violin in durations of five sixteenth notes; the first violin in
durations of three quarter notes plus an eighth-note triplet, or ten
eighth-note triplets; and the viola in steady quarter-note triplets. (In
terms of duration, the instruments range from viola to cello, to second
violin, to first.) In the course of the quartet, the instruments move from
this extraordinary diversity to unified ensemble rhythms. They ap-

proach one another in the ensuing *allegro scorrevole;* in the *adagio* the lower two instruments are pitted against the higher pair. By the end of the final variation movement, the instruments are in the same temporal universe and often play in rhythmic unison.

This unidirectional motion, not surprisingly, is handled in an unusual manner. The breaks between the sections do not coincide with the ends or beginnings of the four "movements." The first continuous section of music comprises the opening fantasia and the beginning of the scherzolike movement, the *allegro scorrevole*. The second section includes the end of the *allegro*, the *adagio*, and the beginning of the final movement. The last movement and the last section overlap most closely, emphasizing the establishment of stability at the end of the quartet and mirroring the stability built into the variation form as such. This is all, obviously, making more explicit the continuity between movements that Carter used in the Cello Sonata. Its effect is to reinforce the notion of continuous time, through the pauses, and in combination with the quartet's beginning and ending, its transpiring in what Carter calls "dream time."[12]

The First Quartet begins with a cadenza in the cello, starting in its tenor register, moving down to its lowest note, C (m. 7), and then moving upward two and one-half octaves to the beginning of the first movement proper (m. 22 in Ex. 2.1). At the end of the quartet, some forty minutes later, the final variations yield without cadence to a cadenza in the first violin that recalls that of the cello and then continues to move upward, to the high E two octaves about the staff. In his notes to the recording of the First and Second Quartets by the Composers Quartet,[13] Carter compares this procedure to Jean Cocteau's film *Le sang d'un poète,* which is framed by the collapse of a tall chimney, the collapse beginning before the film proper starts and ending after it is over. This bookend device is an attempt at a sort of temporal layering, which is also intimated in the beginning and ending of the Cello Sonata—establishing a frame within which a (seemingly) completely different time scheme transpires. And as with the Cello Sonata, one may be inclined to hear the frame as general rather than as a dominant or dictating gesture. The cello and violin cadenzas move through the pitch range of the entire quartet, from lowest to virtually the highest, and they serve again as that general frame of reference within which the quartet takes place, ultimately unifying the quartet in a single gesture as it has been gradually unified in the course of the four movements of the quartet proper.

The effect of such works as Carter's Cello Sonata and First String Quartet resides to a great degree in what might be called their dramatic unity. In this regard, Carter's works resemble those of Beethoven: by the end of the piece, listeners imagine they have been somewhere, have lived through some experience, have learned something.

EXAMPLE 2.1. Carter, String Quartet No. 1, mm. 13–32. Copyright ©1955, 1956 by Associated Music Publishers Inc. (BMI). International Copyright Secured. All Rights Reserved. Reprinted by Permission.

AMP-95544-119

(continued)

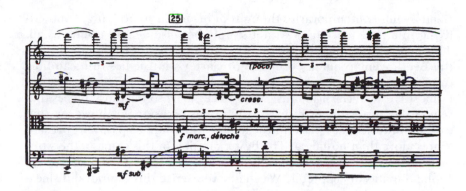

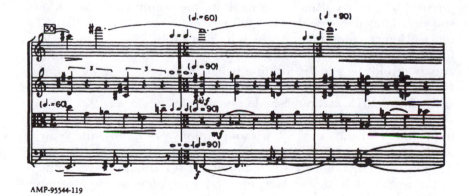

Beethoven's contemporaries thought of his music as edifying,[14] and edifying in a fairly specific way, not simply because beauty uplifts us all. This may be too much to ask of any composer besides Beethoven. But the Beethovenian quality of much of Carter's music lies in its audible drama and the irreversible time in which it transpires. This is a feature of most Western classical music, and necessarily so for those pieces that seem to be dramatic narratives. It happens occasionally, however, that program music takes place in the past, or in a mix of past and present that is more than nostalgia. The best examples of this come in the work of Charles Ives, as we saw in the discussion of the First and Fourth Violin Sonatas in chapter 1. We shall experience this temporal dislocation again in chapter 6, in Ives's Second String Quartet.

Scenes outside Time: Debussy and Stravinsky

It also happens, if more rarely in Western music, that pieces depict extramusical scenes or events outside a linear chronology. In the most common instances, the duration of the work is simply the extension of a moment and the music is an audible evocation, through whatever musical means, of a scene, usually (though not always or necessarily) from a single perspective: two examples are Claude Debussy's "Syrinx" for solo flute and the second of Igor Stravinsky's Three Pieces for String Quartet.

The legend of Syrinx is well known: she was the nymph loved and pursued by the satyr Pan. To escape him, she ran into a stream, where she was changed into reeds. Pan cut these reeds to fashion for himself a pipe—whence panpipes—on which he played out his continuing love for the nymph. The story was a favorite in turn-of-the-century France, and is retold as a ballet-within-a-ballet in Ravel's *Daphnis et Chloë*. Debussy's "Syrinx," written as a competition piece for the Paris Conservatory in 1913, was published only after his death, in 1927. It consists of four sections, each relatively brief. The first section begins high in the flute's second octave, slowly and sinuously descends, and returns to the opening register. The second section begins with the same melody as the first, but an octave lower. It rises, though never so high as the first section, descends again, and moves almost imperceptibly (with low, repeated triplets) into the third section, the least "melodic" of the piece in that it has the least sense of direction and the least smooth contour. The last section returns to the opening melodic figure and makes a long, slow descent to the final note.

In no way does "Syrinx" tell the story of Syrinx and Pan; its subject is the syrinx as panpipe, a meditation on the flute itself. The piece resembles the opening flute solo of Debussy's *Prélude à l'après-midi d'un faune* (1894), circling around a few pitches, repeating melodic motives and ideas, much more complex than it sounds.[15] Here the circling, the rhythmic variety, and the tonality unstressed until the final D♭, all contribute to the contemplative quality of the program: Pan playing his flute while remembering his love for the nymph.

In the same way, the second of Stravinsky's Three Pieces for String Quartet is also a static portrait, in this case of the contemporaneous English clown "Little Tich." Written in 1914, these three pieces were performed from manuscript in the 1915–16 season under the title "Grotesques"; when they were transcribed as three of the Four Studies for Orchestra, their titles were "Dance," "Eccentric," and "Canticle."[16] Stravinsky's portrayal of a clown, a physical performer, although a world away from *The Rite of Spring*, is constructed with the same techniques as much of that ballet score. The principal technique, sometimes called "moment form," is better characterized as modular: a succession, without transitions, of highly contrasting sections made up solely of repetitions or extensions of a single principal figure. A superficial analogy can be made to the analytic cubism of Braque and Picasso; perhaps a better one is Japanese prints, in which Stravinsky had been interested for some time.[17] The question, in the visual medium, is one of space and perspective. In music we hear a number of repetitive figures, all distinct from one another in makeup as well as in time, but with some shared characteristics. These include, beside repetition, rhythmic clarity and metrical asymmetry; frequent unisons among some of the instruments; largely chordal, and nontriadic, sounds; and the absence of dynamic gradations, reinforcing the lack of motivic and rhythmic transitions. The work as a whole lacks any sense of narrative, any sense of forward motion or linear development. It is thus a portrait rather than a story about Little Tich, the eccentric. The American Virgil Thomson made similar portraits throughout his life. He composed them at "sittings," like a painter. They also tend, like the Stravinsky, to be brief and static rather than narrative and dynamic, but there is no reason to believe that Thomson was here following in Stravinsky's path. His portraits are entirely original with him, and in his own markedly idiosyncratic style.

Hearing Time Stop: Messiaen

Such evocative works are not new with the twentieth century, any more than the narrative sort of program music. In contrast, a work that is inconceivable before 1913, before a changed view of temporality, is Olivier Messiaen's *Quartet for the End of Time* of 1940–41. A more apt title is impossible to imagine. Not only is Messiaen's quartet *about* the end of time as depicted in the Apocalypse, but it *embodies* an end of linear chronology as well. The latter is achieved not through any sort of programmatic device—we are not *told* that time stops—but through Messiaen's manipulation of rhythms and durations, elements equaled in the hierarchy of his musical language only by melody.

The various stories associated with the *Quartet for the End of Time* are well known. Messiaen wrote the piece in a German prisoner-of-war camp for fellow inmates who were musicians: a violinist, clarinetist, cellist, and himself as pianist. The work is inspired by a vision of the angel who announces the end of time, from Revelation 10:1–7. The quartet is in eight movements: seven because of the number of days in the week and because it is the perfect number, the six weekdays followed and "sanctified," in Messiaen's word, by the divine Sabbath, plus an eighth movement for eternity, the prolongation of the Sabbath into pure light and peace.[18] The titles of the eight movements are "Liturgy of Crystal," "Vocalise for the Angel Who Announces the End of Time," "Abyss of the Birds," "Intermezzo," "Praise of the Eternity of Jesus," "Dance of Fury, for the Seven Trumpets," "Clusters of Rainbows for the Angel Who Announces the End of Time," and "Praise of the Immortality of Jesus." In his preface to the score, Messiaen provides a narrative description, almost of religious ecstasy, for each movement; the descriptions serve as verbal metaphors for the musical events and are thus in a sense secondary to those events. What interests us is the musical embodiment of the end of time, and of the religious ecstasy that Messiaen invokes in his preface. To examine this we shall consider some techniques at work in the quartet and trace their overall course through the eight movements; and we can see, as did Boulez and other composers who studied with Messiaen in Paris and at Darmstadt, that seemingly abstruse techniques of musical manipulation can lead to extraordinary aesthetic effects that are anything but abstruse.

The first movement, "Liturgy of Crystal," sets the tone for the entire quartet, but it is unusual among the movements for the number of its "precompositional" elements or techniques. The piano part consists of two ostinati, a harmonic ostinato of twenty-nine chords and a rhythmic ostinato of seventeen units. Both are prime numbers; once started, the two pedals do not coincide for the duration of the movement. The cello line also consists of two ostinati, a melodic ostinato of five pitches from one of the two whole-tone collections (C, E, D, F♯, B♭) and a rhythmic pedal of fifteen units; three repetitions of the melodic pedal thus coincide with one of the rhythmic. The violin and clarinet parts are freer, but the violin uses five different melodic cells, and the clarinet a succession of closely related scales and melodic patterns. All this makes for an unusually thorough coherence of musical material, yet without sacrificing variety, which results from the overlapping of the different ostinati and the free temporal placement of the violin and clarinet melodies. In addition, the harmonic language is fairly restricted: melodic patterns tend to describe the tritone or (less frequently) the perfect fourth; the piano chords combine triads with pentatonic collections; and the octatonic scale is omnipresent. The piano part also emphasizes the pitch class F, using it as the lowest pitch in the first twelve chords of the twenty-nine-chord pedal, then ascending to the F an octave above (with a neighboring F♯), and finally descending again to the original F. Yet the music of this movement sounds anything but meticulously calculated; rather, it is extraordinarily depictive. This quality comes principally from the bird sounds in the clarinet and violin, enveloped by the soft, thick sounds of the piano and cello. It also stems from the low dynamic level, which makes the music seem introductory, and from the combination of variation and literal repetition that comes from the overlapping ostinati. The movement is in fact entirely introductory, for the quartet as a whole is built from just such elements and with just such effects.

The sense of time in the quartet seems to be one of defining durations while nevertheless avoiding regular metrical schemes. Because of the sectional nature of the eight movements and the similar qualities shared by several of them, we sense a linear continuity less evolving than Carter's but less developmental than Schoenberg's—among the earlier masters, closest perhaps to Debussy. The forms of the movements and thus of the quartet as a whole are virtually impossible to schematize in any way that corresponds to the experience of hearing the music. Virtually all the movements share common building blocks of scales, rhythms, chord patterns, and kinds of musical language. The fourth movement ("Intermezzo"), the first to be written, uses material that reappears literally in other movements. The solo clarinet movement, "Abyss of the Birds," uses short passages from the other "bird" movements, especially the first. The "Vocalise" and the "Dance of Fury," the second and sixth movements, also have similar outlines. The overall effect of this procedure, again, is of a linear succession, of contrasting elements and sections that form a unitary musical world, in fact the "unity of musical space," which "demands an absolute and unitary perception"—Schoenberg's ideal realized here through very non-Schoenbergian means. This spatial sort of music seems to define durations rather than move through an unrepeatable, Beethovenian chronology. It is for this reason, and through these means—time becoming space by becoming duration rather than progress; the stabilization of our temporal sense through meters and rhythms on the cusp between regularity and ever-new reformulations of irregular elements—that Messiaen can seem to stop time. For if time does not pass, it does not, in our modern Western cosmology, exist. For Stravinsky, music is the medium in which we experience, are coordinated with, the present, but that present is always a new present, never a static and atemporal duration. For Messiaen, time no longer passes and thus no longer exists.

The abolition of time is completed in the final movement, the "Praise of the Immortality of Jesus," which, like the earlier movements, combines a number of elements, both new and traditional. Three elements are specific to Messiaen's musical language: the piano chords, which move in a repetitive rhythm that (because of the infinitely slow tempo and the relative consonance of the sounds) never becomes mechanistic; the movement's form, which, according to Messiaen, consists of a phrase, repeated, followed by a "commentary" on the phrase; and the particular sonorities used, an extension and thickening of Western harmonies, but still not in the standard hierarchy of Western classical tonality. There are also more traditional elements in this movement: it begins very softly, toward the bottom of the instruments' ranges, moves higher and grows louder, then continues to move higher as it grows softer, the last measures marked *ppp* and *perdendosi;* in the Western classical lexicon this progression signifies ecstasy, dying away, ascension to otherworldly bliss (compare, for example, Wagner's *Liebestod* or Schoenberg's *Verklärte Nacht*). The violin does not need to breathe, nor does the piano; the infinitely long phrases reinforce the idea of attaining the otherworldly. The use of the violin with its extraordinary sweetness in the highest registers, not only suggests the ecstatic bliss of immortality but also implies a continuation of the violin's upward reaches, to sounds so high and dulcet that they are beyond the mortal human ear. Finally, the key of E major—or here, an E-major triad as a tonic, enriched by an added sixth, C♯—is often a symbol of religion and of salvation. (Associations of particular keys with particular colors or emotional states are always subjective, not to say impossible to discuss with any pretense of rationality. But E major sounds much different from D major; and Messiaen's own rich metaphorical use of colors in his discussions of his music allows me, I think, to say this.)

The *Quartet for the End of Time* no doubt reflects the circumstances of its composition, Messiaen's imprisonment in a Nazi POW camp. But that is not its point. What the work is really about is Messiaen's extraordinary faith, the assuredness of his vision, and his deep love for the worldly objects that seem to lead him ever back to his faith and his belief in God's love: birds, colors, all sorts of natural phenomena that surround humanity. The quartet is thus not just—or even—a "setting" of the verses from Revelation. One might rather approach the work in the opposite direction, reading the verses as illustrations of the music. This is not Wagner's "deeds of music made visible,"[19] as he described his music dramas, but a programmatic text depicting an event that takes place in the medium of sound. This is music that, as it is about something, embodies that something as well; the apocalyptic texts are separate, if parallel, descriptions, secondary to the heard.

Musical Montage and Ambiguous Signs: Debussy

The relation of the music to programmatic epigraph, to quoted materials, to musical "signs," and thus to networks of meaning, becomes fluid and virtually ungraspable in Debussy's *En blanc et noir* (1915) for two pianos. The structural process at work here approaches montage, in the filmic sense of the word: auditory "images" may or may not be representative, connections are often unstated, and the linearity is from moment to moment, often a matter of succession rather than of progression or relation. *En blanc et noir* raises the most intriguing questions; it is not difficult to discuss how the piece works, as music; but it is extremely tricky to contemplate what the piece is or might be.

One wonders why *En blanc et noir* was not included as the first in Debussy's projected series of six "sonatas for various instruments," since it is a sort of chamber sonata. The principal differences between *En blanc et noir* and the three completed sonatas include its unusual instrumentation and its movement titles and programmatic indications. *En blanc et noir,* "in black and white," refers most directly to the pianos' keyboards, and perhaps also to various genres of the visual arts—woodblocks, etchings, monochromes, photography, black-on-white painting—whose representations are suggestive and elusive rather than directly pictorial. In addition to this extramusical title, Debussy places epigraphs over each of the three movements, a procedure highly unusual for him.[20] They are:

1st movement: Qui reste à sa place
               Et ne danse pas
               De quelque disgrâce
               Fait l'aveu tout bas.

                    (J. Barbier and M. Carré, *Roméo et Juliette*)

               Who stays in his place
               And does not dance
               Of some disgrace
               Makes silent [base] confession.

2nd movement: Prince, porté soit des serf Eolus
               En la forest ou domine Glaucus,
               Ou privé soit de paix et d'espérance

Car digne n'est de posséder vertus
Qui mal vouldroit au royaume de France

(François Villon, "Ballade contre les ennemis de la
France," *envoi*)

Prince, may he be carried by the serfs of Aeolus
To the forest where Glaucus reigns,
Or may he be denied all peace and hope,
For he is not worthy of enjoying these virtues
Who would wish ill to the kingdom of France.

3rd movement: Yver, vous n'este qu'un vilain . . .

(Charles d'Orléans)

Winter, you're but a nasty fellow . . .

Debussy wrote *En blanc et noir* in 1915, at the beginning of the era
when he signed his works "Claude Debussy, musicien français." His
had not been an easy life; and at its end, Germans were bombarding
Paris. We can only speculate about the degree to which *En blanc et noir*
is a product of the First World War. No doubt the tragedy of the second
movement reflects that of the Great War: it is dedicated "To Lieutenant
Jacques Charlot, killed by the enemy, March 3, 1915," and its music is
filled with direct and indirect intimations of combat. In addition, it has
been suggested that the epigraph over the first movement refers to
those (including Debussy himself) who for whatever reasons did not
fight for France.[21] Only the third movement, so far as I can discover,
seems to have no extramusical or musical reference to World War I.
This gives us something further to consider: Why two movements (if
we include the first) about the war, but not the third?

The easiest answer lies in the music itself. Although the structural
process resembles montage, there are really few formal surprises. The
first movement is a kind of sonata-rondo, unusual for a first movement,
but here quite close to a typical sonata movement and, at the same
time, referring perhaps to the dance of the epigraph. In a fast triple
meter, the music is played *avec emportement:* swept away, passionately.
The A section (or the first theme of the exposition) is triadic, arpeggios
sweeping up and down both keyboards, single lines filled out into
chords,[22] undulating between straightforward triple meter and hemiola. The B section (second theme) is slightly slower, *scherzando*, a rhythmic, rising little tune spiked by sudden *sforzando* chords. The A section
returns, not unusually, as the closing theme of the exposition, or as the
truncated second A of a sonata-rondo. The quasi-development section,
the C of the sonata-rondo, plays with the A theme, in fact develops it,
before moving on to new music; this is unusual for Debussy, especially
in his later music. But it sets up the surprise to come: following a *fortis-*

simo climax (at what would seem to be the height of the development) and a decrescendo to lead into a recapitulation (a second climax, separated from the first for its independent effect), that recapitulation turns out to be false. We hear the first theme (A) again, but it quickly moves into remote keys and returns briefly to the new theme introduced for the climax of the so-called development. We then move into a second development section (or a continuation of the first, after the false recapitulation), based on the B theme. And here, too, there is new material: over a pedal of rhythmically falling and rising octaves, Debussy introduces what can only be trumpet calls, as if to battle. The B theme, which had been *scherzando,* is now *marcato* and menacing, kept at the level of *piano* until another *molto crescendo* leads us into the final A, or the final recapitulation, and coda.

We thus have this formal scheme:

Sonata-rondo	A B A	C (A) B	A Coda
Sonata	Exposition	Development	Recap/Coda

This is skewed from the normative scheme for the sonata-rondo, in which the C section would be parallel to a development and the final ABA to a recapitulation. But I cannot believe that Debussy intended here to play on the formal expectations of his listeners: that might well be the case for Schoenberg, who turned received formal schemes to new advantage in *Verklärte Nacht,* his first two string quartets, and his Chamber Symphony, Op. 9. The proportions are wrong in the Debussy for this sort of formal play. The sections follow too seamlessly, and the entire effect, again, is one of linearity rather than sectionality. Debussy's effects, especially that of the trumpet call in the second B section or the development, do not rely on the manipulation of formal norms, but rather on themselves, local events in a long succession and accumulation of local events. Form, again, is a matter of succession rather than of progression and hierarchy.

The first reason for this is Debussy's reliance on melody as his most central musical material—not melody in the sense of songlike tunes, but melody in the sense of arabesques, long, sinuous single lines full of smoothly contoured curves, reminiscent of the lines decorating Arabic paintings (whence the term). These arabesques are widely noted by Debussy scholars, and were an integral part of his essential musical style since at least the *Prélude à l'après-midi d'un faune* of 1894. (That work's principal melody, the opening flute line, is a perfect example.) In *En blanc et noir* and similar pieces, moreover, the arabesques serve to generate the textures: whereas Debussy's music is often characterized by a "layered" texture, in which dissimilar events occur simultaneously in different registers (and, in the orchestra, articulated by contrasting timbres as well), in other works the texture is one of single lines doubled to fill the musical space; or if not doubled, then giving rise to similar lines that fill out the space in the same manner.

Debussy's melodies are not always reducible to conventional scales or modes. In *En blanc et noir* he avoids not only the received tonal hierarchy and authentic cadences but also leading tones and chromatic melodic motion in general. This contributes significantly to the clarity, the transparency, of his music, since the leading-tone or half-step relationship is one of insistence and relentless forward motion. Thus, even though Debussy's harmonies are primarily triadic, his triads seem to derive from his linear melodies rather than to stand in a semi-independent harmonic hierarchy. Sections may be articulated by different tonics (a more exact description than "key"), but these tonics are secondary to melodic and textural articulation.

The second movement of *En blanc et noir*, a ternary form, seems to convey a narrative. But the question remains of what it might be narrating. It falls into at least seven sections. The first sounds introductory, with three figures that recur motivically throughout the movement: a rhythmic pedal on C that also introduces the turbulent middle section; trumpet calls, different from those of the first movement, and which persist in every section; and a diatonic melody in a clear and regular $\frac{6}{8}$ meter, unlike any melody we have heard to this point in the piece. The second, short section has a monophonic melody shared by the two pianos, a passage of widely spaced, serene D-major chords, and an oscillating *sostenuto* melody in seconds (and harmonized by seconds) rising in register and dynamics. This leads to the third short section, which closes the first unit of the movement: again we hear the diatonic $\frac{6}{8}$ melody, again over a dissonant pedal. Without resolving, the music moves directly into the central section, the longest of the movement.

This B section is extraordinarily tumultuous; its swirling arpeggios and pedals, lack of harmonic direction, constantly changing dynamics, and especially its two quotations seem narrative, depictive. (One might be reminded of the "Battle on the Ice" from Prokofiev's and Eisenstein's 1938 film *Alexander Nevsky*.) The first quotation is the trumpet calls, initially mocked by rhythmically jagged figures harmonized with dissonant seconds; these trumpet calls (or horn calls, as if from the *Chanson de Roland*) will later recur. The second quotation is the first three phrases of the Lutheran hymn "Ein' feste Burg": in the Paris of 1915, this must have been literally horrifying. The melody is sounded in octaves, *piano* but marked *lourd* ("heavy"), over a dissonant, *marcato* accompaniment. The melody appears over this accompaniment, the last note of each phrase hanging unresolved (and, in the second and third phrases, even unheard) in the surrounding turbulence.

The referents of the movement are clear enough, but their narrative is not. As proudly French as he was, Debussy was also too aware of the horrors of war to fall easily into jingoism. After the quotations from

"Ein' feste Burg," the rest of the movement repeats the trumpet calls, alternating these with the *sostenuto* melody from the beginning and the ⁶⁄₈ diatonic melody for the third time, but now over a consonant pedal. The trumpet calls cannot be heard as sounding a final victory. Perhaps they are valedictory: the dedication, we remember, is to a man only recently killed by the enemy. The music of this movement is by turns chaotic, martial, serene, joyous. We know, from the dedication and from the music itself, what it is "about": but we do not, and perhaps cannot, know what story is being told here. The music seems to work on the plane of narrative, because of its juxtapositions and recurring motives, because of its central quotation of a profoundly meaningful melody. But the gist of the narrative remains out of reach, unknowable, because (unlike our Carter examples) it lacks a clear framing. The word *montage* springs to mind again, to describe the formal juxtapositions that imply the narrative. It is also perhaps an apt word in that any narrative is filtered through a third-person consciousness that selects and dictates what we hear of the events in question. But the perspective of that third person, and thereby our own, is skewed. We do not know if we are hearing about something that has happened in the past; we do not know if we are in the middle of a depicted scene (as the "Battle on the Ice"). This uncertainty becomes—or is made—part of the emotional and musical affect of the movement; and the overall result is unsettling in the extreme.

The third movement of *En blanc et noir* lacks the quasi-narrative and programmatic elements of the first two movements, and it is much more typical of Debussy's earlier piano music (especially the Preludes). The movement's epigraphic reference is to winter, and the music is full of devices that elsewhere in Debussy serve to depict natural phenomena like rain, squalls, and so on, a much more clement winter scene than his piano prelude "Des pas sur la neige" ("Footsteps in the Snow") or Vivaldi's chilling *Winter* in *The Four Seasons*. The form is, again, sectional and cumulative, defined by texture and figuration as much as by melody or harmonic scheme. Like the first two movements, the third is evocative; but in this case, we seem to know what it evokes. The movement makes a pleasant conclusion to *En blanc et noir,* which raises the only real question about it: What is it doing here, after the first two movements?

The most obvious answer is perhaps the best—the third movement is simply a relief from the exuberance of the first and the emotional journey of the second. The figuration of the movement and its puckish rhythms are too lighthearted for this to be heard as anything sardonic or serious: we are much closer to "Jardins sous la pluie" than to "Le tombeau des naïades," and we are much closer to the eighteenth and later twentieth centuries than to the nineteenth and its obsession with organicism. Yet the pure depictiveness of this third movement may retrospectively tinge our hearing of the first two movements. Perhaps they, too, are more depictive, third-person rather than first-person. But if this is how one hears the first two movements after the third, it can be only in retrospect: they do not work this way *while* one listens to them, even if one listens to the third movement beforehand.

En blanc et noir is a sort of present-tense music, despite its reference to extramusical objects, whereas Ive's Fourth Violin Sonata is a mixture of present and past. This is a result of *En blanc et noir's* creation through montage: its successions and accumulations, which are somewhat analogous to a panning camera, and its manipulations of musical time, which are a matter of juxtaposition and recollection rather than development of narrative. A similar case obtains in Debussy's three sonatas and in much French music of the later twentieth century, especially in the works of the 1950s and 1960s, such as Boulez's *Le marteau sans maître*. Again, the question of musical time and its manipulations by a composer are of central importance to much modern music. But we have now moved rather far from music and literature, the point at which we began this chapter, to tough lightly on visual arts, film, and most important, the musical handling of time and narrative. The following chapter returns to literature. Its first section deals with vocal chamber music and the interaction of specific literary works with musical techniques and procedures. The second is more theoretical or critical, discussing recent developments in the interpenetration of literary or critical ideas and approaches with music, developments of the greatest significance since the mid-1950s.

Notes

1. As with a number of descriptive stylistic terms, *neoclassicism* has no single definition; its meaning depends rather on who is using it. The definition in the *Harvard Concise Dictionary of Music* (Don Michael Randel, ed.; Cambridge, MA, 1978) is as good as any: "A movement of 20th-century music that is characterized by adoption of features of the music of the 17th and 18th centuries. It represents a general reaction against the unrestrained emotionalism of late romanticism." By *neoclassicism* I mean absolute music from the years between the two World Wars that makes conscious reference to earlier musics or that returns to stylistic procedures (forms, textures, and so on) of the Viennese Classical tradition.

2. This is also a time-honored practice. Schoenberg added descriptive titles to his Five Pieces for Orchestra, Op. 16, at his publisher's request.

3. See George Perle, "The Secret Programme of the Lyric Suite," *Musical Times* 118 (1977): 629–32, 709–13, 809.

4. At the 1979 public lecture in which Perle described his findings, the last movement of the *Lyric Suite* was performed twice: first the purely instrumental version, and then with a mezzo-soprano singing the text. The vocal version was

meant simply as a demonstration; Perle was not recommending that the work be performed this way.

5. Elliott Carter, liner notes for Nonesuch recording H-71234 (1969), reprinted as "Sonata for Cello and Piano (1948); Sonata for Flute, Oboe, Cello, and Harpsichord (1952)," in *The Writings of Elliott Carter*, ed. Else Stone and Curt Stone (Bloomington, IN, 1977), 270.

6. Allen Edwards, *Flawed Words and Stubborn Sounds: A Conversation with Elliott Carter* (New York, 1971), 90–94.

7. Carter, *Writings*, 271–72.

8. Cf., in this light, Schoenberg's conception of an absolutely unified music space (see chapter 1).

9. Igor Stravinsky, *An Autobiography* (New York, 1962), 54.

10. Stravinsky, *Poetics of Music in the Form of Six Lessons* (Cambridge, MA, 1970), 41–43.

11. The return comprises not just this exchange of the opening roles. In addition, the piano from m. 157 of the last movement (immediately after the metrical modulation to the tempo and $\frac{4}{4}$ meter of the first movement) repeats two of the central motives of the first movement, the syncopated octaves and a melodic motive (mm. 159, 166–67, 172–73 of the last movement, mm. 19–21 and passim of the first) that has always sounded to me like a reference, intended or not, to Ives's *Concord* Sonata.

12. Carter, *Writings*, 277.

13. Ibid., 274–79.

14. See Joseph Kerman and Alan Tyson, *The New Grove Beethoven* (New York, 1983), passim, especially p. 108 (Tovey's use of the word "edifying").

15. For analyses of both these pieces, see William W. Austin, *Music in the 20th Century* (New York, 1966), 7–23, and Claude Debussy, *Prelude to the Afternoon of a Faun*, Norton Critical Edition, ed. Austin (New York, 1970), 3–19, 71–96.

16. Eric Walter White, *Stravinsky: The Composer and His Works*, 2d edition (Berkeley and Los Angeles, 1979), 234.

17. See chapter 3 for a brief discussion of his 1913 *Three Japanese Lyrics*.

18. Messiaen's notes published in the score (Paris, 1942).

19. Quoted in Curt von Westernhagen, "Wagner," *The New Grove Dictionary of Music and Musicians*, ed. Stanley Sadie (London, 1980), 20:113.

20. It seems important that the epigraphs appear *above* their movements. In Debussy's two books of preludes for piano, the titles appear at the end, as if they were afterthoughts or footnotes, only incidental to the music.

21. Harry Halbreich, "Analyse de l'oeuvre," in Edward Lockspeiser, *Claude Debussy: Sa vie et sa pensée* [Paris], 1980), 609–10.

22. David Lewin, "Some Instances of Parallel Voice-Leading in Debussy," *19th Century Music* 11 (Summer 1987):59–72.

CHAPTER THREE

Music and Literature II: Vocal Chamber Music

If modern programmatic chamber music raises questions of temporality and voice, the genre of vocal chamber music, works for voice and chamber ensemble, deals with issues of the direct interplay between words and music, issues of structure and comprehensibility, and a new theatricality in music. Here I will ignore works for voice and piano and for voice and guitar, topics so vast that they demand their own treatment. I will also pass over settings of poetry in which a voice is accompanied by a small chamber ensemble as it might be by a single pianist. (I am thinking here of works such as Samuel Barber's *Dover Beach,* a setting of Matthew Arnold's poem for voice and string quartet, in which attention is focused on the voice; or like Heitor Villa-Lobos's *Bachianas Brasileiras* No. 5, for soprano and eight cellos, again a piece for voice and a subordinate, if striking, homophonic accompaniment.) In this chapter I am concerned rather with works such as Boulez's *Le marteau sans maître,* discussed in chapter 1, in which there is a real interplay between the voice, as an instrument, and the surrounding chamber ensemble; and in works that show direct and indissoluble links between poetic material—whether technical, structural, or aesthetic—and the music composed on that material.

Before World War I: Schoenberg and Others

Schoenberg's Second String Quartet (1908) is a sonata cycle: first movement in sonata form, second movement a scherzo, third movement a slow theme and variations, and the last movement a through-composed finale. But the work also falls into the category of cyclic pieces whose antecedents include Liszt's B-Minor Sonata and Beethoven's Fifth Symphony, in which all movements are bound together through the use of the same material, and in which—especially in the Liszt sonata—all four movements form a through-composed entity. Chapter 6 deals with the first two movements of the Schoenberg Second Quartet, as part of the discussion of the modern string quartet as a genre. The point of interest for now is the role of the soprano in the last two movements, her interaction with the string quartet, and the import of her text.

The last two movements of Schoenberg's quartet are settings of poems by Stefan George, a disciple of Stéphane Mallarmé. The verses embody the longing for elsewhere and the psychic and physical pain of existence found most outspokenly in Baudelaire but pervasive throughout nineteenth-century European Romanticism. The third movement's text is "Litanei":

Litanei	***Litany***
Tief ist die trauer,	Deep is the sorrow
die mich umdüstert,	which overshadows me,
Ein tret ich wieder,	I enter again,
Herr! in dein haus . . .	Lord!, into your house . . .
Lang war die reise	Long was the journey,
matt sind die glieder,	weak are my limbs,
Leer sind die schreine,	Empty are the shrines,
voll nur die qual.	full only the torment.
Durstende zunge	Thirsting tongue
darbt nach dem weine.	is famishing for wine.
Hart war gestritten,	Hard was the battle,
starr ist mein arm.	stiff is my arm.
Gönne die ruhe	Do not begrudge peace
schwankenden schritten,	to unsteady steps,
Hungrigem gaume	For hungering mouth
bröckle dein brot!	crumble your bread!
Schwach ist mein atem	Weak is my breath
rufend dem traume,	calling to the dream,
Hohl sind die hände,	Hollow are my hands,
fiebernd der mund.	feverish my mouth.
Leih deine kühle,	Lend me your coolness,
lösche die brände,	extinguish the flames,
Tilge das hoffen,	Blot out my hoping,
sende das licht!	send your light!

Gluten im herzen
    lodern noch offen,
Innerst im grunde
    wacht noch ein schrei.
	Ardors in my heart
	    still glow openly,
	In my innermost depths
	    lives still a cry.

Töte das sehnen,
    schliesse die wunde!
Nimm mir die liebe,
    gib mir dein glück!
	Kill my longing,
	    close the wounds!
	Take from me my love,
	    give me your happiness!

The poem falls into eight quatrains, each self-contained syntactically but structurally identical to the others. Each line is a double dactyl in which the last beat is suppressed ($\smile\smile\smile\smile\smile$). The rhyme scheme of each quatrain is *abcd*; the *c* of each becomes the *b* of the next. Given the incantatory rhythm of the poem, any more-obtrusive rhyme structure would have made it doggerel. But this linking of rhymes contributes to the progression of the poem, from the supplicant's entry into the Lord's house (church or heaven or both), to the plea for the sacraments, and for the healing and peace that the sacraments represent. Each quatrain is a step closer to the godhead, each a more urgent and desperate cry.

This is precisely the musical structure of Schoenberg's setting: a progression of steps "forward," growing in complexity and agitation, in chromatic distancing from a home key, in dynamics, and in the soprano's range. Schoenberg's "Litanei" is a theme and variations, stable and repetitive in its insistence on a small number of motives and their developments, unstable and forward-moving in all other aspects. Beyond his predilection for the developing variation as a basis for musical discourse, the choice of a theme-and-variations structure was carefully considered on Schoenberg's part:

> I was afraid the great dramatic emotionality of the poem might cause me to surpass the borderlines of what should be admitted in chamber music. I expected the serious elaboration required by variation would keep me from becoming too dramatic.[1]

"What should be admitted in chamber music" is a telling phrase. Perhaps Schoenberg should have written "what should be admitted into the string quartet," for in *Pierrot lunaire*, completed only four years later, he certainly broke all bounds of what had been admitted into chamber music before 1912. And it is equally striking that Schoenberg was concerned about becoming "too dramatic" in a chamber work. His *Verklärte Nacht* was sufficiently "dramatic" to enable the listener to follow easily the narrative of Dehmel's poem. In the case of the quartet, what Schoenberg presumably meant by drama is not enacted narrative but the inappropriate transgression of formal boundaries. Given the formal structures of the first two movements, he did not want a free rhapsody, which would perhaps have been perceived as a distortion of the poem. The fourth movement, "Entrückung" ("Rapture" or "Transport"), is through-composed and free in form: but that was a far less serious matter in the finale of a sonata cycle, and Schoenberg moved in that direction smoothly by introducing in the third movement the soprano voice and a musical form that followed a poetic model.

"Litanei" begins with the string quartet playing the theme of the movement (Ex. 3.1), a theme made up of four motives, each derived from an earlier movement. Motive a (viola, mm. 1–2) is from the first theme of the first movement, b (1st violin, mm. 2–3) from the bridge of that movement, e (viola, mm. 3–5) from the second movement, and d (2d violin and cello, mm. 5–10) from the second-theme group of the

EXAMPLE 3.1. Schoenberg, String Quartet No. 2, Op. 10, 3d movement, mm. 1–10. Used by permission of Belmont Music Publishers, Pacific Palisades, CA 90272.

first movement's exposition (although by its first appearance in that section, it has been heard to develop gradually from yet an earlier motive).[2] Each strophe of the poem is set with motive *a*, develops by spinning out the motives and the new music to which they give rise, and closes with a variation of motive *d*. Schoenberg's variation techniques include rhythmic augmentation and diminution, inversion, and chromatic elaboration of the basic form as well as the resetting of that basic form in new textures and with new accompanying figures. Note that motive *d*, which closes the theme and each variation, achieves only a half cadence on the dominant B♭, and never progresses to the tonic E♭ minor. Each variation is thus open ended (as the supplicant continues to approach the godhead), but moves smoothly into the next, since B♭ is also part of the tonic triad.

The first variation begins as if repeating the theme, but with the motives reassigned to other instruments; thus the soprano enters as the cello begins motive *d*, its sustained notes now broken up into shorter, repeated ones, the rhythmic changes mirroring the text's anguish. The soprano's melody, doubled in the first violin, is a variation and spinning-out of motives *a* and *e*. This is the technique of all the variations. The second variation begins in the second violin while the soprano and first violin finish the melody of the first variation; this procedure is observed throughout the movement. Variations 2 through 5 continue in similar fashion, growing in chromatic and rhythmic intensity. The last three variations are run on, without the intervening rests in the voice part that separate the earlier variations from one another. The lack of rests stems from the text: the last three stanzas are a direct plea and are thus set apart from the first five. These variations are also the climax of the movement, beginning softly and in the same register as the theme and the first variation, building slowly to the soprano's high G♭ on *schrei* ("cry"), which crescendos and slides up to the dissonant, *fortissimo* G natural for *Töte* ("Kill") to begin the last verse, the last variation, the last plea. This plea climaxes on the two-octave downward leap, *fff*, on the word *liebe*, "love," the supplicant's goal.[3] The final line of the text is set to a variation of the opening motive, but this is a coda and not another variation. Motive *e* is not heard. The coda rests on motive *d*, final triadic simplifications of motive *a*, and motive *b* resolving emphatically into the final E♭-minor triad. We are left with the last supplication, "gib mir dein glück!"

The fourth movement represents Schoenberg's first extended move into atonality.[4] Although the movement ends clearly in F♯ major, it begins with such chromaticism—in *ppp*, muted, scurrying string figures from the cello through the atmospheric first violin—that one is hard pressed to hear the beginning of this movement in any particular key. Indeed, the body of the movement avoids any overall sense of tonality until the end. But the impression made by the music is certainly not one of chaos—which would seem to be implied by the term *atonality*—but rather of constant motion, interrupted only three times (and these in the first half of the movement) by lines or chord progressions that seem, in contrast to their immediate context, timeless and motionless.

The reason for this is programmatic. In his "Notes on the Four String Quartets," Schoenberg wrote:

> The fourth movement, Entrückung, begins with an introduction, depicting the departure from earth to another planet. The visionary poet here foretold sensations, which perhaps soon will be affirmed. Becoming relieved from gravitation—passing through clouds into thinner and thinner air, forgetting all the troubles of life on earth—that is attempted to be illustrated in this introduction.[5]

The introduction is, moreover, a foreshadowing of the entire movement. The motives of the first three movements are left behind, as the earth and its difficulties have been. All is new here, including Schoenberg's rhapsodic treatment of the poetic structure of Dehmel's text.

That structure is, like that of "Litanei," very straightforward. Here tercets follow a rhyme scheme of *aba*, with the *b* of the first stanza also that of the second: *aba cbc ded fef,* and so on. All the lines are in iambic pentameter. Each stanza is fairly self-contained except that the second moves directly on to the third, and the seventh to the last. After a first line, with a full stop, which introduces the poem as a whole, the first three tercets take leave of earth. The fourth stanza begins the transfiguration, the rapture of the speaker, and the last four stanzas, the last half of the poem, are the speaker's transport into vast, eternal realms, into the mystical union with the godhead, thus a resolution of the third movement's "Litanei":

Entrückung	*Rapture*
Ich fühle luft von anderen planeten	I feel the air of other planets.
Mir blassen durch das dunkel die gesichter	Through the darkness faces grow pale to me
Die freundlich eben noch sich zu mir drehten.	which even a moment ago turned to me in friendliness.
Und bäum und wege die ich liebte fahlen	And trees and paths which I loved are dim
Dass ich sie kaum mehr kenne und du lichter	so that I hardly know them, and you, light
Geliebter schatten—rufer meiner qualen—	beloved shadow—who called forth my torment—

Bist nun erloschen ganz in tiefern gluten	are now extinguished in the deeper incandescence
Um nach dem taumel streitenden getobes	so that after the frenzied, warring confusion
Mit einem frommen schauer anzumuten.	you will rise again with a pious thrill.
Ich löse mich in tönen, kreisend, webend,	I dissolve into tones, circling, floating,
Ungründigem danks und unbenamten lobes	with ungrounded thanks and unnamed praise
Dem grossen atem wunschlos mich ergebend.	to the universal breath, will-less, surrendering myself.
Mich überfährt ein ungestümes wehen	A furious blowing passes over me
Im rausch der weihe wo inbrünstige schreie	in the transport of the consecration where fervent cries
In staub geworfner Beterinnen flehen:	of praying women, cast into the dust, beseech:
Dann seh ich wie sich duftige nebel lüpfen	Then I see how fragrant mists arise
In einer sonnerfüllten klaren freie	into a sun-filled, clear freedom
Die nur umfängt auf fernsten bergesschlüpfen.	sliding over the distant mountains.
Der boden schüttert weiss und weich wie molke.	The ground shudders, white and soft as whey.
Ich steige über schluchten ungeheuer	I rise above enormous chasms.
Ich fühle wie ich über letzte wolke	I feel that above the highest clouds
In einem meer kristallnen glanzes schwimme—	in a sea of crystal brilliance I swim—
Ich bin ein funke nur vom heiligen feuer	I am only a spark of the holy fire
Ich bin ein dröhnen nur der heiligen stimme.	I am only a resonance of the holy voice

Schoenberg no longer follows the poem's strophic form, for his intention now is to transgress formal boundaries, to set the transport of the poet from the earthbound to the ecstatic. The first line is thus set by itself; coming as it does after the departure depicted in the introduction, it is the movement's first instance of wondering stasis. The verses are then set continuously through the end of the third tercet, when we hear a recall of the introduction and a rebeginning with the line "Ich löse mich in tönen." (In a sort of musical pun, the second syllable of *löse,* "dissolve," resolves to an F♯-major triad, the eventual tonic triad of the entire work.) This is the second instance of stasis. The third instance is, like the first two, the poet's surrender to mystical union, the word *ergebend* at the end of the fourth tercet (and of the first half of the poem). Here the resolution is into a C-major chord, marked *espressivo (Ton!)*: expressively, and with a full, strong tone. (The first theme of the first movement also moved strongly from F♯ to C. Schoenberg's use of these two chords again for his resolutions into stasis is another example of his careful planning of the quartet's overall structure.)

Hereafter the music moves continually forward, spinning out new variations on the few motives that set it in motion, the fleeting figure of the introduction and the music heard in the strings just before the first entrance of the soprano. For programmatic reasons, the music must be constantly developing, if Schoenberg is to depict the transport (meaning, like the word *rapture,* both the mystical ecstasy and the movement toward it) of the text. Nor does this motion stop at the end of the text. After the ecstatic climax in the voice, supported by *fortissimo* tremolos and arpeggios in the strings, the music sinks into a long coda that gradually establishes real stasis, real motionlessness, after the sustained moving-in-place of the vocal climax. The poet—at once the singer, and composer, and hearer—is subsumed into yet a further realm, arriving on a long F♯-major triad that begins *pianissimo* and fades finally into silence.

We must wait until chapter 6 to consider the role of these two movements in Schoenberg's quartet as a whole. Having considered them briefly, as an early twentieth-century rapturous recycling of Liszt or Wagner, it is now time to turn to perhaps the seminal work of twentieth-century music, Schoenberg's *Pierrot lunaire,* Op. 21, of 1912. Much more radically than *Verklärte Nacht* or the second quartet, *Pierrot* is the cusp between the nineteenth and twentieth centuries, between Romanticism and modernism. The work was an immediate event in 1912, first in Berlin and then throughout Europe. It gave rise to Ravel's *Three Poems of Stéphane Mallarmé* (1913) and Stravinsky's *Three Japanese Lyrics* (also 1913), transmuting Schoenberg's "expressionism" into a contemporary French idiom. It resonates still through Boulez's *Le marteau sans maître* of 1957 and thereafter. *Pierrot's* control—textual, motivic, and instrumental—of its new atonal language was of profound importance in the expansion of tonal possibilities in all contemporary musical languages. Its *Sprechstimme* gave contemporary music a new timbral resource. Its theatricality led, especially from the 1950s, in the work of the youngest generation of composers of that era, to new sorts of vocal music (Boulez's *Marteau,* for example, and the works of Berio, Ligeti, and Crumb discussed at the end of this chapter) and ultimately to an entirely new genre, the so-called theater piece. It is impossible to overstate the importance of *Pierrot lunaire* for the twentieth century. Of both momentary and lasting importance, it resembles *Ulysses* and *Les demoiselles d'Avignon* in its impact on the modern world.

Schoenberg chose his texts from a group of some fifty poems by Albert Giraud and translated into German by Otto Erich Hartleben. Of these, Schoenberg selected twenty-one, or "dreimal sieben Gedichte," "three times seven poems." (Numerology plays a part in *Pierrot lunaire*, as it did in Schoenberg's life; thus he was careful to publish *Pierrot* as his opus 21, or 3 times 7.) Each poem is a *rondeau*, with thirteen lines in stanzas of 4 + 4 + 5; the first two lines return as the last two of the second stanza (that is, lines 7–8), and the first one alone returns as the final line of the poem. This form is important for three reasons: first, the poem begins with its most striking image, which runs motivelike through the short verse and serves even as an epigrammatic conclusion.[6] Second, the strict, repetitive poetic form gives Schoenberg his musical form. He observes the poetic repetitions in his music, as he observes the poetic divisions into stanzas with intervening musical articulations. Moreover, since the voice is always the predominant element of *Pierrot*'s texture, her part alone ensures the balance of variety and repetition that contributes to a pleasing sense of shape. Finally, the repetitions within each poem embody the nightmarish, obsessive, and ironic images of the texts—all heightened by Schoenberg's music.

Schoenberg arranged his selection of three-times-seven poems into a narrative that is elliptical but nonetheless mythic and primeval. Pierrot, the stock character from the Italian commedia dell' arte, is "moonstruck" and "moon-drunk." In part 1, the first seven poems, his condition is ridiculous and endearing, but underlain with horrifying changes in the natural world around him—due, no doubt, to the moon. Part 2, by contrast, is entirely dark and terrifying: in a black, nocturnal world, Pierrot descends into a crypt, bent on robbery; he is horribly frightened and threatened with a painful and terrible death. Part 3 returns Pierrot to the earth's surface and to the gentle moon and light colors of the first part; chastened by his experience, he returns to Bergamo, his home, and—the last line of the past poem and of the cycle—the "old aroma of once-upon-a-time," the "alter Duft aus Märchenzeit."

But Pierrot is only half of the story of *Pierrot*. The first song, "Mondestrunken," is a third-person poem about a Poet, and that Poet is also the subject of *Pierrot lunaire*: in telling Pierrot's story, the Poet tells his own as well. Figure 3.1 summarizes the characters, the points of view, and the colors at work in each number of *Pierrot* and charts the course of the Poet's journey, hand in hand, as it were, with Pierrot. The Poet is as moon-drunk as Pierrot, as he begins to tell Pierrot's story. When the horrors begin to creep in, with the fifth number, the texts are the Poet's own. The latter numbers of part 2 are Pierrot's, as are the first six of part 3, but in the last number of each, the Poet and Pierrot are confused and conflated; they become one. Secondary characters drop out (although Cassander makes painful appearances in "Gemeinheit" and "Serenade"), and we are left with Pierrot. His relief and recovery from terror are those of the Poet, who has journeyed into the

Title of Song	"Poet";	Pierrot;	Other	Colors (or Moon)
Mondestrunken	3d			Moonlight
Columbine			3d	White moon (also murky; auburn)
Der Dandy		3d		Fantastic/crystal/wax moon; ebony, bronze, red, green
Eine blasse Wäscherin			3d	White, silver moon (and arms, linen
Valse de Chopin	1st			Watery blood; icy white
Madonna	1st			Red; absence (of milk, of flesh)
Der kranke Mond	1st			Feverish white moon; black night; colorless blood
Nacht	3d			Black
Gebet an Pierrot	1st			Black (flag); moonlit snow (Pierrot)
Raub		3d		Red; pale (fear)
Rote Messe		3d		Red, gold, candlelight
Galgenlied		3d		–
Enthauptung		3d		Moon on black cushion (cf. nos. 3, 6, 7); "pain-dark night"
Die Kreuze	3d			Blood, blindness; gold, red, sunset
Heimweh		3d		Crystal; pale moonlight
Gemeinheit		3d		White skin
Parodie		3d		White, gray, red; moonlight
Der Mondfleck		3d		White moonlight on black jacket
Serenade		3d		(Night)
Heimfahrt		3d		Moon, waterlily, pale green (dawn)
O alter Duft	1st	1st		Sunlight

FIGURE 3.1. Point of view and colors in Schoenberg's *Pierrot lunaire*.

night world of creation and revilement for that creation, and who has returned from his quest wiser and resigned. We, the audience, have made the journey as well. *Pierrot* must be acted as well as declaimed; at the premiere, the actress Albertine Zehme, who had commissioned the work, was alone at center stage, while Schoenberg conducted the instrumentalists behind a scene. Doubtless the empathy created by a good actress plays a role in drawing an audience into the story.[7] Like many works of the nineteenth century, *Pierrot lunaire* is intended to be cathartic. This is the aspect to which Stravinsky objected so strongly, and it is certainly an aspect of the work that comes from the dying era of German Romanticism, not the rising modern age. But in this case, a modern musical language and a dying aesthetic are in no way incompatible.

Before addressing that question of language and aesthetic directly, it is necessary to consider one final textual element that helps to shape the work as a whole: the use of colors and the motive of the moon throughout *Pierrot* (see Fig. 3.1). The beginning and end of *Pierrot* are in serene, clear light, the first four numbers in moonlight and the last again in calm moonlight giving way to dawn and the warmth of the day. The third number, "The Dandy," introduces other colors as it introduces Pierrot—his black dressing table, the bronze echoes of the fountain, his red and green makeup, the "fantastic" moonbeam. These colors continue in the second and third parts. More important, though, are the colors of blood and icy whiteness also introduced at the end of part 1. In these verses about the Poet, creation is also annihilation, as the Poet is gripped and held by an otherworldly feverish intoxication and crucified on his poetry. (The refrain of number 14, the last poem of part 2, is "Heilge Kreuze sind die Verse," "Verses are holy crosses.") The second part of *Pierrot* revolves around these colors—the full blackness of night, the moon as a scimitar to decapitate Pierrot (No. 12), the excessively rich red and gold. Then, without transition, we return to the more innocent world of the beginning. Part 3 opens with a "crystal sigh from Italy's old pantomime," the moon is again shining palely, and we return to the whiteness and light colors, all placid, of earlier times, the *Märchenzeit* of long ago.[8]

Four of the poems—Nos. 1 and 3 from part 1, 10 from part 2, and 18 from part 3—summarize these literary elements. Each poem is regular in meter and unrhymed. Each is organized around the recurrent image of the refrain. The first three are full of the overripe imagery and diction of the fin de siècle, reminiscent of Aloysius Bertrand's prose poems, which Ravel used as the basis of his *Gaspard de la nuit*. We see Pierrot in a series of still pictures as a comic character; in this he contrasts with the Poet, whom we first see "moon-drunk," but always thereafter in agony. This difference serves to distance Pierrot somewhat; his identification with the Poet does not quite hold fast. Pierrot may return happy and relieved to Bergamo, but the Poet will never be able to return unsullied to the *Märchenzeit* that he and Schoenberg evoke so fondly.

1. Mondestrunken

Den Wein, den man mit Augen trinkt,
Giesst Nachts der Mond in Wogen
   nieder,
Und eine Springflut überschwemmt
Den stillen Horizont.

1. Moon-drunk

The wine one drinks with one's eyes
The moon pours down nightly in
   waves,
And a spring tide floods
The silent horizon.

Gelüste, schauerlich und süss,
Durchschwimmen ohne Zahl die
   Fluten!
Den Wein, den man mit Augen trinkt,
Giesst Nachts der Mond in Wogen
   nieder.

Der Dichter, den die Andacht treibt,
Berauscht sich an dem heilgen
   Tranke,
Gen Himmel wendet er verzückt
Das Haupt und taumelnd saugt und
   schlürfter
Den Wein, den man mit Augen trinkt.

Longings, ghastly and sweet,
Swim numberless through the
   floods!
The wine one drinks with one's eyes
The moon pours down nightly in
   waves.

The Poet, whom devotion impels,
Intoxicates himself on the holy
   drink;
Toward heaven, in raptures, he turns
His head and reeling sucks and
   laps
The wine one drinks with one's eyes.

3. Der Dandy

Mit einem phantastischen Lichtstrahl
Erleuchtet der Mond die krystallnen
   Flacons
Auf dem schwarzen, hochheiligen
   Waschtisch
Des schweigenden Dandys von
   Bergamo.

In tönender, bronzener Schale
Lacht hell die Fontäne, metallischen
   Klangs.
Mit einem phantastischen Lichtstrahl
Erleuchtet der Mond die krystallnen
   Flacons.

Pierrot mit dem wächsenen Antlitz
Steht sinnend und denkt: wie er
   heute sich schminkt?
Fort schiebt er das Rot und des
   Orient Grün
Und bemalt sein Gesicht in
   erhabenem Stil
Mit einem phantastischen
   Mondstrahl.

3. The Dandy

With a fantastic ray of light
The moon illumines the crystal
   flagon
On the black, all-holy dressing
   table
Of the mute dandy from
   Bergamo.

In resounding bronze echoes
Brightly laughs the metal sound of
   the fountains.
With a fantastic ray of light
The moon illumines the crystal
   flagon.

Pierrot of the waxy visage
Stands pensive and thinks: how shall
   he paint himself today?
Immediately he pushes away the red
   and the Oriental green
And paints his face in elevated
   fashion
With a fantastic ray of
   moonlight.

10. Raub

Rote, fürstliche Rubine,
Blutge Tropfen alten Ruhmes,
Schlummern in den Totenschreinen,
Drunten in den Grabgewölben.

Nachts, mit seinen Zechkumpanen,
Steigt Pierrot hinab—zu rauben
Rote, fürstliche Rubine,
Blutge Tropfen alten Ruhmes.

10. Robbery

Red, princely rubies
Bloody drops of old renown,
Slumber in the caskets
Below in the vaulted tombs.

At night, with his cronies,
Pierrot descends—to steal
Red, princely rubies
Bloody drops of old renown.

Doch da—sträuben sich die Haare,	But there—his hair stands on end,
Bleiche Furcht bannt sie am Platze:	Pale fear fixes him to the spot:
Durch die Finsterniss—wie Augen!—	Through the darkness—like eyes!—
Stieren aus den Totenschreinen	Stare from out the caskets
Rote, fürstliche Rubine.	Red, princely rubies.

18. Der Mondfleck | ### 18. The Moon Spot

Einen weissen Fleck des hellen Mondes	With a white beam of the bright moon
Auf dem Rücken seines schwarzen Rockes,	On the back of his black jacket,
So spaziert Pierrot im lauen Abend,	So promenades Pierrot in the mild evening,
Aufzusuchen Glück und Abenteuer.	Off to seek happiness and adventure.
Plötzlich stört ihn was an seinem Anzug,	Suddenly something on his suit disturbs him,
Er beschaut sich rings und findet richtig—	He looks around himself and right enough finds—
Einen weissen Fleck des hellen Mondes	A white beam of the bright moon
Auf dem Rücken seines schwarzen Rockes.	On the back of his black jacket.
Warte! denkt er: das ist so ein Gipfleck!	Wait!, he thinks, that is a plaster chip!
Wischt und wischt, doch—bringt ihn nicht herunter!	Wipes and wipes, but—he cannot get rid of it!
Und so geht er, giftgeschwollen, weiter,	And so he goes on, swollen with fury,
Reibt und reibt bis an den frühen Morgen—	Rubs and rubs until the early morning—
Einen weissen Fleck des hellen Mondes.	A white beam of the bright moon.

Even though this nostalgia belongs to the dying fin de siècle rather than the rising modern aesthetic, by no means should we hear the work, even the parallel thirds at the very end, as Schoenberg's nostalgia for tonality. If Schoenberg had wanted to write *Pierrot* in the tonal or post-tonal style of Strauss, he would have done so. Schoenberg was thoroughly committed to the modernist movement, from personal predilection and from his belief in its historical necessity. He was more interested in the nostalgia, we can believe, as a symbol of the artistic alienation from the modern bourgeois world, which he felt very deeply throughout his life. His nostalgia is not Ives's: Ives was nostalgic for a world that he truly believed had existed, in his forebears' time, and that he was evoking through music. Schoenberg had no such primeval Eden to contemplate. Moreover, given Pierrot's identification with the Poet, the nostalgia for the Bergamo of long ago is simply a foil for the horrific tortures that the Poet undergoes in the present. More than the Poet, Pierrot as a character is thus again somewhat distanced from us and made a figure of fun. But the distancing in *Pierrot lunaire,* both of Pierrot and of the Poet, is always somewhat uneasy; it is never made entirely clear when we are to contemplate the characters and when we are to empathize with them, where the boundaries lie between identification and irony. This dilemma is not solved, for it is literally underscored by the music.

The principal musical technique at work in *Pierrot* is that of *Verklärte Nacht,* motivic development. Each of the twenty-one settings is based on a small motive or group of motives, spun out for the brief duration of the number, and returning fairly intact at the returns of the poetic refrain. There are some instances of more familiar compositional devices: No. 8, "Nacht," for example, is a passacaglia; No. 17, "Parodie," is an accompanied fugue in three and four parts; No. 18, "Der Mondfleck," is a triple fugue in the instrumental parts that midway turns around on itself, so that the second half is the retrograde of the first. No. 4, "Eine blasse Wäscherin," is an example of *Klangfarbenmelodie,* the "melody of tone colors" in which Schoenberg was interested during these years, repeated chords with changing timbres. For the most part the music of *Pierrot lunaire* supports, and often exemplifies, the images and emotional world of the text. At the very beginning, for example, we hear ostinati in the pizzicato violin and the piano and a high, fleeting melody in the flute; everything is *pianissimo.* This is "the wine which one drinks with one's eyes," the intoxicating moonlight. When the poetry concerns the moonlight, the various motives continue to develop; when the poetic subject turns to the Poet, most noticeably at the beginning of the third stanza, the music changes radically. In this case, the piano ostinato is now heard in the flute while the piano has thick *forte* chords and the violin and cello play new music. Since the Poet is looking at the moon, and since this brief piece offers no radical changes that need to be reintegrated into the music, the continuation of the ostinato serves both musical and extramusical ends.

Other examples of musical tone painting are everywhere in *Pierrot.* The *Klangfarbenmelodie* of "Eine blasse Wäscherin" matches the silent silver moonlight in which the washerwoman washes linen in the river. The "Valse de Chopin" is a distorted parody. The "Heimfahrt," the homecoming in No. 20, is a barcarole, music associated with northern Italy, and the full return in the last number is signaled by the sweetness of the constant parallel thirds in the instrumental parts. Even the most abstruse device, the retrograde fugue of "Der Mondfleck," is a musical joke: this is the poem about Pierrot's spinning around and around, trying to brush the moonbeam off his black jacket, and so the music turns around as he does. (The reversal occurs at the beginning of line 7, where Pierrot spies the moonbeam.)

Earlier I called the depiction of Pierrot's journey a series of still photographs rather than a continuous narration, and this is true of the musical setting. Each number is discrete, sharply contrasted with its neighbors. Virtually the only repetition is the recall, in the instrumental coda of No. 13 leading into No. 14, of the flute melody of No. 7, "The Sick Moon," a transition between the moon about to behead Pierrot and the sacrificial altar of the Poet's verses. Schoenberg's music is locally incisive; but for the large-scale form in *Pierrot,* he relies on his texts.

Brief, incisive miniatures were in fact the sort of music favored by the Second Viennese School between ca. 1908, the advent of atonality, and ca. 1923, Schoenberg's development of the twelve-tone method. (Even the Five Pieces for Orchestra, Op. 16, are individually rather brief.) The music coheres through motivic devices, returning to an opening motive often and regularly enough to create shape, a sense of expansion and return to stability. This musical shape is allied to a poetic form that is immediately perceived, so that each reinforces the other. A tonal structuring is not necessary here. The music is atonal, a result of the pervasive chromaticism that had been growing in "progressive" German music since Wagner. It is so thoroughly chromatic, in the view of the pianist and scholar Charles Rosen, that one could transpose any of the parts by a minor second, and it would make no aural difference.[9] Tonality in *Pierrot lunaire* is, ultimately, neither here nor there. The atonality, though, is a distinctly modern characteristic of *Pierrot.* The other two characteristics are the instrumental ensemble (a point taken up in chapter 4) and the ethos of the work as a whole. If *Pierrot lunaire* indulges in the irony and morbidity of the Romantic fin de siècle, as do the music and worldview of Mahler, Schoenberg's primary hero, the work is still meant as a definitive farewell to that world of sickness. Furthermore, *Pierrot* is a self-consciously theatrical work, in which the personae of Pierrot, the Poet, and the performer—but not Schoenberg—are inextricably intertwined.[10]

I have mentioned the Poet's identification with Pierrot, an identification completed in part 3. But in the listener's mind, the two remain distinct personalities: the Poet is intensely emotional, excruciatingly sensitive, possessed by Verse; but Pierrot is a dandy and a fop, not particularly bright or brave, and not a little cruel (in Nos. 16 and 19 he tortures Cassander). The performer must be both characters, separately and together, and she can do this best by emphasizing the theatricality of the work, its artificiality, and at times, its preciosity. The *Sprechstimme,* the semispoken imitation of a sung line, is one technique that enables her to achieve this. In addition, the work must be enacted, and the listener to a recording must imagine such an enactment.[11]

Pierrot is a thoroughly modern work in this way. Self-consciously theatrical, never unaware of the Poet/Pierrot/performer complex of personae, it yet does not impose upon itself a final resolution or consolidation of its musical variety. Schoenberg remains outside that complex. He is the omniscient narrator, obviously enjoying the story and his telling of it, using the richest, if most concentrated, means of his devising. When the performers follow Schoenberg, the result is a work that entices us while making us aware of its complete artifice, that leavens its macabre aspects with (sometimes sardonic) humor, that focuses our attention on the trials of the Poet—a nineteenth-century device—while at the same time making us extremely uneasy about him—an effect rather more common in the twentieth century.

Pierrot's children are many. Its impact on Schoenberg's contemporaries was considerable. Stravinsky heard *Pierrot* in Berlin in the winter of 1912–13, and later, in Paris, told Ravel about it. Each composer reacted with a suite of poems set for soprano and instrumental ensemble; Ravel used three poems of Stéphane Mallarmé, Stravinsky three Japanese lyrics. Both composers called for an ensemble of two flutes, two clarinets, string quartet, and piano—a group much larger and more orchestral than Schoenberg's "pit band" of five. In part because of Ravel's and Stravinsky's homophonic textures, in part because the soprano sings rather than declaims, the sound of the Ravel and Stravinsky works is quite unlike that of *Pierrot*. In his *Autobiography*, Stravinsky refers to his first hearing of *Pierrot*:

> I did not feel the slightest enthusiasm about the aesthetics of the work, which appeared to me to be a retrogression to the out-of-date Beardsley cult. But, on the other hand, I consider that the merits of the instrumentation are beyond dispute.[12]

Using similar means to a new end, Stravinsky produced his *Three Japanese Lyrics* of 1912–13. To cite his *Autobiography* again:

> In the summer [of 1912] I had read a little anthology of Japanese lyrics—short poems a few lines each, selected from the old poets. The impression which they had made on me was exactly like that made by Japanese paintings and engravings. The graphic solution of problems of perspective and space shown by their art incited me to find something analogous in music. Nothing could have lent itself better to this than the Russian version of the Japanese poems. . . . I gave myself up to the task, and succeeded by a metrical and rhythmic process too complex to be explained here.[13]

Visual effects translated through the verbal into the musical: this is a process superficially similar to that in the works discussed in chapter 2, such as Debussy's *En blanc et noir.* But Stravinsky's solution to the new problems of perspective and space in music is quite different from

Debussy's. Instead of arabesques, the *Japanese Lyrics* employ a modular construction, or handling of melodic fragments and rhythmic patterns, which results paradoxically in a music of some stasis. (In this regard it resembles the second of Stravinsky's Three Pieces for String Quartet.) But the repetition of the words and images of *snow* and *whiteness* emphasize, not the progressive changing of the seasons, but the instant of the coming of spring, the momentary cusp between one season and the next.

As strikingly different from *Pierrot* as Stravinsky's repetitive melodic figures and rhythms are, the most important difference is found in his handling of the nearly orchestral accompanying ensemble. Stravinsky treats his instruments as subordinate to the voice, but often in a heterophonic texture that is closer to Webern than to any other contemporary. The players cannot think and act, in these brief pieces, like a chamber ensemble, but must follow a conductor and think orchestrally. Yet the delicate translucency of the texture still keeps us in the realm of chamber music, presumably in response to the nature of the texts.

Ravel's reaction to the *Japanese Lyrics,* and perhaps to *Pierrot* through them, is quite different. Ravel sets longer texts than Stravinsky's, and his musical forms follow those of Mallarmé's poems precisely. What is of interest here, however, is not questions of form or tonality, but of the ensemble. While his ensemble is the same as Stravinsky's, Ravel's treatment is truly orchestral, using instrumental families as units, and creating a continuous and homophonic texture as the setting for the dominant vocal part.[14] If Stravinsky still keeps to the chamber-music sound of *Pierrot lunaire,* despite his larger ensemble, Ravel (who had not heard *Pierrot*) treats the ensemble as a true chamber orchestra; in fact, if the *Trois poèmes de Stéphane Mallarmé* belong in this study at all, it is simply because of their proximate relationship to *Pierrot.* The treatment of the instruments in families rather than as soloists in an ensemble whose colors perpetually shift and re-mix, the dominance of the voice, the distanced treatment of the text, placing it in a setting rather than making it seem an immediate statement and making the setting a part of it—all these factors place the *Trois poèmes* in the world of the orchestral song rather than chamber music. But through its novelty, even such a distant transfiguration attests to the inescapable contemporary impact of *Pierrot lunaire.*

Old and New after 1945:
Stravinsky and Berio

If *Pierrot* was a product of a dying, highly self-conscious Romantic aestheticism, as Stravinsky thought, the *Three Japanese Lyrics* and *Trois poèmes de Stéphane Mallarmé* are harbingers of the French neoclassicism that began in the second decade of the century and reached its apotheosis, indeed its "classical" position, in the twenty-five years from the end of World War I through the end of World War II. This era saw little music for voice and chamber ensemble, and certainly little in which the interactions of poetic and musical elements are so intertwined and cross-fertilizing as in the music written before 1915. By contrast, since 1945 vocal chamber music has become one of the most central genres. The remainder of this chapter examines a handful of representative pieces.

Stravinsky's *Three Songs from William Shakespeare* ("Musick to heare," Sonnet 8; Ariel's "Full fadom five" from *The Tempest;* and "When Daisies Pied," from *Love's Labour's Lost*) and *In Memoriam Dylan Thomas: Dirge–Canons and Song,* on Thomas's "Do Not Go Gentle into That Good Night." The Shakespeare songs, from 1953, are scored for voice, flute, clarinet, and viola. The Dylan Thomas setting, from 1954, is for tenor, four trombones, and string quartet. Both sets are truly chamber music in the clarity of their textures and interaction among equal partners. They are in some ways more like the *Three Japanese Lyrics* than Stravinsky's symphonies or *The Rake's Progress,* but they are still the work of a composer concerned with clear traditional forms. The interplay of literary and musical forms, the first point to consider here, reflects the habits of an older composer, rather than the new generation of the 1950s.

The most highly structured poem of the Stravinsky settings is Dylan Thomas's "Do Not Go Gentle," and it is this music as well that depends the most on the literary form. That form is the villanelle, appropriate to the subject, intensifying and insisting on the rage that the poet is urging on his father, and that is his own rage. Stravinsky follows the villanelle's stanzaic structure precisely: each repeated line is set to virtually identical music (although the notes of the accompanying lines are sometimes changed in rhythm, register, or instrument), and each stanza is set off by a refrain in the string quartet. The more freely set sections offer a greater musical complexity. This provides the only sense of musical development—as opposed to constant, static variation—in the setting of the poem. The second stanza's first two lines are set as a three-voice canon (tenor, cello, viola); the first two lines of the third stanza make use of the full complement of instruments and voice for the first time in the setting; and the fourth and fifth tercets' first two lines are set, respectively, as two-voice and three-voice canons (tenor and first violin; tenor, first violin, and cello), providing a transition to the full texture for the last stanza (the quatrain) and an increasing intensification, which sets off Stravinsky's marking the beginning of each stanza ("Good men," "Wild men," "Grave men") with similar and accumulative melodic beginnings.

Do Not Go Gentle into That Good Night	*Stravinsky's setting*
	String quartet refrain
Do not go gentle into that good night,	A
Old age should burn and rave at close of day;	x
Rage, rage against the dying of the light.	B
	String quartet refrain
Though wise men at their end know dark is right,	canon a 3 (tenor, cello, viola)
Because their words had forked no lightning they	
Do not go gentle into that good night.	A¹
	String quartet refrain
Good men, the last wave by, crying how bright	full texture
Their frail deeds might have danced in a green bay,	
Rage, rage against the dying of the light.	B
	String quartet refrain
Wild men who caught and sang the sun in flight,	canon a 2 (tenor, first violin)
And learn, too late, they grieved it on its way,	
Do not go gentle into that good night.	A
	String quartet refrain
Grave men, near death, who see with blinding sight	canon a 3 (tenor, first violin, cello)
Blind eyes could blaze like meteors and be gay,	
Rage, rage against the dying of the light.	B
	String quartet refrain
And you, my father, there on the sad height	String quartet refrain in instruments
Curse, bless, me now with your fierce tears, I pray,	x
Do not go gentle into that good night.	A²
Rage, rage against the dying of the light.	B
	String quartet refrain

Opposed to this intensification of feeling through manipulation of texture is the intensification arising from insistence, like the probing of a wound. This insistence results both from the musical reinforcement of the verbal repetitions and from the recurring refrain in the string quartet. The intensification also comes from Stravinsky's musical language, derived (at some remove) from serialist techniques.[15] More to the point than the similarity to or difference from classical serial techniques is the audible result, the continued cycling among a very reduced vocabulary of pitches and melodic contours, which are constantly shared among instruments and voice. This cycling constitutes the song's most essential unity and the sense that even if we hear a certain development or progression throughout the song's setting, we are really simply examining the same material more intensely from different angles, turning it in our hands and minds' eyes as Thomas and Stravinsky have turned their materials, as the son in the poem has turned his grief. Every note in the song, vocal or instrumental, is a replication, a next-of-kin, to every other note—through the very small number of serial manipulations (melodic note orderings) and specific pitches (lack of transpositions), and the restricted range of the tenor's part.

The song is framed by two "Dirge-Canons," similar to each other and to the central setting. These "Dirge-Canons" are purely instrumental, and both alternate different settings of the same material derived from the song. The prelude alternates a canon in the tenor and bass trombones, whose sound echoes the most solemn liturgical music, with a brief episode in the string quartet, employing the same row that forms the basis of the canon's subject. The form of the prelude is thus $A^1BA^2BA^3$: the A sections are the trombone music, each time a different canon on the same material; the B sections are for string quartet. The postlude follows the same structural idea as the prelude, but with the ensembles reversed. If we retain the letters of the prelude, the form of the postlude is BA^2BA^1B, with B now played by the trombones and A by the strings. The trombones begin with what had been the contrasting episode of the prelude, with notes and rhythms the same, but the registers adjusted. The strings again play the contrasting internal sections, but these are now the canonic dirges of the prelude, and in reverse order (A^2 and then A^1, the same row forms and textures as in the prelude, but at different levels of transposition). Stravinsky thus observes the principle of unity and variety that he had used in the setting of the poem itself. The trombones begin and end this postlude, as they had the prelude. But whereas the prelude had begun and ended with the canons and used the sustained sections as an interlude, the postlude uses the canons as the interludes and begins and ends with this sustained, solemn music. Although we cannot say that the sustained sections constitute the dirge and the others the canon of the title, since the solemnity and the tradition of the canon are part of the point and the effect here, it cannot be denied that the sustained music in the trombones makes a far more effective closing than the metrical, almost processional, canons would. This ending of the postlude, in addition, echoes the ending of the central song, where the string quartet's refrain is repeated for the final time, but with the first violin and viola parts exchanged, so that the melody at the top of the texture is of a contour more associated with closure, and more similar to the tenor's melodies (specifically that of the line "Do not go gentle") than it had been during the song proper.

All this adds up structurally to a kind of formal manipulation similar to that of Stravinsky's *Three Japanese Lyrics* of some forty years earlier, the modular rearrangement of a restricted number of musical cells. The principal difference in this case is that all the contrasting cells are in fact derived from the same basic material, making the music solid and firmly architectonic. At the same time, the poem and its musical reflection give *In Memoriam Dylan Thomas* a linearity, a temporality, which the *Japanese Lyrics* avoid; and the instrumentation of *In Memoriam*, the kind of music played and the way in which the instruments are handled, has none of the quasi-French ethereality of the earlier music. *In Memoriam Dylan Thomas* is truly Stravinsky's music in a way which the *Three Japanese Lyrics* are not.

This is also the case with the *Three Songs from William Shakespeare*, although their textures differ from that of the *In Memoriam*, as does their emotional world. In each case, however, the form of the song is taken directly from that of the text: "Musick to heare" follows the three-quatrains-plus-couplet of the sonnet, with hints of strophic structure (the beginnings of each stanza) and even a sort of ABAB (A the first and third quatrains, B the second quatrain and final couplet), which results in a combination of through-composition and repetition that mirrors the theme of the text. Ariel's song from *The Tempest*, "Full fadom five," is through-composed. The final song, "When daisies pied," from *Love's Labour's Lost*, is formally the simplest and most traditional: a cheery strophic form with a short coda.

The note-to-note musical handling in the Shakespeare songs is much like that in the *In Memoriam Dylan Thomas*. Again, Stravinsky uses a relatively small number of pitch configurations, which are slightly varied by shifts in register. In the first song, the basic melodic cell is a four-note group, B–G–A–B♭. The cell does not completely fill in the major third it outlines, however; and since Stravinsky often uses sevenths and ninths instead of major and minor seconds, the sound is less chromatic and less dense. The second and third songs employ different basic melodic cells; "Full fadom five" has a seven-note cell (C–F–B♭–A♭–E♭–A♭–G♭), and "When daisies pied" is really a segmenting of tonal colors and areas rather than a melodic ordering, with notes associated with A♭ opposed to those associated with C.

The handling of these basic cells differs in each song as well. In "Musick to heare" the melodic phrases follow upon one another as in the Dylan Thomas music, with little deviation from the cell in the opening flute and following vocal melodies (Ex. 3.2). But the separation between the voice and the other instruments focuses our ears on the melody, as a principal melody generated from a small number of units. In contrast, in the second song, the basic seven-note cell is introduced virtually simultaneously in all instruments and the voice with the first

EXAMPLE 3.2. Stravinsky, "Musick to heare," from *Three Songs from William Shakespeare*, mm. 1–14. © Copyright 1954 by Boosey & Hawkes, Inc; copyright renewed. Reprinted by permission.

Dedicated to EVENINGS ON THE ROOF *(Los Angeles)*

THREE SONGS
from William Shakespeare

IGOR STRAVINSKY
1953

I. Musick to heare

line of the text. Thereafter, the song pursues a much more canonic course than the first, with a great deal of imitation and question-and-answer among the voice and three instruments. In particular, the minor seventh of the melody ("Of his") and the frequent quasi-shake between two notes a minor second apart (the first syllable of "coral" in the second line and "pearls" in the third) are directly repeated by instruments after the voice. The result is a thicker texture than in the first song, far more interactive among the voice and instruments, but even more integrated in the derivation or spinning-out of each melodic event from a single basic unit, seven notes continually undergoing the sea change into something rich and strange. Finally, the texture of the third song is, like the song itself, the simplest of the three. Again, the melodic focus is on the vocal line, with the instruments providing a full homophonic backdrop, flute and clarinet working together, the viola a separate quasi-ostinato behind and above them. This changes in the refrain of each stanza, from the taunting word "cuckoo," when the flute takes over for the voice while the other two instruments play a guitar-like accompaniment, a caustic serenade.

The rhythms of the settings are likewise divorced from the "natural" declamatory rhythms and the equally "natural" adherence to a given meter. Thus, in the beginning of "Musick to heare," the line sounds much more true to its spoken English rhythm than it looks on the page. In a certain sense, however, the rhythms are abstract, not simply because Stravinsky is trying to be difficult; rather, their abstraction is a function of the theme of these songs and the aesthetic experience Stravinsky provides for the listener. The conceit of Shakespeare's sonnet, for example, is one of artifice, and the plea of the poetic persona is not the Romantic, heartfelt one that many readers find in other sonnets. Here the voice is, if not exactly playful, at least more flirtatious than entrapped in the coils of love. It is a scene reminiscent of courtly love: the poet uses his lute as a prop, as an example of the sort of marriage he propounds. He is teasing his audience, singing a song about love (of "Unions married") that is at the same time about the very act of singing and accompanying himself. Stravinsky's music is of an identical type—focused, concentrated, direct, but at the same time self-contained (in its melodic repetitions and its form) and self-aware. He has found a musical clothing precisely appropriate for his text.

These Shakespeare songs are in no way a cycle: musically, there are no connections from one song to another beyond the general language that Stravinsky employs. There are no thematic connections among the texts, and no continuity in voice or persona. The ordering is standard in that the most complex of the works—complex in language, theme, and musical handling—comes first, and the songs thereafter are progressively less intricate. This, too, is a turn away from the standard practice of the nineteenth century. The songs are also a sort of return to the world of the late Middle Ages and the Renaissance, when people readily found pleasure in small, brightly colored and finished artifacts. These songs are a product of the same part of Stravinsky that so deeply loved Gesualdo. They are still "neoclassical," in the broadest and most abused sense of that term as meaning a return to an earlier canon, the canon here being that of the sixteenth century rather than the eighteenth. They are Apollonian rather than Dionysian, this being a function of Stravinsky's compositional personality rather than of era or general aesthetic. They are most Stravinskian, and most modern at the same time, in this artificial beauty—the reader will understand that I can mean nothing derogatory here with the term *artificial*—and, more specifically musically, in the ensemble, the broken consort unified by range, and in the cellular formative procedures. These songs are works of High Modernism, as it would be called in literary circles, compositions by a master in full enjoyment of his powers, at the same time emblematic and self-contained in their beauty.

A set of songs contemporary with Stravinsky's Shakespeare and Dylan Thomas settings is Luciano Berio's *Chamber Music* of 1953, for voice, clarinet, cello, and harp. The texts of Berio's work come from James Joyce's book of poems of that name; they are "Strings in the earth and air," "Monotone," and "Winds of May." Unlike Stravinsky's Shakespeare songs, these three poems form a cycle, about love. In the first, love is "by the river where / The willows meet," again like Stravinsky's lover "All softly playing / With head to the music bent, / and fingers straying / Upon an instrument." The second poem might be Love's lament. In the first person singular, it describes and identifies with the waters' monotone moaning without surcease: "I hear the noise of many waters / Far below. / All day, all night, I hear them flowing / To and fro." In the third poem the winds of May are dancing on the water, on the sea. Its envoi is "Welladay! Welladay! For the winds of May! Love is unhappy when Love is away!"

As the texts in Berio's cycle create a poetic persona in ways that Stravinsky's do not, Berio's settings also are evocative rather than distanced. The interplay of melodic motives and curves is similar in both sets, but Berio's texture is thicker than Stravinsky's, and there is more interplay sustained throughout in *Chamber Music:* Berio's title is not simply taken over from Joyce, with its implications of intimacy and unpretentiousness; the title also indicates the mode of the songs themselves. If Stravinsky's musician/poet plays the lute, Berio's plays a combination of clarinet, cello, and harp, and her voice anticipates and echoes these in an indissoluble ensemble. She becomes part of the ensemble most literally in the first song with her vocalises, sung *quasi bocca chiusa* ("as if with the mouth closed,"), but the constant overlaps of melodic fragments and various melodic manipulations tie the voice tightly into the texture of the whole. The most striking example of this is the second song, "Monotone." For the first two-thirds of the song, up to the word "monotone," the voice and all three instruments sustain a single pitch, the A below middle C. Berio's note in the score reads, "Always with the maximum continuity of sound and a slight *sforzando* on the attack of every note." The constant *ping* of these entrances, their irregularity in attack points, the timbral changes indicated for the clarinet, prevent "Monotone" from becoming monotonous, and insist on its intensity. At the word "monotone," the obsession breaks, and the harp begins *glissandi* (sliding the tuning key up the G string) up a minor ninth from the common A to the B♭ in the octave above. The harp then adds chords to its A pedal, and at the words "the cold winds are blowing / Where I go," the cello as well has rising *tremolo* chords. The rhythms also intensify. The instruments' music is the flow of waters, the monotonous rhythmic flowing and blowing, which the poet/singer hears. Her only departure from the common A comes at the very end, a sudden and precipitous ascent and descent through an octave and a half on the words "To and fro," marked *scivolando senza espressione* ("sliding, without expressiveness"). The surprise of this gesture is so strong as to be theatrical.

The combination of theatre and music in Berio's compositions is never incidental or tangential. He was married for many years to the American mezzo-soprano Cathy Berberian, for whom he wrote *Chamber Music* and many other works. She was a singer of unsurpassed presence and flexibility, and capable (as at this point in "Monotone") of making truly dramatic, theatrical gestures with her voice alone. This sense of theatre, of chamber music that becomes dramatic, is one of the principal distinguishing characteristics between the generation of High Modernism and that of the post–1950s, the first generation of what became postmodernism.

After the 1950s: Chamber and Chamber-Theatre Pieces

The remainder of this chapter treats other post–1945 vocal chamber works in pairs. The pairings point up differences in dealing with texts, in the choice of texts by composers of differing tendencies, and from one pair to the next, a range of the styles coming to the fore or dominating the landscape in the 1950s and 1960s. The three pairs discussed here are Karlheinz Stockhausen's *Stimmung* and John Cage's *Aria;* two theatre pieces (or quasi-theatre pieces) by Berio, *Circles* and *Sequenza III;* György Ligeti's *Aventures* and, very briefly, George Crumb's *Ancient Voices of Children*.

Stockhausen, although a contemporary and close colleague of Pierre Boulez and other post–Webern serialists, took a very different route from theirs in the late 1950s and 1960s. *Stimmung* (1966) is unmistakably and absolutely a work of its era, involving a fascination with the East (because of the work's origins at the Osaka Fair, because of the European music community's interest in Asia, going back continuously to 1889, and because of the temper of the 1960s and its most volatile, energetic community—young people); a sort of comparative mysticism; an acceptance or even celebration of the role of chance, improvisation, and interaction in any activity; and a temporal world unusual in the West, unusual especially for the younger generation. The sounds of *Stimmung* are easily described, as are the process of the piece and its time world. (*Stimmung*, in fact, is one of the principal forebears for the "process" pieces of the 1980s.) More complicated are the work's relationship to chance and its conception of the role of chance. For this discussion, we will turn to a representative work by the grand master of aleatoric music—and the emphasis is on *music*—the *Aria* of John Cage (1958). One might question the inclusion of *Stimmung* and *Aria* in a book about chamber music. But *Stimmung* is a vocal sextet, and *Aria*, as it is recorded with Cage's *Fontana Mix*, is a work for soprano and "accompanying" electronic tape. Their means are new, but otherwise they are as much chamber music as Stravinsky's *Three Songs from William Shakespeare*. In addition, *Stimmung* and *Aria* are essential works in discussing theater pieces, a principal medium of the late twentieth century.

As its name implies, *Aria* is a generic piece. Its starting place is two principal concerns of Cage in the 1950s, the relationship of sound to silence, and the anonymity of the composer, that is to say, the separation of the sounds of a piece of music from the biographical or psychological contingencies of an individual human being. Both of these are new to Western musical aesthetics; they have to do—one is loath with Cage to assign anything to a biographical or psychological "cause"—with Cage's growing up in California, removed from traditional music centers and traditional musical training; his work with Henry Cowell, another inventive composer; and his study of Zen with D. T. Suzuki in the late 1940s in New York.[16] They also have to do with Cage's individual characteristics: his extremely sensitive ear, his love of sound, and his great personal modesty. The essential here, though, is neither Cage nor his idiosyncrasies, but his music.

Cage's concern with sounds demands that we accept them for their own sake and not assign or attribute any external value to them. It is this, and not the use of chance procedures, that is really the most difficult aspect of Cage's music for listeners to understand and accept. This refusal of value implications is the furthest stance from aestheticism, for it is the furthest position from the egotism that Cage finds rampant in Western music: it is the refusal to impose one's personal intellect or emotional complexes on the natural world outside. What we are left with is sound itself, occurring successively or simultaneously in a continuous, unidirectional time. A common reaction to this is the following dialogue: *But what's the point?* (There isn't any beyond the experience.) *So why should I listen?* (Why not?) It is necessary, in listening to Cage's music, to abandon all those intention-laden impulses and reflexes that we normally bring to the concert hall or to the playing of a recording. We are to attend, fully, to the music for the course of its duration; when it is over, we may attend to other things. What we may attend to, during a Cage piece, will include the individual sounds, for their own sakes; the combinations of colors that the performers have brought to the realization of the score, and the range of sounds, whether continuous or discontinuous; the dramatic rhythms of the work, especially in the interaction of sound and silence; the frequent appearances of Cage's wit; and sometimes the work, not as a commentary, but as a sort of analogy to extramusical phenomena. It is important to note, as well, that many of Cage's compositions are as close to the theatre piece as they are to what is often taken to be a purely musical composition. The dramatic, performing aspect of any Cage work is not to be overlooked. Finally, it is frequently senseless to try to discuss any Cage score, that is, to try to approach his composition through its notation, precisely because the piece is its realization. *Aria*, however, does lend itself to written discussion, and its vocal elements are preserved in Cathy Berberian's recording.[17]

The score of *Aria* is written in graphic notation (see Ex. 3.3). In what is called "space equals time" notation, the singer moves at an even pace from left to right across each page, and each page is to last the

EXAMPLE 3.3. Cage, *Aria*, p. 3. © 1960 by Henmar Press Inc. Reprinted by permission of C. F. Peters Corporation, New York.

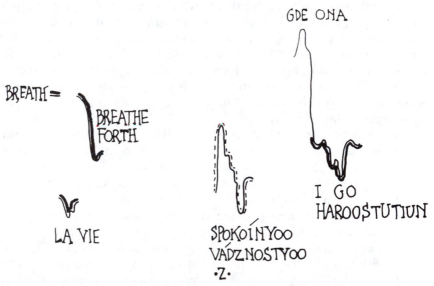

same real-time duration. (Cage suggests, but does not insist on, thirty seconds per page.) The lines on the page are indications of melodic contour and of relative pitch (the higher on the page, the higher the pitch). Where there is blank space, the singer does not sing. Black squares, as the one at the bottom of Example 3.3, are noises such as " 'unmusical' use of the voice, auxiliary percussion, mechanical or electronic devices."[18] These are chosen by the singer. Different colors and parallel dotted lines indicate singing styles, also chosen by the singer; in Berberian's performance, those in Example 3.3 are, from left to right, baby, Marlene Dietrich, baby, (noise = bird call), *Sprechstimme*, dramatic, jazz, and nasal. Finally, the text of *Aria* consists of sounds and words from various languages: Armenian (a tribute to Berberian's heritage), Russian, Italian, French, and English.

As improvisatory and aleatoric as Cage's composing of *Aria* is, the performer has to prepare and practice. The first step is to choose singing styles for the various colors and noises for the black boxes. (A sympathetic performer will choose these in as random a way as possible.) But then one has to rehearse. This performance must, like any other, be convincing, seem real; and that precludes any stuttering or unease along the way. Equally important, a singer must rehearse to ensure that she is realizing Cage's score as it is written, and not indulging in the habits built up by her traditional education and her training for the performance of other sorts of pieces. One potential pitfall concerns the ratio of sound to silence. In Western classical and many other musics, sound is privileged; silence exists only in rests, whose very name is indicative of function. In Cage's universe, however, silence is not the context of sound, but its equal.[19] It is difficult for the performer coming to Cage's music, and for the listener as well, to give silence its full measure. Because the silences are full, and not simply rests for breath or for the articulation of phrases, the performer may become painfully aware of them and undercut them. This is fatal for the piece, for it emphasizes unusual sounds performed in a seemingly normal and traditional manner, and the music becomes senseless. To sustain a silence, and to listen to it as well, becomes central to the singer's work.

Given all this, what does *Aria* add up to? It is many things. It is a succession of sounds, at the most obvious level, alternating with silences and with "nonmusical" sounds or noises, and in some performances superimposed on the tape piece *Fontana Mix* (as on Berberian's recording) or as part of Cage's *Concert* (for piano and orchestra) or any part thereof. In combination with the *Fontana Mix* (also 1958), *Aria* is a sort of duet, two simultaneous successions of sound unrolling through time. Here again, it may be these sounds and nothing more, or the listener may want to hear the two separate pieces as interacting, commenting on and responding to each other. *Aria* is also a virtuoso showpiece, allowing great latitude to a singer's individual strengths and taste, and to her wit and intelligence. Cage specifies in his instructions to the score that "all aspects of a performance (dynamics, etc.) which are not notated may be freely determined by the singer"; since this will also include concert dress, lighting, physical movement about a stage, and so on, the singer has an enormous amount to think about in preparing her performance. The piece also requires a serious performer to consider deeply Cage's aesthetic, from a sympathetic point of view. *Aria* is at once an example of the genre and a commentary on it. But nothing in Cage's score, including his directions, or in any of his writings and *obiter dicta* allows a singer or an audience to approach *Aria* simply as a parody. Cage himself was an extremely witty man; a performer of *Aria* has, as well, ample opportunities for witty gestures. But this does not give her leave to use the work to make fun of operatic arias or operatic singers; no more does it give her and her audience leave to make fun of Cage and this kind of music. A faithful performance, well realized, will, among many things, provide sounds for sensuous pleasure, move back and forth between performance and commentary on performance, and occasion thought on the listeners' part.

Cage's influence began to be deeply felt in Europe in the middle and late 1950s, when the young, post–Webern generation of composers began to feel dissatisfaction with the total serialism they had turned to from about 1948 in an effort to maximize the organic intraconnections of their pieces (an element of this music often dismissed as pseudo-mathematics). Composers also realized that the budding electronic medium offered the best opportunities both for absolute compositional control and for the creation and exploitation of new timbres; it thus seemed pointless to attempt such new sounds and their controlled exploitation in compositions for human performers on acoustic instruments. The human performers, however, had become extraordinary virtuosos, spectacularly endowed and very highly trained; it made sense to many composers to incorporate them into the new music in innovative ways. Cage's European tours with the pianist David Tudor encouraged the freeing up of European music in the 1950s; Stockhausen was one of the principal beneficiaries.

Stimmung, premiered in 1968, is not entirely a site-specific work, but its genesis did spring from a specific event, an international exhibition in Osaka, Japan.[20] The word *Stimmung* is extremely rich as a musical title; it can mean *agreement, mood,* and, in the technical musical sense, *tuning.* All three of these meanings come directly into play in the work. The piece is for six solo singers, three men and three women (SSATBB), who sit in a close circle at the center of the performing space. In Osaka, this was a spherical hall suffused with blue light; the singers sat in a small circle at the center of the hall's floor, with the audience situated around and above them. The work itself is a multiple game: each singer has a sheet with a number of "models" on it, directions for singing patterns of rhythmicized phonemes, and a sheet of "Magic Names," for example, Wakantanka, a Sioux god of thunder; Elohim, god of the Hittites; Kala, the Hindu Earth Mother; Diana the Huntress; Tlaloc, the Aztec rain god; and Maui, a Polynesian trickster god. (I have taken one name from each of the six parts. The gods from any particular sheet come from the same family of religions or from the same area of the world.) A formal schema directs the succession of these interacting phonetic models and allows for the insertion of Magic Names into the text. One of the games that make up a performance of *Stimmung* is the interaction between the various models and the interaction (or lack thereof) between the models and Magic Names, for example, the reduction of a Magic Name to its phonetic elements so that it submerges into the singers' text and the god becomes part of the subtext. In addition, two poems are read during the performance, and the phonetic elements of these may also become part of the other singers' declamations. All of these games, and the others called forth by the score and directions, depend directly on the initiative and the ensemble playing of the singers. Each singer has opportunities to lead the group; the others have a choice of whether to follow or not—one of the exemplifications of the title *Stimmung*.

   Stimmung is also the game of the notes the singers sing, the music, which sounds like nothing else on earth. The basic sonority of *Stimmung* is a B♭⁹ chord: B♭, D, F, A♭, C. This sonority is prolonged for the entire length of the work, which is unspecified but which must be at least sixty minutes. The basic sonority is built up only at length, and appears and disappears through the performance. The singers are instructed to go in and out of tune, but especially to bring out certain overtones of their basic note by singing particular vowels and focusing the note they sing in a particular part of the "mask," the lower part of the face from chin through the sinus cavities where the voice, in the term of classical vocal technique, is "placed." The range of timbre and the resulting alterations of intonation are uncanny, sometimes enormously beautiful, sometimes thoroughly weird. And as the singers have the option of reacting to another's phonetic pattern or Magic Name, they have the option of altering their own particular note in response to what another is singing. Within the parameters set up by Stockhausen's score, each performance will be different, reflecting the mental, emotional, and physical state of its performers on a given day, at a given time. The B♭⁹ chord thus does not pall, because it is so rarely a straight, unadorned sonority. It is established, hinted at, and part of the play of the piece is the long build-up toward a pure tuning (*Stimmung*) of the sound that we hear in so many variations.[21]

   Variety and unity also come from the mediation of the singers' sounds. The score directions indicate not only that the singers should sit in a small circle, so that they can hear all the other singers clearly, and in a physical disposition that replicates the process and goals of the piece, but also that,

> if necessary, each voice should have a microphone and be amplified over a loudspeaker in order to make its finest nuances audible. The loudspeakers should be placed near the singers, so that the amplified sound mixes well with the original and that all the voices are heard equally loud.
>
> It is recommended that each singer be given his own microphone, to be held very close to the mouth. The six microphone potentiometers are to be controlled by an assistant, who continuously balances out the individual voices during the performance.

Note that the use of electronic mediation is for the purposes of clarity, not volume. Stockhausen further specifies that the singers must not use vibrato (which would confuse the intonation) and are to sing in the longest breaths possible at a minimal loudness. He writes, finally, "A singer may also pause [i.e., besides pauses for breathing, which are to made inaudibly] in order to listen to the pitch of the model or to hear how the other singers sound."

This is at the core of *Stimmung,* to hear how the other singers sound, and to attune oneself to that. This is chamber music at its purest, and the processes that all good chamber musicians employ are here put into the foreground and become thematic, in both the technical and the general sense of that word. *Stimmung,* in all its connotations, becomes the physical and aesthetic experience of the work, an experience that the singers realize and the audience shares. *Stimmung* is also meant to be an inclusive work, through its use of the Magic Names from religions around the earth. (The blue interior of the sphere in which the work was performed at Osaka also recalls our planet.) The reader who remembers 1968 will realize how Stockhausen's *Stimmung* gives voice to so much of that era: the belief in grassroots democracy rather than government from the top down; the belief in the possibility of *Stimmung,* agreement among individuals; the appeal to cultures and peoples theretofore outside the European-American mainstream; the importance of contingent, individual feelings and, at the same time, the importance of consensus and sharing; the centrality of mood and its opposition to what was felt (the word is chosen pointedly) to be sterile intellection; the renascence of mysticism, also in part a reaction against what was felt to be the soulless narrow-mindedness of midcentury. The Deutsche Gramophon recording of *Stimmung* is now out of print and unavailable. It is not likely that many singers will want to modify their techniques and put in the extraordinary rehearsal time that *Stimmung* requires, but a revival or new recording of the work in our own era would be a welcome opportunity to consider our contemporary world in its light.

This chapter closes with the theatre piece. That the theatre piece is a hybrid genre, of hybrid origins, need not detain us. More important is its treatment of the relationship of words and music. The works from the beginning of this chapter are formal compositions that unfailingly point up their own artifice, their existence as reembodied or recreated works of art. This artifice is central to most Western music. The theater pieces of the second half of our century, in contrast, deny to their audiences the safety of formality. They address, even attack, the audience theatrically, and with a theatricality that is highly involving, even coercive. There can be no Brechtian, ironic, or Apollonian detachment from a modern theatre piece; rather, the theatre piece is meant to invade us directly, through the combination of words (or wordlike utterances), music, and gesture. The first and last of the theatre pieces we will survey here, Berio's *Circles* and Crumb's *Ancient Voices of Children*, lie on the musical side of the theatre-piece spectrum. They are chamber works with strong theatrical elements and literally dramatic effects. The other two works, Berio's *Sequenza III* "for female voice" (one notes that Berio does not specify "for solo actress") and Ligeti's *Aventures*, are primarily theatrical, even operatic. But their musical techniques, their handling of text, and their emotional languages come directly from chamber music, from an expanded view of the nature and possibilities of chamber music. These theatre pieces are chamber music made, for better or worse, human: not at all debased or lowered, they depict real stories about real people. *Pierrot* vacillates between first and third persons, sometimes one and sometimes both. The last two movements of Schoenberg's second quartet are a first-person narrative, although that first person entails the entire ensemble, not just the singer. The protagonist of Berio's *Sequenza III* is a character not dissimilar to that of Schoenberg's second quartet or of his monodrama *Erwartung*, but her story is different because her music is different. What had been a few isolated works in the early twentieth century has now become a major genre in the later years: the intimacy and directness of chamber music have been retained; the immediacy of narration and of the theatre has been added.

Circles (1960) and *Sequenza III* (1965) rise directly from their texts. Those of *Circles* are three poems of e. e. cummings, "Stinging gold swarms upon the spires," "riverly is a flower," and "n(o)w the how dis(appeared cleverly) world." Berio's music is, at a superficial level, an intensification of cummings's typography, the reveling in sounds and their impregnating with extraphonetic meaning. Berio lingers on vowels, consonants, and even punctuation, his singer/actress moving between denotative meanings, inchoate utterances, and purely musical sounds that ally her with her instrumental partners. Although Berio made little use of such devices in *Chamber Music,* here he is very indebted to the language of *Ulysses. Circles* also uses many of the same procedures—albeit for a virtuoso live performer—that Berio had exploited with striking results in his 1958 *Tema: Omaggio a Joyce,* a *musique concrète* work whose theme (*Tema*) is Cathy Berberian's reading of the first page of the "Sirens" episode of *Ulysses.* These procedures are one of the two elements in *Circles* that push the work in the direction of the theatre piece: Berio's expansion of what constitutes "musical" language, as well as his use of an accompanying chamber ensemble, removes *Circles* from the first-person or third-person narrative world that had marked much vocal music before the current era. The singer of *Circles* does not just sing and portray a story, but enacts it.

Just as the use of language and the exploration of its capacities for generating meaning are one of the elements that make *Circles* a theatrical as much as a musical work, so too are the treatment of the singer and the chamber ensemble. The singer occupies three positions on the stage during the performance of *Circles* (see Fig. 3.2). At each position she has her own percussion instruments—glass chimes, finger cymbals, wood chimes, and claves. In the course of the composition, she be-

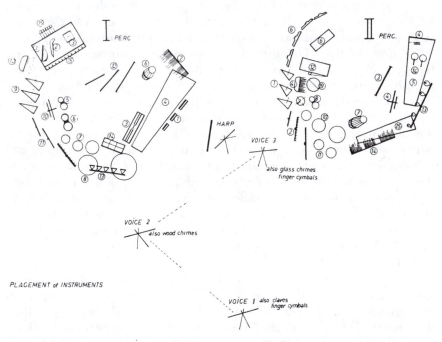

FIGURE 3.2. Placement of instruments, Berio's *Circles.* © Copyright 1961 by Universal Edition (London) Ltd., London. © Copyright renewed. All Rights Reserved. Used by permission of European American Music Distributors Corporation, sole U.S. and Canadian agent for Universal Edition (London) Ltd., London

comes part of the chamber ensemble, which, for the first half of the work, is physically behind her. During the performance, she moves nearer and nearer to its place on the stage, in an indirect path, and at the end is visually and musically a closer part of the group. In a sort of counterpoint to this motion, the latter part of *Circles* recomposes the first two poems, in reversed order. The piece progresses toward freedom and improvisation and then toward a reintegration of stability, all visually reinforced with the singer's stage movement.

The first song of *Circles,* with the singer stage center and a few feet in front of the chamber ensemble, is set for voice and harp; its musical language is more dissonant than the 1953 *Chamber Music,* but again, the emphasis is on the vocal effects and the continuity of word to syllable to phoneme. (This is like the more aleatoric text of Cage's *Aria.* Berio's florid vocal line at some points recalls Boulez's in *Marteau.*) At the end of "stinging gold swarms," the percussion enters, the players surrounded by their instruments of an enormous variety of timbres, inherent volumes, pitched and nonpitched instruments. The percussion is first heard underneath the harp, then moves to the forefront; and the second song (with the soprano still—literally—front and center) is a largely homophonic setting, with a great deal of interaction among the instruments but with the vocal part yet predominating. The singer has still not used her percussion instruments while she is singing; she has played her claves in the interlude before the second song, and the finger cymbals at the end of the last line of the text of the song, "sly slim gods stare." But all this changes, and the composition of the music with it. She repeats the last line, accompanying herself with the finger cymbals, and the music flows into the beginning of the third song, a section of improvisation on given materials (see Ex. 3.4). In this section Berio indicates pitch, particular percussion instruments, dynamics, vocal timbres, and relative durations (space equals time). He does not indicate rhythms or the number and order of notes played; these are left to the percussion players. Results will, obviously, vary; but on the Cathy Berberian recording—presumably "authentic," since Berberian was not only an experienced virtuoso performer of this sort of music but was married to Berio at the time as well—this is by far the most active, even the most frenetic section of the piece. This is also the point at which the singer begins to confuse her roles as the predominant member of the group and as singer. After the text of the poem has been sung, she continues to sing, but now uses phonetic sounds drawn (initially) from the sounds of the cummings text. At a point precisely marked in the score, she turns and walks to the second stand (see Fig. 3.2), where she plays her wood chimes and begins a brief interactive, call-and-response passage with the two percussion players. At the second stand, she again sings "riverly is a flower," but the song is newly composed in all its elements. Thus the songs continue: for the most part, this double of "riverly" is either sung with harp accompaniment,

EXAMPLE 3.4. Berio, *Circles*, p. 19. © Universal Edition (London) Ltd., London, 1960 © renewed. All Rights Reserved. Used by permission of European American Music Distributors Corporation, sole U.S. and Canadian agent for Universal Edition (London) Ltd., London.

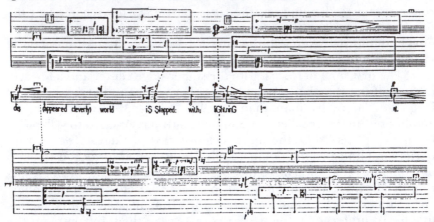

like the first song of the work, or as if improvised among all instruments, like the third, yet briefer and more repetitive than either. The singer than moves to the third stand for a second setting of "stinging." This is the most static song of *Circles,* with repetitive rhythms and repeated chordal sonorities. Its vocal line, especially the declamation, is much more straightforward and simple than that of the first setting, working essentially as a long final cadence, fading finally away into sustained *pianissimo* melismas on "wind," "sea," and "dreamS."

    Circles realizes its title in the recompositions of the three songs (in the order 1–2–3–2–1); in the move from entirely notated music to largely improvised sounds and back to notated composition; in the concomitant move from relative stability and a homophonic texture through great rhythmic, textural, and textual confusion, back to a sustained melodic line in an equally sustained and quiet homophonic texture; and in the circle that the singer describes in her move from stand to stand. It is this last circle that edges the work into the realm of the theater piece and away from that of "pure" music. We watch, through the first three songs of the work, a progressively disintegrating musical texture built on progressively more crazy-quilt verse (crazy-quilt both in typography and in syntax). One of the functions of the last two songs is the reintegration of the musical world by aligning the singer more centrally into the instrumental ensemble; she is a sort of Orpheus, taming the percussionists of the third song by joining in their improvisatory games, but only to a small degree (specific duration of her syllables). As she approaches them physically in the fourth song, she makes a gesture toward improvisation, for a few lines where the ordering of words and notes is given a certain license, but this gesture of agreement effects rather the instrumental return to the singer's world in the first two songs. This comes full circle in the last song, as the singer assumes her new place in the contracted circle of performers, midstage, between the harp and the second percussion player.

The texts Berio chose to set lie between a verse of denotative meanings and the concrete, "musical" use of phonemes and typography to create meaning by example and allusion; similarly, his setting conflates communication and action. *Circles* is thus qualitatively different from other vocal chamber music, even a work of the same era such as Boulez's *Marteau*. If *Circles* is less unorthodox than Cage's *Aria,* it still provokes and requires the same sort of response as that piece, one dependent on the visual, theatrical aspects of a performance. *Circles* is a hybrid work, combining the concrete elements of the visual and the much less fixed, much more fluid messages of its text and music. It is a new sort of piece, possible only after *Marteau* and Berio's own *Omaggio a Joyce,* but still of a type that feeds back into purely instrumental music with, for instance, Crumb's *Vox balaenae* or *Black Angels* (see chapter 6), Stockhausen's *Zyklus* (see chapter 4), and Elliott Carter's Third String Quartet—pieces that call attention to their performers as performers, whose physical actions inform the music one watches them play.

By contrast, Berio's *Sequenza III* (1966) is much more traditional in concept and genre. It is a grand scena for solo female performer, who depicts a traditional type of story for a solo woman on the Western stage, that of the abandoned woman teetering on the edge of madness. Berio's starting point is a text by Markus Kutter:

> give me—a few words—for a woman—
> to sing a truth—allowing us—to build—
> a house—without worrying—before night comes

The text, which associates words with truth and with shelter, is built in small elements that may be rearranged or recombined without an essential change of meaning. This is made to order for such a theatre piece as Berio's, given his interest in the widest possible spectrum of vocal sounds and the alignment on that spectrum of verbal and onomatopoeic meanings. Berio uses sounds pulled from the text, syllables and vowels extracted and rearranged, and only gradually through the piece allows first words and then phrases to emerge from the stream of sounds. At the same time, the emergence of words parallels the emergence of singing, as opposed to the use of the voice to produce "noise," the individual phonemes and nonverbal sounds. The arc of *Sequenza III* is from incomprehensible muttering, a little frightening in its senselessness, through the gradual emergence of sung snatches of phrases, to comprehension of the text (though not in the order in which it appears above) through those sung snatches and their repetition, finally to a sort of establishment of peace, the singer returning to the bottom of her range and repeating, softly, the words "to sing." The singer begins her muttering offstage and comes on only after her verbal wanderings have begun. In contrast, she stays onstage when the piece is done: a specifically shaped ending that reinforces the peace about which she has been singing.

This is all straightforward and rather traditional; but for the specific sounds and noises Berio requires of his singer, it could be a mad scene from Donizetti. Yet this link with the past is obscured somewhat by a sentence of Berio's quoted in the liner notes of Cathy Berberian's recording of the *Sequenza*. Berio notes the various affective adjectives that are used in the score, such as "urgent," "distant and dreamy," "witty." (These are in English in the score.) But then he goes on to say, "The singer should not interpret these indications as a form of actorish mimicry, she should not exhibit (*darstellen*) despair or dreaminess, but rather she should interpret these essentially as indication of rhythm and accent." Since a performance of *Sequenza III* will seem to an audience so immediately emotional—and with such specific emotions evoked or at least seemingly indicated—and since an audience with some experience in the theater will associate this piece quite quickly with traditional mad scenes, Berio's sentence gives one pause. The affective indications, in fact, may have nothing to do with the words or sounds that the singer enunciates at any particular point, and the same sounds may return with different indications in the course of the piece. We are dealing here not with Brechtian alienation but with a representation of a mind running on several tracks at the same time. A structuralist analysis (on the model of Roland Barthes's *S/Z*) could separate these various tracks, chart the course of each, and draw conclusions from their intersections or maintenance of different paths. For the present purposes, it is enough to point out the frequent occurrence of repeating ideas in a different context and with different "clothing," of timbre or rhythm or texture. This aspect of *Sequenza III* reflects its musical, rather than dramatic and narrative, essence.

Another response to Berio's sentence is to consider what might happen if such a warning were not given. The score is precisely notated in terms of relative and absolute durations, melodic contours, and timbres. A singer who takes the affective adjectives too seriously, who allows them too much importance, may begin to distort the other parameters of the performance. She will concentrate on making one passage "dreamy" and the next "urgent." For some actors, such evocations, and the switch from one to another, take time to be created. But this luxury is not possible here, for it would destroy the temporal relationships of the piece, and the concomitant changes in dynamic levels would only distort the music. Again, Berio's warning to the singer is in reality an insistence on the musical essence of the *Sequenza*, a forbidding to treat it as a theatrical tour de force.

Thus *Sequenza III,* if certainly a theatre piece, is still at its heart a musical work, one whose drama and effect lie in its music and not its words or its verbal devices, which are in themselves musical. The other side of this coin is exemplified by Ligeti's *Aventures* of 1962. Indeed, in his annotations to the score, Ligeti writes:

> The entire piece should be performed very expressively, at places with exaggerated expressiveness and correspond-ingly heightened mime and gesture (this applies above all to the singers). The barred and "senza tempo" sections are per-formed in an equally free manner; since the bar lines serve only to orientate the synchronization, no essential differenti-ation should made between the character of the "senza tempo" and that of the "a tempo."

> To realize fully the expressive and dramatic nature of the piece, it is recommended that the singers perform their parts from memory.

Expressive, dramatic, using mime and gesture: the only elements of standard music drama missing here are a comprehensible text and the primacy of "musical" singing. This piece is essentially theatrical, using musicians for a dramatic performance.

The musicians of *Aventures* include three singers—soprano, alto, and baritone—and seven instrumentalists—flute, French horn, percus-sion, harpsichord, piano doubling on celesta, cello, and double bass. The virtuosity required of the singers is extreme, in pitches, melodic leaps, rhythms, tempi, enunciation of phonemes, and so on. All of this is directed toward a purely dramatic goal: the exaggeration of the al-ready exaggerated elements of opera, melodrama, or vividly staged performance. Two of the individual "scenes" in *Aventures* are labeled in the score, one marked "Conversation" (among the three singers, unac-companied) and the other marked "Action dramatique." There is also a solo "aria" for the baritone, immediately after the "Conversation," marked to be performed as if the singer were entering the scene of the action and bringing an important message. (Despite that indication, the recording of *Aventures* makes this sound like nothing so much as a traditional rage aria.) At the end of the piece, the alto has a solo of her own in which, again according to the directions in the score, she ex-presses constantly growing fear and despair. "Her questions remain unanswered, She is completely alone. Her actions give the impression that it is becoming more and more dark and cold." The other singers and the instrumentalists are motionless and expressionless, and when the alto's part disappears into a sigh of nothingness, she also remains frozen on the stage, silent, for fifteen to twenty seconds before the piece is completed.

It would no doubt be possible to construct any number of scenarios for the score of *Aventures*. Any performance will be primarily theatrical, imitating and enacting particular emotional and dramatic states, the music serving to enhance and characterize those states. I have included a few words on *Aventures* here only to indicate the continuity of the progression from what is uncontestably an instance of vocal chamber music, a work for small ensemble of solo players in which a singer and a text are musical elements among many others (*Le marteau sans maître; Circles*), to a piece on the cusp between music and theater, but whose essence is found in the former (*Sequenza III*), finally to a work of music theater in which the theatrical unquestionably predominates (*Aventures*). The blurring of distinctions between one genre and another is one of the hallmarks of our era. This does not signal a breakdown in communications among people (or between artist and audience), it does not mean the end of chamber music (or opera) as we know it, it does not represent decadence, nor it does mean insensitivity on the part of composers and other musicians to their tradition. In general, the blurring of distinctions is a sign of dynamism and the continuing will to communicate, to speak directly to the senses in fresh ways. More specifically, this continuum of expression points to a central element of recent art, that of art precisely as performance, not just as the physicalization of something (a score, for instance) in which the performer is an all too concrete medium. This emphasis on performing returns in chapter 6, about the most august genre in chamber music, the string quartet, when we look at the Kronos Quartet.

This chapter closes with a brief turn to a popular American vocal chamber work, George Crumb's *Ancient Voices of Children* (1970). This piece, which has enjoyed a tremendous vogue in the United States since its creation, has been widely performed, widely written about, and even (especially for new music) widely taught. It seems to touch a nerve, to make a deep impression on many people.

The work is written for soprano, boy soprano, oboe, mandolin, harp, electric piano, and three percussion players, on Spanish texts by Federico García Lorca. As in *Circles,* the nonpercussion players have their own unusual instruments to play as well. The mandolin player doubles on antique cymbals and musical saw, as well as using a glass rod and metal plectrum for "bottleneck" playing. The oboist plays a small harmonica with a chromatic lever. The pianist plays toy piano. The soprano has two mounted glockenspiel plates; both she and the boy soprano use cardboard speaking tubes as megaphones. All these instruments and devices, as well as the myriad percussion instruments that I have not named, lend Crumb's music an extraordinarily wide range of sounds, and their compellingly evocative qualities are one reason for its popularity. Crumb notes in his brief introduction to the score of *Ancient Voices* that one of his desires was to fuse various unrelated stylistic elements, and this he has certainly done—elements of flamenco, Appalachian folk song, quotations from Bach, allusions to Mahler (and specifically to Mahler's references to the Orient, as in *Das Lied von der Erde,* and to childlike simplicity, as in the Fourth Symphony and some of the songs). All of these styles, couched in Crumb's rich, bell-like, fantastic musical world, immediately create a self-contained but spacious musical universe. One element of the work's appeal is its creation of a kind of dream-world, with which each member of the audience can connect precisely because of the variety of musical references and the coloristic writing.

The texts of *Ancient Voices* are extremely Romantic in their quest for lost innocence, the equation of children with the Christ child and his purity, and in the evocation of the tragedy in a child's death. This sort of text is peculiar to Crumb, who has set many García Lorca poems, if not to the United States in general; the Romantic yearning here is worlds away from the less individualized, less personal poetry set by contemporary European composers. Just as Crumb's audience is attracted by the sensuous beauty of his music and specific references to familiar musical traditions (especially traditions such as Lutheran hymns or Anglo-American folk songs), the unworldly imagery and emotional directness of Lorca's poems similarly make an immediate, but complementary, appeal.

Finally, the work is very much of the moment, seemingly an emotional quest of the soprano (in company with the instrumentalists and with a dancer, if one is used) that is taking place as we see it on the stage. All of Crumb's works, vocal or not, are "dramatic" in the sense of seeming to be an emotional traversal of some type. And in this instance, Crumb turns to movement as well. At the beginning of the piece, the soprano sings directly into the open body of the piano, as if singing into a well. As her sound reverberates with the sympathetic vibrations from the piano, introducing the fantastic world of the piece, her posture must indicate a leaning forward, a seeking out. She is answered, at the end of the first piece, by the boy soprano singing offstage, and the physical world is defined as well. She and the boy soprano continue to sing to, and past, each other until the very end of the piece, when he enters slowly to take up a position close to the soprano beside the piano. The two singers end the piece with the lines of one leading to the other's, calling and fading together into silence. In the meantime, during the last song, the oboist has slowly walked offstage, to the side opposite the boy soprano, and from there plays an echo of what he or she has just played onstage, the quasi-Orientalist Mahlerian music. This is then echoed again when the oboist moves even further away offstage, still playing the same lament. The appearance of the boy soprano onstage is thus not a victory, not the successful discovery ending the soprano's search. It seems rather to leave us in suspense, to denote the

impossibility of resolving the Romantic yearning evoked from the beginning of *Ancient Voices*. Although the boy soprano appears onstage, he
and the soprano remain separate; and the disappearance of the oboe,
playing its Mahlerian sighs, reinforces the continuation of the yearning. A sound similar to the voice of the child disappears; the ensemble
remains unintegrated.

The resigned sadness, even the desolation, that one seems to hear
in most of Crumb's music flows at full force through *Ancient Voices* and
strikes an immediate and deep chord in many audiences. And radically
different as the two works are, *Ancient Voices* shares some of the characteristics of Schoenberg's *Pierrot lunaire*. Both works create new, precisely individualized sound worlds. Both involve a search for security in
an alien world, their seemingly modern angst really a part of the
Romantic tradition. Both appeal to traditional elements, Schoenberg in
his forms and in some local devices, Crumb in his quotations and references. They are most different, of course, in tone, the light sardonic
quality of Schoenberg far removed from Crumb's heart-on-the-sleeve
directness. But if *Pierrot lunaire* was radically new in 1912, *Ancient Voices
of Children* was not in 1970. In the latter's amalgamation of widely disparate stylistic elements and forces, it was very much of its time. Music
has changed again in the ensuing decades, and *Ancient Voices* is now
really a repertory piece, no longer as firmly in the mainstream as it was
in its earliest years. More recent pieces that have followed the tradition
of the Schoenberg Second Quartet, *Marteau, Circles,* and the theatrical
pieces of Ligeti are beyond the scope of this book. Their existence indicates the integration of the singer into new musical worlds, a sign of the
maturation of those musical languages. That maturation is evident in
new instrumental musics, as well.

Notes

1. Arnold Schoenberg, "Notes on the Four String Quartets," in *Schoenberg,
Berg, Webern: Die Streichquartette der Wiener Schule, Eine Dokumentation,* ed. Ursula
von Rauchhaupt (Munich [1972?]), 48.

2. The motives are lettered here in accordance with the table of motives
given in chapter 6's discussion of the quartet.

3. No doubt coincidentally, this is reminiscent of Kundry's climactic "lachte"
in *Parsifal,* her horrified recalling of laughing at Christ's agony.

4. See Schoenberg, "My Evolution," in *Style and Idea,* 86–88; "Hauer's
Theories," in *Style and Idea,* 209–13; and "Problems of Harmony," in *Style and
Idea,* 268–87.

5. Schoenberg, "Notes on the Four String Quartets," 49.

6. The fact that the first two times one hears the first line, one hears a second as well, does not affect the climactic last line. The concrete image of each
first/last line ensures that none of the poems lacks closure.

7. In this light it is inexcusable that performances of *Pierrot lunaire* are almost invariably done in German. Schoenberg's express desire was that the work be performed in the language of the audience, to involve them more closely with the story.

8. I am always intrigued by the "pale washerwoman" of No. 4. She never reappears in *Pierrot*. With Columbine (No. 2) and the Dandy (No. 4), her function seems to be to introduce various aspects of the moon, or of the people who live beneath it. Because of proximity and the use of the first person, one can easily associate Columbine with the poet. The Dandy, of course, is Pierrot. But the washerwoman never comes back; she is eternally washing her linen in the pale moonlight. Although she antedates her Dublin sisters by some twenty-five years (though if Joyce knew *Pierrot lunaire* he must have loathed it), she reminds one of the washerwomen in *Finnegans Wake*.

9. Rosen, *Arnold Schoenberg* (New York, 1975), 50. This view is anathema, of course, to those students of the German tradition who preach that each note in music from Bach through Webern is there because it *must* be, that each is organically connected with all the rest. But Rosen is probably right. Since the music lacks tonal centers, pitch relationships are of a different order in these pieces, and in fact are of far lesser importance than motivic relationships or text setting.

10. See Edward T. Cone, *The Composer's Voice* (Berkeley and Los Angeles, 1974), and "Poet's Love or Composer's Love?" in *Music and Text: Critical Inquiries*, ed. Steven Paul Scher (Cambridge, 1991), 177–92.

11. Some years ago, for example, I saw a performance of *Pierrot lunaire* by the wonderful American soprano Bethany Beardslee and a group of free-lance musicians from New York. Beardslee wore black trousers and a large white overblouse with black pom-pom buttons down the front, in striking reference both to formal concert wear and to Pierrot's traditional costume. Standing in the midst of the instrumentalists, she delivered the text as a consummate singer-actress, often using what seemed to be stylized gestures to articulate the text's content and structure. These stylized gestures also turned out to be Beardslee's conducting the instrumental ensemble. (*Pierrot lunaire* is normally performed with a conductor.) This was an extraordinary effect. A singer-actress such as Beardslee will naturally enlist an audience's sympathy and identification with the subject of her text and music, yet her costume and her gestures helped to distance us from Pierrot and the Poet, to emphasize herself as a performer and the theatricality of the work. The result was an extraordinarily layered, but still always clear, performance. The musicians brought out the contrasting worlds of pathos, irony, and humor in *Pierrot* or caught the constantly shifting accents among these.

12. Stravinsky, *Autobiography*, 43–44.

13. Ibid., 45.

14. Ravel wrote the first of the *Trois poèmes* on a visit to Clarens, Switzerland, Stravinsky's home, in early 1913. He wrote the other two later in the spring and summer of 1913. The first of the *Trois poèmes*, "Soupir," is dedicated to Stravinsky. Each composer also dedicates one of the brief songs to Maurice Delage, a contemporary French composer to whom both were close. The remaining number of each set was also dedicated to a contemporary French composer, Stravinsky's to Florent Schmitt and Ravel's to Erik Satie.

15. As elsewhere in this book, I am not interested in discussing specific serialist techniques; here I will bypass the question of Stravinsky's manipulation of such techniques, which are amply discussed in Eric Walter White's *Stravinsky: The Composer and His Works*, 2d ed. (Berkeley and Los Angeles, 1979), and many other works.

16. "What I do, I do not wish blamed on Zen, though without my engagement with Zen (attendance at lectures by Alan Watts and D. T. Suzuki, reading of the literature) I doubt whether I would have done what I have done. I am told that Alan Watts has questioned the relation between my work and Zen. I mention this in order to free Zen of any responsibility for my actions" (John Cage, foreword to *Silence* [Cambridge, MA, 1961], xi).

17. *Aria* is dedicated to Berberian, who was also the first singer of *Chamber Music, Circles,* and many other examples of the "new vocalism," testimony to the importance of the performer in Cage's music, its cooperative and democratic aspect.

18. *Aria* score directions.

19. Cage was perfectly aware that absolute silence is impossible to achieve. In some works, such as the famous and infamous *4'33''*, the ambient sound is part of the piece.

20. My descriptions of *Stimmung* are based not only on the score and the recording but also on a visit Stockhausen made to the New England Conservatory of Music in the early 1970s, when I was a student there. The tape he played of a performance of *Stimmung* was not that of the recording released by Deutsche Gramophon.

21. There is a wonderfully funny and surprising moment on the Deutsche Gramophon recording—although not on the tape Stockhausen played at New England Conservatory—when the singers suddenly and very quickly build up the Bb^9 chord from the bottom up, in standard intonation, to the triumphant word "Barbershop!"

CHAPTER FOUR

New Ensembles, New Works

Music for the "broken consort," to carry that term up from the Renaissance, or for a mixed group such as might play a Baroque chamber sonata, was not unheard of in the nineteenth century, but it was unusual. It also falls only uncertainly into the rubric of chamber music. Beethoven's Septet, Op. 20 (1799–1800), for clarinet, French horn, bassoon, violin, viola, cello, and double bass, sounds much like the serenades and cassations of the late eighteenth century, light music for mixed ensembles. Schubert's Octet of 1824 is modeled, at least in some respects, on Beethoven's septet; in addition, it was a commission for the specific instruments involved, as was much of the subsequent chamber music that used nonstandard groups of instruments. The most famous example is Brahms's chamber music for clarinet—two sonatas for clarinet and piano; the Trio for Clarinet, Cello, and Piano; the Clarinet Quintet—all written for the clarinetist Richard Mühlfeld.

This situation changes completely after 1912. New instruments, especially from the percussion family, move into prominence. And later, new means of sound production are invented—the tape recorder, the synthesizer. For various historical or musical reasons, composers begin to hear new timbres and new timbral combinations, which are as important to the new music of the twentieth century as the so-called breakdown of functional tonality or the inclusion of the voice or of literary or dramatic programs in the previously "pure," absolute genres of chamber music. Works that were new in many ways, such as Schoenberg's *Pierrot lunaire*, sounded that much newer, and were that much more important historically, because of their new sounds.

This chapter begins with brief discussions of three works of the early twentieth century for unusual, at that time sui generis, ensembles: *Pierrot*, Stravinsky's *L'histoire du soldat*, and Debussy's Sonata for Flute, Viola, and Harp. We will then look at a few works commissioned and composed for specific ensembles: Bartók's *Contrasts* (1938), for clarinet, violin, and piano, commissioned by Benny Goodman; Messiaen's *Quartet for the End of Time,* written while he was in a German POW camp in 1940; and Milton Babbitt's *All Set,* for jazz ensemble (alto saxophone, tenor saxophone, trumpet, trombone, double bass, percussion trap set, vibraphone, and piano), composed for a Brandeis University music festival in 1957. We will also discuss works that include percussion in the chamber ensemble, and works involving live performers and tape, especially Barbara Kolb's *Solitaire* and Mario Davidovsky's series of *Synchronisms.* (We will not discuss anywhere in this study purely electronic music or *musique concrète.*) Finally, the last half of the chapter will cover a fairly large and varied sampling of music for nonstandard ensembles, encompassing not only a variety of groups and sounds but also an equally wide variety of musical styles and concerns.

Three Early Modern Works: Schoenberg, Stravinsky, Debussy

Schoenberg's original commission for *Pierrot lunaire,* from the actress Albertine Zehme, was for recitation and piano, or a so-called melodrama. The final ensemble is five players and eight instruments: flute (doubling on piccolo), clarinet (bass clarinet), violin (viola), cello, and piano. Schoenberg developed this ensemble not as a self-conscious gesture of modernism but because he heard these instruments in his mind's ear and needed them to tell his story.

The ensemble is treated as a real chamber ensemble, that is, as a group of potential soloists, not as a mass. Schoenberg does not write for the instruments as winds versus strings versus piano, for instance; rather, he exploits the varieties of colors. The basic instrumentation emphasizes the high, clear timbres of the flute, violin, and clarinet, contrasted with the lower registers of the cello, and Schoenberg largely uses single-note melodies in these instruments as a contrast with the usual chords in the piano. In other words, Schoenberg uses all eight of his instruments in completely standard ways; it is their combination that struck his contemporaries and successors.

In addition, the instrumentation helps depict the story, in general and in some local details. In part 1 the instruments play high in their ranges, the soft, clear sounds depicting the clear and nonthreatening moonlight. As Pierrot makes his quest underground and the Poet goes through the horrors of his trials, the lower instruments and lower ranges prevail, with thicker textures. With the return to Bergamo in part 3, the instruments return to their higher ranges and the less cluttered textures of part 1. In the meantime, there are individual instances of using instruments in a narrative fashion—the cello solo in the "Serenade," No. 19, whose text refers to Pierrot playing a viola with a grotesque giant bow; the solo flute, usually associated with pastoral scenes and easy pleasure, here in anguish in No. 7, "Der kranke Mond"; the rolling pizzicatos in cello and violin for the barcarole of No. 20. And there are the new sounds, such as the *Klangfarbenmelodie* of No. 4, "Eine blasse Wäscherin," where the same chords recur but voiced differently among the three instruments (flute, clarinet, violin), so that the ear is drawn less to the particular chord itself than to its shifting timbres.

Perhaps most striking about the instrumentation of Pierrot, however, is its shaping—not merely its depiction—of the story. Just as Schoenberg begins with the high registers and gradually expands, he gradually uses more players in any particular setting. The specific combination always changes, from number to number and occasionally within numbers, so that the timbres are always new and fresh. But all five instrumentalists play together only once in part 1, at the climax of No. 6, "Madonna," the final refrain "Mutter aller Schmerzen!" ("Mother of all pain!"). In part 2, two numbers involve all five instrumentalists: No. 11, "Rote Messe," and No. 14, "Die Kreuze." Like "Madonna," both are about the Poet, and both express his religious agony. By contrast, all of the numbers of part 3 except No. 17, "Parodie," use all five instrumentalists; moreover, the last number, "O alter Duft," uses all eight instruments. If Schoenberg has not found it necessary to construct an overarching tonal or formal scheme for *Pierrot* beyond its narrative, he has given it a clear shape through its instrumentation. This strategy illustrates the broader fact that as tonal functions lost their preeminence in the first ten years of this century, tonal hierarchy ceded its function to other musical devices, in this case extramusical narrative and large-scale musical shaping through timbre and texture. In this way as well, *Pierrot lunaire* was a liberating and groundbreaking work for the twentieth century, solving problems of expression and cohesion that had been only superficially probed to that point.

Stravinsky's *L'histoire du soldat* (1918) was not written on commission, but it was certainly composed in the hopes of earning enough money for Stravinsky to live. Stravinsky, his family, and some of his friends were virtually stranded without resources in Switzerland during the First World War. As he relates the story in his *Autobiography*,[1] the idea was to compose a music-theatre piece with which a small ensemble could travel around Switzerland, singing for their supper. The result was *L'histoire*, a bleak antiwar story with a heavy debt to the Faust legends. Here we will deal, not with the verbal part of the work, or even with the music in terms of its stylistic or technical devices, but only with its instrumentation.

The ensemble consists of seven players: clarinet, bassoon, cornet, trombone, percussion, violin, and double bass. The percussion set includes side drums with and without snares, a small drum with snare, bass drum, cymbals, tambourine, and triangle. The piece requires a conductor; it is musically not a chamber work but an orchestral work writ small. Two aspects interest us here: the first is the small mixed ensemble, for even if it did not engender other music for these specific instruments, even if there is no *"L'histoire* septet" as there is a *"Pierrot* quintet" in the subsequent history and repertory of modern music, here for the first time percussion is included as an important musical—not simply programmatic—instrument in a small group. The other instruments—pairs of high and low woodwinds, brass, and strings—suggest theatrical pit bands: the orchestra stripped to its essentials.

Second, the soloistic writing for the violin often strikes the unsympathetic ear as "unviolinistic," unidiomatic for the instrument. The rough-hewn writing is far indeed from the Romantic violin idiom, but it is in fact thoroughly suited to the instrument. The violin here symbolizes the Soldier of the title and his struggles with the Devil; given *L'histoire*'s almost Brechtian quality, a violin part in the manner of Tchaikovsky (whom Stravinsky worshiped) would not serve. Yet the violin writing is not only programmatic or dramatic but at the same time a new compendium of modern sonic possibilities. The violin stays almost entirely in its lowest two octaves, its throatiest and least brilliant register. The pervasive double-stops greatly restrict the player's use of vibrato, as well as emphasizing the rhythmic (and not lyric) aspects of the part. The brusque, repetitive rhythms require a lot of downbows and short bows; if the bass occasionally sounds like the foundation of a jazz band, the violin sounds like folk fiddling. (As is often remarked, the tango of part 2 is gypsy music, the waltz is Viennese, the march is Spanish, and the "ragtime" is American.)

L'histoire du soldat is not particularly shaped by its instrumentation, which is rather a realization of the work's dramatic elements. The piece is a moral fable, *faux-naïf* in its verse forms, diction, kinds of music (marches, dances, chorales), and kinds of instruments. Many of its musical characteristics—as with *The Rite of Spring* and the *Three Japanese Lyrics*—are intimately bound up with these programmatic elements. Perhaps this particularity prevented the *L'histoire* ensemble from achieving the model status of the *Pierrot* quintet, as it may have been one reason why Stravinsky's style of the years from 1909 (e.g., *Petrushka*) through 1918 never attained the dominance of Schoenberg's, which was clearly rooted in German Romanticism, or Stravinsky's own so-called neoclassicism following upon the Octet, at the apex of a real international style for some thirty years. It cannot be denied, however, that the particular sounds of *L'histoire*—the marches or the duets between violin and percussion—echoed strongly through the ensuing years in Europe.

Less fixed historically but equally idiosyncratic are the last works of Debussy. His Sonata for Flute, Viola, and Harp (1915) was the second in a projected series of six sonatas for various instruments. The first of these was for cello and piano, the third (Debussy's last completed work) for violin and piano. The fourth, for which a very few sketches exist, was to be for oboe, French horn, and harpsichord. Because of the beauty of its sounds—invariably called "autumnal"—the second sonata (sometimes called the Trio) has in recent years become quite popular; as with *Pierrot*, in fact, it has given rise to chamber groups who make it the center of their repertory, adding on other instruments for other works.

The American musicologist and Debussy specialist William W. Austin hears in the Sonata for Flute, Viola, and Harp "the last word in the vein of the [*Prelude to the Afternoon of a*] *Faun* and *Syrinx*, with both the voluptuousness of the former and the austerity of the latter."[2] He might have gone on to mention the pastoral qualities a listener always associates with the flute (panpipes) and the harp (a shepherd's harp or lyre, an Aeolian harp), conjoined here by the throaty sound of the viola. Like most of Debussy's music, the sonata has few progeny. Debussy's works are always too individual, too specific in a way, to engender imitators. Although this sonata and the other two of the series are contemporary with *En blanc et noir*, discussed in chapter 2, there are few meaningful points of convergence among them. The most important reason for this is the specificity of their sounds: these works of Debussy could not be transcribed for any other instruments. Their construction was of interest to the composers of the 1950s, composers as different as Boulez and Crumb; their sounds may have contributed to the characteristic sounds of such composers as well. Although the lessons of the sonata may not be directly applicable to other chamber works discussed in this book, even other sonatas of Debussy, there are no apologies to be made for that: individuality is itself one of the hallmarks of twentieth-century music, and the Debussy sonata is representative exactly by virtue of not being so.

The first movement is entitled "Pastorale," an evocative word that yet means only slightly more than the titles of the second and third movements, "Interlude" and "Finale." (The second movement is also marked *Tempo di minuetto*.) A pastoral may be any of a number of things: according to the *Harvard Concise Dictionary of Music*, it is an "instrumental or vocal piece written in imitation of the music of shepherds and their shawms or pipes. . . . Typical features are $\frac{6}{8}$ or $\frac{12}{8}$ meter in moderate time, suggestive of a lullaby, and dotted rhythms."[3]

The *topos* was loosened in the nineteenth and twentieth centuries, presumably as the artistic and bourgeois attitudes toward the rustic and the "natural" changed: the most commonly noted pastorals of the early nineteenth century are Beethoven's Sixth Symphony (1809) and the third movement of Berlioz's *Symphonie fantastique* (1830), the "Scène aux champs." We can pass lightly by the Beethoven, since Debussy did not share the nineteenth-century French love for that composer, noting only that even in Beethoven's symphony the organic and tightly organized forms are meant to sound relaxed, at ease, not obsessive like those of the Fifth (and others). More immediately important are Debussy's own earlier pastorals, those noted by Austin, the *Prelude to the Afternoon of a Faun* and "Syrinx."

The Sonata's most patently pastoral element is the instrumentation. In addition to the well-established pastoral associations of flute and harp, the viola acts as a timbral mediation between the other two instruments: it is close to the range of that equally rustic woodwind, the English horn, but shares its string sound with the harp. Other principal elements of the first movement are the continuity of its melody—Wagner's "endless melody" or Debussy's arabesques—and its reliance on melody, texture, tempo, meter, and rhythm to define form, much more than on harmony and harmonic relationships. This movement resembles the first movement of *En blanc et noir* in that its seeming sectionality eventually becomes a sort of linearity instead: rather than hearing an ordered series of discrete musical sections, as one might expect from formal diagrams, one hears the music progressing through time as if with differing routes through the same family of melodies. (This becomes an express conception of musical form in the music of Pierre Boulez some forty years later.) The difference here is not just semantic, for it leads to a way of hearing unlike that required for music that is primarily sectional and hierarchic.

A formal schematization of the pastorale will demonstrate its own inefficacies. The movement falls into three sections: mm. 1–25, where all three instruments reach a melodic cadence and the harmony has moved to C, the "dominant" of the movement's principal tonal center, F; mm. 26–47, a new and contrasting section, even in a new meter and a new tempo; and mm. 48–83, the seeming recomposition of, or return to, or recapitulation of, the first section. Figure 4.1 shows that each segment of the final section derives directly from one in the first section of the movement. But the ordering in this final section is unrelated to that of the first section; rather, the segments here are recombined into an order that is new yet reassuringly familiar.

This recomposition is not what is expected, given the previous two sections. The first, mm. 1–25, is comparable to a standard sonata exposition, beginning with a melody shared among harp, flute, viola, and flute again, marked successively *lento, dolce rubato; mélancoliquement; doux et pénétrant; en serrant;* and *en rentrant au mouvement.* This arabesque melody spins constantly forward and reaches a first cadence, on F, on the downbeat of measure 9. It establishes this tonal arrival as much

Measures		Seeming function; or, mm. 48–83, relationship to mm. 1–25
1–25		"Exposition"
	1–9	1st theme
	9–17	bridge
	18–25	2d theme, cadence on C
26–47		"Development" or contrasting middle section
48–83		"Recapitulation" or "Recomposition" of mm. 1–25
	48–49	Retransition
	50–53	mm. 4–5 plus a cadence on C (V?)
	54–56	mm. 4–5 again to a half cadence on C (V)
	57–62	mm. 14–17 (although the harp plays a B♭ in m. 59 instead of D), plus a two-measure extension
	63–66	mm. 18–20, the last measure recomposed, and the cadence from mm. 8–9
	66–71	mm. 9–12, plus a different extension
	72–83	m. 1 extended and composed out, then melodic cadences from mm. 14–15 and m. 8

FIGURE 4.1. Formal schematization, Debussy's Sonata for Flute, Viola, and Harp, "Pastorale."

melodically as harmonically—that is, with stepwise motion rather than triads around the circle of fifths—and reinforces the arrival with the slight *accelerando* and return to tempo Debussy calls for in its last two measures.

After the briefest of breaths, what seems to be a bridge begins, with open fifths in the viola and harp, a new timbre in the viola (the fifths played on the fingerboard), and a flourish in the flute that describes the least stable of harmonies, the fully diminished seventh chord. This moves directly, however, into a much more defined phrase, with fully melodic phrases and motives. The harp, and then harp and viola together, repeat a stepwise descending figure, and the flute turns what had been the end of its flourish into a new melody (simply by slowing it down and matching it to the meter of the section), which also uses the descending motive. Again we move to a cadence, much like the one in measure 9, and again on F: we have not modulated, as one is supposed to in a bridge, and it is clear to the ear that the essential matter and methods of this sonata movement do not lie in its harmonic structures. At this point, m. 18, we move without transition into a final section, or second group, in a new tempo (*amimando*) and a new meter (⁷⁄₄, and then ⁸⁄₈, after a meter of ⁹⁄₈ to this point). The texture is fully chordal, for the first time in the movement, and the melodies are both more rhythmic and energetic and more single-mindedly directed up and down the scale. For the final time in this section we come to a cadence, having returned to the opening ⁹⁄₈ meter, the instruments again moving by step and in unison rather than by fifth and in harmonies; and we close on C, the "dominant" of the key center of the movement to this point. (I cannot call F a real key because it works only as a center of other more or less directly related chords and tonal areas; it is not at the pinnacle of a tonal hierarchy, like the F major of Beethoven's *Pastoral* Symphony.)

The music of mm. 26–47 is completely new, *vif et joyeux*, its opening viola figure marked *nettement rythmé*, and centering (unlike the first or third section) on a single principal melody and oscillating accompanimental figures in a simple homophonic texture. This is not a "development" in the sense of working out material from an exposition. It fits the sonata pattern in being a contrasting middle section shorter than the first and, indeed, the shortest of the movement as a whole.[4] This section fades and slows, rather than reaching a cadence, and melts into an unaccompanied viola line that acts as a retransition to the final section.

Beautiful as the final section is—but this may be a large part of what makes it so beautiful—it is confusing. Debussy retains the clarity and continuity of succession that hitherto has been broken only at the juncture of the first two sections. But the clarity of division, the articulation among phrases and subsections that we heard in the first section is gone. As Figure 4.1 indicates, things come back in changed orders, and we hear fragments of earlier sections rather than the complete item. A few earlier passages, notably the "second theme" material from mm. 21–25, never reappear. Moreover, in this section, which is surprisingly the longest of the three, the longest subsection is its last, a coda that begins with the reprise of the striking and memorable beginning of the sonata, now extended and newly composed out, and closes with the cadences that we had heard midway through the first section, at the end of the so-called first theme (mm. 8–9) and even in the middle of the bridge (mm. 14–15). Thus the proportions at the end of this movement are in no way what we have been led to expect. The content is changed, too, re-formed as it is re-presented: present in a new guise but still to my ears essentially absent. The material of the first section of the movement is not, as it would be in an earlier sonata, reworked into a new unity that transcends an earlier one, but rather disintegrated into a (still seamless) continuity that specifically denies the organic coherence of the first section. One result of this is the extraordinary nostalgia that the last third of the movement causes to well up: things cannot return. Shards may resurface, beauty may well be always there, we may seek what lies in the past; but things cannot return. This tough-minded nostalgia (tough-minded because Debussy could, of course, simply repeat and rework his earlier material, but chooses not to) informs even the movement's final cadence, with its unresolved major seventh (E natural) in the flute. In all principal cadences of the movement—mm. 9, 24, 53, 58, 66—the cadential point of arrival is always completely triadic. Only here, at the end, do we have a full cadence with an "added," or nontriadic, note. The E natural in the flute is not just a simplistic yearning toward F, toward resolution, however; it is a final blurring of the basic material of the movement, the denial to the chord of F major any clear and articulated existence. Even the simplicity of the major triad is removed from us.

Thus far ignored in this formal description is the movement's tone: not its timbres, but its light, almost nonchalant character. A result of tempo, texture, timbre, and phrase shapes and successions, this lightness is of a piece with the movement's tough-minded nostalgia, and with its formal process, exploring differing routes through the same family of melodies. If things cannot return, that is of no real or crucial import. Music is of necessity transient; by the time it has registered in our minds, it is gone. The quasi-spatial hierarchical structures of, say, German music from Haydn through Schoenberg are essentially chimeras, aesthetic constructs on which musicians and listeners have learned to agree. Debussy denies these constructs, in virtually every work he composed, and it is here that he is a true modernist and a deeply original composer. He insists on music's loyalties to its own nature, for as tones disappear, so do melodies, phrases, sections. Obviously, one cannot say that Debussy's music is for this reason better than Schoenberg's; but these two composers represent different views of the nature of music, and of the relationship of music to the world about it. In this particular instance, it is Debussy who introduces the new era, Schoenberg who lives still in the old.

Yet all this is not to say that Debussy's music simply disappears into the ether. The function of the finale is ultimately tonal and metrical grounding in F major (again, the chord as tonal center more than the key) and common time. The second movement, the interlude, begins to move in this direction of clarity and stability. Its textures are simpler and more straightforward than those of the first movement, its harmonies more triadic, and its rhythms more firmly mixed into a metrical framework. But the interlude has still some connections to the pastorale. Its forms, from the phrase level to the most general, are successive and additive, like those of the first movement. In addition, Debussy frames the movement proper with a particular and evocative harmony that, if it does not confuse the tonality of the movement, lightens the insistence on F as a tonal center and keeps the listener, as it were, on point.

A quasi-modal scale, heard in the flute's melody at the very beginning of the interlude and again in the flute and viola at the end (see Ex. 4.1), is essentially a Phrygian scale on F; yet it employs both E♭ and E natural, the E♭ both descending and ascending (mm. 1 and 3, with leaps in both instances) and the E natural descending, interposed be-

EXAMPLE 4.1. Debussy, Sonata for Flute, Viola, and Harp, Interlude, mm. 1–4.

tween F and C (m. 4). Given that mm. 4–7 function as a dominant upbeat to m. 8's arrival on F minor as a tonic, the E natural of m. 4 seems
to be merely the usual chromatic inflection that is inherent in the minor mode. But its pleasing contradiction of the E♭ emphasizes the G♭,
which makes this a quasi-Phrygian scale, tending toward F but never attaining it directly. Likewise, the D♭ of mm. 1 and 2 always appears in an
ascending phrase, never descending through C natural to F. Debussy is
not working against the "natural" tendencies of E natural, E♭, D♭, and
G♭; he is just not treating them obviously. As E natural and G♭ want to
converge on F, E♭ and D♭ want to descend to C. Since D♭ is to C as G♭ is
to F, each reinforces the other, and we are left neatly balanced between
F as the ostensible tonic and C as its apparent dominant. At the beginning of the interlude, this is quite clearly the case, since seven measures
of C pedal resolve to F in measure 8. But at the end of this movement,
Debussy resolves his harmonies to F minor, first through G♭ and then
through C, only to end on unison Cs in all three instruments. The tonic
is established, only to be erased slightly, smudged around the edges, or
perhaps leavened. We are on point again, balanced lightly between F
and C.

The finale is, like that of *En blanc et noir,* more straightforward and
standard, with clearer harmonies and harmonic progressions, repeated
melodies spun out from incisive motives, unequivocal formal articulations, all in a sort of "Jardins sous la pluie" texture. At the end of the
movement, however, suddenly we hear the framing melody of the pastorale; and here it is in a way resolved. In this context, the tragic quality
of the first movement, however lightly it was stated there, is removed
completely. The expression of transience has itself become a memory.
This is not a denial or a contradiction of the first movement. On the
one hand, the opening of the sonata is one of its most beautiful and
striking gestures, and one always wants to hear it again—especially
since Debussy was so chary of it in that movement. In a technical sense,
its reappearance at the end of the sonata works directly and most effi-

ciently for overall closure. We know here that we are not going to reex-
plore an old idea, since it appears so suddenly in what is otherwise
quite clearly the end of the movement; the recall thus acts quite un-
abashedly as review and conclusion. Moreover, the recall here in a new
and different context of an idea that seemed to symbolize transience in
a way now embodies that transience. Things cannot remain the same,
and indeed the connotations of this phrase of the music have not remained the same. The wistfulness of the first movement, its sense of ir-
revocable loss, has itself been lost. If one returns at this point directly to
the opening of the sonata, it doesn't "work"; the opening idea has lost
its effect. This is not the case with, for example, Schoenberg's *Verklärte
Nacht,* perhaps because in that case the motives are so consistently
worked through and developed that the change from beginning to end
is audible, even the focus. Here the change takes place while we're not
listening, while our ears are elsewhere, and we are aware of it only
when the initial situation is past forever.

Contrasts and Duets

Contrasts: Bartók, Messiaen, Babbitt

Other works for unusual ensembles are the results of commissions
or unusual circumstances. These do not form a body of musical pro-
genitors in this century, as indeed they rarely do. But three such works
make for an interesting conjunction. The first is Béla Bartók's *Contrasts,*
for clarinet, violin, and piano. *Contrasts* was commissioned in 1938 by
the clarinetist Benny Goodman, best known as a jazz musician, who
also performed classical pieces.[5] The title refers to the differences
among the three instruments, primarily, but also among the various
dances that make up the work and the musical material within the
movements. It is a genial and unassuming work, but nonetheless one of
charm and attractiveness.

Bartók the composer assumed modesty for Bartók the pianist in
Contrasts, giving pride of place to Goodman and the original violinist,
Joseph Szigeti (these three premiered the work in January 1939). The
two wide-ranging, virtuosic melodic instruments, both treble, are thus
accompanied by a less assertive piano part. The writing for the two
melody instruments is brilliant and utterly idiomatic. Bartók's innovations come in many arenas: formal conception, new ways of arranging
compelling tonal hierarchies, new rhythms and meters, and the assimilation of the ethos of eastern and southeastern Europe into the traditional language of western Europe.

Each melody instrument is assigned material that shows it off to
great advantage—arpeggios in the clarinet, multiple stops in the violin,
trills and tremolos, exploration of registers, and so on. And each has an

extensive cadenza, the clarinet's in the first movement and the violin's in the third. The work gives the impression of an accompanied duet precisely because of the differentiation, the contrasts, between the violin and clarinet. But because the writing for each instrument is so idiomatic, so natural, the listener's attention comes to focus not on the instruments but on melodies, harmonies, and rhythms of the dances and the intervening "Rest" movement. As in an orchestral work or, for example, Brahms's Trio for Clarinet, Cello, and Piano, the contrasting instruments or instrumental groups combine to form a cohesive whole. This is the opposite of what happens in *L'histoire du soldat* or *Pierrot lunaire*, as well as in Bartók's string quartets or the Sonata for Two Pianos and Percussion, in which the composer seeks out diversity within a family of instruments as well as the cohesion of sound and timbres that unites them. The instrumental writing in *Contrasts* is most similar, among the pieces discussed in this study, to the works of Francis Poulenc, for the most part traditional and forbidding neither to the less-than-virtuoso player nor to the popular audience. This accessibility accounts to some extent for the popularity of *Contrasts* among both players and audiences: it is a grateful piece, attractive, and does not require the philosophical seriousness of much modern music, including much of Bartók's own. It contains many of the stylistic traits of Bartók's other music of the 1930s, and of the music of that era in general, in its rhythms, its textures, its clear (if nontriadic) harmonies, its precisely contoured melodies, and its unmixed instrumental colors, without demanding the constant concentration and active listening that other works do.

Just as Bartók's *Contrasts* is a good example of his compositional style, if a more modest piece than some of its contemporaries, Messiaen's *Quartet for the End of Time* is an extraordinary example of its composer's style, a musical statement about time and religious certainty, and a piece of immediate and lasting historical impact. I discussed the context and the compositional elements of the quartet in chapter 2. Here I would like to make only a few remarks about the instrumental writing in the quartet and its contribution to the whole. The ensemble is made up of those instruments available to Messiaen in the German POW camp: violin, clarinet, cello, and piano. Messiaen uses, before anything else that strikes the listener's ear, the sounds and timbral possibilities of the instruments to create the world in which time will end. (According to his notes for the work, this movement, the "Crystal Liturgy," takes place at between three and four o'clock in the morning, and represents the harmonious silence of heaven.) The clarinet enters "comme un oiseau," sounding like a bird, either a blackbird or a nightingale. Then comes the piano, its chords drenched in pedal so that all attacks are softened and we are more aware of individual chords than of the rhythmic and harmonic ostinati that organize them. Next the cello enters, exploiting high harmonics in combination with vibrato and a glissando connecting the last two notes of each five-note melodic pedal. Finally, the violin is another bird, singing away independently of the other two instruments. Once established, this early-morning world is neither explored nor expanded: it simply exists, and it forces itself on us, or invites us in, through its duration alone.

A new world comes with each movement, though some begin to resemble earlier ones as we move through all eight movements. The "Vocalise, for the Angel Who Announces the End of Time" is framed by a "robust," "quick, almost joyous" passage in which the instruments work against or across each other more vigorously than in the first movement. The piano plays big, crashing chords, *fff*, as the clarinet continues its birdlike arpeggios and syncopated figures from the first movement (though here *fortissimo*), and the strings play aggressive sixteenth-note scalar figures two octaves apart. The "Vocalise" proper is played by the violin and cello, still two octaves apart, while the piano repeats clusters of descending chords, again drenched in pedal. Yet this is different from the first movement because its repetitive figures are much more readily heard to be so, and because the texture emphasizes the violin and cello's melody of long and ecstatic phrases, which finally reaches a cadence simply through repetition and insistence on a final figure and through repeated arrivals on a final high D, *ppp* in the muted strings and *pppp* in the piano. The framing music from the beginning then reappears, descending and reascending, and the instruments are now brought in one by one (strings, then clarinet, then piano), here maintaining the sense of ensemble that was missing in the beginning but was the point of the "Vocalise" proper.

Each movement has its own instrumental profile. The third movement, "Abyss of the Birds," is a clarinet solo that uses music from both earlier movements, but also uses an idiomatic and strikingly expressive possibility on the clarinet, beginning a high E (concert pitch) below the threshold of human hearing, increasing its volume so that it is at first vaguely heard as ambient sound, vibrations coming from somewhere in the concert hall, then localized as the clarinet, and continuing its crescendo to as loud a sound as possible, marked in the score as *ffff*. This is not possible on any other instrument, and its effect is breath-stopping for the listener.

The "Abyss" is followed by an "Intermezzo," the earliest movement of the quartet to be composed. This is the least demanding movement for the listener because of its texture—the three melodic instruments essentially playing in unison at the beginning and end, and in straightforward homophony in the central section, the piano remaining silent—and because of what we hear as repeated music from earlier movements. This texture of instrumental unisons is repeated in the sixth movement, the "Dance of Fury, For the Seven Trumpets." But here the sound is "decided, vigorous, granitic," *fortissimo* throughout except for a brief passage toward the beginning that returns even more briefly at the very end. This sixth movement is the ne plus ultra of instrumental unity in the quartet, 180 degrees from the world of the opening movement. Here attention shifts from particular instrumental qualities to jagged melodies, with their extreme register shifts and the pervasive "added values" (the term is Messiaen's), which work to loosen meter by extending the duration of individual beats or groupings of beats.

The seventh movement, "Clusters of Rainbows, For the Angel Who Announces the End of Time," continues the cello and piano duet begun in the fifth movement, with new material that yet sounds reminiscent of earlier music. This first theme of the movement alternates with a second theme, drawn from the framing music of the second movement. As each of these themes is repeated, it is simultaneously varied by changes in instrumentation, change of mode, or other standard means of musical variation. Since this movement directly follows the unisons of the "Dance of Fury," we hear it as a relaxation but simultaneously as a new cooperation among the four instruments, each of the four brining its particular voice to shared material. It constitutes an instrumental succession, and a very clear one, but not a progression in the sense of a unidirectional line toward a common goal. This is one of the working methods of the quartet perhaps taken from Debussy, the repetition of elements (beginning already in the second movement) but not in a linear or obviously cumulative way.

The only exception to this pattern is the suggestion of motion in the closely related fifth and eighth movements, and even here the succession is broken by the entirely different sixth and seventh movements. The progression here is one of ecstasy, in the symbolic E major triad with an added C♯, beginning in the cello and continuing three movements later in the violin. At the start of the fifth movement, the cello is high in its range, already on the B above middle C, but the piano is playing in its richest low register. We also have the contrast of the "majestic, contemplative, very expressive" (Messiaen's description in the score) cello melody with the repeated, organlike chords of the piano. As this through-composed movement grows out of the opening phrase, the instruments rise in pitch and dynamics until a sudden *ppp* marks the final section. The movement ends with the instruments almost where they were at the beginning of the movement, the piano only adding a low E to its opening chord, and the cello on the E a fourth above its opening B.

In the final movement, the "Praise to the Immortality of Jesus," the piano begins in a slightly higher register than in the fifth movement. The violin begins on the same B that the cello had, though, with its leaner timbre, it sounds higher than that cello B, and it promises still higher registers to come. In gradual stages, sometimes returning to the opening registers only to rise again, the through-composed movement rises to the highest possible registers, ending on a high E, *ppp* and held to infinite lengths, over repeated *ppp* chords in the piano, *perdendosi* (dying away). The piano chords are so high that it is difficult to distinguish the pitches; the violin's E is in such a high register that we may think that we are imagining it rather than really hearing it—a reaction that may suggest the "harmonious silence of heaven" mentioned with the first movement.

Thus the very instrumentation of the *Quartet for the End of Time* becomes programmatic. It is not just that the clarinet and violin can imitate birds convincingly, but that Messiaen uses the various capabilities of his four instruments to depict the stopping of time and the creation of ecstatic and timeless stasis. We begin in what seems to be the most perfect earthly time for Messiaen, the beginnings of the day's awakenings, in an extremely variegated instrumental universe. From there we move through a kaleidoscopic succession of textures and colors, instrumental unisons and oppositions, but ultimately aiming for unisons (the "Vocalise" section of the second movement; the fourth movement; the seventh). Each of the melodic instruments has a solo movement, and their order moves from the unaccompanied clarinet, still earthbound, through the accompanied cello and violin movements. This is why the final movement works in fact to stop time, and why it always seems in a good performance that the movement is played by the whole ensemble. In hindsight, it seems as if Messiaen has been working from the beginning to the final E of the violin, though never in a direct line. We are almost surprised at the succession of movements, their rapture seizing us unaware. For if we are made to know that time will stop, and if we see that end approaching, the chronology set up for us will be so strong that time's arrow will continue and chronology will go on. As much through instrumental means as through repetition of devices or reprise of earlier music, we are to realize only after the fact that time has already stopped. The cello and the clarinet have been subsumed into the melody of the violin in the final movement. The last sounds of the quartet, in an act of real mysticism, point further upward and inward, to that which cannot be seen or heard. It is hard to think of another work in the Western tradition that so embodies a religious experience.

An example much different from Bartók and Messiaen is Milton Babbitt's *All Set*, a response to two of Babbitt's interests, serialism and popular music. The soprano Bethany Beardslee has observed that the most difficult aspect of Babbitt's music is its rhythms, and that Babbitt has always been close to jazz and popular rhythms, which he notates precisely in his own music. The title is itself a pun, combining the attitude of the ready-to-wail jazz group and the piece's basic pitch material, the all-combinatorial set.[6] Babbitt's piece is precisely notated music for a typical jazz set-up, which, given an assured enough performance, will sound marvelously free and even "swinging."

All Set is scored for alto and tenor saxophones, trumpet, trombone, bass, piano, vibraphone, and percussion, the last including small and large tom-toms, snare drum, bass drum, three cymbals, and hi-hat cymbal: a jazz combo of four melody instruments and rhythm section, typical of the jazz mainstream since the 1920s. Moreover, the instruments are deployed as they often are in jazz: over a steady beat, we hear first the ensemble playing all together, the three principal lines in unison in the saxes, the brass, and the piano and vibes. Then follows a fragmentation of the texture and of the melodic materials, in a fluid alternation of solos of varying lengths and ensemble sections often picking up riffs from the soloist and displacing him or her as a principal instrument.[7] These solos and displacing voices move around the various instruments. Some minutes into the piece, a trombone solo leads into a brief passage of chords, or melodic lines in rhythmic unison. The alto sax then, to my ears, quotes Jerome Kern's "All the Things You Are" (in this context an appropriate allusion), and another ensemble section closes out the first half of the piece.

The second half of *All Set* is a sort of reconstitution of the material that is fragmented in the course of the first half. It begins with a trombone solo, soon joined by the trumpet. In this second half, the unisons among instruments increase; the "licks" are longer and more frequent. (This pattern is in opposition to the polyphonic, almost heterophonic riffs of the first section. It is also a structural device that we have seen in the third movement, "L'Artisanat furieux," of Boulez's *Le marteau sans maître*.) After a final solo—that staple of the jazz chart, a bass/drums duet—the unison lines return for an ensemble "out chorus" or conclusion.

I have used jazz terminology in this brief description of *All Set*'s surface in order to emphasize some of its connections to jazz in general, and to certain styles of jazz in particular. Besides its 1920s "Chicago"-style layout of intermixing solos and ensembles, many of the piece's traits are reminiscent of other jazz eras as well. The prominence of the percussion part[8] and its steady, swinging pulse, are like those of the swing and bop eras, and the melodic lines and textures are similar to certain kinds of post-bop. The piece is unlike most jazz in its harmonic and melodic construction—no chord progressions as such, the musical source being Babbitt's all-combinatorial set. Thus, on the one hand, *All Set* is (according to Babbitt) a "conjunction of 12-tone structures (the all-combinatorial set) and jazz-like properties . . . the use of percussion, the Chicago jazz–like juxtapositions of solos and ensembles recalling certain characteristics of group improvisation."[9] But, on the other hand, Babbitt writes in the liner notes to a recording of the piece:

All Set was composed in 1957 for the Brandeis University Arts Festival, which that year was a "jazz festival." Whether *All Set* is *really* jazz I leave to the judgment of those who are concerned to determine what things *really* are, and if such probably superficial aspects of the work as its very instrumentation, its use of the "rhythm section," the instrumentally delineated sections which may appear analogous to successive instrumental "choruses," and even specific thematic or motivic materials, may justify that aspect of the title which suggests the *spirit* of a "jazz instrumental," then the surface and the deeper structure of the pitch, temporal, and other dimensions of the work surely reflect those senses of the title, the *letter* of which brings the work closer to others of my compositions, which *really* are not jazz.[10]

The first statement is an accurate description, while the second reads like a testy reaction to unthinking presumption and hyperbole. But there are pointers here, too, for the listener to *All Set*: Babbitt emphasizes the deep unity of *All Set*'s various "dimensions," thus aligning himself with Schoenberg and Webern in the continuation of German Romantic organicism: the creation and exploration of an essentially unitary musical space.

But no true art work is a sum of its technical elements. *All Set* is, at first blush, a jazzlike High Modern "Classical" composition. Thereafter it is a self-contained and self-defining work, beautiful to contemplate (which is to say, both to hear and to think about, to rehear mentally) as an aesthetic creation; this is very much a modernist, and also Classical, object. From the conjunction of these two comes an aesthetic frisson. Like a late Brahms piano piece, *All Set* is always in motion, its motivic manipulations seeming to point backward and forward in time, up and down in musical space; unlike many of those Brahms pieces, its surface reflects and exploits this constant motion. And the piece does swing. I make no claims to define what *All Set* "really" is, but *one* of the things it is—one of "All the Things You Are"—is an exemplary work of 1950s American music, in its techniques, in its combination of two disparate traditions, in the "American"-ness of its rhythms, in its evident self-satisfaction and self-pleasure. One can hear it as a very inviting self-pleasure, inviting the listener to join in as well. For among other things, *All Set* "really" is invigorating.

Chamber Music with Percussion: Cage, Stockhausen, Carter, Bartók

Three composers are responsible for bringing percussion into modern chamber music: Stravinsky, in *L'histoire du soldat;* Edgard Varèse, with his *Ionisation* (1931) for a percussion ensemble of thirteen players; and Henry Cowell, whose book *New Musical Resources* (written 1916–19, revised and published in 1930) and whose compositions, for example the *Ostinato pianissimo* of 1934, pointed up the timbral and expressive possibilities of percussion. Of these three, only Cowell seems to have been impressed by the Asian percussion ensemble so important for the music of our century, the Indonesian gamelans, an example of which Debussy heard in Paris in 1889.

Another composer who, like Cowell, was from California, acquainted with gamelan music, and interested in the structural possibilities of rhythm was John Cage. Two representative early works of Cage are *Amores* (1943), for prepared piano and percussion, and his *Third Construction* (1941), for four percussion players. Two works could hardly be more different. *Amores* is a suite of four movements remarkable for its delicacy, softness, and restraint. The *Third Construction* is exuberant and exhilarating: it often sends an audience home decided to begin percussion lessons the next day. The reasons for this contrast lie both in the instruments Cage uses and in the sorts of rhythms and rhythmic structures he composes.

The three percussion players of *Amores* each use, in the second movement, three graduated tom-toms, played with the fingers. One of the players also taps a pod rattle, and another plays the tom-toms with a wire brush. In the third movement, the players have two or three graduated pieces of "resonant wood," placed on cloth pads. Cage specifically notes in the score that "what is not desired . . . is the extreme richness of, e.g., the marimba or xylophone, nor, on the other hand, the extreme sharpness of the conventional Chinese wood block." The dynamic range of these instruments is limited; they are capable of fine gradations and delicate accents, but they do not produce much volume. The prepared piano is similar, for the objects placed between the instrument's strings act not only to change the timbres but to mute the piano as well. Cage gives the piano's preparer detailed instruction for the nine screws, eight bolts, two nuts, and three strips of rubber to be used, and describes the results he wants. The sounds produced by muting strings with bolts and screws should be "resonant, rich in harmonics and free of any metallic buzzing." Those produced by using rubber strips will be "dull, thud-like, rather than rich." Moreover, to insist on the particularity of the desired timbres, he writes:

> The total desired result has been achieved if, on completion
> of the preparation, one may play the pertinent keys without
> sensing that he is playing a piano or even a "prepared pi-
> ano." An instrument having convincingly its own character-
> istics, not even suggesting those of a piano, must be the result.

By contrast, each of the four players of the *Third Construction* has six or seven instruments, of enormous variety: rattles, graduated tin cans, drums, cowbells, a large suspended cymbal, claves (solid hard-wood cylinders that are struck together), the so-called lion's roar (a rope pulled through an upturned metal bucket, the friction of the rope's rubbing against the metal producing a "roar" whose volume and relative pitch are determined by the speed of the pull), and even a conch shell. The array of instruments thus includes metallic sounds, woody sounds, rattles, and the single pitch of the conch shell. It is also capable of great volume, the sharpest of attacks, and the most sustained sounds (e.g., the bass drum "roar," produced by rubbing it rather than hitting it, or the rattles). Cage uses the array and its possibilities both for local color and effect and for long-range shape. His rhythms and textures here are quite different from those of *Amores,* in each case directly suited for his instrumental forces.

Three of *Amores*'s four movements are through-composed; the second, a trio for nine tom-toms, is a sort of rondo. The third movement, a trio for seven wood blocks, is a wonderful exercise in displaced rhythms, in which the same figures reappear, but never quite where they were before. The outside movements, for solo prepared piano, are a frame, with material from the first movement reappearing, somewhat transformed, in the last. The first movement is a quasi-prelude, entirely introductory in its brevity, its lack of internal repetition, and its exposition of the sonorous and overtone-laden sounds of the preparations. The fourth movement is much longer and more varied than the first, and, given the restricted range of *Amores*'s ensemble, the loudest as well. In a way, *Amores* is an exemplary case of the well-made piece. It has a clear beginning, middle, and end, with the requisite introduction of materials, variety, and unifying conclusion. It is thoroughly consistent internally, even quite self-restricting in the materials it uses or explores. This concentration is echoed in the work's seeming introspection, the delicate and soft explorations of rhythms and rhythmic combinations in a timbrally continuous texture, and those timbres themselves: a realization of the traditional ideal of unity of theme and expression. Structural skills and an ear for wonderful sounds are in evidence in the *Third Construction* as well, but to wildly different effect. The principal differences between this piece and *Amores*—to stay for a moment at the mundane level of process and materials—are the much vaster dynamic range in the *Third Construction,* its more continually varied timbres, its greater use of crescendos and decrescendos, and its use of ostinatos, even riffs. The work is through-composed, but its overall shape is a dynamic one of growth, its first climax coming at the first entrance of the conch shell, about three-quarters of the way through the piece. From this point as well, the tempo picks up, and the *accelerando* continues to the end of the piece. The effect of the *Third Construction* lies in the joyful floating that comes from the combination of a perceived regular meter, syncopated and highly rhythmic riffs working against that meter, and the fast, propulsive beat. Whether the *Third*

Construction is irresistible because it is so joyful, or vice versa, it is music one does not easily tire of.

If functional tonality and regular phraseology have ceded pride of place as principal building blocks of musical form, then color, attack (that is, how to play a note), and rhythm have assumed greater importance in the various musics of the twentieth century. Percussionists have inspired other musicians to bring their attention more than ever before to these aspects.

Two solo percussion works illustrate the variety of techniques that percussionists are called on to utilize. In addition, these two works differ greatly in the composer's intent, and in the preparation and philosophy that the percussionist has to bring to bear on the music in performance. The two pieces are Karlheinz Stockhausen's *Zyklus* (1957) and Elliott Carter's Eight Pieces for Four Timpani (1950/1966).

Zyklus is an aleatoric piece and, as its name implies, in a circular form. (The work predates Berio's *Circles* by some three years.) Moreover, that form is made manifest by the setup of the percussion instruments and the performer's traversal of them through the course of the piece. The various instruments are arranged in a triangle around the performer, who during the performance will turn 360 degrees in an unbroken arc. This circle also describes the continuum of timbres that Stockhausen uses in the piece, and that make up the percussive arsenal, from pitched sounds through the nonpitched, and over the spectrum of woody and metallic timbres. The percussionist moves through that aural universe in ways largely of his or her own choosing: Stockhausen has arranged his score so that it may be played either "forward" or "backward," which is to say that the percussionist may move in either direction around the circle of instruments. The score has no specific beginning or ending; the percussionist may start at any point in the circle, and the piece will be finished when that point is reached again. Finally, at any point in the circle, the percussionist will determine specifically what events happen and how long they last, within the general rule that in this graphic score (Ex. 4.2), space equals time. Repetitions are possible in some instances, specifically indicated, but not required.

Stockhausen has quite precisely delimited the aural world of this piece and its basic elements: the general sound universe, the general ordering of sounds, and the specific kinds of sound that are to be produced at general points in that ordering. But the making of the piece that is heard is the work of the percussionist, who thus becomes a sort of co-composer with Stockhausen. The percussionist must know the work's structures and possibilities well enough to make satisfying musical choices—where in the circle to begin and end (which will determine the overall shape), and what to do at each moment. This bringing of the performer into the realization of the piece is a development that

EXAMPLE 4.2. Stockhausen, *Zyklus*, sample page. © Universal Edition (London) Ltd., London, 1960 © renewed. All Rights Reserved. Used by permission of European American Music Distributors Corporation, sole U.S. and Canadian agent for Universal Edition (London) Ltd., London.

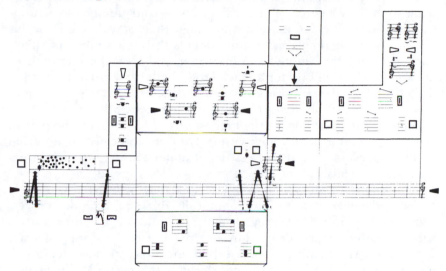

arises from the so-called new virtuosity of the 1950s and later, in tandem with the loosened conceptions of musical structure that came with the aleatoric music of John Cage and the reactions of many European composers in the 1950s against the perceived strictures of total serialism. Its initial effect was an increased drama in musical performance, and often (as here, or in Berio's *Circles*) a visual realization of the musical events. Eventually, such scores led to the inclusion of real improvisation, sometimes within given limits and sometimes not, and also fed back into other post-Cageian developments, such as "happenings," mixed-media events, and performance art. Involvement of the performers in a work's composition or specific realization becomes one of the central tenets of postmodernism: it is a denial of the dictatorial role of the composer; it is a focus on process, as that is determined by "composer" and "performer," the relationship of these two functions no longer being always clear; and it is a musical, or aesthetic, attention to continuity and succession rather than to the predetermined closed form of Western traditions. Finally, as a result, the relationship of work to hearer or to critic is modified as well. We cannot hear *Zyklus* as we can a work of Elliott Carter's, despite Carter's saying that he wants his music to sound as if the players were making it up on the spot.[11] That Stockhausen's percussionist has been a sort of co-composer and is actually acting out his or her compositional choices before us should affect our listening. At the very least, it should remind us while listening to a recorded performance that we are missing a central element of the piece.

It is not a question here of simply acknowledging the expanded role of Stockhausen's percussionist (who is not improvising the performance). It is a matter of musical gestures and audible structures. Carter's music is much more concentrated than Stockhausen's; in his timpani pieces he explores his instruments through a range of effects and emotions, but without the luxuriant and easy thoroughness of *Zyklus*. Stockhausen calls for a much larger battery of instruments than does Carter, and therefore uses it in a different way. Carter's eight pieces are, generically, in the tradition of the nineteenth-century etude, combining the demands for the highest virtuosity with, on the part of the composer, the equally high virtuosity of musical construction from small motives and the use of restricted materials for satisfying large-scale musical ends.

A *saëta* is an Andalusian religious folk song, associated with Holy Week, and normally sung monophonically during a religious procession. The beginning of Carter's "Saëta" (Ex. 4.3a) is a written-out accelerando, the gesture repeated in the third line of the score and again at the end.[12] The ensuing music is a rhythmic, processional extension of the pitches and steady eighth notes of the first measure of the second line. The last line of the first page is the transition to the piece's second section (the piece ternary, with a gradual transition from the B section back to the final A), including an example of metrical modulation. In the next-to-last line of the example, Carter introduces sixteenth notes into the rhythmic vocabulary and begins to emphasize the pitches A and D, breaking up the D–C dyad, which he has been repeating since the beginning, and adding rhythmic variety as well. The first measures of the last line are a cadence, immediately repeated. The durations of the repetition are precisely those of the first sounding, as indicated in the superscript. But then Carter only gradually reinforces the new beat—that is to say, the slightly lengthened quarter note—by writing a rhythm that will sound like that of the first section, the quintuplets of the third measure of the line. (These will sound like two eighth notes and a sixteenth in the original tempo.) The music continues in the new quarters, but rests are not easy for a listener to fix metrically in a transitional passage like this one. The subdivision into triplets, in the next-to-last measure, and the steady rhythm of the next measure help locate the meter in the listener's ear. These same gestures are repeated on the next page of the score, and the transition to a new meter made unmistakable.

The beginning of the third of the Eight Pieces, "Adagio," shows different uses of similar musical procedures (Ex. 4.3b). This piece requires pedal timpani, and on a superficial level is about the exploitation of that instrument for color, for glissandos and harmonics. Using these colors and devices as motives, the piece introduces a particular

EXAMPLE 4.3a. Carter, "Saëta," from Eight Pieces for Four Timpani. Copyright © 1968 by Associated Music Publishers, Inc. (BMI). International Copyright Secured. All Rights Reserved. Reprinted by Permission.

EIGHT · PIECES
for Four Timpani
(one player)

to Al Howard

I. Saëta

Elliott Carter

motive and then extends it and intensifies it. This is also the shape of the through-composed piece as a whole, building to climaxes and then receding only slightly at the very end.

EXAMPLE 4.3b. Carter, "Adagio," from Eight Pieces for Four Timpani. Copyright © 1968 by Associated Music Publishers, Inc. (BMI). International Copyright Secured. All Rights Reserved. Reprinted by Permission.

to Jan Williams

III. Adagio

Elliott Carter

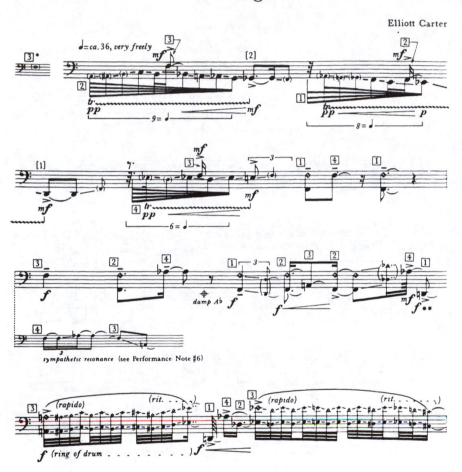

• If this piece is performed after another of the series, it is only necessary to tune Drum 3. Drums 1, 2 and 4 may start on any note and slide into the first notes not in parentheses.

•• The drums played before the harmonic and glissando note should be loud enough to form a ringing background without covering that note. (See Performance Note #6 regarding the production of harmonics.)

Hence the differences in the sounds of Stockhausen's and Carter's works: Stockhausen's musical procedures, no matter how well planned in advance, remain at the level of the general, leaving the specific realizations—the sounds that a listener hears—to the percussionist. A performer of *Zyklus* may set up motivic passages such as we see in the

Carter, but they will be brief and transient. In contrast, no matter how improvisatory or immediate the Carter will sound in the hands of a master percussionist, the very concentration of its motivic devices and construction will militate against our hearing it as anything but carefully and intentionally composed. If *Zyklus* is postmodern, to go back again briefly to this distinction, the Carter pieces are squarely in the modern ethos, in their privileging the composer and compositional devices and in their adherence to fully traditional conceptions of compositional processes and musical construction and structure. The percussionist will thus have to practice *Zyklus* and the Eight Pieces in very different ways, and will need to bring a different mind-set to the rehearsal studio.

Percussion plays a significant role in one of the classics of the modern chamber music repertory, Bartók's Sonata for Two Pianos and Percussion (1937). I am interested here initially in the ensemble and in the relations among the instruments, but the discussion will also anticipate the discussion of the twentieth-century sonata in chapter 5. In addition to the two pianos, Bartók calls for a battery of (1) metallic sounds—both crash cymbals and suspended cymbals, triangle, and tam-tam; (2) nonpitched percussion—bass drum and side drums, with and without snares; and (3) pitched percussion—xylophone and three timpani. The layout of the instruments is given in Figure 4.2. The position of the two pianos is designed for maximum communication among the four instrumentalists, and for the balance of the sounds as well: it is important that the pianos not overpower the percussion instruments, and that neither piano take precedence over the other. It may initially unsettle an audience to watch the pianists' backs rather than their profiles, but the antiphony between the pianos and their changing relationship to the percussion would be less clear in any other disposition. This use of sound space is unattainable in recordings, as well; such a solution as channeling each piano over its own speaker, with the percussion somewhere in between, sounds unnatural and also denies the music the resonance among instruments that is so effective in the concert hall.

The role of the two percussionists grows through the three movements of the sonata. In the first movement—here, as traditionally, the most "serious" and classically constructed—the percussionists are primarily supporting players, and the thematic material is given largely to the two pianos. The second movement gives much larger play to the timbral resources of the percussion and distributes one of the principal motives, the quintuplets describing a minor third, among all four players. In the third movement, the first theme is introduced by the xylophone, and this instrument and the timpani are much more equal participants in the thematic aspects of the movement, not just the rhythmic and coloristic. Surrounding the two percussion players aurally as well

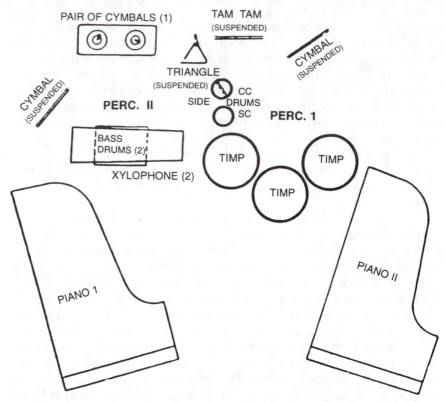

PAIR OF CYMBALS (1)

TAM TAM
(SUSPENDED)

CYMBAL
(SUSPENDED)

TRIANGLE
(SUSPENDED)

CYMBAL
(SUSPENDED)

PERC. II

SIDE   CC
DRUMS
SC

PERC. 1

BASS
DRUMS (2)

TIMP

TIMP

XYLOPHONE (2)

TIMP

PIANO 1

PIANO II

FIGURE 4.2.   Placement of instruments, Bartók's Sonata for Two Pianos and Percussion. © Copyright 1942 by Hawkes & Son (London) Ltd.; copyright renewed. Reprinted by permission of Boosey & Hawkes, Inc.

as physically, the two pianos, both together and antiphonally, exploit many of the standard keyboard devices; Bartók avoids the more unusual textural and pedal devices that he turns to in other works. The only really unusual element is Piano I's double glissandos toward the end of the second movement, rising in thirds on the white keys in the right hand and descending (generally in fourths) in the left.

The Sonata for Two Pianos and Percussion is thus more conservative in sound than Bartók's string quartets, or even his *Out of Doors* for solo piano. Yet it is much richer in sounds than *Contrasts, Mikrokosmos,* or most of the Music for Strings Percussion and Celesta. It is one of the most powerful works of the modern repertory, and one of the most popular, largely because of its very regularity, or rather the balance that Bartók strikes between symmetry and asymmetry at every compositional level, from the scales that form the harmonic background of the music to the most general formal relationships. The first of these formal shapes is the growing role of the percussion across the three movements, which I have just described, growth not at the expense of the pianos, but rather to join them. Another general kind of asymmetry pertains to the lengths of the three movements and their proportions.

Bartók's was a mind keenly sensitive to temporal durations and proportions. Especially in his later scores, he indicates not only tempo character markings (e.g., *assai lento* and *allegro molto* for the first movement of the sonata) and metronome marks, but the lengths of individual sections and entire movements. These provide a double check for the performers and force them as well to think about sectional proportions. According to the indications in the score of the Sonata for Two Pianos and Percussion, the first movement is to last 12′10″; the second, 5′38″; and the third, 6′46″. The first movement is thus virtually as long as the second and third combined.

The second movement is slow (*lento, ma non troppo*) and the third very fast (*allegro non troppo*, but with a great deal of rhythmic activity). Both are sectional in form; both are cumulative, as well, although in different ways. The second movement can be formally summarized ABCA′coda. The A section consists of a long melody, asymmetrical in meter and modal framework, shared by the two pianos and accompanied by the dry sounds of cymbal and side drums. The B section contrasts widely spaced intervals (a minor ninth, a minor sixteenth) in regular half-note rhythms with quintuplets outlining a minor third. Like the first section, it begins very softly, builds to a loud climax, and then falls back again. In the C section, Bartók combines elements of the first two, retaining the quintuplets in the timpani and writing a sliding chromatic, expressive melody in the pianos (in canon) and xylophone (in unison with Piano I) that is reminiscent of the melody of section A. Here, however, the melody is filled out with thick chords, and is much more regular in shape and phraseology than the first melody. Again, the music builds to *forte;* but in this section, the texture thins as the dynamics build, and the music dissolves into murmuring scales, the tempo slowing as well. This C section, retaining and expanding elements from both earlier sections, works as the archstone of the movement's structure; but it does not last long enough or work independently enough to function as a true climax. It yields to a reprise of the A section, the melody of that section in one piano against rapid scales— white notes in one hand, black in the other—in the other piano. This builds to a second high point, the scales turning into glissandos, the melody in one and then in both pianos, which repeatedly builds and fades. This A′ section functions as the real climax of the movement because of its retention and expansion of elements from earlier sections. Each section of this second movement enfolds elements from earlier sections, and the climax fades out to sustained chords and the quintuplet minor third that has underlain the B and C sections.

The third movement combines a similar cumulative sectional construction with reminiscences of the sonata form, this in itself a

reminiscence of the structure of the first movement. (The last movement also returns to the tonal center of the first movement, C, after the
chromatic second movement, which cadences on F. We will discuss
Bartók's harmonic methods in chapters 5 and 6.) Briefly: the movement
begins with a fanfare tremolo in both pianos, recalling the tremolo at
the climax of the first movement, and a rhythmic, straightforward first
theme in the xylophone. Thereafter we hear what could be a bridge and
a second theme, but they are not so clearly articulated as such sections
would be in a "real" sonata form. This is a reference to the idea of sonata
construction, not the thing itself. The ideal of the sonata is duality followed by variety, these then resolved into unity. This sequence happens
primarily (for Charles Rosen and many other musicians)[13] in the harmonic realm, and for such musicians the principal event in a sonata
form is the return to the tonic at some point past the temporal midpoint
of the movement. (This happens in the first movement of the Bartók.)
But it may also occur in the treatment of theme, texture, rhythm, and
meter. The essential in setting up the form is that we hear the duality in
the work's first sections, that they be clearly marked off. This is not the
case in the third movement of the Bartók sonata. It thus asks to be
heard as a sectional form that only refers to the sonata idea.

The reference then continues in what is, in fact, a development
section, expanding and manipulating the ideas of earlier passages in
the movement. There is a climax that serves as an arrival, with the recurrence of the first theme, but not with the "right" notes, not back on
C. This section continues much as the first did, but with a thinner texture and no percussion. All three sections to this point—the A section,
which resembles an exposition, the development, and this final A' section—are of almost equal length. The A' section, which began with the
movement's climax and then faded back (in dynamics, texture, rhythmic activity), yields to a coda that works much as a Beethovenian coda
does, firmly reestablishing the tonic as the movement's last grounding.

The second movement is, then, a cumulative sectional movement
that begins (as we shall see below) with an echo of the first movement's
second theme, a recollection of that section's emotional world, which it
then transmutes into a new and independently viable musical structure. The third movement is formally the simplest of the sonata's three,
a cumulative and propulsive ABA'coda that refers to the sonata model
without adhering to it. The third movement also returns to the tonal
center of the first movement and to one of its musical worlds as well—
its jauntiness—while remaining much more regular in rhythm and meter and in tonal materials. The beginning of the third movement also
quotes, if at a little distance, the climax of the first movement. Thus
here, too, we have a movement that begins with some of the general
ideas of an earlier movement and transmutes them into new music.

This is one of the reasons that the proportions among the first three movements work so well: the first movement is an extended and complex structure, encompassing a variety of emotional states, expansive and concentrated at the same time. The latter two movements are much more single-minded. Spinning as they do off materials from the first movement, they do not need to be longer, to attempt individually to balance the duration of the first movement. Since each of the latter two movements comes out of material of the first, it satisfies the ear that both of these movements together balance the first in duration, in musical devices, in affective states. More would be too much; it would belittle, in retrospect, the extraordinary first movement.

This movement is a benchmark of modern classicism in its combination of formal tradition and formal reinterpretation, and especially in its canny balance of symmetries and asymmetries in virtually every musical element. In this last matter, the movement resembles Mozart more than Haydn or Beethoven: luxuriant in its ideas, rather than single-minded in its aims, and so full of pleasurable contrasts that the very idea of lightly balanced contrasts becomes one of the themes of the work. This character may be seen first in the melodies that form the main themes of the movement. In accordance with standard sonata procedures, these themes might be labeled (Ex. 4.4) as introductory theme, first theme, bridge theme, second theme, and closing theme.

EXAMPLE 4.4. Bartók, Sonata for Two Pianos and Percussion, first movement, Piano I. © Copyright 1942 by Hawkes & Son (London) Ltd.; copyright renewed. Reprinted by permission of Boosey & Hawkes, Inc.

(a) mm. 1–2

(b) mm. 32–34

(continued)

EXAMPLE 4.4. (*continued*)

(c) mm. 84–85

(d) mm. 105–6

(e) mm. 161–62

   The introductory theme and the closing theme are circular, turning back on themselves, but are otherwise dissimilar. The introductory theme does not repeat a pitch, and its first four measures use only these notes. Its characteristic half steps are balanced with a diminished fourth, a perfect fourth, and a minor third, none of these larger intervals repeated. Answered by the second piano in canon, this theme seems to be a coiled spring; and that is what it will prove to be, in the transition into the *allegro molto* exposition and in the development section. The closing theme also resembles the so-called bridge theme in their initial descent; they will be similarly treated in the development section. The bridge theme does not reappear in the recapitulation.
   The closing theme is of less importance than the first theme, that which begins the *allegro molto,* and the second theme, beginning in measure 105. The latter is striking because of its bounding rhythm and the large interval that begins it: given the close ambitus of the other themes and the dense texture of the movement to this point, this major sixth sounds like a sudden vast opening. The first theme also makes its mark by contrast. Coming out of the semitone-loaded introduction, which has gradually become faster and more insistent, this triadic,

punched-out theme sounds from the very beginning like a triumphant and exultant affirmation. The first theme does not reappear as such for the rest of the movement; to repeat it would be to dilute its impact. Its rhythm (not its exact melody or its triadic makeup) reappears in the development section (mm. 198ff, 217ff, 248ff), the last time in the buildup to the recapitulation. It also reappears, in literally a summary fashion, in the last measures of the movement. Bartók does not repeat the theme as such; he repeats, at the proper moments, its impact and its character. The beginning of the recapitulation is the movement's principal structural point of arrival. As is evident in Example 4.5, it is also a moment of stasis, like the exultant affirmation of the beginning of the *allegro molto*. The C–G–C/B–F♯–B tremolo in the second piano gives an activating sheen to the open fifths of the rest of the texture. Coming from the four different instrumental areas on the stage, the

EXAMPLE 4.5. Bartók, Sonata for Two Pianos and Percussion, first movement, mm. 274–82. © Copyright 1942 by Hawkes & Son (London) Ltd.; copyright renewed. Reprinted by permission of Boosey & Hawkes, Inc.

(continued)

EXAMPLE 4.5. *(continued)*

music seems to surround the audience in this resplendent C major. The harmonic motion is stopped, at least for some measures, the rhythm activated by the tremolo in the timpani and the second piano's echoing the first. Bartók has thus redoubled the effect of the beginning of the exposition, here at the beginning of the recapitulation. Having thus served twice, this gesture cannot be called upon at length a third time. When the first theme reappears at the end of the movement, it is only in outline. It carries with it the baggage of its associations; its meaning need only be pointed at to make its effect. Thus its reappearance at the very end of this first movement (mm. 417ff) sounds more like a coda than like a final recapitulation, a reminder and a reaffirmation of the effects of the C-major arrivals at the beginning of the exposition and the recapitulation.

Of course, these themes do not exist in a vacuum. Working at the same time are the formal and harmonic outlines of Bartók's sonata scheme, and the textures and balances inherent in the sonata idea. This is not the venue for a detailed harmonic analysis of this movement.[14] But it is worth noting here Bartók's opposition, at the beginning of the movement, not of C and its dominant, G, but of C and F♯, a tritone. Bartók uses the tritone as a sort of substitute dominant, using a literally opposite pitch (the tritone bisects the octave) in lieu of an ersatz one. This works as a sort of double asymmetry. We cannot hear the tritone as a dominant, precisely because it is not a perfect fifth. We are led to hear it in fact as unstable, since it is the harmonic interval between the two pianos in their canon at the beginning of the introduction, where we are denied any sense of harmonic grounding. But at the same time, this introduction serves as a large-scale upbeat to the movement proper, and F♯ as a large-scale dissonant harmonic area that is resolved by arrival on C. This relationship exemplifies Bartók's canny balance of symmetries and asymmetries. In combination with his formal schemes, it creates the classicist aspect of such pieces as this sonata; at the same time, it revivifies the sonata procedure in creating a thoroughly modern form.

That form, like the Classical sonata form, is a function of thematic and harmonic work, the handling of texture, the completeness or incompleteness of musical ideas or gestures, and the duration of sections. Figure 4.3 shows the first movement's basic formal subdivisions and their lengths in measures and time, the latter taken from the score. The introduction lasts thirty-two measures, through an oscillating C–F♯ in the timpani, which is the final anacrusis to the exposition's first theme in the two pianos in m. 33 (see Ex. 4.4). The exposition lasts from m. 33 through m. 174, for 5'46". The recapitulation lasts from m. 274 (see Ex. 4.5) through the end of the movement, m. 443, at 3'55". (If one hears the final appearance of the first theme as a coda instead, this coda lasts from m. 417 to the end, some 37".) It is possible to find a number of golden-section relationships in the durations. The climax of this movement, m. 274, does not fall at the golden section of the movement; but the length of the recapitulation and that of the introduction and exposition fall into that approximate ratio. The length of the development is in a similar ratio to that of the recap. In addition, the exposition is by

Measures		Section	Duration
1–31		Introduction	2'35"
32–174		Exposition	3'11"
	32–83	1st theme	1'35"
	84–104	bridge	35"
	105–32	2d theme	31"
	133–60	3d theme	26"
	161–74	closing theme	26"
175–273		Development	2'29"
274–443		Recapitulation and coda	3'55"
	274–91	quasi-1st theme	37"
	292–331	bridge (inverted)	1'11"
	332–416	2d theme	1'30"
	417–43	coda, on 1st/2d themes	37"
			12'10"

FIGURE 4.3. Formal subdivisions, Bartók's Sonata for Two Pianos and Percussion, first movement.

far the longest section; if one includes the introduction (as one no doubt should, since its principal music constitutes one of the main themes of the movement), the ratio of the exposition to the development and recap is very close to equal, and it approximates the ratio of the first movement of the Sonata as a whole to the latter two movements. If, on the other hand, one abstracts the introduction from the movement proper, the exposition stands in a close golden-section ratio to the remaining length. In this way, each subsection of the movement falls into the same durational proportion to the next longer subsection.

Many people believe strongly in the functioning of such golden-section proportions in Bartók's mature music. Others wonder about their real impact on a listener. A real question is the degree of precision required for sections to stand in a golden-section proportion. The calculations in the previous paragraph are by no means precise. Are they good enough? Answers depend perhaps on individual performers and listeners. I raise the question because many careful analysts of Bartók's music find such relationships to be meaningful in their hearing of the music, and because these calculations do point to the extreme care that Bartók gave to the relative durations and weights of his formal sections. These weights are also a function of what music reappears, and how it is used.

The exposition, as we have seen, is straightforward in its succession of themes in contrasting characters, contours, rhythms, textures, and harmonic areas. The development section, the shortest section of the movement, works with motives from the introduction (mm. 175–94 work as an introduction to the development section, as the introduction itself did to the movement as a whole, but with material from the latter part of the introduction; the principal motive of the introduction, at the tempo of the movement proper, appears in m. 195) and from the first and closing themes of the exposition. These are cut down to their minimum, retaining only the smallest characteristics of the original themes. The recapitulation presents the themes in reverse order. The arrival at the recap, as we have seen, is not a reprise of the first theme, but a re-creation of its effect. In m. 292 we hear the exposition's closing theme (mm. 161ff of the exposition), in inversion. In m. 332 we hear the second, jauntiest theme, which thus retains its central position in the section. This theme continues for quite some time in the recapitulation, longer than in the exposition. (It did not appear in the development.) And finally, the first theme, or its characteristic outlines, recurs in the final twenty-six bars of the movement. Thus, in another balance of symmetry and asymmetry, all the principal melodies return, though not in their original order (and one of them inverted as well) or their original proportions.

All of this makes this movement the epitome of what we shall call, in the next chapter, the modern classical sonata procedure. It is classicist in its proportions (within movements or between them), its adherence to and dependence on the tradition of the sonata form, its use of such traditional practices as tonality, motivic development, and so on. The work is modern in its handling of these elements: the tonal relationships, especially the crucial one of the tritone, are modern, as are the rhythms and the use of percussion. Even the use of the sonata idea may be modern. No truly Romantic music of the nineteenth century, with the possible exceptions of the symphonists of central and eastern Europe at the end of the century, uses the sonata as a vehicle.[15] This assurance in the renewed viability of the sonata procedure, as we shall see, is one of the marks of modernism in the twentieth century, though here without irony or self-consciousness, a characteristic more common to composers like Stravinsky, who always emphasizes his and his music's individuality in opposition to any shared characteristics.

Chamber Music for Performers and Tape; Duets for Live Performers

A combination popular with composers and performers from the 1950s through the 1970s, that of live performer and tape, seems to have died out in recent years. The reason for this languishing of the medium may be that composers got tired of it, or that—paradoxical as it might seem—the vast possibilities of tape music soon became larded with clichés, and it became hard to imagine a fresh music coming from this medium. Another possibility, and one more likely to be the reason, is that tape pieces presented logistical difficulties for performers. Few concert halls in those years had adequate playback and amplification equipment. A performer would find it difficult to cart around equipment of his or her own, and the cost of renting it for a single performance might be prohibitive. According to the composer Elliott Schwartz, performers may express a preference for a piece with piano or harpsichord accompaniment, or with no accompaniment at all, over a piece with tape, on the basis that they will not be able to perform the latter.[16] Moreover, in today's current state of electronic sophistication, live electronics have largely replaced the use of prerecorded tape.

Nonetheless, the medium of tape and live performer was common for more than two decades and gave rise to some important works of new chamber music. We will look at two examples, one for live piano and prerecorded music (piano and vibraphone), Barbara Kolb's *Solitaire* (1971); and one for piano and synthesized music, Mario Davidovsky's *Synchronisms* No. 6 (also 1971). (The *Synchronisms* is one of a long series for live performers and synthesized tape.)

Both *Solitaire* and *Synchronisms* No. 6 are conceived not as duets between piano and tape but as solos, music for an extended performer. In his notes to the score, Davidovsky writes, "The electronic segment should perhaps not be viewed as an independent polyphonic line, but rather as if it were inlaid into the piano part." To that end, he directs that the loudspeakers be placed very close to the piano. Similarly, Kolb's title reflects the technique of her piece, "a game of solitaire with neither motivation nor intent but to exist for and by itself; growing singly or separately; not forming clusters or masses."[17] In the case of the Davidovsky, this conception works less well in live performance than, say, a performance of a piece for prepared piano or a piece in which the pianist uses the body or the interior of the instrument. In the Kolb, it works very well because the taped music is manipulations of the same music that the live pianist is playing (though not necessarily at the same time): one hears it as sort of a temporal overlapping within a single sensibility.

The Davidovsky is, further, another example of a classicist work in a modern mold. The opening gesture of *Synchronisms* No. 6 foreshadows the work to come: a G played on the piano and imperceptibly taken over by an identical G from the loudspeakers, which crescendoes as the piano's fades away. Thereafter, as Davidovsky indicates, the piano and tape parts are almost of a piece, sharing motives and rhythms, engaging in call and response, approaching each other or distancing themselves in timbre. (For example, the piano uses two effects that move its sound closer to the electronic world, plucking the strings directly and also stopping them with the hand.) The shape of the overall piece is one of steady and progressive growth, rather than of juxtaposition and contrast, and its arc is the familiar one of increasing to a *ffff* climax of density and volume with an aftersection that is spare, quiet, and a final hearing of many of the work's gestures. All of these characteristics are those of the mainstream musical tradition of at least the last two hundred years; *Synchronisms* No. 6 represents a successful extension of that tradition into a modern genre, the use of electronic media.

The Kolb is also a traditional work, but of a less mainstream tradition. This is the tradition of Romantic musing, the solitary figure alone with his or her feelings, the tradition of the Chopin preludes or the late Brahms intermezzi. Even the title exemplifies this conceit: the pianist as composer, solitary in her music room, and laying out before her like cards the various sections of the work, combining and recombining the music she plays with that she hears in her inner ear (and which we hear as if transmuted, through the speakers). The score is a sequence of different sections marked with upper- and lowercase letters. A performance is to follow a general scheme in moving through these sections; any number of specific realizations is possible. Kolb states in her "Instructions for the Performer," however, that "although it is possible to have more than one performance scheme, the complexity of creating a new tape for each scheme is such a monumental procedure that I have chosen one preferred version." This is the version performed on the recording by Cheryl Seltzer and, in fact, the only one that I have ever heard, recorded or "live."

Solitaire begins with a circular vamp figure, simply setting and prolonging a particular introductory scene. This vamp forms the underlying texture of much of the music to follow, which overlaps among live piano, taped piano, and taped vibes. Most strikingly, we hear quotations from other music, especially Scarlatti and the Chopin Prelude in A♭ Major, Op. 28, No. 17. The Chopin quotations come to form the core of the musings by the pianist-composer persona, and they are (with the basic vamp figure) what stays in the mind after hearing *Solitaire*. Through the course of the piece, the Chopin comes to overpower the newly composed music, and even moves against itself at different tempi. What is extremely apt and effective here is that Kolb is doing in her own piece what Chopin himself does in his prelude. That prelude also begins with a pedal or vamp, the repeated A♭ triad in second inversion, its most unstable position. The melody seems to grow out of that chord, which continues as a vamp underneath, as the melody avoids cadences and grounding. As the A♭ chord in second inversion changes to a V^7 (E♭^{7}) chord, the implication is that we will arrive on and establish A♭ as the tonic of the piece. The cadence moves, however, not to A♭ but to A♭^{7}, or V^7/IV, and we are propelled directly into a D♭ harmony, our definitive cadence sidestepped. This is the working method of the rest of the prelude. In addition, it also shows some use of musical overlapping, as when toward the end the melody is heard *pianissimo* and *sotto voce* over repeated *sforzando* A♭s in the bass, A♭s that boom forth and are caught by the pedal, no matter what the specific harmony above them might be. Finally, the Chopin seems to fade back into the ether whence it arose, its last sonority again the A♭ triad in second inversion, dying away over the final *sforzando* A♭ in the bass.

The general processes of the Chopin A♭-Major Prelude and its affective world of the composer-pianist musing alone at the keyboard are precisely those of *Solitaire,* which displays both the modern love of organicism and a new and fresh-sounding musical world. *Solitaire* is a striking piece, especially in live performance, precisely for those qualities that seem to make it an improvised, truly living performance. Its surface sounds are quite beautiful, and the "scenario" of the performance is at once compelling. The work uses contemporary technology to say something that would otherwise be impossible to utter: performing this piece with a second live piano and vibes, for example, would destroy the effect of the taped music as heard through the music of the live piano, through the inner ear of the pianist-composer. It is possible that the piece might strike some ears as retrogressive, "useless" (as Boulez said in the early 1950s of all new music that did not take full account of the heritage of Webern). To these ears, *Solitaire* might use new technologies to serve an outmoded aesthetic. Here the question is what constitutes the outmoded, for one of the "new" aesthetics to arise in the late 1960s and early 1970s was what is now referred to as neo-Romanticism, a return to the conception of music as primarily expressive and emotional rather than as a classicist architecture in sound. In that sense, *Solitaire* is exemplary of its era. What makes it seem dated now is its medium: performers have become less interested in playing pieces with tape. Performers' interests have moved into new areas, including working with synthesizers or computers (these used in composition or live in performance) and the expansion of contemporary musical language by including various kinds of crossover, from American popular music or from world musical traditions. *Solitaire* and *Synchronisms* No. 6 stand up very well as compositions; but hearing them takes a listener back to a musical world that has disappeared as other musical worlds—that of the string quartet, that of the "*Pierrot* quintet," that of such ensembles as New York's Da Capo Players or Speculum Musicae, San Francisco's Kronos Quartet—continue to thrive.

There is one last category of unusual ensemble to consider before we turn to a general and more chronological concluding overview. The duet of two melody instruments, without a chordal instrument such as piano, organ, or guitar, is largely a twentieth-century phenomenon. There are a number of such pieces, perhaps the best known being the series of forty-four violin duos by Bartók, intended (like his *Mikrokosmos* for piano) both for instruction and for musical performance. Two other examples are Zoltán Kodály's Duo for Violin and Cello of 1914 and Heitor Villa-Lobos's *Bachianas Brasileiras* No. 6 for flute and bassoon, written in 1938. As it happens, both these pieces allow us to consider the uses of national or ethnic materials in concert works of a generally neoclassic bent: the Kodály is a fruit of his efforts in the collection and study of Hungarian music, and the Villa-Lobos reflects the composer's conscious intention to merge Baroque and Classical techniques with the melodies and even the timbres of the native instruments of Brazil. These ethnic elements, which correspond to the non-Germanic elements in European music of the late nineteenth century, are a hallmark of music from the years between the wars. Depending on one's point of view, they constitute a contemporary element in contrast to the more generally traditionalist aesthetic of musical modernism, or a distinguishing characteristic of that modernism. (Other writers find these elements to be simply nonessential surface colorations.)

In 1921 Bartók wrote that Kodály possessed

> rich melodic invention, a perfect sense of form, a certain predilection for melancholy and uncertainty. He [Kodály] does not see Dionysian intoxication—he strives for inner contemplation. . . . His music is not the kind described nowadays as modern. It has nothing to do with the new atonal, bitonal and polytonal music—everything in it is based on the principle of tonal balance. His idiom is nevertheless new: he says things that have never been uttered before and demonstrates thereby that the tonal principle has not lost its raison d'être as yet.[18]

The Duo of 1914 is an example of all that Bartók says. It is new, but not in the contemporary progressive—that is, German or Stravinskian—sense. All its movements are squarely tonal, although their tonality is rarely defined by the hierarchy of fifth relationships. The melodies are more modal than tonal (that is, their constituent notes are reducible to scales other than the major and minor, though they may use those as well, and they often lack the leading-tone/tonic and dominant/tonic axes of definition). Chords are often triadic but not used in functional progressions. Despite Bartók's disclaimer, this was in 1914 a sort of modernity, as were his own and Stravinsky's references to ethnicity in his first two string quartets and *Allegro barbaro* and Stravinsky's Three Pieces for String Quartet. Even the modality in Kodály's music is not unmodern: it is the same sort of modality found in Debussy, whose music had a lasting effect on Kodály's, and in the music of Ravel such as his 1903 String Quartet (see chapter 6).

The work is in three movements: *allegro serioso, non troppo; adagio;* and *maestoso e largamente, ma non troppo lento—presto.* The first movement is in sonata form, defined here primarily (as Bartók suggests) by melody; for the movement, like the work as a whole, is a succession of striking melodies, usually in a clear homophonic texture. The opening is a resolute melody in the cello, sweeping down two octaves from first note to last, accompanied by rhythmic chords in the violin. The roles are then reversed, although the cello's accompaniment is one of broken chords that turn into an oscillating ostinato, which will underlie the first theme of the sonata and much thereafter. This introductory section defines the music that will follow throughout the Duo, in the handling of texture and in the emphasis on strong and wide-ranging melodies. It also helps to define the structure: it returns at the end of the exposition as a transition to the development section, and in a highly varied form at the end of the movement.

The second movement is ternary, its sections set off in the traditional way by melody, texture, and rhythmic activity. The third movement, after the slow introduction (which brings back music from the second movement) is a *perpetuum mobile* with contrasting sections of a joyful, *scherzando* character not unlike the strange interpolations at the end of Bartók's Fifth String Quartet. Like the first movement, these are articulated principally by melody—specific tunes, types of tune, melody in various textures, repetition or contrasting melodies—this articulation in turn supported by harmony. Almost invariably the harmony of any given section is one implied by its dominant melody: that is, the chords are usually made up of the same set of pitches or intervals that constitute the melody. But again, these harmonies seem to be abstracted from the melodies; they seem simply accompanimental, and they do not work in the traditional European functional ways. For these reasons, the Duo sounds exotic and intriguing to ears attuned to the traditions and heritage of central Europe. This is not necessarily the case for our point of comparison, Villa-Lobos's *Bachianas Brasileiras* No. 6 for flute and bassoon.

The two woodwinds are meant to be reminiscent of native Brazilian instruments, and this is the most exotic—in fact, the only exotic—element of the music. Kodály's instruments are used in traditional ways, while his textures and his way of relating harmony and melody are untraditional. Villa-Lobos's work, by contrast, is thoroughly in the European traditions, enhanced with some slight local flavor. His harmonies are always clear, D minor in the first movement, a modal C yielding to C major in the second. His texture has all the correctness of European counterpoint, independent melodies moving sometimes in different rhythms (as at the beginning of the first movement, a *perpetuum mobile* in the flute against a slower and more lyrical melody in the bassoon), sometimes together, yet each voice essentially self-defining. The harmonic language is also that of European tradition, functional tonality whose chords are defined by fifth relationships and leading-tone/tonic successions. The forms are clear and, again, traditional, a slow aria followed by a faster second movement. To a degree, the *Bachianas Brasileiras* No. 6 can be defined by what it is not: it does not have the organicism of music from the Germanic tradition or the rhythmic pointedness and grace of French or Spanish music; it does not quote native music, as some American music does during our so-called Jazz Age, or as the music of Carlos Chávez does. It does have contemporary music's textural clarity and formal and harmonic simplicity. It has the immediate charm of the best incidental music. It shows the contemporary desire, most pronounced in Hindemith's *Gebrauchsmusik*, to expand the repertory of good music for the less common instruments. Its historical place probably lies in these last two elements, and it will no doubt stay in the repertory because of them.

Sui Generis Ensembles

This chapter concludes with the sort of music with which it began. By far the largest category of modern chamber music is the class of works for a mixed ensemble specifically devised by the composer. The model provided to composers by *Pierrot lunaire* and *L'histoire du soldat* was less the actual makeup of either group than the idea of compositional freedom in a work's instrumental requirements, the idea that virtually all sounds are available and may be combined at the composer's desire. The experience of modern chamber music players is that ensembles are fluid: in such groups as Speculum Musicae, the Fires of London, and Tashi, players are added to and subtracted from a core group according to the requirements of the repertory chosen. The symbiosis between composer and performer continues, but perhaps in a less restrictive way.

We continue here with four works from the post–World War I years: Stravinsky's Octet (1923), Varèse's *Octandre* (also 1923), Virgil Thomson's Sonata da Chiesa (1926), and Webern's Quartet, Op. 22, for violin, clarinet, tenor saxophone, and piano (1930). These four works neatly exemplify the mainstream modernisms that dominated music until the late 1940s: the quasi-French in Stravinsky and Thomson, the continuation of the Germanic tradition in Webern, the new progressivism, the most direct continuation of European music before World War I, in Varèse. The Thomson Sonata da Chiesa also reflects its era's interest in national flavors, although this is not the work's principal focus. The three works that include traditional elements (all but the Varèse) do so in markedly different ways; all four pieces are "modern" in different ways as well.

First, the ensembles. Each work is for a unique ensemble of players. The Octet is scored for flute, clarinet, two bassoons, two trumpets, and tenor and bass trombones, a balance of four woodwinds and four brass. Like the Beethoven Septet and Schubert Octet, the piece is reminiscent of Classical serenades. The Stravinsky Octet's polar opposite in this respect is Varèse's *Octandre*, for flute, clarinet, oboe, bassoon, French horn, trumpet, trombone, and double bass. In traditional terms, this is a woodwind quintet plus trumpet, trombone, and bass; or three-fifths of a brass quintet plus woodwinds and bass. But the sound of *Octandre* has nothing of those standard ensembles. As we shall see, it is much more like a reduced orchestra for a work like *The Rite of Spring*. Thomson's Sonata da Chiesa is written for E♭ clarinet, the smallest and clearest in timbre of the clarinet family; the trumpet in D (or C, but specifically not the most common trumpet, in B♭), also clear and light in timbre; viola; French horn; and trombone. Of these instruments, the viola, at the center of the overall range and the most individual in timbre, is perhaps the *prima inter pares*. Webern's use of the tenor saxophone in his Op. 22 Quartet is a rare instance of that instrument in classical music; in fact, in 1930 the saxophone was only beginning its road to dominance over the clarinet in jazz. The tenor saxophone has the obvious assets of timbral continuity with the clarinet in Webern's quartet, as well as a distinctive enough sound to separate it from the rest of the polyphonic texture. Beyond this, the Op. 22 Quartet is typical of serial Webern, crystalline in its textures, highly organized and highly lyrical at the same time.

Webern's lucid textures are one of his traditional elements, in this case the tradition being Renaissance polyphony. Yet this "tradition" was as unusual in the early years of this century in Europe as the exotic musics of the Far East were. Music from the eras before J. S. Bach was still the province of musicologists, and remained so well into the middle of the century. Webern, of course, was a trained historical musicologist. Not surprisingly, his taste in one sort of music reflects his taste in others: while the limpid textures and ametrical rhythms of his own compositions do not sound like Renaissance motets, the general procedures and characteristics are similar. Webern combines these elements with the organicism he inherited directly from Schoenberg, and which goes back to J. S. Bach. Although the tone row of this particular composition is asymmetrical, Webern's use of it is thoroughly organicist, so that literally every note in the work belongs to a repetition, retrograde, or inversion of another figure that is (usually) heard simultaneously. Webern's recourse to dynamic structural models prevents this sort of constant cross-weaving from resulting in a static time sense, analogous to the examination of a single crystal from various angles. His first movement is reminiscent of mid-eighteenth-century sonata form: a brief introduction, a first section (which is repeated), a second section (also repeated), and a coda. The introduction directly prefigures the theme of the first section, the tenor saxophone's melody. The first half of the second section constitutes a development of the first section, its textures and phrases fragmented and more densely combined, with a contrast in dynamic levels that leads to a real climax, *fortissimo*, directly before the return of the original melody. This recapitulation divides the melody among the violin, clarinet, and tenor saxophone, recreating the opening textures in an even sparser way. After its repetition, a coda echoes the introduction.

Not only do the melodic figurations reflect each other in a web of related forms, but the various musical elements combine (as they do in Beethoven and Schoenberg) symbiotically. Even the slightest surface details contribute to Webern's balance of precompositional materials and dynamic structure. For example, the pitch class C rarely occurs in the same octave in close temporal proximity, while F♯ recurs repeatedly in the octave above middle C. The repeated F♯s are always a structural articulation of some kind, not simply an intersection of simultaneous row forms (the repeated F♯s in the clarinet at the very beginning of the work are an intersection of the two row forms, I_0 and P_{10}, which have been running in the other three instruments). The repeated F♯s at the end of the first section mark it as a cadence. In m. 21, we hear four F♯s on successive sixteenth notes; this is the beginning of the development's (and movement's) high point of tension. The end of the development section begins with two repeated F♯s in the piano, and the recapitulation begins with the same two F♯s in the midst of the piano's phrase. Finally, the F♯s return as the end of the second section, marking its cadence as they did the end of the first, and to begin the coda.

In contrast, Webern seems positively to avoid juxtaposing Cs in the same register, although this would be no more difficult than it was to juxtapose F♯s. Since the texture is organized symmetrically around an axis in the middle register, the avoidance of repeated Cs becomes quite notable. Again, careful listening suggests that Webern is using the pitch class C to define for the movement a curve from the beginning through a climax at the end of the development section and back to an ending that resembles the beginning. At the beginning and end we hear C^4 and C^5 (middle C and the octave above it) in close temporal proximity in the piano. By contrast, at the movement's climax we hear C^7 in the violin and C^2 in the piano in successive sixteenth notes, immediately after we have heard the four successive F♯s; that is, we hear the central F♯s almost immediately followed by the highest and the second-lowest Cs on the piano keyboard. The range of the movement's music has been expanded to its fullest; the recap and coda return from that most extended range to the restricted middle registers of the beginning.

Webern's serialism is thus both atomistic and organized in a thoroughly inclusive, coherent way. While seeming in this movement to think in terms of individual pitches and two- or three-note motivic groupings, he is also organizing his basic materials in such a way that each musical element reflects the others, and their combination results in a musical structure that grows and regroups through time. This structural procedure is possible because of the sparseness of Webern's textures. His traditional elements—neo-Renaissance polyphony and recourse to the Germanic sonata ideal—become part and parcel of his modernism. If one removes a single element of this three-part conjunction, the whole structure collapses. Similarly, the second movement of the Quartet is a fantasialike enchaining of melodies drawn from the work's row, again in a quasi-Renaissance polyphonic texture. Here the preexisting model is not the sonata form but the Renaissance motet.

Stravinsky and Thomson handle tradition differently. Both of these composers, working in France and Switzerland in the 1920s, use a sort of quasi-tonality in stark contrast to the contemporary Viennese and the immediately earlier music of Debussy and Stravinsky himself. Since the Octet and the Sonata da Chiesa both use tonal centers, and the Octet is full of triads, it is easy to try to hear these pieces as tonal in a traditional, functional way. But ultimately they are not. The tonality of the so-called common practice era (eighteenth and nineteenth centuries) is based on the dominant/tonic axis of chord relationships and the leading-tone/tonic axis of melodic successions. This is not the case in either Stravinsky or Thomson. Their music is, rather, a sort of antithesis to the music from the latter years of the nineteenth century. They use much of the same material as that music, but not in the same ways. Their textures are much less dense. Their colors are sturdy rather than brilliant. Thomson's music, in particular, exemplifies the well-made piece, music that has a goal and gets there in a direct and satisfying way. Stravinsky's may be more brittle, more sectional and given to quick changes, but he, too, prefers the sort of construction whose building blocks are clear.

The three movements of the Octet are "Sinfonia," "Theme and Variations," and "Finale." The sinfonia is, like the first movement of the Webern Quartet, a reminiscence of mid-eighteenth-century genres. In this case, a slow introduction sets up the dominant of E♭, the key of the first movement, and introduces the shifting accents and meters that characterize the movement and the entire work. The movement proper begins with a strongly metrical melody, in unison. This is the fount for the melodies of the rest of the movement, spun out continuously, in various instrumental textures and combinations. Stravinsky derives the movement's material from this melody and its accompaniment, from the scales that close the introduction and underlie principal melodies, and from a new tune heard first in the trumpet. But this is not strictly a sonata procedure. There are two distinct melodies in the first section of the movement, and then a sort of development section, with textures and melodic lines fragmented, and a reprise of the first theme. But the second theme, introduced by the trumpet, does not reappear at the end of the movement, and the syncopations and rhythmic angularities of that theme, especially in its treatment in the central section of the movement, are never resolved into a metrical context. The movement is incomplete thematically and metrically; and this incompleteness will be picked up in the finale.

The second movement is a theme and variations and at the same time a quasi-rondo. There are five variations, lettered A through E in the score, with variation A recurring after variations B and D. Each variation is based on the melody of the theme, its notes regrouped into new phrasings, set over new harmonies, or differently rhythmicized. By far the longest movement of the Octet, and its musical heart, this second movement leads without a break into the last movement, as the slow introduction to the first did to the movement proper. The finale is infectiously jaunty, building up from a syncopated melody over a sort of walking-bass line in the bassoons to a final section of syncopations in rhythmic unison that at last ground—if still with great energy—the metrical asymmetries and ambiguities of the first movement.

Stravinsky's is a constructivist method of building in the Octet, based on clearly differentiated musical sections that follow one another and sometimes refer to one another, but that do not have the continuity of line that weaves through music of the Germanic tradition, including Webern. One hears his music in chunks, as it were, and the varying proportions and continuities among these affect both the local level, our immediate hearing of the music's surface, and the larger level, our sense of each movement's and each work's cohesiveness. What is omitted from such a description of Stravinsky's formal means, though, is any sense of what the music actually sounds like. In the case of the Octet, the swing of the rhythms and tunes of the first movement is irresistible. In the second, the contrast of the swirl of Variation A, the recurring refrain, with the more reserved and stately theme and single variations creates a headiness of compressed energy that is finally allowed to burst forth in the finale. Stravinsky shares with Beethoven the ability to use similar musical processes to different effects in different pieces. In the Octet we have the freshness of a new musical language that Stravinsky himself had helped shape in the years since L'histoire du soldat. In chapter 5 we shall see with his Concerto for Two Solo Pianofortes similar constructivist means put to other musical ends.

Virgil Thomson's Sonata da Chiesa is no less interesting. It assumes a certain musical sophistication and capacity for enjoyment on the part of its listeners, and it delivers on its assumptions. Like the Stravinsky Octet, it speaks a new musical language, one that retains its newness while it makes use of very old materials. Historically, the sonata da chiesa was a work typically in four movements, slow-fast-slow-fast, often but not necessarily for two treble melodic instruments and continuo. Thomson's three movements—"Chorale," "Tango," and "Fugue"—suggest some of the Baroque sonata's salient features: slow opening movement, fugal writing, and sectional dance forms (in the

Baroque usually a binary gigue; Thomson's tango is ternary). What makes this music so unusual and so attractive, besides the novelty and the clarity of its instrumentation, is its mix of materials from various eras of music history, not only the Baroque. In the chorale, the voices move largely by step, doubled in open fifths, the sort of faux-organum one hears in movies set in the Middle Ages. The phrase lengths, the rhythms, and the meters, like the doublings in fifths, are meant to sound archaic, but not really to fool the listener for a moment.

The second movement is a sort of reverse on the same ploy, a false historicizing of a contemporary dance. An unmistakable tango quality pervades the music, in the throaty sound of the low viola, the syncopations, the undulating phrases. But Thomson's tango is full of metrical shifts, moving almost with every measure from $\frac{4}{4}$ to $\frac{5}{4}$ and even to $\frac{3}{2}$ and $\frac{3}{4}$, and the sinuous rubatos are precisely notated with brackets that indicate "3 in the time of 2," "4 in the time of 3," and so on. The harmonies, based on seconds and sevenths, are closer to those of contemporary concert music than to popular music. These combinations, like those of the chorale, serve at once to locate the music in a particular era and to distance it—to take it out of history.

The fugue is the most traditional movement, in its treatment the most contemporary as well, and the most straightforward, since its function is to close off the work as a whole. The tune is a classic fugue subject, a so-called wedge theme whose high and low notes continually and regularly move further apart. Moreover, the end of the fugue subject is a trill on the second scale degree, resolving down to the tonic, repeated, in a rhythm of dotted quarter-eighth-quarter, the last on a downbeat. These traditional elements reflect the 1920s interest in writing "objective" music, constructivist compositions eschewing any sort of personal or subjective expressions on the part of composer or performer. The perceived historical model was Baroque music's lack of "expressive" directions to the performers. Although Thomson was far too musical to think that music can be entirely "objective," he recognized the fugue's ability not only to echo the historicism of its preceding movements but also to work on every level toward closure. It returns to the same tonal center as the first movement, and it matches the traditional final movement in tempo and straightforward character, in clear textures and clear progression toward a known conclusion. A summary and a settling, it returns its listeners to their own contemporary musical world.

In most ways, beyond this general historicizing element, Thomson's music is far removed from Webern's and closer to the neoclassical music of Stravinsky. (Even Stravinsky, though, lacks Thomson's straightforwardness, which I attribute to his being from the American midwest.) All of these composers are a world away from Edgard Varèse, who stands alone in twentieth-century music history.

Octandre (1923) is in three continuous movements, *Assez lent, Très vif et nerveux,* and *Grave—Animé et jubilatoire.* None of these movements falls into a precompositional genre or formal procedure, and none is functionally tonal. The first movement is, in a small way, reminiscent of the beginning of *The Rite of Spring,* opening with a solo double reed, moving to a section of overlapping lines and entrances, then to a heavily accented rhythmic section with much repetition of pitches, and ending with the briefest of reprises of the opening melodic material (but not a return to the opening pitch level). There is nothing in the way of true motivic development, the spinning out of a small cell into longer lines, the use of a single germ to engender new ideas, the combination and the articulation of voices and textures through motivic manipulations. The result is a music that seems spatial or sculptural rather than temporal, as if the music were a three-dimensional object, and the time of performance and hearing were the time of examining it in space, walking around it to observe it from all possible angles.

This metaphor leads us to a question of musical time that is new in the twentieth century. Edward T. Cone and Jonathan Kramer have discussed what they call "moment form";[19] other writers, especially those concerned with contemporary minimalism, speak of "vertical listening" (the term is Kramer's), as opposed to the "horizontal" listening implied and required by composers as otherwise different as J. S. Bach, Beethoven, and Debussy, where the musical form and experience are shaped by what happens to musical ideas through time, as if in a drama or a process of organic growth. The metaphor for music such as Varèse's is that of an object already fully formed that we apprehend through time, not one which takes shape temporally. This impression is created through those characteristics already noted as well as through the "abstract" shape of the basic musical ideas, their angular melodic contours, asymmetrical rhythms, and unpredictable phraseology. The result is a sort of musical objectivity, but not that sort meant by the contemporary modernist term "New Objectivity" (*Neue Sachlichkeit*). It shares with the New Objectivity its eschewal of music as personal expression by the composer. But Varèse does not share the mechanistic aspects of such music, the procedures that seem to propel themselves in the manner of a workmanlike Baroque concerto grosso. Varèse's music is not predictable, for it is not regular. Varèse followed the road that Stravinsky had retreated from, and he himself was forced into a sort of retreat, a silence imposed on him by the discrepancy between the music he wished to compose and that which was possible on existing concert instruments. It was only in the 1950s, after the anonymous gift of a tape recorder, that Varèse began to compose again. His last completed work was *musique concrète* for the Philips Pavilion at the Brussels Exposition in 1958, the *Poème électronique,* in which he follows the same procedures as in his earlier, instrumental music, but to further ends. Basic material was manipulated and changed, but it was also made (because of the architecture of the pavilion and the placement of speakers) literally to move through space rather than just trying to create that impression. The French term *musique concrète* is apt, for the *Poème électronique* is like a concrete object that subsists through time, and the time of our musical apprehension is given over not to a process of creation and growth so much as it is to perception.

It is hard to imagine how far this approach might be followed. Varèse has few successors, though many admirers, among later composers. Electronic composers have continued to make pieces that are progressive, dramatic, narrative—in some way linear and unidirectional. Nonelectronic composers have largely adhered to the common musical languages of neoclassicism, the post-Webern serialism of young composers after 1945, and so on. The guitarist and composer Frank Zappa was a major exponent of Varèse's music for years and made Varèse as well-known a classical composer among the counterculture as Charles Ives, but one cannot hear much of Varèse in Zappa's own music. Even the so-called process music of recent years, which requires the sort of "vertical," nondevelopmental listening that writers have propounded, is still a product of quasi-organic procedures. The music of Terry Riley, Steve Reich, John Adams—different as these are one from another—is also referred to as "phase" music, in which incremental changes are gradually introduced to a basic undulating texture, the resulting sounds moving outward and overlapping in phases often compared to the ripples of water in a pond. The processes are not necessarily goal oriented; hence the concept of "vertical" listening, in which one attends as fully as possible to the totality of where one is at a given moment, rather than where one has been or will be. But this, too, does not match the experience of listening to Varèse. His music demands one's attention; it is extremely dynamic; it is weighty, ponderous, monolithic in its textures and repetitiveness.

It is because of Varèse's different conception of musical time, and the resulting change in the nature of musical perception, that his path has not been followed. Changes in musical style may come quickly, as they have in this century and as they did in the eighteenth century. But changes in deep perception, the "paradigm shifts" of Thomas S. Kuhn,[20] come much more glacially. Varèse remains an example of musical modernism, but one apart from the common herd. He shares many traits of pre–1945 modernism, but not the deepest ones. Like the three composers yet to appear in this chapter, he cannot be put meaningfully in any general musical category.

Those three composers are Stefan Wolpe, Joan Tower, and Lee Hyla. Their resistance to categorization stems from two causes. Wolpe's music, like Varèse's, is too individualistic. Tower and Hyla are, for the purposes of sweeping historical observations, too contemporary. As part of the living musical scene, they are still as much individual voices as they are representatives of larger issues.

Wolpe is unfortunately known primarily to academic composers; his music has not been played and championed as it deserves. In his life, Wolpe went through a number of different compositional styles, including folk- or ethnic-derived pieces such as the Oboe Sonata, intensely chromatic atonal writing, a kind of structuring through the accretion of pitches and intervals sometimes called pitch-field composition, some rather neoclassicist works, and a final period of great freedom and imagination, which produced idiosyncratic and fascinating music. The two pieces discussed here come from this last period, the Piece in Two Parts for Violin Alone of 1964 and the Solo Piece for Trumpet of 1966. (A piece for solo violin does not necessarily fall under the rubric of "new ensembles"; solo trumpet is rather unusual. Both pieces, however, are individual enough to warrant inclusion in this chapter.)

Both pieces are rather light in character. The verbal directions for the two movements of the trumpet piece, in fact, are "Graceful, talking" and "Not too big, intimate." Both are the products of the fantasy and imagination of an old master: focused, the utterance of a single self-assured voice, yet relaxed, not intense or insistent, full of uncomplicated pleasure. The source of this affect lies in the phrasings and the developing shapes of the pieces. In the Solo Piece for Trumpet, the phrases are rhythmic but not metrical, and they grow as if conversationally, a phrase growing smoothly from the one before, continuing its shape, expanding it, or just using a few of its notes to make a new response. Repetition occurs, but unpredictably: often enough to give a pleasing moment-to-moment coherence, not so often as to become patterned or conventional.

Yet each of the pieces, and each of their movements, is different. The second movement of the trumpet piece is a true bagatelle, a brief and affectively unified piece that grows outward from an opening antecedent-consequent phrase. The first movement is longer and more sectional; its sections grow from motives (spun out and developed, or contrasted, alternated, juxtaposed) and differ from one another in generative phrase shapes, rhythms, and rhythmic groupings. The two movements of the Piece in Two Parts for Violin Alone are longer, and they involve more structural repetition than the trumpet piece. Still, they are "fantastic" in the nineteenth-century sense of the word, a composer's inventions on a fairly limited collection of basic materials or basic ideas. As a help to the performer, Wolpe includes at the end of the score a listing of the "materials used" in its composition, a set of five combinations of notes and intervals, plus transpositions of these materials to pitch levels where the five share "many common notes" and to pitch levels with "least common notes." These "materials" point up structural relationships that are analogous to modulation and the tonal hierarchy in functionally tonal music. One also sees the unformed note successions that Wolpe has then made into melodic phrases and themes.

The overall form of each of the two movements is a function of repetition and alternation, both of these in varying degrees. As with the trumpet piece, phrases grow from earlier phrases directly enough to provide coherence and cohesion. Structural repetition—that is, closer repetition of larger phrases and gestures—continually reminds the hearer of the seminal material as we move forward to new developments and variations. Wolpe's exploitation of the violin's possible timbres becomes structural as well. Bowing *col legno,* the use of rapid tremolos, the juxtaposition of pizzicato, spiccato, and arco playing are unified with specific melodic configurations and then brought so to the fore that they become much more than local timbral decorations. Rhythmic gestures are developed similarly: initially associated with given melodic figures, they take on independent life and become, in a certain sense, the means of change to which the melodies, the notes and intervals, are submitted. But although one can hear the piece being made before one's ears, as it were, the music never approaches the constructivist mode. It is too continuous, too seemingly organic in its successions and developments, and its combination of sectional structural clarity with the immediacy of its musical gestures gives it a classicizing air that transcends construction. Wolpe's music, especially of this era, has the clarity in every musical parameter that is associated with classicist language, including modernist neoclassicism and midcentury serialist classicism. In a rare confluence, this clarity and classicism exist at the service of an individual voice and an idiomatic language.

Joan Tower's liner notes to the recording of "Platinum Spirals" for solo violin read:

> *Platinum Spirals* (1977) was commissioned by the National Endowment for the Arts and dedicated to the memory of my father, who was a geologist and mining engineer. Platinum is a mineral whose internal properties reveal a very malleable and flexible set of characteristics. It is said that an ounce of platinum can be stretched into a mile. A lot of this piece is about the stretching of lines of ten upward in "spirals." Other times, there is a quiet kind of "rocking" pattern that "holds" the action in place.[21]

Tower aptly points out two of the most immediate characteristics of "Platinum Spirals." She might have mentioned others, as well: the extraordinary beauty of the piece's use of major and minor thirds, the continual upward striving of those spirals, and the overall shape of the piece as created by all of these. Tower's pervasive use of thirds in "Platinum Spirals" does not work as any sort of neotonality, or pseudo-postmodern reference to tonality. It is necessary, of course, that we hear these thirds as consonant; we must also hear them, in their consonance, as points of arrival, not simply as unprivileged intervals among many such; but this is not tonality. All musical language is built on relative consonance and dissonance, whether established contextually (that is to say, within the confines of an individual piece) or by a more general common system. With the 1970s, the common language of music began to readmit sounds and intervals that had been avoided in the previous fifty years as too redolent of major/minor tonality. Tower's music here is a perfect example: the thirds are gestures of consonance, stability, and beauty. But they are not more than that.

Tower's spirals do more than just move upward. They seem to reach upward, to strive. The reasons for this lie in their contrast to the so-called rocking patterns, and in their rhythms, most often in the quickest notes of the piece. (This is not the case in the central section.) The highest notes of the spirals are points of arrival, sustained, emphasized through their dynamics, often followed by a caesura. The final cadence of the piece is a series of three such spirals, of which the last is the most stretched out. The result is music that itself seems to be striving toward the ineffable, toward unearthly heights. In this "Platinum Spirals" resembles the last movement of Messiaen's *Quartet for the End of Time*. The shape of the piece is one that wakens gradually, that moves back and forth between its active, upward-moving sections and its more static, "rocking" patterns. As the piece goes on, the latter give way more frequently and decisively to the former. But the material that pervades the piece—the thirds, but other gestures as well—are stretched from one section to another, so that we hear them as essentially unitary.

A completely different effect is created by Tower's *Petroushskates*, her 1980 work for the Da Capo Chamber Players. Tower's notes to the score read:

> *Petroushskates* is an amalgam of two diversified ideas: the pure rhythm of figure skating in the Olympic ice games, and obviously, the patterns of Stravinsky's *Petroushka*. However, this work is not a pastiche of Stravinsky, but a musical tribute in the form of a memoir with only a few passing references to his works: the opening hurly burly of *Petroushka*, a violin solo passage from *L'Histoire du Soldat* and fleeting suggestion of the chord spacings of *Rite of Spring*. But in all aspects this is an original work, freshly conceived and executed. The "borrowing" of Stravinsky is used in the same way he himself "borrows" from other composers, resulting in an entirely different musical atmosphere and composition. Also, like Stravinsky this work is balletic for it is inspired by the movements of the body in motion.

We come here full circle to the dichotomy with which we began this chapter, with a piece based on Stravinsky but composed for the "*Pierrot* quintet," now an established genre. The work is, as Tower states, not a pastiche or an imitation. Tower's rhythms are much more fluid than Stravinsky's, and her sounds less hard-edged. It is the holiday cheerfulness of *Petroushka*—and of Olympian, self-assured ice skating—which she evokes here. Unlike *L'histoire*, *Petroushskates* is very much an ensemble piece, not a chamber concerto for violin. The instruments are used for their brightest colors, and much of the music lies in the higher registers. It is a piece that seems completely unproblematic and untroubled. And in this, too, it is representative of its era, for our composers seem largely to have left behind them the conviction that every work of art must be self-consciously serious, philosophical, and deep. It is one of the legacies of French and American neoclassicism that some works of art can be fun, in addition to being artistic.

This chapter closes with a piece that summarizes a number of the musical developments of recent years, Lee Hyla's *The Dream of Innocent III* (1987), for amplified cello, piano, and percussion. The obvious characteristics that put the piece in this chapter are the amplification of the cello and the important percussion part. It is also typical of much of today's music that Hyla wrote the piece with specific performers in mind: the cellists Rhonda Rider, Ted Mook, and Tom Flaherty; the percussionist James Pugliese; and himself as pianist. Finally, the music could have been written only in the late twentieth century, given the influences and sounds that Hyla has sought out.

Hyla's notes to the score are extensive:

> From the time I started work on the piece I conceived of the cello as the protagonist, with the piano and percussion offering a variety of commentaries which often strongly contrast with the cello's voice. The piece opens elementally, with the cello playing primarily open strings and natural harmonics while the piano and percussion define their initial roles in whaps and thuds. The decision to amplify the cello actually came from the nature of this opening, and is an effort to gain more unity of attack between the cello and percussion. This combination of open sonority, along with a sense of long line in the cello part, and heavily articulated rhythm form the basis for the development of the piece.
>
> *The Dream of Innocent III* is in three large interrelated sections, the first two ending with extended amplified cello solos of contrasting character. The third section (and the piece) ends with a transfiguration of the riffs and tunes that have been the focus of the piece throughout, and with an intensification of the dramatic roles of each instrument.

The title is borrowed from a Giotto fresco that is part of the "Scenes from the Life of St. Francis" cycle in Assisi. The piece, recurrently, was inspired by the fresco, which depicts Pope Innocent III, in full papal regalia, dreaming that the Church is being literally upheld by Francis. The tilted dream image of Francis propping up the church of St. John Lateran evolves seamlessly out of the papal bed chambers, and the surreal intensity and simplicity of that image had a deep impact on me while I was working on the piece.

What these notes do not convey is the extraordinary intensity of the music, as with all of Hyla's compositions. This intensity reflects some of Hyla's musical tastes—Beethoven, James Brown and other soul artists, the composer and pianist Cecil Taylor. There is no sense of the specifically personal in Hyla's music, but there is always an irresistible musical drama worked out before our ears, a drama that takes place in deep and intense colors.

As Hyla implies in his notes, *The Dream of Innocent III* is essentially a linear and developmental piece, beginning with the roles of the three instruments established in the opening minutes, and continuing with motives that are continued, extended, modified, and intensified over the work as a whole. The percussion battery is large and, for the most part, unpitched. The piano writing is percussive, and at times seems a sort of mediation between percussion and the amplified cello. The music is not always a matter of contrast and confrontation, however; it happens as well that all three instruments combine in unison statements that are as rhythmic as they are melodic or motivic. The overall sense of the piece is constant forward motion, constant heightening of the rhythmic and melodic impulses, interrupted and set off by passages (primarily in the cello) of the most beautiful serenity. Yet even this serenity is not that of earlier musics: it may be a sort of cantilena, it may be rhythmically more static than other sections of the piece, but the serenity is ecstatic. Hyla's music contains the variety and intensity of Cecil Taylor's and the sense we have in Beethoven that each note is essential, even the sense that each movement is simultaneously thematic and transition to something else. This concentration—emotional and technical—I connect to the fresco of Hyla's title, the "surreal intensity and simplicity" to which he responded in Giotto. Hyla's music sounds like no one else's. But the confluence of other sounds in his work, the artful artlessness of his composing, the overwhelming visceral impact of the rhythmic, motivic, and developmental play, place Hyla squarely in the late twentieth century, a composer fully alive in the present yet very much aware of Western music history. The very individuality of Hyla's voice makes him in some ways an exemplar of music today.

Finally in this chapter we turn to a development in classical music that became very pronounced in the last decades of the twentieth century, music with roots in both Asia and the West. Asian-influenced Western classical music is nothing new, of course: as far back as the 1930s, Colin McPhee (1900–64) was exploring Balinese music and incorporating its sounds into his own compositions, and John Cage and other composers from California were also familiar with Asian musics, ensembles, and aesthetics. Stockhausen, as we saw in chapter 3, found Asian inspiration for his *Stimmung,* premiered at the Osaka international exhibition in 1968. The Chinese-born composer Chou Wen-chung (b. 1923) was Edgard Varèse's protégé in New York and has been extremely important in both new-music and intercultural circles. There have also been a number of other Asian composers reasonably well known in the West, especially the Japanese Toru Takemitsu (1930–96) and more recently, the Chinese-born composer Tan Dun (b. 1957), perhaps most widely known at present for his score to the movie *Crouching Tiger, Hidden Dragon.* In all, a growing number of Asian composers have become prominent, and a new kind of "crossover" or "world music" sort of influence has become popular. Our examples here will be Takemitsu's 1966 *Eclipse* for shakuhachi (a kind of Japanese recorder made of bamboo) and biwa (a large lute played with a plectrum), two interconnected works by the Chinese composer Bright Sheng (b. 1955), and the Chinese-American cellist Yo-Yo Ma's (b. 1955) "Silk Road Project."

Perhaps the most striking characteristic of Takemitsu's *Eclipse* is its "live"-ness, the listener's constant and vivid awareness of this music being made in the *Now.* This is not a function of any exoticism that European-American ears might hear in its instrumentation; I think the same effect would occur if it were performed on flute and guitar. Rather it is a function of the musical materials and their handling. The listener is always aware of the shakuhachi player's breathing and the biwa player's physical motions. The two instrumental parts constantly circle around one another, seeming less to converse in any call-and-response sort of way than to complement each other, to "speak" the same message, constantly approaching and frequently coming together. This in turn has to do with the fairly restricted melodic material that Takemitsu employs in this work and with his use of it. He does not "develop" his basic materials, that is, the basic scale and melodic patterns, in any Western sense of that word, but extends them, plays them out. Moreover, the large-scale events of the work are aleatoric, determined by the performers; and this contributes as well to the feeling of absolute presence in the music.

"Absolute presence" is probably what some commentators and writers describe as the "timelessness" of much Asian music. *Eclipse,* for example, lacks any or the long-range sense of tension and release that is elemental in much Western classical music. In the recording by Katsuya Yokoyama (shakuhachi) and Kinshi Tsuruta (biwa) (Philips 432 176–2,

1991), there is a very loud, tense, rather frenetic passage at about 80 percent of the way through the piece; but this has not been "prepared" as it would have been in Western compositions, and does not constitute a climax which is then resolved. The chain of events to that point prevents such a hearing, for our ears are always directed to the present, not to the past or future. Moreover, much of the piece is a kind of audible turning of basic materials in the mind's ear, with constant explorations of timbre, pitch ornamentation, and paths from one note to another. We are in motion, and the motion is both auditory and physical (the players' performing and our sympathetic cooperation in their actions). Any goal is not predicted, deferred, eventually reached; on the contrary, the goal is the sounding in the present.

Bright Sheng is a very active and highly visible composer of accessible and beautifully wrought works that draw on both his Chinese heritage and his advanced Western training. The first movement of his 1990 *The Stream Flows,* for solo violin, and the last of his *3 Chinese Love Songs* of 1988, with the same title, are based on the same Chinese folk song. The violin piece is a long-breathed expansion of the basic melody, clearly stated at the outset, sometimes reminiscent of Joan Tower's *Platinum Spirals* in its handling of register for extension and variation of emotion and to establish points of arrival in the unfolding line. There is minimum use of extended techniques (although the music is obviously not easy, does not play itself) or unusual coloristic devices; perhaps the only technique it has in common with the Takemitsu *Eclipse* is the frequent use of glissando and portamento more associated with Asian singing and melodic writing than with Western work. The vocal version of the song sets the melody forth more straightforwardly, in two strophes not identical in rhythm, ornamentation, or phrasing. The singer is accompanied here by a viola playing, for the first half of the song, virtually the same melody in canon a perfect eleventh below the voice line and three eighth notes ahead, then (from m. 11) a minor seventh below the voice and following her by two eighth notes, then in a freer counterpoint that still mimics the quasi-heterophony of the first stanza. The piano plays only three notes during the entire song, a D♭ (three octaves below middle C) in the brief interlude between stanzas and then the neighboring C♯ at the end, all struck directly by the finger on the string, with the right pedal depressed. Sheng rounds off the song with a recollection of the opening vocal sigh and by a melodic resolution and unification of all three parts, as each cadences on C♯ and then the viola on a high harmonic G♯ *in alt* over the piano's final low C♯. The sound of the voice and viola can remind one of the flute/voice movements of Schoenberg's *Pierrot lunaire,* though obviously without its Expressionist angst and queasiness, and Boulez's *Marteau sans maître,* or also of Berio's *Chamber Music* in its interweaving of melodic lines and the wistfulness of its texture.

The second movement of the solo violin *The Stream Flows* is a much faster work, based on open fifths and an almost obsessively repetitive working and reworking of a three-note motive sounded at the very beginning. Listeners will immediately hear similarities to the folk-based music of Béla Bartók in its building, dance-like frenzy, although Sheng uses a smaller vocabulary here than Bartók usually does. The movement is a stirring end-piece to the song of the first movement, and some three-quarters of the way through recalls the textures and melodic arcs of that movement before calming to a surprisingly quiet and grounded close.

The first two of the *3 Chinese Love Songs* are also both strophic, and built on pentatonic melodies varied and lightened by changing ornamentation and rhythms. (In the second song, "At the Hillside Where the Horses Are Running," the second strophe is sung a minor third higher than the first.) Here, unlike the third song, the viola and piano parts are more independent of the voice, with the viola concentrating on open fifths and minor sevenths in the first song and repeated seconds, ninths, and harmonics in the second. The piano uses the same intervallic material as the viola in both, but in its own rhythms and phrasings. These songs thus sound more "modern" or more "Western" than does the third, but the three work together as a cycle in their basic intervallic materials, in their lyrical themes, in the roughly slow-fast-slow *tempi* of the three, and in a kind of narrowing of focus, from the sight of a beautiful girl in the first song, "Blue Flower," to the love between a boy and girl in the second, to a direct text sung by the lover to the beloved in "The Stream Flows."

The cellist Yo-Yo Ma, an American of Chinese extraction born in Paris, is a musician of wonderful curiosity and enterprise. His Silk Road Project attracted a great deal of attention from music writers as result of a recording done in 2001 (*Silk Road Journeys: When Strangers Meet*; Sony Classical SK 89782) and concerts in 2001–2. As *New York Times* critic Allan Kozinn wrote, such a project "could easily seem a matter of surfing on the popularity of world music, or a classicist's belated attempt at fusion, in the style of Paul Simon's adventures in South African and Latin American music."[22] He quickly goes on to say that these fears are ungrounded. Similarly, a review by Alex Ross in *The New Yorker* is lavish in its praise of Ma and the musicians and works performed at the Carnegie Hall concert reviewed by Kozinn.[23]

As this music represents or combines elements from many traditions, it also stands on the border between chamber music and music for a larger ensemble, similar to Varèse's *Octandre* or Boulez's *Le marteau sans maître*. The recording is masterfully arranged, with the newly composed works squarely in the context of music from the traditions from which they newly spring. (One does wonder, however, about the Finnish folk songs reworked by the Japanese composer Michi Mamiya. This is a long way from the Silk Road; but the music is beautiful.) The spirit which rises from the recording, and if the reviews are to be believed from the concerts as well, is one of individuals in deep collaboration, not, as might be feared, one of some sort of quasi-aesthetic globalization. Projects like this are no doubt very expensive to realize, and will probably have less impact on Western classical music (chamber or otherwise) than individual composers who bring their own extra-classical influences to play in their works. But the Silk Road Project was eminently worthwhile and, one hopes, can perhaps spur individual broadening on the part of performers and listeners as well as encouragement to adventurous composers.

Notes

1. Stravinsky, *Autobiography,* 70ff.
2. Austin, *Music in the 20th Century,* 46.
3. *Harvard Concise Dictionary of Music,* 374.
4. These questions of sectional relationships and proportions are taken up in chapter 5.
5. He performed and recorded the Mozart Clarinet Concerto and Clarinet Quintet, for example, and commissioned concertos from Aaron Copland and Patti Hindemith.
6. All-combinatoriality: "The capacity of a collection to create aggregates [i.e., collections containing all twelve pitch classes] with forms of itself and its complement under both transposition and inversion." Milton Babbitt, *Words about Music,* ed. Stephen Dembski and Joseph N. Straus (Madison, WI, 1987), 193.
7. A riff is a repeated melodic, rhythmic, or harmonic motive that continues throughout (and may serve as the basis of) a musical section or composition.
8. At least in the performance by the Contemporary Chamber Ensemble, Arthur Weisberg, conductor, Nonesuch H-71303.
9. Quoted in Elaine Barkin and Martin Brody, "Milton Babbitt," *The New Grove Dictionary of American Music,* ed. H. Wiley Hitchcock and Stanley Sadie (London, 1980), 1:105.
10. Nonesuch H-71303. Emphases in original.
11. See Allen Edwards, *Flawed Words and Stubborn Sounds: A Conversation with Elliott Carter* (New York, 1971), 78.
12. Although this is an effective opening gesture, Carter specifies in his "Performance Notes" to the score that "Saëta" should be neither the first nor the last played in a selection from these *Eight Pieces.*
The circled *N* in the score indicates normal playing position, the circled *C* playing at the center of the drum head.
13. See Rosen, *Sonata Forms,* rev. ed. (New York, 1988).
14. I direct the curious reader to other analyses such as those in Erno Lendvai, *Béla Bartók: An Analysis of His Music* (London, 1971), and Elliott Antokoletz, *The Music of Béla Bartók: A Study of Tonality and Progression in Twentieth-Century Music* (Berkeley and Los Angeles, 1984).
15. It may be that music historians overgeneralize when we characterize the period from Schubert through Mahler as Romantic. Art and literary historians are far ahead of us here, and a new history of the nineteenth century separating out Romanticism from other cultural trends would be extremely welcome.
16. Personal communication from Schwartz.
17. Kolb, liner notes to *Solitaire* (Turnabout TV-S 34487, 1972).
18. Quoted in László Eösze, "Kodály, Zoltán," in *The New Grove Dictionary of Music and Musicians,* ed. Stanley Sadie (London, 1980), 10:139.

19. Seminal writings include Cone, "Stravinsky: The Progress of a Method," in *Perspectives on Schoenberg and Stravinsky,* ed. Benjamin Boretz and Edward T. Cone (New York, 1972), 155–64 and Kramer's magisterial *The Time of Music* (New York, 1988).

20. Thomas S. Kuhn, *The Structure of Scientific Revolutions,* 2d edition (Chicago, 1970).

21. Joan Tower, notes to CRI recording SD 517 (1985).

22. Allan Kozinn, "Music Review: At a Cultural Crossroads, Yo-Yo Ma Becomes a Spice Trader," *The New York Times* (May 9, 2002), pp. B1, B7.

23. Alex Ross, "Musical Events: Journey's End," *The New Yorker* (May 27, 2002), pp. 122–3.

CHAPTER FIVE

The Modern Sonata

The term *sonata* has no single meaning: that is one reason why Charles Rosen entitled his 1980 book *Sonata Forms,* in the plural. The sonata is both a genre, originating in the seventeenth century, and a form, crystallized in the latter half of the eighteenth. In purely formalist terms, the nineteenth-century sonata is a received structure no longer inspirited with the original impulse. In the twentieth century, particularly in the hands of the so-called neoclassicists, the sonata has enjoyed a remarkable renaissance. In particular, the sonatas of Debussy and Bartók are true reinventions, and not of the wheel. Ravel, Ives, and Carter have also succeeded, not just in writing sonatas that resemble those of the eighteenth century, but in writing true chamber sonatas.

In the seventeenth century, sonatas were pieces that were "sounded" (the past participle of *sonar*) rather than sung. During the second half of that century, a principal form of the sonata was a work in four movements, slow-fast-slow-fast, with alternating characters articulated by these tempi and by texture, meter and rhythm, derivation from particular dances, and so on. Individual movements of these Baroque sonatas are monolithic, emphasizing unity and continuity, the genius of their invention lying in their extended spinning-out of their given material. Contrast comes from one movement to another, and the overall structural rhythm is usually one of great regularity, each movement holding its place in a scheme of roughly equal proportions. Although material may be shared among the instruments, the melody instruments are often the more important, and the keyboard instruments are relegated principally to accompaniment.[1] This format of the Baroque sonata as a multimovement work for one or more instruments continues into the twentieth century.

The Classical sonata differs, first of all, in its evolution of the one-movement sonata form, an unfolding musical drama of internal growth and balance, a combination of diversity and unity. What bears emphasis here is the organic quality of this sonata form: it is not simply a succession of three or four contrasting sections that somehow add up to a coherent whole. A Classical sonata is a drama of sound in motion with a beginning, middle, and end. The workings of any specific sonata are often peculiar to that sonata, and this is as true of twentieth-century music as of Classical music. But a general schema needs to be drawn before we can turn to individual works.

Classical sonata form is a cumulative series of large-scale musical gestures. The first is the *exposition,* which introduces not just the themes of a given movement, but the duality, the contrasts, the unfinished business of the drama. The exposition opens up the musical energy that has to be grounded over the course of the movement. The *development* is as aptly named as the exposition. It is a section of variety, of dissolution and recombination, fragmentation and new composition, the exacerbation of the tensions erected in the opening section. The resolution of these tensions and the grounding of musical energy take place in the *recapitulation.* Themes are reconstituted, tonality is reestablished, successions are simplified. Sometimes there is a closing section, or *coda,* depending on the requirements of the music. Whether the Classical sonata form in question is a fast first movement, a slow second or third movement, or a fast final movement, it is heard as an argument or a drama. It is a creative procedure in which weight accumulates across time, and the easing of that weight in a listener's mind requires an active attention to the musical drama.

This one-movement sonata form is the major structural procedure of the Classical and Romantic sonata cycle, the multimovement scheme that stood at the top of music's firmament from the 1770s (Haydn) through World War I (Schoenberg). The sonata cycle is found in instrumental pieces called sonatas, whether for piano solo or for another instrument and piano; symphonies; string quartets and quintets; piano trios, quartets, and quintets; and concertos. The scheme is this: a first movement, moderate to fast in tempo, in sonata form, often the weightiest and most complex of the work's movements. Of the middle movements, one is a minuet or a scherzo, a sectional form in a moderate-to-fast triple meter, and the only remnant in the Classical sonata of the dance forms so popular in the Baroque. The other middle movement is a slow movement, in one of various forms, such as sonata form, ternary form, theme and variations, or rondo. The last movement is invariably fast, and is usually clearer in texture and form than the first movement or the slow movement. Its most common forms are the sonata form, theme and variations, and rondo. As music moved through the Romantic era, the weight of the sonata cycle gradually shifted across the entire work. Instead of the "serious" first and slow movements, then lighter dance movement and finale of most Classical and early

Romantic sonatas, each movement began to assume more equal proportions in the balance of the whole. The impetus for this was, as for so much else, the music of Beethoven, primarily the symphonies, but also the piano sonatas and the string quartets.

Twentieth-century neoclassicists leaped back across the Romanticism of the nineteenth century and recreated, in more or less contemporary musical language, the sonatas (or sonata ideals) of the Baroque and Classical eras, the earlier and latter halves of the eighteenth century. We have also had in this century sonatas that seem completely contemporary in their handling of inner chronology and the drama central to the sonata ideal that I have posited. This chapter treats these various kinds of sonatas according to the historical period they most resemble: the modern "Baroque" sonata, the modern "Classical" sonata, and the modern sonata *tout court*.

The Modern "Baroque" Sonata: Bartók

In chapter 4 we considered Virgil Thomson's Sonata da Chiesa of 1926, an "early Baroque" sonata in its forms (chorale, dance, fugue). The modern "Baroque" sonata par excellence is Bartók's Sonata for Solo Violin (1944). It is a direct tribute to the solo sonatas and partitas of Johann Sebastian Bach in its forms, textures, choice of instrument, and manner of its musical developments. It is also in some ways reminiscent of late Beethoven—that is, the Beethoven most indebted to Bach and Handel. At the same time, it is thoroughly of its era, a product of the musical language of the European tradition of the 1930s and 1940s, and of Bartók's idiosyncratic late style.

The sonata is in four movements, marked *Tempo di ciaccona* (in the time of a chaconne, a stately triple meter); *Fuga, Risoluto non troppo vivo* (Fugue; resolutely, not too quickly); *Melodia, Adagio* (Melody, broadly); and *Presto*. Thus, only the last movement is fast. In addition, only the last movement is not tightly, even rigorously, structured. The gravity of the slow tempos and the inexorably laid-out structures is underscored by the sonata's tonalities. The movements are neither in standard functional keys, nor "on" pitches, to use Halsey Stevens's terminology,[2] that is, with a tonic note but not the conventional scaffolding that creates the sense of tonic in earlier music. This sonata is more triadic than Bartók's music of the 1920s and 1930s, for example the Sonata for Two Pianos and Percussion (see chapter 4), or the Third, Fourth, and Fifth String Quartets (see chapter 6). This "triadicity" may reflect the general directions of Bartók's music during the 1940s, as in the Third Piano Concerto, the Sonata's place in a tradition of tonal pieces, and the nature of the violin and of writing for a solo melody instrument (it is easier to establish a clear tonal hierarchy by using chords, or a mix of chord relationships and voice-leading melodic relationships, than by using the latter alone). Bartók's chords are not the standard triads of functional tonal harmony, but Bartók uses them to establish a sense of harmonic relationships that is entirely analogous, chords that sound like a dominant or a subdominant, key areas that do the same. And as with the rigor of the forms, this use of chords to define keys and key areas loosens somewhat across the four movements, from the first movement, which is almost entirely in double-, triple-, even quadruple-stops, to the concluding *presto*, written largely in single notes with double-stops only as intensifications.

Despite its title and the implications of its first measures—the unwarned listener who knows the great Chaconne in D Minor by Bach will start in recognition—the first movement is in a strict sonata form. The form is also reminiscent of late Beethoven in its constant motivic work; its distinguishing of sections by texture, figuration, and thematic and tonal clarity; and its constant evolution from similarity to difference. The first theme presents the characteristic chaconne rhythm; a brief duet emerges in which the chaconne's ornamental fillers become melodic and primary. The bridge, as long and important here as in Beethoven, alternates double-stops with single notes; the tune is less defined in melodic contour than either the first or second themes, and its figuration is often used throughout the movement to define a modulatory section, focusing, for example, on the dominant of the key to which the music modulates. (This is an example of Bartók's using a texture to define a formal element previously established by tonal movement.) The second theme is a descending single-note melody, in triplets, and in a quasi-submediant (E♭) tonal area: all these elements are in contrast to the first theme, and to the bridge. This second theme ends with an upward-spiraling line that inverts and then repeats the beginning of the tune and leads to a cadence. This upward-moving figure, the inversion of the second theme, prefigures the principal melody of the third movement. Thus begins the interweaving of movements through repeated themes and ideas.

The development begins with the chaconne figure of the first theme, and fragments, recombines, and intensifies elements from the first theme and the bridge theme. The texture is almost entirely two-voiced, either as double-stops or as a call-and-response with the same motive. This two-voiced texture is relieved only by repeated single notes (which then expand to double-stops), a foreshadowing of the principal material of the fourth movement, and by the more expanded texture of the climax of the development, the three-part "duet" between one line doubled at the distance of a third and single notes in contrary motion below. The climax broadens into the final section of the development, which moves gradually back to the recapitulation. The recap achieves its sense of unification and resolution through its seeming simplicity. It has more internal repetitions than the exposition, its sectional divisions are much clearer, and its textures are concomitantly less thick. In addition, it incorporates the repeated-note figure from the development section, the repeated notes here being octaves rather than unisons, and combines this with the bridge theme. The second theme is heard in a simplified form as well, now moving in steady eighth notes and with a clearer contour.

The process of simplification and relaxation does not continue directly with the second movement, however. This fugue is as thick and intense as the exposition and development of the first movement. In addition, the treatment of the fugal procedure gives at least equal attention to the episodes (and their spinning-out of motivic material) and the expositions of the fugue subject. The balance shifts here from what we are used to in a Bach fugue, the alternation of thematic material with brief episodes of contrasting music, to a scheme of more continuous extensions and developments, occasionally hung from a scaffolding of the subject in a clear texture and tonality. This can be readily seen from the lengths of the fugue's sections:

mm.	1–21	exposition 1 (four entries of the subject, on C, G, C, and G successively)
	21–37	episode 1
	37–44	exposition 2
	44–62	episode 2
	62–76	stretto, the subject against itself
	76–84	exposition 3, original key
	85–107	coda

After the initial exposition, clear statements of the fugue subject are rare, even incidental. What we hear is a linearly expanding extrapolation of the subject with a climax not in the stretto of mm. 62–76 or the final exposition, in the original key, but in the coda. This coda works as a summary of much that we have heard before: motives and textures from earlier in the movement, and from the first movement as well; pitch registers and dynamic ranges; bits of the fugue subject; and even a reminiscence of the first theme of the chaconne. Despite its quasi-Baroque format, this movement moves toward the classicist ideal of variety within an overriding unity: the fugue, although less than half as long as the opening movement, seems to balance it in weight and intensity. It begins with completely new music, a subject unlike any theme from the first movement, but by its end has reminded the listener of the world of that first movement. The beginnings of the first two movements are clear signifiers of seriousness of purpose. But it is Bartók's treatment of form, theme, and texture in the two movements that maintains that depth of character, intellect, and affect.

The last two movements move clearly into the quasi-Baroque world implied by the first two, if overlaid with Beethovenian forms and affects. Structures in the third and fourth movements are much simpler, more clearly articulated, and less interwoven. The third movement, "Melodia," is a ternary form whose main theme begins like that of the slow movement of the Brahms Double Concerto for Violin, Cello, and Orchestra. The movement's long phrases are made by motivic extensions and developments, the contrasts of harmonics and normal playing, and the use of register to give phrase direction; all traditional means. The fourth movement, *presto*, is a sort of rondo, ABA'CA''/coda, the coda incorporating music from the B section. This form, its sections of almost equal proportions, the very fast tempo, the lightness and clarity of texture, are all traditional elements for the last movement of a sonata, both in the Baroque and in the early Classical eras. The A sections, a sort of *perpetuum mobile,* include the repeated single notes and double-stops first heard in the development of the first movement. The B section is largely in double-stops, and its main theme alternates between the simple triple meter of the A sections and a contrasting hemiola. The C section presents yet another melody, moving upward rather than down (as did the B melody), an expansive and stable tune. These sections are also slightly overlapped; they are not kept so separate as the sections of, say, a Mozart or Haydn rondo. The movement fulfills its cadential function through tonality (G, quasi-minor at the beginning of the movement, moving into a less clouded quasi-major), and its recall of material from the first movement (the repeated notes and double-stops).

Yet this sonata is not excessively interwoven and all of a piece. It would be difficult for a solo violinist, and for the audience, to maintain the intensity of the first two movements across an entire sonata cycle. The format requires more variety, which Bartók supplies in greater abundance as the sonata progresses. Bartók has revivified in this work the tradition of the Baroque solo sonata, but not without recognizing what has happened in music since the Baroque era. The sequence and shape of the four movements are Baroque. The use of sonata form in the first movement and such intermovement references as there are are Classical. The harmonic language is contemporary. The means of building phrases and sections is equally contemporary, but in a tradition that goes directly back to Beethoven and his predecessors. In phrase structure and proportions, the Baroque and the modern era meet. The playing techniques are modern (as is the instrument, obviously), but in the tradition of virtuosity that goes back to Bach's solo suites for violin and cello. If one listens to a Bach solo partita and then to the Bartók sonata, one hears the latter as a sort of homage to the Baroque in a thoroughly modern guise. But if one listens to the Bartók and then to such solo works as we discussed in chapter 4, Wolpe's pieces for solo trumpet and solo violin or Tower's "Platinum Spirals," one then hears in the Bartók a deeply and pervasively traditional piece, a work that in fact emphasizes its indebtedness to the Western musical heritage of the past two hundred years. In this sense, although I have been approaching this sonata as a quasi-Baroque work, it is a masterpiece of neoclassicism, recombining the traditional and the contemporary in assured and inextricable ways. No great composer of the twentieth century but Bartók has truly achieved this mix. For, as we shall see in the next section (and in the treatment of the string quartet in chapter 6), most other works are "too" traditional, and not particularly thrilling to the modern ear, or "too" modern, more emblematic of their era than of the sonata tradition.

The Modern "Classical" Sonata: Prokofiev, Ravel, Stravinsky

Rarely in this century do we find the sort of dynamic two-part process described by Rosen's *Sonata Forms*. Nevertheless, many successful modern sonatas are similar in design or motivation to the late eighteenth-century sonata. We can arrange these pieces in groups: first, those sonatas closest to the Classical mold, for example Sergey Prokofiev's Sonata for Flute and Piano, Ravel's Piano Trio, and Stravinsky's Concerto for Two Solo Pianofortes. Next are Debussy's Violin Sonata, neoclassic in its own way, and two works that seem to spring from it, Bartók's First Violin Sonata and Francis Poulenc's Clarinet Sonata. All these sonatas provide some idea of contemporary composers' use of the form and their attitudes toward its use in earlier centuries. These sonatas also demonstrate the ultimately untenable status of the term *neoclassicism*. Finally, the sonatas give a broad view of many compositional procedures and concerns in the middle years of this century.

The Prokofiev Flute Sonata (1943), the very model of a modern "Classical" sonata, need not detain us long. The piece is still popular with flutists and violinists (who play it in arrangement), although it is no longer regarded very seriously by critics, composers, or academics. The reason for this is twofold, I think. First, this style has gone very much out of fashion in the last twenty years, much more so than the contemporary styles of Stravinsky or Bartók. Prokofiev's homophonic textures, relentlessly regular phrase structure, and what used to be called its "wrong-note" chordal structures—that is, with added notes, but here "spicy" rather than "spiky"—have come to seem like a modernistic imitation of Classical *Kleinmeister* like Kuhlau or Clementi. The style has not gained depth with age, but rather the reverse.

The second reason for the decline in the stock of pieces like the Prokofiev lies in the listener's perception that the composer seems to be following the sonata procedure by recipe, rather than allowing his material to give rise to an original and dramatic musical form. On the broadest level, Prokofiev's use of standard forms in each of his movements seems mechanical rather than necessary. Everything follows in the prescribed order, from the phrase level to the succession of movements. But one is hard pressed to find (that is, to hear) an inner reason for any particular musical event. For example, key relationships are used as signposts, but without necessarily being established as key functions. In the exposition of the first movement, the first theme is in D major and the second theme arrives in the key of A, even though we have not heard to this point any tonic/dominant relationship to which we can relate the two keys. Prokofiev moves from D major to A major not to expand, on a larger canvas, a tonal relationship already established in microcosm. There is no compelling internal reason to move to A major rather than any contrasting key. The reason he does so is in deference to procedures common some two hundred years before.

The point is not whether Prokofiev obeys the "rules," whatever they might be. The point is that Prokofiev is writing in a genre and with forms that imply certain procedures, and he is neither following these literally essential procedures nor replacing them with something original. It is a case of filling up an empty pot labeled "sonata form" (or "rondo," or whatever) with whatever comes to hand, or adhering to "sonata form" as if it were a train schedule. Like many other sonatas of its era and persuasion, the Prokofiev is not unpleasant to listen to. But it has become one of the bonbons of the chamber repertory, not a real staple.

Much more enduring are French works—or works from a Francophile tradition—in the first half of this century. One example is Ravel's Trio for Violin, Cello, and Piano (1914). Like his String Quartet of 1902–3 (discussed in chapter 6), Ravel's Piano Trio falls into four movements in standard forms. Beyond that, however, little is reminiscent of earlier works in the mainstream European (i.e., Germanic) musical tradition. The first movement is a sonata form descended, in a way, from Schumann in its handling of key and rhythms. The entire exposition is in A minor, or rather, a highly modal version of A minor; it does not modulate, although there is a great deal of harmonic activity, and the sonorities by themselves are extremely rich. The harmonies move, but the stark contrast of keys supporting contrasts of melody and texture is missing. In contrast, the recapitulation—which, as in many works of this era, is more aptly called a reconsolidation—begins with the second theme, at the same pitch level as in the exposition, but now reharmonized, and then modulates to C major (or, again, a modal collection of pitches centered on C). This modulation, like the retransition into the recapitulation, is effected with the first theme of the exposition. Thus a primal unity that is established in the exposition and fragmented in the development is reestablished in the reconsolidation/recapitulation. But the reconstituted unity is a new one, not that of the exposition. The new key, C major, has been reached with the expectations and realizations implicit in the sonata form—the listener never believes, even with the one-key exposition, that this is not a sonata form—and with the particular working-out specific to this movement and this material. Unusual for the quasi-Classical sonata, but not for the nineteenth-century variety, is the lack of complete closure at the end of this movement. The delaying of the reconsolidation of unity, and the new essence of this unity, leave us still floating at the end. More music is required.

Like the formal treatment, the rhythms of the first movement are also heard as moving freely over a firm ground. The movement is written in $\frac{8}{8}$ time, but each measure of eight is grouped as 3 +2 + 3; moreover, the first two groups include dotted rhythms, and the last is a Lombardic (short-long) pattern (see Ex. 5.1). Because of the moderate speed, the basic unit is the eighth note, not the quarter or dotted quarter. The effect is one of floating above a fixed meter, very supple but never completely untethered.

The second movement is scherzolike in character and in its sectional form, but corresponding only inexactly to the received scherzo form. In this movement, too, rhythm is treated with a certain freedom. The movement's title, "Pantoum," apparently refers to the Malayan *pantun,* which Ravel heard at the famous Paris Exposition in 1889.[3] Written in triple meter, like the traditional scherzo, the main theme of the movement alternates measures with accents on the first and second and first and third beats (that is, the internal patterns alternate 1 + 2 and 2 + 1). This pattern contrasts with the second major theme, heavily downbeat-laden but with a crescendo in every measure to the third beat, the upbeat to the next downbeat.

The third movement is a passacaglia. The 8-measure theme, marked *très large* (very broadly), is stated first in the lowest register of

EXAMPLE 5.1. Ravel, Piano Trio, first movement, mm. 1–8. © 1915 Durand S.A. Editions Musicales, Editions A.R.I.M.A., and Durand S.A. Editions Musicales Joint Publication. Used by Permission of the Publisher.

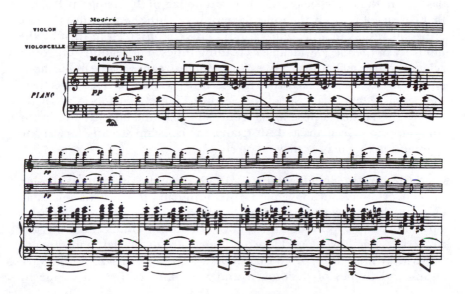

the piano, then in the cello and the violin. This exposition is followed by increasingly thickly harmonized variations on the melody, and then a conclusion that reverses the exposition: the first violin accompanied by the cello; then the theme in the cello, with a piano accompaniment that thins from three voices to single notes; and the theme finally in the piano, again in the lowest octaves.

The last movement is another sonata form. Ravel adheres to the standard Classical procedure of using the last movement of a sonata cycle for the clarification and grounding of elements from earlier movements. Its first themes, in $\frac{5}{4}$ and $\frac{7}{4}$, recall the rhythmic patterns of the first two movements. The second theme contrasts with the rhythmic first theme and is equally striking: its ecstatic trills in the two strings over *fortissimo* piano chords resemble the climactic moments of Messiaen's *Quartet for the End of Time*. The trills and chords serve the same purpose in the Ravel Trio, acting as the climaxes of the recapitulation and the coda. In this way, the last movement does indeed act as a finale, simplifying and summarizing elements from earlier movements, and building to a climax of texture and dynamics that surpasses anything heard in those movements.

For all its traditional features, the Ravel Trio does not sound like either a mainstream nineteenth- or twentieth-century work. It is the kind of modernism that, as Bartók said of Kodály's (see chapter 4), would not be admitted as such: tonal, consonant, and filled with melodies whose regularity is belied by suppleness of rhythm and contour. But all these elements are treated in an idiosyncratic way. The tonality is not major-minor functional tonality, but heavily modal. Also, the tonality is often a tonality by implication, for Ravel from the opening measures uses extended pedal points: harmonies shift above a sustained bass (or, in the finale, below the inverted pedals of the strings' trills), but that bass itself is rarely the tonic harmony. As with the rhythms, this use of pedals results in a floating, lapping effect, reinforced in turn by the modality of the piece, which lacks leading tones. The leading tone/tonic relationship, which was at the center of mainstream European harmony in the nineteenth and early twentieth centuries and which led directly to the pervasive chromaticism of the Second Viennese School, was anathema to the French, whose music generally lacks the angst found in the contemporary Germans and Austrians, the constant striving forward to a resolution that may or may not arrive.

Different again is our last "Classical" modern sonata, Stravinsky's Concerto for Two Solo Pianofortes (1935). Like the previous examples, the concerto has four movements, including an idiosyncratic sonata allegro, a slow movement entitled "Notturno," a set of four character variations, and a prelude and fugue. Unlike the other sonatas is the concerto's Beethovenian character, especially in the last movements. (Stravinsky himself reported that he had "steeped himself" in the variations and fugues of Beethoven and variations of Brahms while he composed the last three movements of the concerto in 1934 and 1935. The first movement had been composed in 1931.)[4] The treatment of the two pianos also resembles the music of Brahms (e.g., the Variations on a Theme by Haydn) or certain concerted works of the Baroque era, in which the instrumental forces—soloist and orchestra, *concertino* group and orchestra, members of the *concertino,* as in Bach's Fifth "Brandenburg" Concerto—at times share material but at other times play contrasting music. Here the treatment of the two pianos differs considerably from that in Debussy's *En blanc et noir* (see chapter 2): there the two were almost completely separate instruments, whereas in the Stravinsky, the separation alternates with the effect of a single large keyboard, played four-hands.[5] The modernity of the Stravinsky concerto comes from its rhythms, nonfunctional tonal structures, and black-and-white polyphony; all these bespeak the taste of the interwar years for clean lines, energy, immaculate surfaces, and strong, coherent architecture.

In a talk he delivered at the 1935 premiere of the concerto, Stravinsky referred to the second movement thus:

> I have entitled the second movement, which takes the place of an *andante,* 'Notturno'. I was thinking here not of those dreamy character pieces, without predetermined form, such as the nocturnes of Field or Chopin, but of the eighteenth-century pieces called *Nachtmusik,* or better still, of the cassations so frequent in the compositions of the era. The only difference in my case is that the different parts which generally formed the works in this genre are condensed into a single movement.[6]

Paul Jacobs wrote that Stravinsky had described to him the first-piano part of this movement as "une ballerine representée par un harrrpseechorrd."[7] Given the movement's homophonic texture of highly decorated melodic lines over repetitive chordal accompaniments, one does, pace Stravinsky, hear Chopin. One can also hear the slow movement of Beethoven's *Hammerklavier.* The term *cassation* is not particularly informative, beyond referring to a certain idea of eighteenth-century music: a cassation (like a serenade or divertimento) was a suite of pieces of various and contrasting characters, sometimes intended for outdoor performance. As long as we are amassing verbal and pictorial analogies for the Notturno, we might also think of the paintings of Watteau, all elegance and grace, beautifully composed and drawn, with the airy wistfulness noted by Verlaine ("Mandoline," "Fêtes galantes").

Musically that character is determined principally by the melody and its texture. The movement falls into three sections, ABA', the last of which is greatly foreshortened. (The first A is 35 measures long, the B section 53, and A' only 5.) The principal melody of A and its first ornamented repetition are shown in Example 5.2. In steady beats with

EXAMPLE 5.2. Stravinsky, Concerto for Two Solo Pianofortes, "Notturno," mm. 1–13. © B. Schott's Soehne, Mainz, 1936 ©renewed. All Rights Reserved. Used in the world excluding the U.S. by permission of European American Music Distributors Corporation, sole U.S. and Canadian agent for B. Schott's Soehne, Mainz.

II
Notturno

(continued)

only the gentlest of syncopations, after three measures the principal voice of this movement (Piano I) indulges in filigree decorations, always soft and unvirtuosic, on top of and not part of the secondary melodies and accompaniment of Piano II. With an elided cadence (the lengthened m. 8, where the first piano's cadential figurations resolve into the second piano's statement of the principal theme in m. 9), the main phrase begins again, but after only a measure and a half, with a striking decoration of rhythm and color in the first piano, moves directly into an abstracted and ornamented version of that melody, in both instruments. The phrase lengths and their relationships approach the miraculous: never regular or predictable, they yet never sound inelegant or badly proportioned. This has to do with the slowness of the tempo and the steadiness of the beat, so that we hear these both individually, or "locally," and as a concatenation of phrases and sections.

In m. 14 Stravinsky begins another variation and decoration of the principal melody; and a similar approach continues until m. 35, when with a cadence and surprising shift of key (from C up a step to Db)[8] we move without further transition into a contrasting B section. The principal contrast in this section is in its material. But the handling of that material—its variation, the texture of its melody and accompaniment, and the detached figures—is carried over from section A. This middle section becomes the weightiest of the movement; on the other hand, the outline and character of section A were etched strongly enough in our ears that only the briefest reference to that melody, five measures in length, suffices as a closing section.

Instead of the more usual dance movement (minuet or scherzo and trio), Stravinsky chooses for the third movement a set of character variations. The Beethovenian referent in this instance is the "Diabelli" Variations. Stravinsky's variations do not quote Beethoven, nor are they in a specifically Beethovenian style, but their process is much like that of Beethoven and the German Romantics who followed him. Each of the four variations is formed on a single given melody (which is not stated on its own in the movement), but the handling of that melody—its ornamentation, accompanying figures, harmonic treatment, and so on, everything but phrase structure—is so different from variation to variation that each has its own individual character. In addition, the accompaniment figures in the first and the last variations recall the development section of the first movement: a gesture that, if not really enough to label the sonata cyclic, is nevertheless a gesture toward a more unitary perception of the work. Even the repetitiveness is a stylistic trait, at every level from the accompaniment figure up to the sectional. The first movement, as we shall see, is both a forward-moving sonata form and a monolithic sectional construction with a great deal of repetition. The accompaniment figures of the second movement are pervasively repetitive, and the melodic ornaments and decorations seem placed on those repetitions as whorls and filigree on solid masonry. This repetitiveness allows Stravinsky to recall only the opening measures of the A section as a final section, enough to stand in for a longer, self-sufficient section. The third movement has the obvious repetition of the theme from variation to variation, although this is (as in the second movement) so different in character in each variation that early listening may not perceive the theme as such. The accompaniment figures are repetitive, except for the second variation, to the point of using an ostinato bass line in the fourth. (This accompaniment recalls that of the first variation as well.)

One could hear a progressive sharpening of focus across the sonata, in its repetitiveness and handling of material. In this hearing, the prelude and fugue of the last movement form a fitting conclusion. The prelude connects the fourth variation to the fugue and serves as introduction to the latter. The unstated theme of the variations is now presented clearly as the fugue subject. This movement is also the most developmental of any of the sonata's movements, dealing almost exclusively with the subject or with its accompaniment (again *martellato* repeated notes). As in the late fugues of Beethoven, Stravinsky employs a four-voice texture, but voices are sometimes doubled, and the texture is extremely dense because of the thick counterpoint and the extreme rhythmic activity. The fugue goes about its business quickly, from the opening statement of subject and accompaniment through the introduction of all the voices, the alternation of subject expositions with concentrated episodes, to a series of climaxes. The concluding section of the fugue offers an inversion of the subject, with a brief development, and then final stretto statements of the subject, *fortissimo* and *marcatissimo*, in a call-and-response pattern between the two pianos.

The impression of this final fugue is one of great rigor activated internally by its rhythms, its debt to Beethoven's late piano sonatas and the "Diabelli" Variations. Stravinsky's finale also offers a tremendous contrast to the world of the first movement; again as with Beethoven, this gives the impression that the listener has traversed great distances in the sonata, that the music has conveyed an emotional (or aesthetic) and even existential journey. To appreciate that, we need to look now at the first movement, an idiosyncratic sonata form that combines the forward-moving and the monolithic in a highly interesting construction, and that, in contrast to the later movements, is distinctly unlike the Classical sonata in its formal handling.

The movement is simultaneously a sonata form and a compound ternary structure. Unlike the first movements of Debussy's *En blanc et noir* and the Ravel Trio, where diverse formal schemes do not coincide, these simultaneous forms are not skewed in the concerto:

Exposition			Development			Recapitulation		
A			B			A′		
a	b	a	c	d	c	a′	b′	a′
m. 1	55	74	92	109	154	169	208	227

The exposition begins with a 10-measure introduction that sets forth the two principal melodies of the movement with their characteristic accompaniments. (As in later movements, the accompaniment figures and textures are much more similar than the thematic material in the foreground.) We then hear a first theme, an arpeggiated, highly rhythmic tune in clear phrases over a running accompaniment of arpeggios and repeated notes. This leads to a bridge that, as if to imitate the Classical style, is built on sequences and conveys a sense of rhythmic and harmonic instability. The bridge leads to the second theme, much less clearly contoured than the first theme, and audible as a true theme only because of its presentation in the introduction. The statement of the second theme is the shortest section of the exposition. It is followed by a *fortissimo* restatement of the first theme (not uncommon in the Classical era), at the same pitch level as before but now reharmonized. The section ends with an unresolved cadence figure, a loud and repeated motive from the first theme suggesting a climax and arrival at closure, in the event not realized.

The development section begins, irresistibly seductively, with an accompanimental chordal figure from the exposition now in a changed rhythm: Stravinsky changes from $\frac{2}{4}$ to $\frac{12}{16}$, so that the rhythmic groupings are now three and six rather than two or four. This resembles the sort of metrical ploy that some French composers borrowed from jazz in the 1920s, and the effect is not dissimilar to a sort of syncopated swing. This $\frac{12}{16}$ music constitutes the outer sections of the ternary development, the *c* of the above plan. The central section of the development returns to $\frac{2}{4}$, but at a slower tempo than the exposition or recapitulation. In addition, beyond the rerhythmicized accompanimental figure, no material from the exposition appears in the development. There is a family resemblance in the rhythms, the contours of the accompanying figures, and the dotted rhythms of the tunes in the development section, but this resemblance, strictly speaking, is not a development of the material of the exposition. This central section is a development rather because of its language: the lack of clearly stated themes, the more unstable texture, the more varied harmonic world, especially in the motivic spinning-out and motivic play (as opposed to thematic statements) that characterize the Classical development. That the movement does not exemplify the common harmonic scheme of the Classic or Romantic sonata (as do some modern sonatas, such as Bartók's Sonata for Solo Violin) is owing to Stravinsky's conception of sonata form not as the two-part, contrast-and-return schema described by Rosen,[9] but rather as the three-part, duality-variety-unity outline more popular in the nineteenth and earlier twentieth centuries. The point here is less a harmonic *agon* than a scheme of variety within unity, conveyed through specific material and the handling of that material. In this sense (and, again, unlike such pieces as Debussy's *En blanc et noir*), this central section of the first movement does constitute a development section.

The recapitulation begins with a literal reprise of thirty-seven measures from the beginning of the movement (mm. 5–41, the latter part of the introduction and the first theme/bridge, reappear as mm. 169–207, the retransition and the corresponding part of the recap). This reprise is unusual, for Stravinsky individually and for the major composers of the neoclassicist era. But the literal reprise does create the sense of a double and simultaneous formal scheme in this movement. First, it works as the return to the final *a* section in the compound ternary scheme. Second, its literalness increases the sense of return and recapitulation necessary to the idea of the sonata: since neither theme of the exposition has been heard in the development, the note-for-note repetition of the first theme and the beginning of the bridge here reestablish the language of stability, which constitutes the essence of the recapitulation necessary for a sonata form. Paradoxically, the literal repetition of so much music consequently allows Stravinsky to omit the exposition's second theme. It is implied by the bridge; but this section, in the recap, does not move to a different harmonic area from that of the first theme. Instead, it is simply a passage of contrasting motivic material that incorporates the accompanying music from the exposition's second theme, the repeated sixteenth notes. The amorphous second theme itself is never heard. Stravinsky insists, rather, on the granitelike solidity of his arrival, his reestablishment of the harmonic and thematic starting points, so that he moves directly on to the closing theme, again a *marcato* statement of the first theme.

Stravinsky's Concerto for Two Pianos and Bartók's Sonata for Solo Violin present two different ways of dealing with the heritage of the latter eighteenth century, Beethoven, and the sonata tradition. Bartók moves from the most intense and concentrated to the least, from his sonata reminiscent of the chaconne through a fugue spun out horizontally rather than vertically (built up by the entrance of voices), to a simple ABA slow movement and a straightforward final *presto*. Stravinsky, in contrast, begins with a sonata form more sectional than Bartók's and less rigorous in its handling of themes, motives, and harmonic areas. The concerto then becomes progressively more concentrated, moving in the direction opposite to Bartók's, across the ternary slow movement to the four variations, and to the final fugue, whose subject is the variations' theme. Each of Stravinsky's movements becomes progressively more traditional, more rigorous, in its approach to received forms, its harmonic language, and its textures, from the geniality of the first movement to the Beethovenian (or Brahmsian) absoluteness and certainty of the final fugue. The weight of each work is thus completely different; Bartók's is more similar to the distribution of weights in the eighteenth century, Stravinsky's to that of Beethoven and the nineteenth century. Together these pieces might constitute two poles of the neoclassic sonata.

The Modern Sonata: Debussy, Bartók, Poulenc, Carter

But there is yet another sonata tradition in this century, one that stems from Debussy. This tradition shares the textural and harmonic clarity of modern neoclassicism; indeed, with other French music of the late nineteenth and early twentieth centuries, it is one of the roots of modern neoclassicism. This tradition also conceives of the sonata as a multimovement work for concerted instruments (neither Debussy nor Ravel, for instance, wrote a sonata for piano solo) that is in some ways more cohesive than Baroque trio sonatas or such a neo-Baroque work as Thomson's Sonata da Chiesa. But these sonatas do not necessarily adhere to the movement scheme of the Classical tradition, nor do they necessarily have movements in sonata form. Such sonatas as Debussy's always have signposts that link them to sonata form, to the Classical sonata format, to the style(s) of eighteenth-century music, especially eighteenth-century French music. But they are thoroughly and primarily modern in their insistence on compositional freedom and invention in form and harmonic relationships, on newness in texture and phraseology, on a kind of motivic coherence that avoids the developmental language and the progressive organicism of contemporary Germans and Viennese in favor of something much more difficult to pin to the page, something that appeals almost subliminally to the ear.

Debussy's Sonata for Flute, Viola, and Harp (1915; see chapter 4) was the second in a projected series of six sonatas "for diverse instruments," as the title pages of the individual sonatas read; the first was for cello and piano. *En blanc et noir*, as I noted in chapter 2, could be seen as a sort of pre-first sonata in this series; it shows many of the same musical procedures as the three completed sonatas, and it shows the same nationalistic fervor on Debussy's part. In these works the composer consciously returns to some of the elements of eighteenth-century French music. Moreover, he signs the sonatas "Claude Debussy, musicien français," a musical taking-up of arms against the Germans. In both *En blanc et noir* and the Sonata for Flute, Viola, and Harp, Debussy adheres to the model of a three-movement work, the first movement moderate or fast in tempo, the second a slow movement, and the third an animated finale. But in the Sonata for Violin and Piano (1916), his last completed work, he does not. This seems to be the earliest instance of a newly free sonata conception that continues through at least the middle years of the century.

The first movement of the Violin Sonata varies considerably in tempo. Although marked *allegro vivo* (with a *meno mosso* in the central section), because of the nature of its melodic material, it does not sound *allegro vivo* continuously throughout. In fact, one is not aware of a basic tempo until the music is well past the first principal theme of the movement. The second movement is scherzolike, labeled "Intermède" ("intermezzo") and marked *fantasque et léger*. The last movement, marked *très animé*, begins with figuration not unlike that of the last movement of *En blanc et noir* or of one of Debussy's "weather" pieces (the piano prelude "Le vent dans la plaine," for example, or "Jardins sous la pluie"), but a recurrence of the first principal theme of the first movement upsets the sense of temporality, obscuring any clarity of tempo and meter. Although there is no slow movement as such, slow sections are scattered across each of the three movements. These sections give relief and contrast to the otherwise faster tempos; more important, they change the formal perception of each individual movement as they bind all three movements together into a coherent whole.

In addition to these temporal vagaries, each of the three movements is a sectional form. No two are alike in their sectional contrasts or successions; none follows at all closely a conventional form. In this sense, the sonata resembles *En blanc et noir* more than it does the Sonata for Flute, Viola, and Harp; but that is more a family resemblance than real identity.

A listing the sections of the movements will begin to demonstrate the coherence of Debussy's Violin Sonata. Although a schematization does not account for the moment-to-moment continuity and coherence of melodic and textural connections, it should reaffirm that coherence, which is more pronounced and effective than a simple prose description might imply. As Figure 5.1 demonstrates, although the sonata has some of the benchmarks of a sonata form, these are only the most general signs, directed at conventional expectations about format, kinds of musical language, and so on. More essentially, the sonata is a linear and continuous spinning-out of melodies, and the logic of their appearance and use is not that of the sonata idea, whether conceived of as a dramatic scenario or as a more purely musical scheme of the move to a foreign key and a return to the original tonic. Motives are introduced that later gain importance through repetition, although their first appearances had given no intimation of this. Conversely, music that seems to occupy a conventionally important place—the apparent second theme of mm. 42–63—does not reappear at all.

Yet Debussy is not "deconstructing" sonata form, commenting on it, even turning a traditional genre to modern uses. The real working method of the movement is integration: not the duality/variety/unity scheme of more traditional sonata forms, but a move from multiplicity

mm. 1–63		"Exposition"
	1–21	1st theme (including, in mm. 18–21, an important cadence/climax figure)
	22–41	bridge
	42–63	2d theme (which will not reappear); mm. 56–59, the cadence/climax figure
64–83		transition (although sounding very static); *portamento* (glissando) first appears in violin, mm. 72–73
84–149		"Development" (new material; some will reappear in the "Recapitulation")
150–255		"Recapitulation"
	150–85	analogous to mm. 1–27
	186–95	new "bridge" (not that of mm. 22–41)
	196–215	alternation of the first theme (mm. 1, 150) with figure from the end of the "Development" (mm 133–45), repeated notes and *portamento* up a whole step and back
	226–55	2-part coda: mm. 226–37 using the cadence/climax figure originally from mm. 56–59; mm. 238–55 on the repeated note/*portamento* figure originally from mm. 133–45; the final cadence is plagal (iv–i or IV–i), not authentic.

FIGURE 5.1. Formal design, first movement, Debussy's Sonata for Violin and Piano.

to unity that takes place in the last half (or slightly less) of the movement. The first sign of this comes not in the "exposition" proper, but in what I have called the transition of mm. 64–83, a section that seems quite motionless. The function of this section is to defuse the first section of the piece, to separate it from the "development" after m. 84 in order to emphasize the newness of the latter. Because of this wealth of different music, then, the last section of the movement is not a recapitulation, nor a reprise and reconsolidation (except perhaps on the harmonic level), but an integration of previously unrelated material and a concentration on a reduced number of earlier themes. The transition from the "development" into the "recap" maintains the same figuration, simply introducing the movement's first theme on top of it. Instead, of reprising the contrasting second theme of the "exposition", Debussy insists on two other figures, from the end of the first theme and the end of the "development." From rather distant places earlier in the movement, both figures have functioned as cadential figures; Debussy continues to reintroduce them more frequently so that they become, together, the cadential figures for the movement as a whole.

Time, in this piece, seems unidirectional, rapidly flowing, and absolutely unrepeatable. The principal musical concentration here seems to be not on the harmonic but on the melodic and motivic.[10] Tunes and their characteristic sections follow upon one another, internally spun out from small figures and linked more or less closely by transitional figuration that is analogous to harmonic modulation, one thing gradually becoming another. What happens at the macrolevel, the structural level, is similar. Recapitulation is impossible, since the necessary disintegration of material has not taken place. Literal repetition is equally impossible, since that implies a static (or even nonexistent) time. Rather, Debussy retains three ideas from the first half of the movement: the first theme (mm. 5–14), the oscillating figure that functioned as a climax and cadential gesture (mm. 18–21), and the repeated note/*portamento* that appears at the end of the "development" and becomes another gesture of closure. Moreover, Debussy retains not only these three ideas but their function as well. The first theme remains a primary melodic theme. The other two, neither particularly melodic, are cadential, and insistence on them brings the movement as a whole to its close. That these two cadential figures are first heard at widely separated points in the movement and are now juxtaposed creates the integration that seems to be the structural function of the last section of the movement, and that gives the movement its satisfying closure.

The structural layout of the second and third movements is, mutatis mutandis, not unlike that of the first movement (see Figs. 5.2 and 5.3). Both employ sectional forms, their sections defined by melody, rhythm, texture, and tempo as much as harmonic framework, a linear succession of ideas whose sense of cohesion comes from the smooth

mm. 1–8   introduction (*fantasque et léger*)
  19–26   A
  27–45   B (*scherzando*)
  46–59   A' (*au mouvement*)
  60–82   C (*scherzando; portamento* marked *doux et expressif*; at m. 72,
                  violin and piano two octaves apart, repeated thirds in
                  between, marked *expressif et sans rigueur*)
  83–100   A'
  101–12   C' (*meno mosso* figure from end of C, mm. 72ff.)
  112–35   A'/C" (from mm. 56–57); the coda, mm. 130–35, reminiscent
                  of the coda of the first movement, a plagal cadence in G
                  with a long, spiraling descent in the violin

FIGURE 5.2. Formal design, second movement, Debussy's Sonata for Violin and Piano.

transitions from one section to the next and from the occasional repetitions and recompositions of earlier material. The biggest surprise in the sonata comes at the beginning of the third movement, when we hear the reprise of the first theme of the first movement, in a completely new context. Here that first theme functions as an introduction, and its contrast to the principal melody of the third movement lends the latter even more regularity and stability than it might otherwise have had: the theme of the first movement points up the regularity of the new theme. The rest of the movement is not, at the most general level, dissimilar to the first movement, a succession of sections that focuses in its last half on a reduced, concentrated vocabulary. If the second movement is the most radically unintegrated sectional form of the three movements, this return to the methodology of the first movement brings about a sense of integration at the largest level that is analogous to that of the first movement individually.

Debussy's sonata form, then, seems to be a reinvention of the genre. It is not new wine in old bottles, for no specific model exists in

mm. 1–28   introduction (including first theme of first movement)
  29–44   A (regular, scalar melody in $\frac{9}{16}$)
  45–66   B
  67–84   A'
  85–99   C (twice as slow as A and B; completely new material)
  100–115   introduction, but recomposed
  116–45   A/first-movement theme, recomposed
  146–53   A (as originally done)
  154–71   A''' (new accompanimental figure in the violin, A in
                   augmentation in the piano)
  172–207   coda and final cadence, based on A melody

FIGURE 5.3. Formal design, third movement, Debussy's Sonata for Violin and Piano.

earlier music, no model that matches more than a single feature of Debussy's work. A sort of sonata ideal, absolute music for concerted instruments, has been retained. The idea of eventual unity achieved through integration (however accomplished) is also apparent. But completely absent from Debussy's sonata, unlike Ravel's sonata forms or the contemporary Viennese compositions, is the idea of a formal hierarchy as a structural agent. The latter depends on a sense of time that can move forward and backward, where memory of past events is essential to comprehension, even apperception, of current events and the prediction of the future. Debussy's sonata seems singularly unpredictable; one does not know at any given point in the sonata what is likely to happen next. Rather, all one's attention is directed to what is currently taking place. This is why the last parts of the first and third movements achieve a sense of unity through integration rather than recapitulation. We have not heard a theme or motive "worked"; rather, we hear repeated and then convincingly juxtaposed themes. Memory has not been thrown by the wayside; it is always essential to any sort of musical perception at all. But since Debussy's sonata is neither dramatic scenario (thesis-antithesis-synthesis) nor rational argument, the sort of memory that these require is irrelevant. This is the essential part of Debussy's modernism, to which later composers responded. He insisted on the present as the locus of activity and the focus of perception; yet the present is always the vehicle of constant change. To fix this in a "form"—by its very definition static—is impossible. To exploit the continually new present by insisting on it is a modern device: one does not establish a unity after the fact, since that cannot really be done. But if one focuses on process rather than object, the problem seems to disappear. The continuous spinning-out of arabesques is such a technique; its essential structural quality is its very continuity. That this occurs at every level of Debussy's Violin Sonata, from the phrase through the section to the movement to the sonata as a whole, achieves through new means the integration of elements that is at the core of a Classicist aesthetic. It is Debussy's particular genius to combine this Classicist unity with a seemingly paradoxical focus on the present and the contingent.

A slightly later sonata in the same mold is Bartók's First Sonata for Violin and Piano (1921). In his cogent discussion of the work, Halsey Stevens makes a number of points about its procedures.[11] The first of these is that there is little exchange of material between violin and piano in the first movement—peculiar enough in a concerted chamber work. The second is the filling up of the chromatic vocabulary and the frequent lack of pitch repetition, something Stevens hears as incipient serialization, and indeed the sort of handling of pitches that did precede Schoenberg's arrival at serialism in the early 1920s (i.e., at precisely the time of the Bartók sonata). Stevens also mentions the frequency of octave displacements in Bartók's melodic lines, moving a particular note from its "right" register to the octave above or below; he hears Schoenberg again in this, but he also quotes Bartók's study *Hungarian Folk Music* on the Hungarian peasants' free use of octave displacement in their singing.

A more debatable point is this statement by Stevens: "With the exception of [one] motive, the materials [in the first movement of the sonata] are merely varied upon their reappearance; they do not grow organically, and consequently they violate the fundamental ethos of the sonata idea."[12] As we have seen in this chapter, and will see again in chapter 6, there are sonata ideas and there are sonata ideas. The "idea" of Bartók's First Violin Sonata—its way of proceeding, of ordering and organizing its materials—falls under the general rubrics of statement, development, and reunification (reconsolidation, but including further variation and recomposition). It is a post–Beethovenian sonata idea, and especially a post–Debussyan one: precisely because of the emphasis on continuing variation, and because of Bartók's harmonic procedure here as well, the listener's ear is directed constantly to the event at hand, to the eternal *now* of the music as it flows past. The sonata is an essentially linear work, not a hierarchically structured one, as one might find in Schoenberg or Ravel. It is no less a sonata for that; but it is a modern, not a neoclassic, sonata.

The harmonic scheme at work in this piece is one of polytonality, a phenomenon that needs commentary. Polytonality, far from being the pervasive technique that many scholars find in the music of the 1920s, lies, I believe, rather in the ear of the listener. My own ears, for whatever reasons, are slow to pick up any intimations of polytonality. The principal reason for this, I think, is that true polytonality demands the audible working of different tonal hierarchies and progressions at the same time, and my ear rarely hears this sort of textural stratification. What I hear (and, therefore, what I find in scores) is a particularly rich chromatic harmony of varying densities; that is, I hear complex simultaneities rather than simultaneous simple structures. One example is the so-called *Petrushka* chord, a simultaneity consisting of the C-major and F♯-major triads. Although people describe it this way, and sometimes even call it an instance of polytonality, it is impossible in the experience of Stravinsky's *Petrushka* to hear two simultaneous keys at work; one can hear a complex extended sonority, even a polychord, but not polytonality. (We may also be dealing with a historical phenomenon here. What sounded more clearly like polytonality in 1920 or so, to ears still surrounded by tonality, may sound quite different to ears of the late twentieth century that have experienced the musics of the postserialists, Cage, and the "classical" atonality of the 1950s and beyond.)

That said, we can touch briefly on the harmonic scheme of the Bartók sonata. According to Stevens, the sonata is in C♯ minor. Stevens himself is drawn to a polytonal hearing of the sonata. He points out its final cadence, in which the violin plays an E-major triad, the pianist's right hand C♯ major, and the pianist's left hand C♯ minor. Polytonality is certainly an available option, for the harmonic vocabulary and combinations of the entire sonata may be heard as the imbrication of different harmonic planes. But ultimately, the perception of polytonality, unlike that of atonality, lies in the listener's ear.

Beyond these questions, Bartók's First Violin Sonata is quite straightforward: the first (sonata) movement is an extremely flexible *allegro appassionato,* the second movement a slow sectional form with highly lyric materials, and the last movement a sectional dancelike *perpetuum mobile* based on Hungarian rhythms (and perhaps ethnically derived modes). But these do not make the sonata a modern "Baroque" or "Classical" work. It is, rather, a modern sonata pure and simple, modern in its handling of the sonata idea—or in the handling of *its* sonata idea—and in its ever-continuous temporality, the concentration always on the present moment that seems to be a hallmark of the modern era. In this way the sonata follows the example of Debussy, although I am not about to claim any direct influence of the French composer on this particular work. We will see in chapter 6 how this temporality translates into Bartók's six string quartets, of which two had already been written by the time of this sonata. Before we pass to the string quartet, however, we will look at another directly post–Debussyan sonata, Poulenc's Sonata for Clarinet and Piano (1962), and a fully modern sonata by Elliott Carter.

The Poulenc Clarinet Sonata is both post–Debussyan and, in a loose sort of way, post–Stravinskian. Its movements are sectional, the first more conventionally so than the latter two. It is tonal, and almost functionally so, but spiked with Poulenc's characteristic seventh and ninth chords. It last movement is highly rhythmic, its regularities countermanded by abruptly elided phrases (as the phrases in the slow movements are often unexpectedly lengthened). The sonata is almost entirely homophonic, and largely melodic in focus: we hear tunes with striking accompanimental harmonies rather than a hierarchical harmonic scheme articulated by melody.

At the same time, the sonata is highly individual. Its three movements are marked *allegro tristamente, romanza* (*très calme*), and *allegro con fuoco* (*très animé*). Each movement has a sectional form. The first movement is ternary, superficially resembling both a traditional sonata form and a Debussyan sonata form. Its first A section is a miniature ternary form, like that of Stravinsky's Concerto for Two Solo Pianofortes, but its middle B section does not develop material directly from the first A. The final A section, much the shortest of the three, recalls the two principal themes of the first A section in reverse order. One might better hear this final A as an elided reprise of only the final sections of the first

A. In any event, the movement works not as a sonata form but as an ABA. It falls into the sonata tradition because it is a concerted work of absolute music, and because after Debussy, insistence on first-movement sonata form is much less rigorous.

The second and third movements are even more sectional than the first, and their sections are more closely interwoven. After their presentation, the two principal themes of the second movement alternate at frequent intervals through the middle of the movement until the first principal theme returns in the final section. The movement is thus also an ABA, in which the first A has two themes stated separately, the B is a closer alternation of the motives of these themes, and the final A is the first theme alone. One might hear this pattern as another variation on the general scheme of the first movement. The third movement of the sonata is rondolike in both form and character; its central section is in great contrast to the other main themes, and the treatment of the whole resembles the sonata rondo. Since this latter form—ABACABA—can also be heard in the most general sense as an ABA, once again we have another variation on a similar form for each of the sonata's three movements. These large-scale formal resemblances between individual movements are another characteristic that makes the work cohere as a sonata, for these resemblances do not normally occur in modern suites or simple sets of pieces.

One final aspect of the Poulenc Clarinet Sonata is its borrowings, in the principal themes of the first and second movements, from other works. The main lyrical theme of the first movement (from rehearsal no. 2) comes from Poulenc's one-act opera *La voix humaine* (1959, on a play by Jean Cocteau), where it is heard most clearly and in its entirety at the very end. The single character of *La voix humaine* is a young woman who has been deserted by her lover. The opera consists of an extended, interrupted telephone conversation between the woman—in turn loving, forgiving, pleading, hysterical, resigned—and the lover, whose voice is never heard. At the end of the opera, where this particular melody is heard, she seats herself on her bed, holding the telephone in her arms, tells her lover that she is strong, and asks him to hang up quickly as she continues to say that she loves him. The clear implication is that she dies.

The second movement's principal theme is related to the fifth movement of Poulenc's *Gloria,* the "Dominus Deus, Agnus Dei." In neither case, however, is there any sort of thematic connection between the sonata and the original source of the two melodies. Nothing in the sonata points to *La voix humaine* or to the *Gloria,* to their ideas, their musical treatment of the same material, or their existence as, respectively, musical narrative and musical ritual celebration. One can only assume here that Poulenc had written two melodies that pleased him and that he wanted to enjoy further. Both are well suited to the clarinet and may have given rise to the idea of composing a clarinet sonata; or the desire to write such a sonata may have reminded Poulenc of them. At any rate, they have been turned here into absolute music.

The final sonata under the "modern" rubric is one already discussed, Elliott Carter's Sonata for Violoncello and Piano (1948). In chapter 2 I discussed the work only in terms of its handling of time and in its aspect of dramatic scenario. Here, at the end of this chapter, we can look rather at the sonata as an exemplar of the modern incarnation of the sonata ideal. Although Carter's music of the 1930s and early 1940s—before the Piano Sonata and the Cello Sonata—was in an American neoclassicist (i.e., post–Copland) vein, with these two compositions he apparently no longer felt constrained to compose the music of his immediate tradition, but instead to invent something new. This is one of the essential qualities of modernism, as it had been of Romanticism 120 years earlier. If the sense of a score as a dramatic scenario is not entirely modern—one has only to think of Beethoven, or the Brahms piano concertos—Carter's construction of that scenario certainly is. But most of all, it is the sense of time created by Carter's Cello Sonata—the sense of time it conveys to, even imposes on, the listener, and the sense of time necessary for its very composition in the first place—that places the work squarely under the modernist rubric. Carter's models (the word is too strong) may have been Debussy and, conceivably, Ives; certainly his piece would be impossible without them. But the sonata is essentially a work of its era, and a work that is generative, fertile, rather than a summary revivification or reexamination.

Thus the sonata in our century. It has been many things to many composers since the beginning of the twentieth century, and it is best dealt with conceptually (various types of sonatas ideas and ideals) rather than chronologically. I have omitted many sonatas from this chapter on precisely these grounds: the sonatas of Hindemith, for example; the various chamber works of Shostakovich; Cage's Sonatas and Interludes (1948) for prepared piano; Boulez's neoclassic, in fact neo-Schoenbergian Sonatina for Flute and Piano (also 1948). All these fall into the categories I have laid forth in this chapter with the most telling examples I could find: the modern "Baroque" sonata, closer to the earlier eighteenth century than to the later; the modern "Classical" sonata, those most indebted to Mozart and especially Beethoven (early and middle); and the modern sonata, beginning with Debussy and Ives, resuming in Carter. Of these three principal types, the second or the modern "Classical" sonata is by far the most numerous, even overwhelmingly so. The least common is the genuinely modern sonata; as we have seen in previous chapters, the interests and preoccupations of twentieth-century composers have moved in different ways. Few modern composers besides Carter (and perhaps Boulez) have found a sonata idea that matches their musical predilections. It is possible, however, to follow the sonata in combination with a particular genre, the string quartet, and cover quite a bit of the musical history of twentieth-century chamber music. That is the burden of our final chapter.

Notes

1. In the later eighteenth century, this was often reversed: in Mozart's violin and piano sonatas, the piano is the more important instrument and the violin embellishes and ornaments.

2. See Halsey Stevens, *The Life and Music of Béla Bartók*, rev. ed. (London, 1964), 171–72.

3. Arbie Orenstein, *Ravel: Man and Musician* (New York, 1975), 183.

4. Eric Walter White, *Stravinsky: The Composer and His Works*, 2d ed. (Berkeley and Los Angeles, 1979), 390.

5. Paul Jacobs, liner notes to his recording (with Ursula Oppens) of Stravinsky's music for two pianos and piano four hands (Nonesuch H-71347, 1978). Jacobs also mentions in these notes the double piano Stravinsky had built for him by Pleyel, "with a keyboard at each end, the two frames set over a single soundboard."

6. White, *Stravinsky*, 584. "Le second mouvement, qui tient lieu d'andante, je l'ai intitulé *Notturno*, en pensant, non pas aux morceaux de caractère rêveur et sans forme déterminée que présentent, par exemple, les nocturnes de Field ou de Chopin, mais aux pièces du XVIII⁰ siècle appelées *Nachtmusik*, ou, mieux encore, aux cassations si fréquentes chez les compositeurs de l'pépoque. Seule ment, chez moi, les différentes parties, qui formaient généralement les ouvrages de ce genre, sont condensés en une seule." My translation.

7. Jacobs, liner notes. This is a very Mallarméan—or perhaps Valéryan—conceit.

8. Stravinsky simply shifts up, from a C-major seventh chord, C–E–G–B, to a D♭-minor triad, D♭–F♭–A♭, the E of the first chord becoming the F♭ of the second, and then to D♭ major, D♭–F♮–A♭.

9. Rosen, *Sonata Forms*.

10. David Lewin, "Some Instances of Parallel Voice-Leading in Debussy," *19th Century Music* 9, no. 1 (Summer 1987): 59–72.

11. Halsey Stevens, *Life and Music of Bartók*, 205–9.

12. Ibid., 208.

CHAPTER SIX

The String Quartet

Despite the modern predilection for new ensembles, the string quartet is still Parnassus for twentieth-century composers. It is a challenging and rewarding genre, with four instruments of the same family offering overlapping ranges and an enormous variety of available sounds. It demands thoroughly professional compositional skills. Finally, composers often want to join their colleagues in a conversation of and in music, across time. To join those composers who have addressed themselves to the string quartet, to address oneself to them, to hear what they have to say, is to make a contribution. Lest this sound too mystical, I quote Pierre Boulez:

> "Some people," [Michel Butor] writes, "may think that, while intending to write about Baudelaire, I have only succeeded in speaking of myself. It would certainly be better to say that it was Baudelaire who spoke of me. *He speaks of you.*" If you question the masters of an earlier period with perseverance and conviction you become the medium of their replies: they speak of you through you.[1]

This can happen not only in writing criticism of an earlier writer or composer, but in considering the art of another while creating one's own. The occasion of the Boulez passage, for example, was his large work for soprano and orchestra *Pli selon pli*, presented as a "portrait" of the French poet Stéphane Mallarmé.[2] Composers undertaking a string quartet often consult earlier examples, especially Beethoven's,[3] not only to review ways of handling textures, but also to establish oneself firmly in the territory of the string quartet. The resulting work may become, on any number of levels, a conversational musical response to an earlier work.

Before World War I: Ravel, Schoenberg, Webern, Stravinsky, and Ives

The first string quartet considered here is an example of this musical response. That is the String Quartet of Maurice Ravel (1902–3), in some ways a response to the 1893 quartet of Claude Debussy, but as modern a work as Debussy's is Romantic.

The Ravel Quartet adheres precisely to the schemes for the sonata outlined in chapter 5. It is a cyclic work in four movements: an *allegro moderato* sonata form, *très doux;* a scherzo and trio, *assez vif—très rythmé;* an ABA' slow movement, *très lent,* incorporating phrases from the first movement; and a rondolike finale, *vif et agité,* alternating sections of ⅝ and ¾ meters, and also recasting material from the first movement. As is usual with Ravel's music, the forms are not at all difficult to hear, despite Ravel's own verdict that formally this quartet was not realized entirely successfully.[4] What is more interesting to consider is the musical space that the quartet defines, musical space as Schoenberg meant it (see chapter 2). Here, too, as in Schoenberg's *Verklärte Nacht* and his Second String Quartet, we have an absolutely unified musical space, unified through the cyclic use of themes, thematic transformation of motivic materials from the themes, and similar harmonic and textural devices throughout the four movements of the work.

Example 6.1 gives the principal motives from the first, second, and fourth movements of the quartet. Motives *a* through *c* come from the first theme group, motive *d* comes from the bridge, *e* the transition into the second theme, and *f* from the development. These last two are examples of the sort of transformation and smooth motivic development pervasive in Ravel. The transition into the second theme (motive *e*) was the principal motive of the first theme, treated heterophonically in the two violins. The repeated pitch A is the most important note of that first theme, and Ravel repeats it with the rhythms associated with the theme (triplets are first heard in conjunction with the first theme in mm. 31, 33, and 38, midway through the bridge). The doubled eighth notes in the violin, a sort of written-out *ritardando* in contrast to the preceding triplets, move us smoothly into the second theme. This theme retains some of the contour and rhythms of the first, but at the same time, it changes the function of the note A. In the first theme, A was a stable pitch, the third of the tonic triad, the first note of the melody and the one to which the melody immediately returns. In the bridge motive *d*, a rhythmic transformation of the beginning of motive *a*, the pitch can still be heard as rather stable melodically (because of the repetition), although part of a harmonically unstable chord. In the second theme, by contrast, the note A serves as a sort of launching pad for the melody, which jumps up a perfect fifth, turns down again, but never

EXAMPLE 6.1. Ravel, String Quartet, first movement. © 1910 Durand S.A. Editions Musicales Editions A.R.I.M.A. and Durand S.A. Editions Musicales Joint Publication. Used by Permission of the Publisher.

(a) Violin I, mm. 1–2

(b) Violin I, mm. 9–10

(c) Violin II, mm. 21–23

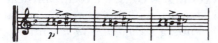

(d) Violin I, mm. 24–25

(e) Violins I and II, mm. 47–57

(continued)

(f) Viola, mm. 102–5

(g) Violin I, mm. 1–2

Assez vif – Très rythmé

(h) Violin I, mm. 13–16

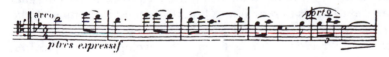

(i) Cello, mm. 89–93

(continued)

Example 6.1. (*continued*)

(j) Violin I, m. 44

(k) Violin I, mm. 54–56

regains the original A until the very end of the theme (after the melody has dropped farther down and returned upward to the pitch).

There are two major changes here: the melody tries to return downward to A, but never does, reaching only B♭ and thus setting up a tension analogous to the leading tone/tonic tension in a rising scale. This tension is partly what gives the melody its melancholy sweetness. The other change is that this melody, unlike the first theme, is not in a major or minor mode, but in the Phrygian mode on A. This sets up a tantalizing harmonic dichotomy: the notes of the Phrygian mode on A are precisely those of F major, the key of this movement and of the quartet as a whole, and of D minor, the relative minor of F major and the key of this second theme. So the melody somehow sounds distanced from its surroundings, and yet is not alien to them: its pitches are the same as its underlying harmonies, but its principal note (its "tonic") is A, whereas the harmonic tonic of this passage is D. When the second theme reappears in the recapitulation, the effect is essentially the same, but minimized. The melody returns at exactly the same pitch level as in the exposition, but the harmonies underneath it are now in F major, the tonic of the entire movement, not D minor. The harmonic ninths of the exposition are now sevenths—relatively more consonant and stable. Although the A that begins the melody is the third of the tonic triad, the melody is in the Phrygian mode, and the B♭ wants to return to A but never does; if attenuated, the melancholic sweetness of the theme persists.

Motive *f* in Example 6.1 is from the development of the first movement. A new theme, it is obviously derived from the accompaniment figure *c*, from the end of the first thematic section of the exposition, and the second theme; its end resembles motive *b*, part of the first theme itself. Motives *g*, *h*, and *i* are from the second movement. Motives *j* and *k* are important motives from the last movement, and are obviously derived from the first theme of the first movement. Motive *j* works as a transition from the ⅜ principal section of the movement to the ¾; motive *k* is the second principal theme of the last movement.

It would be easy to analyze the entire Ravel quartet from a perspective of motives and motivic development. But the first real difficulty of such an approach would be—as it is with Schoenberg—isolating what is motivic and specific to this piece from that which is more generic, more an element of Ravel's musical language or the language of the music of his time and place. For example, a great deal of the bass motion in the quartet is scalar, and the chords move by stepwise root progression, not around the circle of fifths. (There are also important passages where the chords are a third apart.) The opening cello line introduces this pattern; its first four measures are an ascending F-major scale through two octaves, its next four (the consequent phrase) descending through the same range and primarily by step, but in darker and more unsettled keys (A♭ and F minor) to a cadence on a G-minor triad, approached by half step from above (F minor in its first inversion), perhaps a foreshadowing of the Phrygian elements later. The harmony underlying the second theme is somewhat more traditionally functional—i–♭ii–iv–V–i—but this is the only section of the exposition where such root movement by fifth predominates. The development section begins with a long descent in the cello by whole step—B♭–A♭–G♭–E–D—although because the notes last so long and underlie triadic harmonies, there is no characteristically whole-tone flavor to the passage.

Ravel also avoids even cadential fifth progressions. The last cadence of the first movement is G⁹–F, or V⁹/V to I, without the V. That of the second movement is an augmented-sixth chord resolving outward to the tonic triad, B♭–E–G♯–C–E to an A minor chord. The final cadence of the entire quartet is a string of major triads, rising by consecutive minor thirds and then falling back one, F–G♯–B–D–F–G♯–F. This is motivic, but it is primarily an aspect of Ravel's harmonic language, one he shared with much French music of the late nineteenth and early twentieth centuries. The movement by second and third rather than fifth lends a vaguely modal quality to the sound, although the work itself is not modal except in certain clearly demarcated sections (e.g., the second theme of the first movement). The music, as we have seen, is a mixture of modal aspects with tonal triads and some tonal progressions.

All the aspects of the piece that are not specifically tonal are absorbed into a generally functional framework by the end of the last movement. That movement is the simplest formally of the work's four movements, with only two principal strains. The second of these is the reworked first theme of the first movement, now combined with clear functional harmonies over the circle of fifths and straightforward ii–V–I cadences. The chromatic elements of the second movement, which recur here in the main strain, are resolved into a stable triadic tonality. The rhythmic play of the second movement, ⁶⁄₈ against ³⁄₄, reappears in the contrast (*not* combination in this movement) of ⁶⁄₈ and ³⁄₄, which is resolved strongly in favor of the latter, more stable and more usual meter. This resolution is reinforced by the melody's recapitulation of the first theme of the first movement. Ravel is doing something here that is precisely analogous to Schoenberg's procedure in *Verklärte Nacht,* working all its disparate elements into a clear triadic tonic. The real difference between Ravel and Schoenberg in these pieces lies essentially in two areas: the harmonic language (though not how the language is used) and the relationship of form to texture. Schoenberg's harmonic language is thoroughly chromatic, filling and overfilling a lush musical space. Ravel's language is triadic, modal, and diatonic. There are, simply, fewer pitches in play in any given section.

The second distinction, the use of texture, relates to the larger issues of Romanticism and classicism or neoclassicism. Schoenberg's music is pervasively polyphonic, in the tradition of German Romanticism, of both Wagner and Brahms. (This constant polyphony is obviously a concomitant to the rhythmic instability of so much of *Verklärte Nacht*). Ravel's distinction between homophony and polyphony is the distinction between instability and stability, created through texture. This is a principal element of the neoclassical language of the twentieth century, and also of the tradition of French classicism that Ravel inherited from his teacher Fauré, and that runs from Lully through Bizet to Pierre Boulez. The balance of homophony and polyphony in Ravel's String Quartet, and in other neoclassical works, makes it a completely different sort of piece from *Verklärte Nacht.* The latter is constantly progressing in a unidirectional temporal flow, cumulative and unrelenting, insisting on final resolution, final arrival. Ravel's sections are more in balance: they fall into a hierarchy, of course, but one that drives less insistently to a final resolution. Such works are less relentlessly teleological than the music of German-speaking Europe since Beethoven,[5] and consequently less angst-ridden to many ears. This continuing use of texture to delineate received forms (or allusions to those forms, as in the late Debussy pieces discussed in other chapters) is one of the distinguishing stylistic hallmarks of the early years of this century.

Four other pre–World War I works for string quartet exemplify other important aspects of the music of those years: the so-called breakdown of functional tonality around 1908; the writing of extraordinarily short instrumental miniatures, so brief that they seem static and outside of time, and depending on motive and color for their effect; the use of extramusical programs, but at the same time the rejection of Romanticism. All of these four works—Schoenberg's Second String Quartet, Op. 10, Webern's Op. 9 Bagatelles, Stravinsky's Three Pieces for String Quartet, and Ives's Second String Quartet—come from the five-year period immediately preceding World War I. Such compositional diversity is itself a hallmark of this period; it does not occur again, at least on this grand a scale, until the 1960s. These four works display various aspects of the early modern years, including aspects that many composers, among them all the ones discussed here except Ives, rejected in turn in the years after 1918.

Chapter 3 discussed the last two movements of Schoenberg's Op. 10 String Quartet, which include the setting for soprano of poems by Stefan George. That discussion concentrated on text-music relationships and the question of tonality in the last movement. Here we will discuss the first two movements of the quartet and consider their place in the quartet as a whole.

Every movement of the quartet except the last is in a standard and easily discernable form—sonata form, scherzo, theme and variations. What is new to Schoenberg's Second String Quartet is the interpenetration of classically stable and unstable areas, and his constant development of motives in a pervasively chromatic language.[6] Again, Schoenberg learned this from Brahms.[7] He combines the motivic development here with the desire for a totally cohesive, cyclic work that he found in Liszt and Beethoven.

Example 6.2 gives the principal motives of Schoenberg's Second Quartet. Motive *a* is the beginning of the first theme. Motive *b* is the principal motive of the bridge section, which is almost four times as long as the first theme section. Motive *c,* closely resembling motive *b,* is the second theme; its two halves are developed separately in the movement. Motive *d* appears as cited first in m. 58; but it has developed *ab*

EXAMPLE 6.2 Schoenberg, String Quartet No. 2, Op. 10, first movement. Used by permission of Belmont Music Publishers, Pacific Palisades, CA 90272.

(a) Violin I, mm. 1–2

(b) Viola, mm. 12–15

(c) Violin I, mm. 43–5

(continued)

EXAMPLE 6.2. *(continued)*

(d) Violin I, mm. 58–59

(e) mm. 39–43

(f) mm. 14–17

ovo from an accompanimental figure at the beginning of the bridge. The cadential figure, *e*, appears throughout this movement and elsewhere in the quartet, though it is never subjected to development. Finally, motive *f* is one of the principal themes of the second movement, the scherzo.

Motives *b*, *c*, *d*, and *e* are like the principal motives of Schoenberg's *Verklärte Nacht* in that they begin after the downbeat, which gives them some forward propulsion and permits Schoenberg to place them easily anywhere within a measure or across bar lines. But these motives are far less volatile rhythmically than those of *Verklärte Nacht,* and motives *a* and *f,* the principal themes for the first and second movements, are quite regular rhythmically and melodically. The Second Quartet is less dramatic—less demonic and less narrative in intent—than *Verklärte Nacht,* so its basic materials are necessarily different.

The first movement, and particularly its exposition, gives the listener the material for the rest of the quartet: not simply the motives and their handling, but the harmonic framework and textural devices heard throughout the piece. The exposition begins without preamble, with motive *a* in a clear homophonic setting and even what appears to be a four-bar phrase. But this conventionality is sidestepped and developed. The first violin lands on a B♯, and suddenly, for three measures, all four instruments play a C natural, crescendoing from *pianissimo* to *forte*. C natural is as far as one can get from F♯ in classical tonality, a tritone away.[8] There are more surprises: C natural becomes the third of the key of A minor, in which the theme is repeated, and then A becomes the third of F major, where the first theme cadences. Stable melodically and rhythmically, the first theme is far from stable harmonically. It is also, unusually, by far the shortest section of the exposition. We are almost immediately plunged into the bridge section, a long and developmental section based on two principal motives of its own.

The first of these, motive *b*, is introduced in the viola and spun out into a long, expansive melody before being passed on to the first violin. The second is simply a short five-note accompanimental figure in the second violin, initially oscillating between two notes before a third note is introduced. This little cell also continues to grow, virtually imperceptibly, expanding in range and rising in register throughout the bridge, eventually doubled by second violin and viola. It is briefly interrupted at the end of the bridge by the return of motive *a* in the violins at a climax that yields (with the cadential figure) to the second theme. But this bridge figure will return during the second theme's presentation and, in m. 58, will supersede that theme to lead us to the concluding theme of the exposition.

The second theme, marked *sehr ausdrucksvoll* ("very expressively"), is like the first theme in its chromatic setting—although it is much more chromatic and less triadic than the first theme—and in its replacement by a developing figure, the figure of the bridge. But the second-theme group is much longer than the first, longer indeed than the first theme and the bridge together; and even after its arrival at a *sforzando, fortissimo* closing theme (m. 68) it continues in the same developmental, chromatic, rhythmically propulsive vein, which dies out only gradually. The weight of the exposition thus comes at the end, and it is completely unresolved. This device is repeated at larger levels: the weight of the movement and of the quartet are also at the end, and the first movement seems unresolved, unfinished, at its close. Only with the third movement, a sort of development of the first two, and the fourth, which transcends them, does the quartet finish.

The first-movement development, not coincidentally shorter than the exposition (each of the main sections of this movement is shorter than the one before), continues the developmental practices of the exposition—fragmentation, spinning out, motivic extension, rapid chromatic harmonic motion, contrapuntal textures, and so on—with the additional device of combining motives from different themes. This is, of course, standard practice for a development. The recapitulation is quite out of the ordinary, however, and its treatment is one of the reasons for the movement's lack of resolution or stability. Rather than a reconsolidation of what has been fragmented and dispersed in the development, this recapitulation is in truth a second development, although closer to the exposition than the first, "real," development has been. It begins with the first theme stated fully, but in the wrong key; we do not reach a cadence in the tonic, F♯ minor, until the end of the first theme.[9] The first half of the bridge section follows the same general plan as that of the exposition; its second half newly develops the bridge theme and the first theme, as in the exposition. But there is no second theme section in the recapitulation. When we reach that point, the second half of the first theme is used as a transition figure for a prolonged cadence in F♯ minor, and what follows is a coda made from bits of the bridge theme, the cadential figure, and motive *d*.

This sonata form is thus skewed far from the norm. The proportions of the sections are off—the exposition is 89 measures, the development 57, the recapitulation 55, and the coda 32. Within the exposition, the first theme lasts only 11 bars, the bridge 31, and the second-theme group 47. In addition, the harmonic articulation does not coincide with the thematic or melodic articulation. Within the first theme, we move however briefly from F♯ minor to C major. The recapitulation begins in F major, which also has appeared in the first theme of the exposition, and does not move to the tonic, F♯ minor, until fourteen measures later. Finally, the second theme does not appear in the recapitulation or the coda. There are a number of possible explanations—most importantly, the second theme highly resembles the bridge theme, so that another treatment of it could prove repetitious. The result, however, is that the movement as an entity seems incomplete, insufficient. Contrasts have been set up, and balance and adherence to a norm have been implied (the medium, the genre, the relationship of development to exposition), but that balance and adherence have not been realized. The incompleteness of this movement implies that it will be completed on a larger scale, that the latter movements will in some way finish the trajectory opened by the first movement. Our attention is thrown forward to those movements. And after the second, relatively self-contained movement, the third movement again picks up the threads, and the fourth movement leads us to a satisfying conclusion and resolution.

The second movement is a duple-meter scherzo and trio in D minor. The *b* theme of the scherzo is motive *f* in Example 6.2. This scherzo is probably the most self-contained of all four movements, a closed form with clear articulations and a character completely in the Classical-Romantic tradition. (Scherzos in duple meter are not unusual since Beethoven.) It is more concentrated in material, straightforward in its presentation, and with a rougher surface than any other movement. The rusticity is even pointed up at the end of the trio by Schoenberg's quoting "Ach, Du lieber Augustin" and extending it with the melodic bit that goes with "alles ist hin" ("everything's over"). This has been variously explained as his farewell to tonality and his reaction to a serious crisis in his marriage during the composition of the quartet.[10] Neither theory is particularly satisfying: Schoenberg's musical humor, as we saw in *Pierrot lunaire,* is much more sardonic and less bumptious than this supposed reference to the end of tonality; in the same vein, his biographical references in his compositions are extremely rare (as in his Op. 45 String Trio's depiction of his heart attack) and extremely well hidden. The most rational explanation would see the quotation as a sort of self-mocking reference to the scherzo's down-to-earth and even a little clumsy rusticity.

The third movement, the slow theme and variations, is based on four motives from the first and second movements (see chapter 3). We are now able to sense that this movement has an extraordinary weight in performance, coming as it does after the rough second movement and reprising themes from the first. In a way, this theme and variations is a quasi-development of the first two movements (although the metaphor of development is not to be carried any further, and the fourth movement is in no way a recapitulation): the development that was given rather short shrift in the first movement is expanded here and imbued with a character that deepens the anxiety of the first movement and reinforces its dark colors, but now in a controlled, even almost constricted, format of successive developing variations. If, on the one hand, this is a development of the first two movements, on the other it is a reconsolidation of the musical and emotional world of the first movement, deepened by that contrast with the second movement. It is this reconsolidation that permits Schoenberg (and the soprano) to take leave of earthly surroundings and earthly concerns in the last movement. Having reached an emotional nadir in the supplication of the "Litanei," her prayer is answered in the final movement's mystical rapture, the reunion (or the recognition of unity) with the Holy Fire and the Holy Voice. This fourth movement is a long and fully explored textual and musical conclusion, supplying the first movement and the quartet as a whole with the needed resolution and release. Just as the third movement is meaningless without having heard the first two— one must recognize the musical material and realize that it is now being not only further developed but also supplied with words—so does the first movement remain hanging in midair until we hear the fourth. After two highly structured movements, the fourth returns to the first movement's relative formal freedom; but rather than observe the earlier movement's unsettled formal proportions, "Rapture" is completely linear and unidirectional, moving progressively and almost unhesitatingly forward to the final transport.

The question of tonality remains between two stools in this quartet. On the one hand, the music often moves beyond the boundaries of what may be heard as tonal (organized around a central tone or simultaneity), even further than *Verklärte Nacht* had; on the other, we have not yet moved into the full-blown atonality of Schoenberg's Op. 15 songs, *Das Buch der hängenden Gärten*, or *Pierrot lunaire*. Schoenberg himself wrote about this quartet that in all movements

> there is a clearly recognizable key to be heard at all junctions of the formal structure. But the overwhelming multitude of dissonant sounds could no longer be balanced by occasionally introducing such tonal chords as are ordinarily used to establish a key. It did not seem appropriate to force independent motion into the Procrustean bed of tonality without supporting that tonality at the same time by the harmonic progressions belonging to it. This dilemma was not mine alone, but should have occupied the thinking of all contemporary composers. The fact that I was the first to take the decisive step is not generally held to my credit—which, although I regret it, I must ignore.[11]

Although Schoenberg does not here describe his solution of the dilemma of dissonance and tonality in his Op. 10, it is the same solution we have seen in his formal treatment, in which an initial complexity is interrupted by seemingly unrelated, highly tonal movements, and finally resolved into concord at the end of the fourth movement. The first movement, again, is not really resolved tonally: F♯ minor does return in the coda, but since not all the thematic material returns, and the first theme (which does return) is heard in a different key, the tonal drama of the first movement is never closed. The second and third movements are clearly in single keys, D minor and E♭ minor respectively. The fourth movement begins in an ungraspable atonality and makes it real tonal arrival (albeit in midphrase and even midword) on "löse," in the sentence "Ich löse mich in tönen" (see chapter 3). Schoenberg is only stating the case when he observes that he does not "force" tonality without supporting it with some thoroughness. But the nature of his tonality in the first movement especially, and also in the third and to some degree the second, is such that we can move without shock into the atonal world of the beginning of the fourth movement, and the tonal resolution at its end. Schoenberg's voice leading here, as in *Verklärte Nacht*, is pervasively chromatic. Even the approach to tonal points of arrival is often by half step in the bass as well as in other voices.[12] The shift from the first three movements to the fourth is thus a matter of degree, not a change of language. Omnipresent chromaticism and the establishment of a tonal center only to avoid it thereafter lead us smoothly into the seemingly free-floating tonal world of the last movement. Furthermore, in both the first and last movements, Schoenberg establishes C major as a strong tonal contrast to F♯—at the very beginning of the first theme of the first movement, for example, and at the word "ergebend" (surrendering or yielding) in the last movement. In standard harmonic theory as far as one can get from a tonic F♯, C major works in this quartet both as a sort of substitute dominant (as F♯ does for C in Bartók's Sonata for Two Pianos and Percussion) and as a tonal antithesis. Even if one's sense of pitch does not realize that the same keys are being contrasted, the same key relationship is audible.

In the last analysis, though, we must view Schoenberg's step into atonality in this quartet as being completely interdependent with his text, and thereby with a program for the quartet as a whole. As with *Das Buch der hängenden Gärten* and *Pierrot lunaire*, the musical means are inseparable from the textual material (diction, structure, and theme). Conversely, the text is necessary for the comprehension of the work as a whole: the implications of chromaticism moving into atonality are not so strong in the first movement, much less in the second or even the third, that an atonal fourth movement concluding in the key of the first will be structurally satisfying.

Immediately following Schoenberg's breakthrough compositions of 1908–10 (Op. 10, *Das Buch der hängenden Gärten*, the op. 11 piano pieces and the op. 16 orchestra pieces), he and his pupils began writing extremely brief pieces of extraordinary motivic, timbral, and emotional concentration. Webern's music was the briefest of the brief. These works met with incomprehension then, and occasionally still do today. But Schoenberg prefaced the score of Webern's Bagatelles for String Quartet, Op. 9 (1913), with an introduction that may help us find our way into the music:

Though the brevity of these pieces is a persuasive advocate
for them, on the other hand that very brevity itself requires
an advocate.

Consider what moderation is required to express oneself so briefly. You can stretch every glance out into a poem, every sigh into a novel. But to express a novel in a single gesture, a joy in a breath—such concentration can only be present in proportion to the absence of self-pity.

These pieces will only be understood by those who share the faith that music can say things which can only be expressed in music.

These pieces can face criticism as little as this—or any—belief.

If faith can move mountains, disbelief can deny their existence. And faith is impotent against such impotence.

Does the musician know how to play these pieces, does the listener know how to receive them? Can faithful musicians and listeners fail to surrender themselves to one another?

But what shall we do with the heathen? Fire and sword can keep them down; only believers need to be restrained.

May this silence sound for them.[13]

Schoenberg points out three crucial features of the pieces: their concentration, already mentioned; their absence of self-pity; and their expression of what can be expressed only in music. Their concentration strikes the listener most immediately, of course: because of the discreteness of the notes and the extraordinary variety of timbres (harmonics, bowing by the bridge or on the fingerboard, pizzicato), each individual note or brief phrase seems overloaded with emotional import and color.[14] The Bagatelles are also concentrated in their use of the string quartet as an ensemble. Gone here is the concept of melody as separate from other elements in the musical texture. Instead, one hears each note of all four instruments as belonging to a single melodic line, expressed not only in pitches and phrases but in a melody of tone colors as well. This is Wagner's "endless melody," each note essential, none dispensable.

Phrase structure is a critical feature of listening to (or performing) Webern. Given the separateness of many of the sounds and the frequent silences between them, any sense of phrasing must come from the sense that all notes are melodic, and from observing Webern's tempo markings, all too rarely followed by conductors and chamber groups. Virtually every measure in the Bagatelles, as in most Webern, is marked with at least one tempo indication, often one of more or less gradual slowing or speeding of the basic pulse. In order to realize this, the ensemble must hear and feel as a single organism, must hear each note as belonging to a single shaped unit. This ideal is difficult to realize and requires a great deal of rehearsal, but the combination of technical exactitude and musical freedom is literally essential.[15]

The concentration of the music is also, of course, a matter of form. These six bagatelles follow precisely the scheme of a string quartet's sonata cycle in types of music if not in form. The first bagatelle is a *moderato* (*mässig*), as many first movements are. The second and third bagatelles are scherzolike, *leicht bewegt* and *ziemlich fliessend*. The fourth and fifth bagatelles are slow movements, *sehr langsam* and *äusserst langsam*, and almost frozen in their lack of forward motion. The final bagatelle is again faster, *fliessend*, a return to the world of the beginning. This is a much more conventional ordering than, for instance, Schoenberg's Sechs kleine Klavierstücke, Op. 19, which are more similar to a cycle of gradually darkening piano intermezzi like Brahms's op. 118.

Concentration, finally, is obviously at work in Webern's use of atonality. This sounds paradoxical: as with Schoenberg and Berg, Webern's move into atonality was occasioned by a progressive chromaticism that finally moved beyond any vestigial sense of overriding tonal center. But in Webern's case, the sense of pitch in the Bagatelles is not one of extreme chromaticism, as it was in the last movement of Schoenberg's Op. 10 String Quartet, but of a restriction of the possible pitches to a very reduced choice.[16] Each pitch, because of its isolation in musical space and time, timbral individuality, and ultimate place in a melodic phrase shared among the four instruments, seems especially chosen, necessary, and shaped as a single unit from all the pitches available to the composer. This concentration is only increased by the very soft dynamic range: understatement becomes emphasis.

The concentration is the source of the "absence of self-pity" that Schoenberg noted in these pieces, and of their expressing that which can be expressed only in music. Remarkable here is not particularly the absence of self-pity, but that Schoenberg should choose to emphasize it. Schoenberg's own *Pierrot lunaire*, as we saw, is not lacking in self-pity on both Pierrot's and the Poet's part; and that self-pity comes out through the sort of musical devices we have been discussing here—brevity, concentration, chromaticism, and tonal color. Schoenberg's idol Mahler was also capable of immense self-pity, and the pathos of his symphonies and songs is among the most striking characteristics of his musical world. Schoenberg's praise of Webern's lack of self-pity, then, is his recognition of an independent musical voice, perhaps of a nascent modernity moving away from that aspect of nineteenth-century German Romanticism. Yet at the same time, Schoenberg is at pains to point out that these bagatelles are true music—they express that which only music can express—and, however aphoristically, that they will face the same battles as all true music, attacked by heathens and (he hopes) accepted by the faithful.

Whereas German music is developmental, Stravinsky's music in the years before 1918 may be called modular.[17] Historically his art derives from the recent Russian-French "tradition," from Mussorgsky through Debussy: continuous sound, but not continuous music in the sense of constant motivic development; attention to rhythm as an essential musical factor; often small gestures, brief musical ideas; effects through juxtaposition as much as any smooth transition; downplaying of traditional functional harmonic relations and progressions. *Le sacre du printemps* is one example, and Stravinsky's miniature works of the years 1913–18 are as well, if without the violence or the visceral hold of *Sacre*. The differences between Stravinsky and the Viennese in musical time and musical effect are striking, and they are a result of this "modular" construction.

In chapter 2 we looked briefly at the second of Stravinsky's Three Pieces for String Quartet, the "portrait" of the English clown Little Tich. The general characteristics noted there and in the preceding paragraph apply to the first and third pieces as well. The first piece is a sort of Eastern European ethnic dance, reminiscent of Stravinsky's *Les noces* or the music of Béla Bartók.[18] Its basic metrical unit is one of seven beats, $3 + 2 + 2$, articulated by repetitive patterns in the cello and viola. (The viola also sustains a D pedal throughout the entire piece, characteristic as well of this sort of folk dance.) The second violin, too, follows a sort of modular pattern, descending eighth notes on F♯, E, D♯, and C♯. This is done first a single time, every note marked upbow, beginning on the second beat of a seven-beat unit. Then, several beats later, this descending four-note pattern is repeated twice in immediate succession, the first time played downbow and the second upbow on each note. In this second pattern, first downbow and then upbow, the last two notes always overlap the first two of the recurring seven-beat pattern (see Ex. 6.3). Finally, even the dance-tune proper in the first violin is modular. Restricted to four notes, G–A–B–C, it consists of a single melody twenty-three beats long. This melody is highly repetitive, but since its length does not coincide with that of the pedals in the second violin or the viola-cello duo, it sounds slightly different with each repetition.

Stravinsky's modular use of both pitch and rhythm thus strikes a balance between repetition and variety. Each instrumental unit—first violin, second violin, viola-cello duo—has only four pitches; but the only overlapping pitches are C♯ and D♯, in the second violin and the cello, and C♮, in the first violin and cello. At the same time, the three different rhythmic patterns never overlap twice in precisely the same way. The result, on the one hand, anticipates the music of Messiaen (*Quartet for the End of Time*) and his followers and, on the other hand, like the contemporaneous Kodály and Bartók, satisfies two different aesthetic urges, to use the ethnic and the exotic and to be modern. Stravinsky will not sound like this again until the 1950s, in such quasi-serial music as the *Three Songs from William Shakespeare* (see chapter 3).

EXAMPLE 6.3. Stravinsky, Three Pieces for String Quartet, first movement, mm. 1–16. © Copyright 1922 by Edition Russe de Musique; copyright renewed. Copyright assigned to Boosey & Hawkes, Inc. Reprinted by permission.

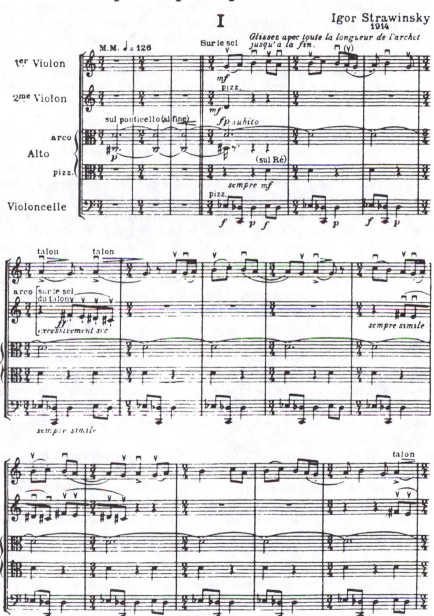

The third piece, "Canticle," is similarly made. Sectional in construction, it alternates, during its first half, between two phrases, which resemble a psalm verse and its antiphonal response. The resemblance is unmistakable: all four instruments play in rhythmic unison; the melodic ranges are very small, and the lines are primarily scalar; the durations are all quarter and half notes; there is a fair amount of internal repetition; and fourths—to modern ears, a "medieval" sound—predominate vertically, especially between the first and second violins.[19] The antiphonal response is set off by a leap upward of an octave to a higher register, a melodic pattern that sounds like a cadential gesture, and a rise in dynamics from *pianissimo* to *mezzoforte* with a small crescendo and decrescendo. This occurs three times, unvaried. The antiphonal response is also played normally on the instruments, whereas the "verses" are all played *sul tasto,* on the fingerboard, for an unearthly, fluty sound. The last section of the piece rises in register but seems to change metrically, to move in slower and statelier steps. The beginning of the first half's "psalm verse" returns, twice as slow, alternating with high cords, in harmonics, to end the piece and the set.

The Three Pieces thus do not exhibit the large-scale unity of the German musical tradition. Each piece uses similar methods of modular construction, but to different results. The three fall into not the most traditional fast-slow-fast scheme, but rather a fast-moderate-slow. Their sound worlds are also far apart, from the ethnic dance of the first through the off-balance and literally eccentric gestures of the second to the extremely static third. On this scale, too, Stravinsky has achieved what he did in the first, the combination of the primeval and the modern. This is the sound that carries Stravinsky from *The Rite of Spring* through *L'histoire du soldat* into the early 1920s, when he began to write in a neoclassical way reminiscent of the eighteenth century and left behind this sound that seems familiar in its parts but, as a whole, almost alien to its time.

If Ravel may be seen as a neoclassicist or an adherent of the continuing strain of French classicism, Schoenberg and Webern as Romantics in the tradition of Wagner and Brahms, and Stravinsky as an "alien" in turning to musical devices and effects unheard in Western European music, Ives is more alien still. He is, in at least one way, a direct heir of a Beethoven tradition, that of the ennobling aspect of music: the belief a great work of music not only depicts but also embodies a great philosophy—for example, the Enlightenment ideals of the perfectability of humanity and the brother- and sisterhood of all people and all peoples in Beethoven's Ninth Symphony. A work such as the Ninth does not merely show listeners what certain goals might be; in its musical effects it moves them by sympathetic example to those ideals. So it is with Ives's Second String Quartet (1907–13). The three movements are entitled "Discussions," "Arguments," and "The Call of the Mountains." A note on Ives's manuscript reads: "S. Q. for 4 men—who converse, discuss, argue (in re 'Politick'), fight, shake hands shut up—then walk up on the mountain side to view the firmament."[20] As we shall see, this happens *in* the music, not through it.

Ives differs greatly from other composers in this chapter because of his compositional devices, both his novel techniques and the sound of their combination or juxtaposition. Not for Ives the "easy" technique of motivic development, knowing (as he said) that cream will turn to butter but still having to watch the arm churn in the process. Ives works differently. Throughout the Second Quartet we hear continuous, through-composed musical discourse, incorporating quotations of great tunes, whether "Columbia, the Gem of the Ocean," Tchaikovsky's Sixth Symphony, or Beethoven's Ninth. We also hear something akin to passage work, sequencing a melodic pattern up and down the scale, but here released from traditional harmonic patterns and sounding entirely new. For these reasons, we need not pore over every note of the Second String Quartet. What one listens for is the overall, global sound and sense of the work, for it is here that the message and the music lie.

In the first movement, "Discussions," the music begins slowly, with one instrument after another presenting a sort of position, a variant of a single motive, while the others sustain long single pitches. Gradually the activity increases, and from that point on, one of three things happens: they play similar material at the same time; they play similar material in imitation, varying it from instrument to instrument; or they play different material. (I list the three types of procedure in increasing order of occurrence.) Some passages seem abstract and optimistically inventive in setting up a pattern of intervals to be sequenced up and down in order to get a certain dense, scurrying texture while avoiding anything so banal as the circle of fifths, avoiding a tonality that could only too tightly circumscribe in the event. For example, when the first violin plays a snatch of "Columbia, the Gem of the Ocean," the second violin and cello play a pattern that runs ascending whole step–descending half step–ascending whole step (e.g., C–D–C♯–D♯–D, and so on). The viola plays the inversion of this pattern. To prevent any possibility of too much cohesion among the three instruments (especially the second violin and cello), all three begin on different pitches as well: the second violin begins on E♭, the cello (playing the same pattern) on E natural, the viola (playing the inversion) on D. This texture continues throughout this brief passage, as quoted tunes appear in one instrument or another, "Dixie" in the viola, "Marching through Georgia" in the second violin, and "Columbia, the Gem of the Ocean" again in the first violin and cello (but a minor tenth apart).

Such techniques appear in all three movements; again, their effect is to draw the listener's ear to the grand design, the large-scale continuity of the music rather than to its small constituent elements. Ives seems taken here with whole-tone scales, rhythmic pedals and developments, the juxtaposition of highly varying sorts of music, the quotation of famous tunes,[21] and the sort of through-composed form that results from these techniques. The unity of the quartet as a whole—for despite musical surfaces sometimes so varied as to be chaotic, Ives was still interested in some sort of overall unity and coherence—derives from this continuity of techniques from one movement to another, from the tunes quoted in the first two movements (and their contrast with the religious music quoted in the third), and from the movements' titles.[22] This is what I mean by listening to the quartet at the large-scale level, and with less attention to details of pitch, motive, or rhythm. One could, in fact, profitably hear this quartet as if one were a participant rather than a passive observer of the discussions and arguments, and as if one hears the call of the mountains, just as do the players.

All this serves to exemplify yet another way of dealing with the remnants of the Romantic tradition: the genre of the string quartet, the concept of program music, the quoting of popular tunes, the creation of new forms for new and immediate purposes, even the very idea of chamber music itself. At the same time, Ives's Second Quartet serves to introduce many of the concerns and developments of American music after 1945, when John Cage and Elliott Carter came into the fore. Without direct influence from Ives, Cage used many of the same techniques, especially the idea of setting up a pattern and contrasting it with another, simply to see what will turn up. Cage also shared Ives's attitudes toward music, notwithstanding the linguistic as well as philosophical differences between the two composers. Neither Cage nor Ives was interested in music as the expression of an individual ego or soul; neither, in fact, believed that that is even possible. Both were caught up in the wonders of sound for its own sake, and with sound as a medium for invention and construction. Unlike Cage, Ives still believed in music's capacity for the expression of something that is not itself music—the expression of human community, for example, or of an Emersonian oversoul, of a philosophy. For Cage, music (like anything else in the universe) simply *is*.

Elliott Carter shares some of these characteristics, but to still different ends. Carter knew Ives and his music as a young man, and has changed his mind about his predecessor several times during his own compositional career. Carter's First String Quartet, discussed later in this chapter, evinces echoes of Ives in its way of proceeding, echoes that are of doubled importance because of Carter's own role as one of the principle definers of an "American" sound in music from the late 1940s to the present.

Schoenberg, Bartók, Shostakovich, Seeger

The styles of the years between the two world wars are very different from those of the beginning of the century; but these styles of the 1920s and 1930s now seem much more similar to one another than they did at the time. I have treated serialism as one current of neoclassicism, for the essential difference between them is simply one of the specific type of control of harmonic material, not control itself, nor the preeminence of pitch among the various musical parameters. What has been called neoclassicism usually involves triadic harmonies (occasionally what used to be known as "wrong-note" tonality) in networks of relationships that approximate the keys of earlier music, although they may not use the typical chord progressions of functional tonality. By contrast, serial music generally eschews the use of triads, privileging all intervals and simultaneities equally. A serial piece may use a great many triads, as for example, the Berg Violin Concerto. Webern's music often uses major and minor thirds pervasively, but Webern's textures and melodic gestures prevent these from combining into functional triads. Schoenberg, presumably because his musical habits and his own ear were trained in the late nineteenth century, often writes serial music that seems to duplicate the most important functions of tonality, especially the tonic/dominant axis that in fact defines functional tonality. (Such protective coloration did nothing to prevent the attacks of unsympathetic critics, however.) In many ways, the various types of neoclassicism seem a retreat from the music of the years before 1918, and that is how they are often treated.[23] "Retreat," of course, is a loaded word; and to other ears, the Apollonian clarity of, say, Stravinsky's Concerto for Two Solo Pianofortes, its precisely controlled and calibrated (if still witty) motor rhythms, are far preferable to the gut-wrenching *Rite of Spring,* as the Brahmsian Variations for Orchestra of Schoenberg are much more familiar, easily dealt with, than, say, his First Chamber Symphony or *Pierrot lunaire.* On the other hand, the music of the 1920s and 1930s may seem, and does to many post–1945 ears, as effete as the arts of the 1890s did to people ten or fifteen years later, a style or approach that has lived beyond its day. We can see this type of neoclassical serialism in Schoenberg's Fourth String Quartet, Op. 37 (1936): thorough serial pitch organization and manipulation, but forms, phraseology, rhythms, and textures that all derive from a classical language, and what even sounds at the beginning like the key of D minor.

The forms of the four movements are like the "modern" sonata-cycle forms of chapter 5. Derived at some distance from the received forms of the Classical era, specifically those of the early nineteenth century and middle Beethoven, they are realized with a great deal of constructive freedom. They are much less a rethinking or revision of earlier means, as Stravinsky's forms may be, than another evolutionary step in the ever-developing progression of the canon (obviously a nineteenth-century, German Romantic attitude). The first movement, *allegro molto, energico,* is a sonata form in its general ideals and procedures, although it does not conform to the textbook sonata forms as closely as do the Fourth and Fifth Quartets of Bartók, for example. The second movement, *comodo* ("comfortably, easily"), is a sort of *Ländler,* a genial dance movement after the demanding first movement. The slow movement, *largo,* is a sort of binary movement. And the last movement, another *allegro,* is a freer finale, with elements of the sonata form and of the rondo. But each movement, at the same time, is pervasively developmental, bordering at moments on the through-composed.

The first movement begins with a strong first theme (Ex. 6.4), which seems to foreshadow the motivic development that comes to constitute the principal compositional technique of the movement. Strongly contoured as an antecedent phrase, downbeat-heavy, the theme is still marked by the rising sequence of mm. 2, 3, and 4 in the recurring eighth-note pattern. This pattern becomes one of the leading motives of the movement and even marks the relatively stable and unstable sections of the sonata form, those that are developmental and those that

EXAMPLE 6.4. Schoenberg, String Quartet No. 4, Op. 37, first movement, mm. 1–6. Copyright © 1939 (Renewed) by G. Schirmer, Inc. (ASCAP). International Copyright Secured. All Rights Reserved. Reprinted by Permission.

are expository, recapitulatory, or some combination of (or transition between) these. The hammered-out eighths may sound in rhythmic unison among the four instruments; they may sound in canon; they may be heard in a single instrument, or in two, as accompaniment to more principal melodies in other voices; they may be audibly transformed into another characteristic rhythmic figure. They serve, in sum, in the same way as does the basic rhythmic motive of Beethoven's Fifth Symphony, with the exception that they are less "characteristic" (in the Romantic sense), less immutable and more malleable than Beethoven's eighth notes.

Once this first antecedent theme has been heard, however, no consequent achieving real closure follows. The first movement is a series of differing melodies—differing in rhythm, contour, length, instrumental context, and character. Closure at the end of sections is achieved not through recapitulation of melodies but through conventional signals that have taken on the meaning "closure" in modern and Romantic music, such as loud, repetitive figures played in rhythmic unisons, or the dissolution of texture and harmony into a cloud of harmonics. The compositional techniques are continuous on either side of these structural articulations, and the sense of stability and instability, of exposition or reprise as opposed to development, is a matter of degree. The development does fragment and recombine motives heard earlier in the movement to a greater degree than does the original exposition, and no new material appears in the recapitulation. But "recapitulation" in the sense of reprise, reconsolidation of melodies, anchoring the forward musical motion, does not occur until the very end of the movement, when we at last hear the first them reconstituted; and at this point, it is initiating the coda.

The latter three movements are similar in their general structural schemes, in the avoidance of literal repetition in favor of continuing development, in the rhythmic and textural suppleness of the music, and in melodic density (both simultaneous and sequential). Yet the characters of the four movements are quite different, even though all four are based on the same series of pitch classes.[24] The second movement, the quasi-*Ländler,* is notable especially for its rhythmic and metrical play, never unsettling but always comfortable and easy (*comodo*), a graceful and even humorous dance. The third movement is introduced and characterized by a stark unison opening statement from the four instruments, a melody that some writers have found reminiscent of Jewish mourning.[25] The last movement, as often in the quartets, symphonies, and sonatas of the late eighteenth and early nineteenth centuries, is the least aggressive, the loosest formally, and the (relatively) lightest in character. The quartet thus is thoroughly traditional in its adherence to received forms, characters, and associations (that is, no programs or sopranos here). It differs from the time-honored Classical quartet in only two aspects, its compositional method (serialism) and the particular compositional and musical personality of Schoenberg.

The techniques we have noted in the Fourth String Quartet's construction—its constant motivic development, the recurrence of rhythmic motives, the constant textural transitions between homophony and polyphony, the "developing variation" technique of repeating some aspects of a melody or motive while varying others markedly, the deferral of closure, the contrast of sections or movements—all these various techniques are precisely those of *Verklärte Nacht* of 1899, almost forty years before. Among all the great composers of the twentieth century, Schoenberg most resembles those of the German tradition in the constant and cumulative development not just of his style, but of his entire musical personality. He came the farthest, over the longest period. Debussy's compositional journey was also far-reaching, but it was relatively short in duration. Stravinsky's career cannot be summarized in the same way, for although he lived longer than Schoenberg and wrought fully as many changes on the music and musical attitudes of our times, Stravinsky's career is not so consistent at all musical levels (aesthetic concerns, general structural predilections, the surface sound of the pieces) as is Schoenberg's. Ives certainly had the range, but his career path, too, seems less single-minded than Schoenberg's.[26] Schoenberg's most immediate successors, Webern and Berg, also follow relatively concentrated paths, but their careers, like Debussy's, are not so long nor so extensive as Schoenberg's. Schoenberg's was the cultivation and further extension of a musical personality complete by the turn of the century. Like Beethoven and Wagner, his career consists of the exploration and exploitation of the capabilities and capacities of that personality: if not quite the universe in a grain of sand, as close as we can come to that in music.

I do not mean to imply here that Schoenberg is, by any stretch, the "greatest" composer of the twentieth century, a nonsense category. Nor do I mean to denigrate other composers at his expense. But I do wish to point out this characteristic of Schoenberg's career and musical personality *as an element of a musical tradition:* in this sense, even Schoenberg's career, not just his serial music, is neoclassical. It follows a path and a model laid down by the greatest composers of the generations preceding him, for all its twentieth-century colorations. When the world and its music changed during the years of World War I, Schoenberg essentially did not. The lives and the music of those composers who came of age after 1918 were fundamentally different from those of Schoenberg; and if German Romanticism died with him in Los Angeles in 1951, so, in a very real sense, did neoclassicism.

I did not mention Béla Bartók in the list of Schoenberg's contemporaries. But Bartók makes a cogent comparison. Moreover, his six string quartets offer a foil, in the first half of our century, to the string quartets of Beethoven in his era. Beethoven's earlier quartets are easily comparable to other contemporary works in the same genre, but over time become more idiosyncratic, more a reflection of Beethoven as an individual composer, less of their chronological era. With Bartók, on the other hand, the first two quartets may be comparable to contemporary works, with echoes of Richard Strauss, Schoenberg, and Debussy, but they are by far the least "Bartókian" of the set. The third quartet is extremely idiosyncratic, almost a work sui generis. The last three quartets approach many of the benchmarks of contemporary styles and of the contemporary string quartet as a genre; instead of diverging from the mainstream, these three quartets rejoin, even exemplify it. Like Beethoven's quartets, Bartók's have established a central position in the string quartet repertory, and have done so only after the composer's death. But whereas all of Beethoven's quartets are heard regularly, and not just during performances of the entire cycle, Bartók's Third, Fourth, and Fifth Quartets are frequently played, and the First, Second, and Sixth more rarely.

Bartók was quite different from other composers of his generation (he was born in 1881, a year before Stravinsky) in the variety of his musical pursuits: first a virtuoso pianist, then a pioneer ethnomusicologist, and then—and only gradually—a major, and later great composer. The first characteristically Bartókian works come in the second decade of the century, from his thirtieth year (*Allegro barbaro* for piano from 1911, the opera *Bluebeard's Castle* from 1918) and continue through the 1920s. His works in the 1930s and 1940s—we have looked at *Contrasts* (1938) and the Sonata for Two Pianos and Percussion (1937) in chapter 4, and the Sonata for Solo Violin (1944) and the First Sonata for Violin and Piano (1921) in chapter 5—are normally taken as exemplars of the richest neoclassicism. The six string quartets (1908, 1917, 1927, 1928, 1934, and 1939) span all but the last years of Bartók's creative life. To do them justice fully would require a book like Joseph Kerman's on the Beethoven quartets.[27] What follows here is less ambitious. For the only time in this study, we shall examine all the chamber music in a given genre of a single composer, by tracing Bartók's various paths in the six quartets, from 1908 to 1939.

In his book about Bartók,[28] Halsey Stevens notes a number of quintessentially Bartókian characteristics in the quartets, which he groups into five categories and which we may summarize here. (The categories are Stevens's, but the examples and exegeses are for the most part mine.)

The first in contrapuntal freedom, which takes many guises. Bartók's contrapuntal lines are rarely constrained by rigid tonal structures or processes. The result of this freedom, as Stevens points out, is not only great textural richness and variety (four independent lines, for example, or the two violins pursuing one melody while the viola and cello accompany them, or pursue another, or a full four-voiced *fugato,* etc.), but also a heightened ability to draw the ear to melody, texture, and often rhythm as the formative elements of the quartets. This contrapuntal freedom is a great generator of musical material and development; it allows a corresponding freedom in the handling of harmony and form, since it assures highly unified melodic and rhythmic contours. It is much more than simply a textural device.

Stevens's second general characteristic is one of the most widely discussed in the Bartók literature, his treatment of tonality. Stevens's position is that Bartók's works, specifically the quartets, are *on,* rather than *in,* a tonality, and that this tonality is a given pitch rather than a given sonority (e.g., a triad) or a key (which implies specific chordal relationships). This approach finds C, for example, as the note on which the Fourth Quartet's tonality is founded, but it tells us nothing specific about how C's centrality is established or treated in the course of the work. Many writers have found various pitch systems (or protosystems) in one or another Bartók quartet (for whatever reasons, most often in the Fourth). But a theoretical system that explains all of the quartets seems as impossible to achieve as one for Debussy. We will therefore discuss tonality and tonal systems here only in specific and fairly isolated instances, taking note of particular local techniques (basic tonal materials, for example) as well as larger systemic procedures.

As various and as striking as Bartók's idiosyncratic tonal process is the rhythmic vitality of his music. This goes hand in hand with Stevens's first category, Bartók's contrapuntal freedom. The most widely noted aspect of Bartók's rhythms is, of course, the rhythms and meters derived from folk music, especially Hungarian and Bulgarian. But beyond these exotic, asymmetrical meters and the cross- or polyrhythms that still seem regular (more so than, say, *The Rite of Spring*), Bartók's rhythmic vitality lies in its variety and unpredictability, and in the flexibility of his phraseology. The latter is again an example of freedom mixed with internal regularity: particularly after the First Quartet, Bartók's phrases are of quite varied lengths, and their textual combinations are not always predictable; but the phrases are invariably carefully contoured, shaped for immediate apperception. The rhythms on every level, from the local sequence of beats to the phrase, the shaping of sections, the large-scale form, are managed with tremendous originality and variety.

The largest rhythmic level leads us directly to the fourth of Stevens's categories, Bartók's "preoccupation" with architecture. (Stevens's choice of words is a little odd. "Preoccupation" implies the neglect of other musical parameters, which is certainly not the case with Bartók. And what serious composer, of whatever era or persuasion, does not give close attention to the questions of formal relationships, large-scale shape, and the connection of detail to whole?) It is here that most writ-

ers find Bartók closest to the neoclassicism of his era and his debts to
J. S. Bach and Beethoven. Bartók's revivifying of sonata form, for example, is as original and as interesting as anything else we discussed in
chapter 5. The organicism of his forms is very much of a piece with his
era, and equally to the taste of many writers about music. Bartók's
through-composed works are fascinating in their temporal constructions. And such a work as the Sixth Quartet is both troubling and com-
forting in the handling of temporality, within its own boundaries manipulating received forms, frequently looking backward, and constantly
bringing the past forward as a constitutive element of the present.
Whether or not Bartók was "preoccupied" with architecture, the formal clarity of most of his work—again, principally after the First Quartet—is beyond question; and the relationship of this formal clarity to
the musical and aesthetic effects of his music is a topic of some variety
and interest.

The organicism of Bartók's forms leads to the last of Stevens's categories, the motivic basis of much of Bartók's music, which underlies as
well much of its contrapuntal freedom and variety. By "motivic basis,"
Stevens means the organic proliferation of motives and the regenera-
tion of phrases from small units of two or three notes, a constant quasi-
developmental compositional technique that, as we shall see, is still quite
different from Schoenberg's or Ravel's precisely because it often seems
so little goal-directed. (This is most true of the first two quartets, and of
sections of the later ones.) As with Stevens's other general categories,
this compositional concern with a motivic basis to music is beyond question, but its realization and its musical effects vary greatly from one
string quartet to another. We have now reached the point where generalizations no longer suffice. It is time to turn to the First Quartet.

The First Quartet (1908) is perhaps the most discursive of the six.
It is in three progressively faster movements, *lento, allegretto,* and *allegro
vivace,* the last preceded by an *allegro* introduction. The first two movements are played without pause, and the third movement (after its introduction) is based on the same principal material as the second. A
long single arc thus extends from first note to last, all the more so because each of the three movements is essentially through-composed.
The first movement is a ternary ABA' whose A' is an elided recomposition of A, not a static reprise. The second movement is anticipated at
the end of the first: the viola and cello play a three-note rhythmic motive, syncopated and accented, which is unlike anything around it except that the two instruments are a third apart; after the movement's final phrase in the two violins, this motive is repeated precisely in the
viola and cello and becomes the beginning of a principal melody of the
second movement.[29] This movement's sectionalized structure is loosely
reminiscent of a sonata form, but only in the most general outline.
After an introduction of some nineteen measures, setting forth three

different motives (including the one from the end of the first movement), the first large section of the *allegretto* comprises several subsections on four or five themes, often in combination with the motives
from the first part of the movement. The central segment of the movement (mm. 140–216 of a total of 367 measures) is a continuous spinning-out and extension of three principal motives from the first 120
measures. It is not really a development, however, in that it uses the
motives not to explore the music of the first large section but as the basis for new music. The final section of the movement includes no new
music per se. But it does not recapitulate the themes of the first section
in anything resembling the original order or completion; it is, rather, a
combination of repetitions (in varied order) and new music on the
same material. Thus the general outlines of the movement resemble
those of a sonata form, but the dynamic of the music is wrong. Trying
to hear it as a sonata form is counterproductive, for one thereby misses
the ongoing discursiveness of the phrases and sections, the emphasis
on newness rather than on the exploration of a more restricted set of
musical material.

The third movement is even more an aggregation of small sections, but here Bartók restricts his material to just four basic themes,
the first of which is a motive from the *allegretto*. He also uses a particular introductory figure, quickly repeated Es (or, in two cases, E–B and
A–E open fifths). As with the second movement, it is possible to divide
the third into larger sections—that is to say, to group the small segments based on individual motives into more cohesive units—but this
does not give us any sort of formal sectionalization more helpful than
the term *through-composed*. The movement is essentially a *perpetuum mobile,* its form a constant tumbling forward of its various sections, broken
only by the recurring repeated Es and (twice) by the last of its four
principal melodies, an *adagio*.

The overall shape of the First Quartet is thus a sort of arc, gather-
ing speed through the second movement and simplifying its trajectory
in the third. The first movement moves continually forward in its contrapuntal intertwining of voices and spinning out of melodies. It completely lacks closure and leads us directly into the sectional *allegretto,* a
plethora of contrasting motives repeated and tossed about in a welter
that resists more general characterization. This movement is followed
in turn by the *allegro vivace,* which retains its exuberance and general
techniques (i.e., repetition, juxtaposition, spinning-out, old motives in
new contexts), but with a much more restricted basic vocabulary. Closure, at the end of the quartet, is gestural rather than formal. Bartók
does not end with recapitulations of previous material, or with grounding of earlier instabilities (since those have not really existed), but with
the repetition of cadential figures, energetic rhythms, and the filling up
of the vertical space of the string quartet.

This end-directed (as opposed to beginning-heavy) motion is unusual for Bartók, especially for the Bartók of the quartets. It is quite in keeping, however, with the contemporary musical scene of 1908, and other features of the First Quartet also seem to mirror more their historical context than the idiosyncrasies of their composer. Although Bartók's musical materials in the First Quartet are not so restricted or obsessive as those of Schoenberg's *Verklärte Nacht* or Second String Quartet, the general end-direction of the music is similar. (This is no doubt in the nineteenth-century Romantic tradition of beginning with slow, dark, or gloomy music and gradually striving for more light.) The beginning of Bartók's second movement, in its gradual and progressive shaping of motives into a full texture of a sweet melody over a steady, simple, but cross-rhythmic accompaniment, is reminiscent of early Schoenberg as well. The spirit of Richard Strauss is everywhere in the first movement, in the frequent climactic use of major tonic triads in second inversion, their most unstable form, and in the pervasive chromaticism. This chromaticism is simultaneously sweetened, almost to the point of being cloying in the first movement, and intensified by the constant pairing of voices in thirds, to the almost complete avoidance of fifth relationships, so that any sense of overriding tonality is confused. Here, too, are echoes of Strauss and Schoenberg, indeed of Liszt and some late Beethoven. There is even a strong echo of Ravel, at the end of the B section of the first movement, a string of first-inversion triads over a cello melody. Finally, the first melody of the quartet is much in the mold of Schoenberg, Strauss, or some Liszt—long, sinuous, chromatic, without clear internal articulations, pulling a listener in rather than setting forth something for us to apprehend.

Certain rhythmic characteristics are more Bartókian. Everywhere in this quartet, except for the principal portions of the first movement's A sections, rhythms and meters are clear, energetic, and what one might call downbeat driven (By that term I mean to emphasize their clarity, but not a regularity that would be implied by the term *metrical*.) Bartók likes to employ the whole range of the string quartet, but he tends to do so in a more continuous manner than, say, Schoenberg or Webern. And although, like every competent composer for the genre, he is very much alive to the possibilities for unity and variety within the ensemble, he seems to lean rather to a balance of independence and cooperation among the four players, not to the overriding polyphony of the Viennese or the principally homophonic textures of Debussy and Ravel. In this sense one might say that he treats the string quartet less orchestrally and more as a chamber group than do the contemporary Viennese; and that (at least at this point) his variety is more textural and less coloristic than the Parisians.

The Second String Quartet (1915–17) is much more "Bartókian." This is hardly surprising, given that the Second Quartet was composed during the cataclysm of World War I and that since 1908 Bartók had been immersing himself in the folk musics of central and eastern Europe. These musics were beginning to make themselves heard in his compositions. A teleological approach to Bartók—for example, the view that the first three quartets are somehow apprentice works leading to the "true" Bartók in his Fourth and Fifth Quartets, and relegating the Sixth to a sort of farewell to chamber music—is not uncommon, but neither is it helpful. It assumes that there is only one real Bartók, that of the years roughly from 1926 to 1939. And it traduces the individual quartets, since it prevents us from hearing them directly.

The quartet is in three movements, a *moderato* in sonata form, an *allegro molto capriccioso*, and a final *lento;* the latter two movements are sectional, cumulative, and through-composed. It is difficult to characterize the quartet as an entity, since, unlike the others, there is so little connection of any kind among the movements, which all seem completely self-contained. The proportions of the movements are not what they appear to be, either, probably both because of internal formal traits and because of the expectations of the listener. When I listen to the Second Quartet, I am always sure that the second movement is the longest of the three and the third the shortest. I am invariably surprised to note that, in fact, the second movement is the shortest and the first is the longest.[30] The second movement seems longest because of its character and position. The first movement is from early on clearly a sonata form. As it progresses, the movement coincides precisely with one's expectations of the events of a sonata form and their temporal proportions. Since the experience agrees with one's expectations,[31] the actual time elapsed seems brief. Following this first movement, the second begins like a scherzo—fast, energetic, rhythmic (and metrical), sectional, and much more "folkish" in spirit because of the melodies and embellishments. (For example, Bartók uses both F♮ and F♯ in a melody based on D, and G♯ and E♯ rather than the G♮ and E♮ of the major or minor scale. The result sounds like a folk mode of eastern Europe.) Yet the movement eventually proves not to be a scherzo. It is sectional, but the sections do not recur in the order of those of a scherzo (such as the second movement of Schoenberg's Second Quartet, Op. 10). There is some repetition, especially of repeated notes as a pervasive element and of some melodic figures. But the movement is overwhelmingly through-composed and forward moving. The lack of close repetition and of clearly balanced sections emphasizes the rhythmic energy of the movement and its constant propulsion; and it seems longer than it is. The last movement is as surprising as the second, for its greater length is disguised by its stillness. Time here seems to stop, as in the last movement of Messiaen's *Quartet for the End of Time;* and time stops to such a degree that one does not expect or need a fourth movement, to round off what might have seemed a sonata cycle of first movement, scherzo, slow movement, and finale. The quartet is not a truncated sonata cycle, a contemporary gesture in the direction of any neoclassicizing trends. It shares with the sonata cycle a first movement in sonata form; but beyond that, it is very much its own creation.

The harmonic language of the Second Quartet is as varied as its formal devices. The first movement mixes the free atonality of the day (in this case larded with half steps, tritones, and fourths) with the sound of modal mixtures, using both major and minor triads, as in the closing theme of the recapitulation (mm. 156–161, four measures before rehearsal number 21 to the second measure of the rehearsal number), where the violins, and later the viola, play the closing melody in the minor mode over the parallel major chords, strummed pizzicato, in the cello. Even within the first movement, Bartók associates specific kinds of musical language with the contrasting sections of the sonata form; that is to say, he uses types of harmonic language to create the stability and instability, tension and closure, that mark the sonata form. In the exposition, the first theme (mm. 1–19) and the bridge (mm. 20–31) are chromatic and atonal, emphasizing the half step (both vertically, in chords, and horizontally, in melodies) and the fourth (primarily melodic). The brief, in fact, is an extension and first development of the basic motives of the first theme. The second theme (mm. 32–61), or from rehearsal number 5 to rehearsal number 10) is much more triadic, using thirds and sixths, but still in a freely tonal context. The closing theme (mm. 62–69) is, as I have mentioned, triadic and modal.

The development is primarily atonal and built with half steps, and it grows more dissonant as it approaches its climax at rehearsal number 15 (mm. 103–106). It is also based on the principal motive of the first theme and its extensions. This then raises the question of the recapitulation—how to differentiate it from the development based on the first theme of the exposition, and what sort of function to assign it in the movement as a whole. The beginning of the recap is an extraordinary moment: Bartók returns to the opening melody of the first theme, but the accompaniment, while similar to the beginning of the exposition, completely transforms it. Instead of the half steps of the opening measures, we hear the tritone A–D♯ in the viola and second violin, completely relaxing the tensions of the first theme in the exposition and of the immediately preceding development. This tritone is sustained (although the pitches are changed) for fifteen measures, almost the length of the entire first theme in the exposition, its rhythms as lulling as the harmony. The tritone in the inner strings is supported by long pedal notes in the cello, these a tritone apart (F and B), but forming seventh chords with the second violin and viola, again a much more stable and "familiar" spacing of the vocabulary of fourths and half steps that have earlier characterized this music. This is sheer Beethoven, transforming material so that it retains its original shape while changing its character and function.

The final pages of this first movement are primarily triadic, a sort of large-scale resolution of the more dissonant and less stable harmonies of the exposition and development. This is not to say, however, that these pages are clearly tonal. The second theme in the recapitulation (from m. 141), four measures after rehearsal number 19) begins with an augmented triad, A–C♯–F, the same chord that closes the movement, rather than with the major or minor triads of the exposition. The end of the exposition is recomposed here for the end of the movement, its scalar half-step melodies now led (and resolved) into triadic contexts, so that all earlier material is now associated with the most stable harmonic language of the movement. Yet the music remains, from a purely tonal point of view, ambiguous. If the movement is "on" A, as Stevens states and for which one can certainly make a good case, the final chord is again an augmented triad, A–C♯–F, in the three upper voices; since an augmented triad trisects the octave symmetrically, it does not have a root. Furthermore, when this chord dies away in the upper strings, the cello continues with a melody (the closing theme) that implies A as a tonic, but ends on E, the dominant of A and not part of the augmented triad of the other parts. The first movement is closed and resolved in that the general harmonic language of its final pages is the most stable of the movement. But Bartók prefers here a sort of fading out, a dissolution of that stable language before (perhaps) it becomes too leaden.

The second and third movements are less interwoven structurally than the first, and so their harmonic languages are less varied as well. The scherzolike second movement is full of repeated eighth notes on a single pitch or octave, and its principal melodies are scalar. This is not to say that harmony, as such, does not exist; but the fifths and tritones of the accompanying parts are as effective in terms of color (again, folklike, scherzolike) as they are for tonal underpinning. The half and whole steps of most of the movement are in fact so pervasive that the essential effect of the last pages, a Bartókian version of a Rossini crescendo, is the result of arpeggios that rise and descend in thirds instead. The last movement is different from either of the first two, although it returns to the general type of atonality that marked the less stable sections (exposition first theme and bridge, development section) of the first movement. The new principal sound of the last movement is chords that are stacks of perfect fourths, used climactically. But these stacks of fourths are eventually resolved to another sound that underlies much of the movement—and in fact that constitutes its first full cadence (mm. 20–22)—the minor third A–C. Major and minor thirds are expressly contrasted with fourths in this movement; the fourths form the climaxes of the music, and the (minor) thirds its resolutions.

But this resolution into thirds is not a reprise of the general harmonic system of the first movement. The harmonic and musical worlds of the two movements are too different for that. Nowhere does the third movement approach the consonance of the first movement; nowhere does it have the first movement's rhythmic activity; most notably, nowhere does it have tunes. The third movement is darker than the first in every respect: a slower tempo, to the point of seeming ametrical, even out of time; thicker textures; the use primarily of the lowest registers, moving higher for the louder climaxes and to set off these low sounds as the more central. The third movement seems much more primeval than the first two, with inchoate sounds that build up into textures of simultaneities rather than into articulated utterances.

Bartók's Second Quartet is thus a child of its time in its very refusal to resemble any contemporary creation. The mark of music from *Pierrot lunaire* (1912) and *The Rite of Spring* (1913), through late Debussy, Scriabin, Ives, *L'histoire du soldat* (1918), up until the early 1920s (Stravinsky's Octet, Schoenberg's development of the twelve-tone method and his first compositions with that technique) is its variety, from one composer or country to another and from one work to another. A listener who presumes to know what a string quartet is may react to this quartet as Schumann did to Chopin's Piano Sonata in B♭ Minor, Op. 35 (the so-called "Funeral March" Sonata):

> The idea of calling it a sonata is a caprice, if not a jest, for he [Chopin] has simply bound together four of his most reckless children; thus under his name smuggling them into a place into which they could not else have penetrated.[32]

That is one reaction, for it is not easy to hear or intuit any sort of concrete relationship among Bartók's three movements, to connect them in a linked succession. To do that, one has to resort to retrospection, and even this may result in a structure of juxtaposition rather than continuity. If Bartók's First Quartet describes an arc, the Second may be heard as a triptych of contemplation.[33] The first movement, in this hearing, is the most traditional. (And indeed, if one thinks back to the first movement after hearing the third, it may seem clear and untroubled.) The second movement is also straightforward, but its world is not that of the first; the latter is the classical music of Western tradition, the former derives more directly from the rustic. The movement is unsettling, because how one is to hear it is in no way clear. While the movement evokes, it simultaneously undercuts; it fails to integrate. The final movement is a retreat from both the first and second "alternatives," for its dark coloration is intensified by contrast with the earlier two movements. I do not want to characterize the mood of the third movement as disillusionment or despair. But I do not mind hearing it, in contrast to the first two movements, as introspection and relative isolation. Whichever approach to the Second Quartet one prefers, the central question is precisely the very existence of irreconcilable ways of hearing it. This is not the case with any other Bartók quartet, and it is not the case with most modern music. The ultimate ungraspability of the Second Quartet is one of its most central characteristics.

As there had been approximately ten years between Bartók's First and Second Quartets, so there is a decade between the Second and Third. Yet despite this elapsed time, the new quartet's intensification of language, and its dramatically condensed—almost foreshortened—form (it is in only one movement, which lasts about fifteen minutes), the Third String Quartet (1927) has still some direct connections to its predecessor. These have to do with shared musical gestures and, to a degree, with form. In some ways, it is as if the second movement of the Second Quartet had been folded into the first movement, and both of these drastically concentrated to make the Third.

The quartet is made up of a *prima parte,* 112 measures of *moderato;* a *seconda parte,* 417 measures of *allegro;* a shortened (70 measures) *recapitulazione della prima parte;* and a coda, 121 measures of *allegro molto.* The material of the coda is drawn more from the *seconda parte* than from the *prima,* but it does not constitute a recapitulation of the *seconda parte.* The *prima parte* is itself an aba'/codetta form, analogous in outline to the quartet as a whole. The *seconda parte* is a through-composed movement on a fairly small amount of basic material, like the second movement of the Second Quartet, but whose last large section (mm. 281–417) is a much condensed recapitulatory section. The *recapitulazione* of the *prima parte* is another, shorter aba'/codetta. The coda is sectional, through-composed, forward driving, and capped by its own codetta. The quartet as a whole thus resembles both a compound ternary form (ABA') and a sonata form, and yet it is binary in its twofold motion from slow music and a certain type of intensity to much faster music and a different (and rather simpler, more direct) type. But this allusive and highly concentrated form does not account entirely for the overriding tension of the Third Quartet as a whole. This comes as much from the quartet's motives, melodies, and gestures, from the harmonic language, and from the coda's combining these elements from the two principal parts of the quartet proper.

The *prima parte* and its *recapitulazione* are formed from a single basic cell, which assumes shape gradually at the outset of the piece. This cell is the three-note rising fourth and falling third that is heard from m. 6 onward; it has arisen from the gradually expanding chromatic opening bars. The lower three instruments first play a chromatic "cluster" spread out through different octaves (C$\sharp$ and D in the cello, E in the viola, D$\sharp$ in the second violin), *pianissimo* and muted. From this come the first violin's first four notes, which anticipate the contour of the movement's basic cell. In each measure of this first phrase, the first violin's range expands until it settles again, in its lower middle range, on the basic motive. The motive pervades the music (see Ex. 6.5), and continues to underlie the movement, even forming the ostinato background to the new music of the first part's middle section. Also apparent in Example 6.5 is what one might call the music's overlapping chromaticism, so characteristic of Bartók: the different instruments play different chromatic collections, but with the aggregate result not of polytonality but of chromatic richness.

This chromatic richness is echoed by the textural richness. When the four instruments of the quartet play contrapuntally, the music is thoroughly imitative, usually a development of music based on the principal motive. Bartók also uses the instruments in pairs, the violins against the viola and cello, playing contrasting music or playing the same music in inversion or in imitation. In the more stable or the most

EXAMPLE 6.5. Bartók, String Quartet No. 3, *prima parte*, mm. 1–17. © Copyright 1929 by Universal Edition; copyright renewed. Copyright and Renewal assigned to Boosey & Hawkes, Inc., for the U.S.A. Reprinted by permission.

climactic sections, he uses all four instruments as a unit, as in the opening five measures, the chords that close the first *a* section or form the
climax of the *b,* and the final measures of the first part. Each of these
types is established smoothly; in this quartet, Bartók is interested in
stark textural contrast only from one large formal unit to the next, between the first and second parts. This contributes to the large-scale formal clarity of the Third Quartet, and it gives the coda its climactic
excitement.

The second part unfolds as organically as the first, but over a
longer duration. The immediate result is a relaxation of tension, since
our ears are not overloaded with new music; nevertheless, the motivic
unity of the second part eventually generates great cumulative tension
built up through repetition, slight variation, harmonic coloration, and
rhythmic intensification (see Ex. 6.6). The example shows four successive sections built on the same material, the scalar motives of mm. 1–10.
Three separate motive elements appear at the beginning: the trill, the
ascending scale (marked *quasi glissando* at its first appearance, in the viola), and the regular, "melodic" theme set in pizzicato triads in the
Dorian mode (the occasional F♯ does not belong in the Dorian mode on
D, but is presumably there to form a minor, rather than diminished,
triad). The trill becomes thematic in its alternation of D and E♭; in fact,
it is in part an extension of the opening sound of the movement, the
D–E♭ trill in the second violin against the *sforzando* and *pizzicato* D in the
first violin and E♭ in the viola and cello. This half-step polarity becomes
one of the principal harmonic elements of the second part. The quasi-
glissando scale in the viola is the proximate introduction to the melody
in the cello, but it also turns into full-scale glissandi at the climax of the
section (mm. 353ff.) and then again in the recapitulation of the first
part. The cello melody is obviously the principal—virtually the sole—
melodic material of the section, and Example 6.6 shows its first transformations. These include rhythmic variety and intensification. The
example also shows the gradual rise in pitch level, both register and absolute pitch, in the first three instances; this encapsulates the shape of
the movement up to m. 182 (rehearsal number 23), the last passage in
Example 6.6 and the beginning of an extended section that climaxes
in a *fugato* (mm. 242–284) before the quasi-recapitulation that begins in
m. 284. (Although the second part is of course not a sonata form, this
section resembles a development in its thematic work, carried on from
earlier sections, and in the climactic *fugato* leading to a sort of restatement of earlier material.)

The recapitulation of the first part is a foreshortened reprise and
recomposition, with two principal differences. The beginning of the recapitulation sounds much more stable than the beginning of the first
part, a function of the more sustained notes, the far more gradual appearance of each instrument, and the fact that the first interval heard is

EXAMPLE 6.6. Bartók, String Quartet No. 3, *seconda parte*. © Copyright 1929 by Universal Edition; copyright renewed. Copyright and Renewal assigned to Boosey & Hawkes, Inc., for the U.S.A. Reprinted by permission.

(a) mm. 1–21

(*continued*)

EXAMPLE 6.6. (*continued*)

(b) mm. 26–29

(c) mm. 96–112

(*continued*)

(d) mm. 182–90

B & H

the tritone rather than the minor seconds of the beginning of the first section.[34] In contrast to this more stable and gradual beginning, however, the recapitulation as a whole is marked by much more sudden textural juxtapositions and a greater build-up of tension than in the first part. The *a'* of the recapitulation is only six measures long, and it emphasizes the chromatic imitative polyphony of the first section, in a final glimpse between the heavy, repeated *martellato* chords of the *b* section and the *perpetuum mobile* of the coda. The coda picks up the repeated notes (now sixteenth notes at an *allegro molto* tempo) and even scales of the second part and continues in a more or less headlong rush to the end. Everything that happens in the coda has happened before; but the melodies that were heard in the second part are for the most part abstracted here (as they were occasionally in the earlier section), so that the lines become elemental rather than developed or shaped. All the gestures of the coda are forward moving: crescendos, piling up of motives, either rising scales or simultaneous rising and descending scales to fill out an extended range, glissandi that last for two entire measures, repeating chords, thickening of texture. All of these devices, compressed into an extremely short time span, bring the Third

Quartet to a close at the top of its arc. Yet, at the same time, the large-scale form is unitary, all of a piece. The chromaticism, rhythmic and metrical devices, and coloristic and textural use of glissandi are all highly unusual for the sometimes retrogressive 1920s, in the century's first infatuation with abstract modern clarity. Bartók's formal scheme here is more typical of the era, but is still highly idiosyncratic, and never repeated even within his own oeuvre. Bartók shares in the Third Quartet the age's liking for formal clarity and abstraction, here even the abstraction of basic musical elements from shaped melodies and phrases, as well as the organic generation of the latter. But little else in the piece matches the general profile of its time, not the case in the Fourth and Fifth Quartets.

The Fourth and Fifth String Quartets (1928 and 1934, respectively) are undoubtedly the most frequently played and written about of the Bartók quartets. This popularity probably has less to do with their status as masterworks than with their combination of stringently modern surface language—such aspects as harmony, colors (some derived from new playing techniques), rhythms, and the combined force of all of these—with Apollonian clarity of outline and form. The Fourth and Fifth Quartets are, in perhaps just a superficial sense, less "problematic" than the other four; they are certainly closer in their structural and formative devices to what we are used to from the canon of string quartets in Western musical history and in the contemporary works of the 1920s and 1930s. Our question here is the musical result of that clarity, and of the apparent contrast between surface language and formal balance.

Both the Fourth and the Fifth Quartets fall into an "arch form": the movements stand in symmetrical relationships to one another. In the Fourth Quartet, for example, the first movement (of five) is a sonata form using a restricted amount of basic motivic material; the fifth movement is a lighter, more rondolike movement (as most last movements of string quartets studied in these pages have been), using two of the principal motives of the first movement. Both movements are oriented about the pitch C as a tonal center. The second and fourth movements of the quartet are both scherzolike in character and function. Although they do not share literally the same material, their themes are built in roughly similar ways (for example, rapid ascending scales). More important is the character imparted through their performance means: the second movement is a *prestissimo*, with the string playing muted throughout, even when the dynamic marking is *fortissimo*. This muted coloration and reduced volume at whatever dynamic level is a striking effect, especially in combination with the scurrying, *prestissimo* eighth notes (the movement is in $\frac{6}{8}$), and in stark contrast to the first movement. The fourth movement uses another, equally striking device, all strings playing pizzicato throughout. In addition, we hear for the first time in the quartets the famous percussive "Bartók pizzicato," in which the string is plucked so strongly that it rebounds off the fingerboard. Beyond these playing effects, there is a tonal symmetry to the second and fourth movements as well. The second movement is oriented around E as a tonal center, a major third above the C of the first movement. The fourth movement is built around A♭, a major third above E and a major third below the C of the last movement. These two inner movements thus trisect the octave from C to C and form an axis around the tonal centers of the outer movements.

Within these movements is the third, the slow movement (although marked *non troppo lento*, "not too slowly"), a sectional and rounded-off example of Bartók's so-called night music.[35] The movement begins with the three higher string building up a cluster at first played without vibrato, and then with vibrato added. The cluster is maintained for twelve measures (that is, almost a full minute) underneath a recitative in the cello marked *espressivo*. The recitative continues for another twenty-one measures, and the cluster beneath it changes quietly and slowly, its top note rising gradually, from G♯ above middle C up a perfect fourth to C♯, as the bottom note (in the first violin as well) sinks from A below middle C down (in the viola) a major sixth to C. The sonority thus maintains the cluster as its pitches expand from an amplitude of a major seventh (A to G♯) to two octaves plus a minor second (C to C♯). Above this, the cello's recitative fills the space from a high D♯ (a ninth above middle C) down to the cello's lowest note, the C two octaves below middle C. Most of the cello's lines descend within this range, and its highest register is used only in the middle of the recitative, for the highest tension. The anxiety of the recitative comes also from the juxtaposition of sustained notes with very brief ones, the repetition of patterns (or almost-patterns) in scales and tonalities that sound exotic and oddly inflected, and the prevalence of dotted notes (i.e., the absence of notes that in themselves define a beat or meter).

This thirty-four-measure cello recitative gives way to a new first violin figuration over a chord borrowed from the cluster supporting the recitative. The violin figuration, repeated notes and major seconds like a night bird's chirping, expands over three octaves and leads directly into a second principal section, an *agitato* (mm. 42–54). This section is defined at first by its color: the first violin, viola, and cello playing *tremolo* double-stops *sul ponticello* (on the instrument's bridge, a raspy or guttural sound) which alternate with *sforzandi* played in the normal position. Here the principal line is the second violin's, but it is equally colored by being played entirely on the lowest string of the instrument, resulting in a throaty timbre that lends urgency to the melody. The *agitato* gradually subsides. It is followed by a section marked *tranquillo* in which the cello again has a recitative; but this recitative is regularized metrically, in $\frac{4}{4}$ time, and in phrasing, 2 +2 + 4 measures. It is answered canonically by the first violin, playing the melody in inversion. Supporting these instruments, the second violin and viola return to the intertwined chromatic chords of the first section of the movement. Having been thus stabilized, the recitative yields to a final few measures that recreate the sound of the opening section of the movement: not the recitative as it had been then, but the clusters, the violin figurations from mm. 34–40, and some sliding scalar and chromatic figures in the cello. The final sonority disappears into the ether, the notes of the chord dropping out one by one from lowest to highest, until all that is left is the first violin's high D, diminishing into silence.

Thus, in crudest terms the third movement of the quartet is an ABA', although it actually sounds through-composed, with only a reminiscence at the end of its opening sonorities. This combination of repetition and the appearance of through-composition we have already seen in the Third Quartet, and it is at the heart of the mainstream Western tradition going back to Haydn. The same balanced combination also stretches over the Fourth Quartet as a whole. The first movement is extraordinarily astringent and gritty in its harmonies, made up overwhelmingly of half steps, both vertically and horizontally, and in its almost obsessive concentration on two basic motives, the opening upward-rising major seconds, which gradually expand in register and interval to constitute the second theme (mm. 15ff.), and the *fortissimo* rising and descending figure first heard in the cello at the end of the second phrase (just before the repetition of the opening, now in canon in all four instruments, m. 7). Bartók uses these motives, in a tremendously single-minded language, to build a sonata form that works like a model of its kind—contrast of stable and less stable areas, here even the stable areas full of harmonic and rhythmic tension; motivic development leading to overall tension and release; a recapitulation that merges into a coda to keep the forward direction paramount until the end. In the fifth movement of the quartet, however, he uses the same basic motives to different structural and aesthetic ends, as a final, grounding gesture rather than an opening one.

Yet this arch structure is not the same as expanding the idea of a sonata form to a sonata cycle, as Liszt had done in his B-Minor Piano Sonata, and Schoenberg in his First String Quartet, Op. 7, and First Chamber Symphony, Op. 9. Nor is Bartók's structure the expansion of a Romantic ternary form over the course of the whole string quartet. The Romantic ternary form, as in the Brahms intermezzi, is essentially a static structure: the final A section is more or less identical to the first one, and the aesthetic pleasure rises from hearing its beauties again, after the contrasting music of the middle section. In contrast, a sonata form normally must work in the moment; it must be conceived and heard as a drama of tension, exacerbation, and resolution. This does not happen in Bartók's Fourth Quartet; one need only turn to Schoenberg's Second Quartet to see how the idea might (and does) work. The Bartók Fourth lies between a symmetrical but static scheme and the balanced but forward-moving and dynamic structure of the Schoenberg Second Quartet. Each of Bartók's five movements is a unit, closed at its end. The structure of the slow middle movement, although it mirrors that of the quartet as a whole, does not imply that overall structure. Likewise, the sonic similarities of the second and fourth movements do not imply that the final movement will resemble the first. Bartók's arch form thus works only after the fact, in retrospect. When we hear the main theme of the last movement, we remember the first movement; we do this even more strongly when we hear the chromatic scalar motive. But we realize simultaneously that we are hearing new compositions of old material, not the final closing of tensions that had been left unresolved. The result is extraordinarily satisfying, of course, and it integrates what must have seemed the most modern musical language in 1927 (and what is, in fact, an exemplary language of modernity) with a large-scale structural scheme that is thoroughly and classically traditional. In retrospect, the listener can give equal weight to all five of the quartet's movements; the listener to Schoenberg's Second Quartet will hear those four movements to be of increasing importance. Furthermore, the equal weighting of the movements removes Bartók's Fourth Quartet to a timeless sphere, where all the movements coexist. This temporal framework is one of the principal qualities that lend the work its impact and staying power.

The Fifth Quartet follows along the same general lines, but to somewhat different effect. It is also an arch form, its five movements symmetrically arrayed, but this symmetry is foreshadowed in the first movement, and the parallelisms are much more direct than in the Fourth Quartet. The five movements are a first-movement sonata form, *allegro;* an *adagio molto,* another "night music" movement; a scherzo, *alla bulgarese (vivace),* using rhythms and meters reminiscent of Bulgarian folk music; another slow movement, *andante,* a sort of variation of the second movement; and a finale, *allegro vivace—presto,* which uses material from the first movement, although to a lesser degree than the fifth movement of the Fourth Quartet.[36]

The most striking structural change in the Fifth Quartet is the sonata form of the first movement. This sonata structure is as clearly articulated as any, with three distinct themes in the exposition, a development that concentrates on the first two, a false recapitulation, and a real recapitulation. The change here is that in the recapitulation, the themes are melodically inverted and appear in reverse order. Whereas the third theme of the exposition was a rising and then falling lyrical scalar melody, in the recapitulation it falls first and then ascends, and it appears at the beginning of the section. The same obtains with the second and first themes, and the movement closes with a coda built principally with elements of the first theme. Bartók thus combines the sonata form with a one-movement arch form. The sonata form continues to work according to its norm, with themes of contrasting character set forth in the exposition, fragmented and worked in the development, and reestablished in a more unitary way in the final section. This particular sonata form also continues one of the traditions of the sonata since Beethoven, that the recapitulation continue the compositional work with the themes of the exposition, and not merely repeat them. (A coda thus serves as a final unifying section.) The arch form is a part of this continued composition; it stands not in opposition to the sonata ideal but as a contributing factor to it. At the same time, it imparts to the movement a symmetry that the sonata form alone cannot lend, and it reinforces the first theme of the exposition as the dominating idea of the movement, as a whole. The combination of simultaneous symmetrical repetition and new composition creates a structural lightness entirely in keeping with the characters of the three principal themes—the language here is much less dissonant than that of the Fourth Quartet—as they set up the symmetries that are mirrored in the overall arch form of the quartet.

These arch forms are quickly dealt with. As is often the case in the sonata cycle, the last movement is much lighter in character and looser in form than the earlier movements, here a sectional form along the lines of a rondo.[37] The themes of this movement bear a slight family resemblance to those of the first; again, the themes are inverted at their repetition. The central portion of the movement is a *fugato* on the first theme of the first movement. The second and fourth movements, as I have noted, are both "night music" movements; the fourth is a kind of large-scale variation on the second, the themes, textures, and figurations returning in more or less the same order and further composed out into new music. The middle movement, the quasi-Bulgarian scherzo, is an ABA, its A (or scherzo) sections in a meter of $4 + 2 + 3$ and its B (or trio) $3 + 2 + 2 + 3$ (note the symmetry of the metrical unit, at the center of the quartet).

The symmetry of the Fifth Quartet works to different effect from that of the Fourth because it is prefigured in the first movement, and because the relationship of the second and fourth movements is much more direct and much stronger than in the earlier work.[38] In this case, the arch form works throughout the quartet as a stabilizing factor, analogous to the conflation of sonata form and arch form in the first movement, and imparts to the quartet at every structural level a sense of security and repose (even in the most jovial or quiet moments) that is quite peculiar to this quartet among Bartók's six. In this way the Fifth Quartet closely reflects not only its historical era but also the reintegration into the modern string quartet of its canon and tradition. If the Fourth Quartet may be heard as Beethovenian in demonic energy, formal innovation, and sense of unerring rightness, the Fifth may seem more Mozartean in its ever-present sense of balance, its melodiousness, the dance form of its scherzo, and the elegance of its slow movements.

The Sixth String Quartet (1939) is an emotionally complex work because of overlapping but distinct structural procedures: a contrast of movement types, which becomes more important as the piece proceeds; the recall in the later movements of earlier material; a degree of harmonic ambiguity in the later movements; and, most striking, a refrain that grows from a slow introduction to the first movement to lengthier, fuller introductions to the second and third movements, to become the principal material of the fourth movement. Of these devices, harmonic ambiguity and the recall of earlier material may be found in the earlier quartets. The combination here of all the devices results in a quartet that is as individual as each of Bartók's other five.

Forms of the individual movements are uncomplicated. The first, *mesto—vivace,* is in sonata form, with the slow introduction, a faster second introduction (or transition), and then a straightforward exposition, development, recapitulation, and coda. The exposition has three separate themes, the third of which recalls a much faster version of the *mesto* melody. The second theme also works as the closing theme, and the exposition sets up D and F as its contrasting tonalities. (This will be important at the end of the last movement.) The recapitulation presents the exposition's three themes in the original order, but not necessarily in the original character. The movement has a certain quicksilver quality, from changes in tempo, general lightness of character, and the fleeting nature of the themes themselves. Like the first movements of Schoenberg's Second Quartet, Op. 10, or Beethoven's Op. 127, this movement is unfixed, open ended. It seems to serve as an introduction to the quartet as a whole.

The remaining movements are all in ABA' forms. The second movement (*Marcia*) uses as its principal theme the melody of the first movement of *Contrasts* (1938). Its A sections are themselves in ternary aba' forms, so that this principal *a* section (or its variants) occurs four times in the course of the seven-minute movement. The A sections are of roughly the same length, rather greater than that of the B section. The same outline recurs in the third movement (*Burletta*): three sections, ABA', the A sections again roughly the same length and of greater duration than the B; here, though, A' is significantly recomposed. The final movement (*mesto*) builds from the material of the slow introductions to each of the previous movements. The *mesto* is also an ABA', but the first A is longer than the subsequent BA' together, and the A' uses material from B as well. In addition, the B section recalls the two most important themes of the first movement, the first two themes of the exposition. (It is also possible to hear material from the first movement in the third, if less definitely outlined, and working perhaps as a foreshadowing for the direct quotations in the fourth movement.) This recall of the themes from the first movement serves to close off that movement and to bind the quartet together. But the end of the quartet, in another reprise of material from the first movement, undermines that closure. The final cadence of the quartet juxtaposes D and F, the two keys of the exposition of the first movement, and it is left unresolved. This final cadence is of great interest; we shall return to it.

This would all seem straightforward: a first-movement sonata form, two scherzolike movements, and a finale that repeats the formal outlines of the previous two movements as it incorporates melodic and harmonic materials from the first. But I have omitted from this description the music that connects all four movements and that gives the Sixth Quartet its aesthetic depth and complexity.

The *mesto* that introduces the first movement is played by the solo viola (Ex. 6.7). At the beginning of the second movement, it recurs in a

EXAMPLE 6.7. Bartók, String Quartet No. 6, first movement, mm. 1–3.
© Copyright 1941 by Hawkes & Son (London) Ltd.; copyright renewed.
Reprinted by permission of Boosey & Hawkes, Inc.

two-part texture, with the melody played by the cello while the other instruments play a single countermelody in three different octaves, all muted (the first violin plays sustained notes; the second violin and viola play *tremolo*). At the beginning of the third movement, the *mesto* is expanded again, now to a three-part texture. At first the first violin has the tune while the second violin and cello accompany. Then, in measure 10, the viola doubles the first violin at the octave below—still a three-voice texture, but now thicker. Finally, at the beginning of the fourth movement, the melody is heard in a complete four-voice texture (the cello at its first entrance playing the melody in canon with the first violin).

The *mesto* thus grows in texture with each hearing. It also grows longer, from 50 seconds at the beginning of the first movement to one minute for the second, and 1′20″ for the third. The listener has no way of knowing, at the beginning of the fourth movement, whether this material will again be introductory. Thus the beginning of the fourth movement is doubly unstable, because of the nature of the music—slow, chromatic, the phrases of the four instruments overlapping in a full polyphonic texture—and because we do not know what is to come.

The music builds to a *forte* climax on a C-minor chord (m. 13), the first real textural articulation; but then it continues with the same sort of music, spinning out chromatic lines from smaller units of the principal melody. Thus the listener realizes only gradually that this introductory music has become the very substance of the last movement. This realization changes the way we incorporate the three preceding movements into our hearing of the fourth, as it affects in retrospect our memories of the first three movements. The progressively thickening and lengthening *mesto* now assumes greater importance in our ears, as the structurally more static and simple earlier movements yield to it.

In addition, the structural functions of the movements change. The sectional quality of the second and third movements requires the ear's memory for their stability; the repetition of sections is a recovery of the past, not an ongoing development. In the fourth movement, this assumption is called into question. The growing importance of the *mesto* makes these substantial movements now seem only way stations. It is rather the reverse procedure but the same effect as in Beethoven's Ninth Symphony, where out of chaos and unstable recitative, music from the first three movements is called forth, summarily cut off, and dismissed, giving way to the triumphant chorale melody for Schiller's "Ode to Joy." No music from the earlier movements proper is heard in the first half of Bartók's last movement. But the growing realization that the *mesto* is taking final precedence serves a similar purpose of downplaying the earlier movements, as the ear relinquishes them in favor of the final movement. Continuous development now seems the essential quality of this quartet. The function of the very end of the piece becomes the integration of the contrasting material of the first movement into a coherent utterance.

The B section of the last movement begins this process by directly quoting the first movement's first theme, but also by thinning out and simplifying the texture and chromaticism of the first half of the last movement. The entire effect is one of closure, of leave-taking. (When the second theme of the first movement is quoted, it is marked *più dolce, lontano*—more sweetly, distantly.) The final A' returns to the *mesto*, now in miniature, but the final cadence is still ambiguous (Ex. 6.8). The viola repeats the *mesto* melody at the original pitch level, accompanied by a descending chromatic line in the second violin. The two instruments end on an E♭ and an A, which is then taken over by the first violin (joined by the second). The cello enters on a G♯, the first note of the preceding viola melody, perhaps as if to begin that again; but it does not. The E♭ of the dyad in the violins descends to D, the A is retained; this dyad seems to become the final tonal center of the quartet, especially when the cello G♯ moves both to the A and the F♯ of the D-major triad. But even this is not the end: the cello, pizzicato, plays the first phrase, and only the first phrase, of the *mesto* melody, filled out in com-

EXAMPLE 6.8. Bartók, String Quartet No. 6, fourth movement, mm. 81–86.
© Copyright 1941 by Hawkes & Son (London) Ltd.; copyright renewed.
Reprinted by permission of Boosey & Hawkes, Inc.

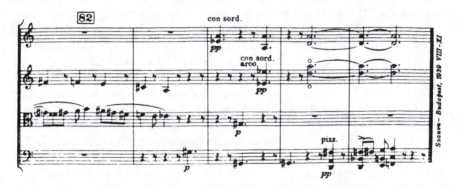

plete triads, and ending not on D major but on F major, as the D–A
dyad continues to sound in the violins.

It is impossible to resolve this cadence into a single chord. The cadence becomes a simultaneity of the first and last units, still separate
(melody versus tonality) but heard together. The final triads in the cello
are of extraordinary sweetness; they disappear into the air rather than
rest firmly on the ground. The combination of these various effects—
sweetness, lack of complete and insistent closure, harmonic ambiguity
(or harmonic simultaneity), incomplete melody, but arrival at finality in
every other way—gives the Sixth Quartet its complex emotional character. Its handling of time is also an essential element of this character,
for all Bartók's other quartets, varied as they are, seem more in line
with the traditional Western conception of time as linear, ongoing, unitary, and unrepeatable. The Sixth Quartet folds or overlaps different
times. The treatment of the *mesto* is progressive, developmental, and
cumulatively deepening. The second and third movements are sectional and static; in retrospect, as the *mesto* takes precedence, they seem
like irruptions into its continuing stream. The appearance in the fourth

movement of melodies from the first brings that open-ended movement back into the arena, now grounded in the stable, central music of
the *mesto* material; but the melodies and textures from the earlier
movement remain as light and ethereal as before. To borrow a phrase
from Mallarmé, they are evoked even as they escape. Despite the seeming finality of the *mesto* music, the last cadence sustains the first movement's lightness and incorporeal quality. We are left with a piece that
evokes several temporal streams at the same time, a work that is hence
aesthetically or emotionally layered, pluralistic, but whose strands cannot finally be disentangled. If there can be an oxymoron in music, it is
this conclusion to the Bartók Sixth, and the emotional world of the
quartet as a whole.

Until recently, Dmitri Shostakovich has been thought of—in the
former Soviet Union and in the West—primarily as a symphonist. In
the last fifteen years or so, however, much attention has been turned to
his fifteen string quartets.[39] The quartets have been recorded several
times, and performers have begun to present them as a complete cycle
over the course of several evenings, like the quartets of Beethoven and
Bartók. Like the sixteen Beethoven quartets in particular, Shostakovich's are now heard as a sort of musical autobiography of the composer, a portrayal of his innermost life in this most intimate of chamber
formats. Indeed, the Eighth Quartet (1960) quotes music from earlier
compositions of Shostakovich, including his musical anagram (D. SCH.,
or the pitches D–E♭–C–B in German nomenclature), which he also used
in his Tenth Symphony (1953).

Much more critical and biographical work needs to be done on
Shostakovich before any reliable accounting of his work, much less any
evaluation of it, can be essayed. Shostakovich's musical styles are many,
often within a single work. He adopts traits from many styles of the
early and middle twentieth century, but to a different effect than other
musically eclectic pieces. His idiom is essentially conservative musically
and more radical personally. He turns more modern characteristics—
for example, sardonic dissonances in a generally tonal context, and especially a remarkably free approach to formal construction—to extraordinarily expressive individual use. Many of his quartets eschew the
four-movement cycle still most common even in our century; many of
his individual movements are original forms. The result is that these
works seem to create their own worlds, much as Mahler's symphonies do.

For some listeners, as with some listeners to Mahler, the worlds of
Shostakovich's quartets are dark and deeply disturbing. This may reflect the state of the earth and its inhabitants during the twentieth century as much as it does Shostakovich's intolerable situation in the Soviet
Union, especially under Stalin: Shostakovich was never one to compose
in a vacuum. The Eighth Quartet is dedicated "to the memory of the

victims of fascism and the war." The last of the series, the Fifteenth (1974) consists of six run-on movements—Elegy, Serenade, Intermezzo, Nocturne, Funeral March, and Epilogue—all of which are *adagio*s. It is undeniably the case that Shostakovich's colors are generally dark. Never nostalgic, he often seems to turn modern musical gestures or usages against themselves, as a kind of bitter reflection on the world around him. His quartets and symphonies make intense demands on the listener; whether the current popularity of Shostakovich's quartets reflects our current situation, or whether they will achieve the seemingly timeless stature of their only modern equivalent, Bartók's six, remains to be seen.

Shostakovich's music seems both highly individual and generally (if also perhaps sardonically) modern, rather than "Russian" or "Soviet." Bartók's music, when not classed as neoclassic, is invariably labeled "quintessentially Hungarian," and its ethnic qualities are not difficult to hear. If Ives's music sounds equally American, it is usually because he quotes American vernacular tunes and sometimes uses ragtime rhythms. Americanness is not always easy to define: one can hear it unmistakably, for example, in the First Piano Sonata (1930) of Roger Sessions, but beyond the piece's syncopated rhythms in the first and third movements, I am not entirely sure why. The same is true of the String Quartet from 1931 by Ruth Crawford Seeger,[40] who was living in Berlin when she composed it. (By coincidence, Sessions lived in Florence and Berlin when working on his First Sonata.) The American quality of Seeger's quartet certainly has something to do with its forthrightness: it does not sound as if the weight of the Beethoven quartets was lying on her shoulders. Seeger's quartet sounds unlike any others of its time; in this, it is somewhat akin to the emergence of Elliott Carter in his First String Quartet of 1951. It became widely popular in the early 1970s, primarily because of a superlative recording by the Composers Quartet, and as part of a general surge of interest in Ives and contemporary (that is, postwar) American music. (The surge of interest in music by women composers did not really achieve momentum until later in the 1970s, or even the 1980s.)

Seeger's most striking conception in the String Quartet is her treatment of the ensemble as four different voices, united only by the commonality of instrumental family. This is not simply a question of texture in the sense of homophony and polyphony; it is a question of texture in a more general sense, as we discussed it in the music of Debussy in chapter 1. The instruments in Seeger's quartet are, in a metaphorical sense, dramatic, four differing characters of a single species, assembled in a single given space, engaged in some sort of (musical) discourse. This concerted discourse is the stuff of the work at its local level and in its basic materials, and it determines the shape of the piece as a whole. We can approach the treatment of the quartet by considering Seeger's treatment of pitch, of rhythms, and of the forms of the composition.

Seeger's treatment of pitch is in some ways quasi-serial.[41] She is less inclined to derive the composition from a row (the fourth movement excepted) than to employ other devices closely associated with the twelve-tone technique. For example, she avoids close repetition of specific pitch classes, especially in a given octave. Indeed, an important issue in this quartet is whether the various members of a given pitch class (all Ds, for example) are in fact equivalent, as they must be in tonal music and as they almost invariably are in the truly serial music of the era. Instead of using pitch-class equivalence throughout the range to privilege harmonic unity and the string quartet as an ensemble, Seeger subordinates pitch-class equivalence to the articulation of registers and the internal differentiation of texture and ensemble.

At the same time that she avoids repeating pitches (and pitch classes) and emphasizing any pitch as a possible tonal center, Seeger does repeat melodic contours with an approximation of pitch repetition. In Example 6.9 the shape of the first violin's first phrase (mm. 1–8) resembles that of the second (mm. 8–15); after the first pitch, the next few (D♯/E♭–E–F♯–C♯–D♯) are identical, the last C♯ comes in the same place, and the two cadential notes are the same. But the specific rhythms of each phrase are different, and these identical pitches are placed differently as the phrase unfolds. These two phrases work as

EXAMPLE 6.9. Seeger, String Quartet, first movement, violin I, mm. 1–15.
© 1941 Merion Music, Inc. Used by Permission of the Publisher.

STRING QUARTET 1931

FIRST VIOLIN

RUTH CRAWFORD

principally similar, two antecedent phrases answered by a contrasting phrase in the second violin (mm. 6–7 and 13–15), its two appearances as mutually differentiated as the two phrases of the first violin. The opening is thus a local example of differing levels of identity (through repetition) and difference (through variation and contrast), distinction of instrument and register, and commencement of a structured musical discourse (through alternation and varied repetition). The handling of pitch, though of course not the sole musical technique at work, is an integral part of the musical construction.

In addition to such approximate phrase repetitions, Seeger also uses more traditional devices. She reuses the opening music of the first movement by repeating the first violin's entrance (mm. 1–4) in exact inversion, beginning two octaves lower (mm. 25–34, Ex. 6.10). This is

EXAMPLE 6.10. Seeger, String Quartet, first movement, Violin I, mm. 25–34. © 1941 Merion Music, Inc. Used by Permission of the Publisher.

another example of exacting unity that is nevertheless understated: the durations of the first six notes in each phrase are the same, but the metrical placement is different; the final two notes in the second example are greatly elongated (as the focus shifts from this melody to the cello line); and the resulting effect is one of continuation, of melodic spinning-out.

A much more unusual, and from a teleological point of view "advanced," technique is that of the fourth movement. This *allegro possibile* pits the first violin against the lower three instruments playing in octaves. Seeger uses here a ten-note series in a "rotational" manner. After the first statement of the series presents all ten notes in order, she then begins the second statement (third note of m. 4) with the second note of the series (E), so that the first pitch (D) now appears as the last of the ten (m. 5). The third presentation of the series then begins with the third note, F, and D and E appear in the ninth and tenth positions (mm. 7–8); and so on (see Ex. 6.11). This seemingly mechanistic treatment of a series presented in even eighth notes for almost the first third of the movement is enlivened by every other compositional device at Seeger's disposal. In this movement, unlike the first, register is not associated with particular pitch classes but with phrase contour; the first five statements by the three lower instruments, for example, have an

EXAMPLE 6.11. Seeger, String Quartet, fourth movement, mm. 1–12. © 1941 Merion Music, Inc. Used by Permission of the Publisher.

IV

overall rising shape. In addition, these first statements are differently phrased: the first four statements all begin with internal groups of 4 + 2 + 4 + 2 eighths, but vary thereafter.

A similarly rigorous device creates the shape and momentum of the movement as a whole. The first statement by the lower three instruments (mm. 3–5) is twenty eighth notes long. The second, mm. 7–9, is nineteen eighths. The third, mm. 10–12, is eighteen, the fourth seventeen, and so on. Each succeeding statement by the lower three instruments is shortened by a single eighth note, so that even though pitch classes are repeated, no melodic phrase recurs exactly. The simultaneous working-through of differing constructive techniques results in an unstoppable, forward-surging musical current.

Of the other critical compositional devices in this quartet, rhythm and texture are the most important. In the first movement, where the texture is one of four simultaneous but separate voices, rhythm is a means of distinguishing among the four. Seeger avoids any sense of metricality: the phrases are of differing lengths, the varied durations of notes sound like rubato playing, tied notes are used to disguise beats and hence avoid regular metrical articulation, and the four instruments often vary quite strongly in their particular rhythmic vocabulary. When the solo line passes from the first to the second violin in the sixth measure of the first movement, for example, not only does the tempo increase slightly, but the second violin's rhythms become more brusque in the shortness of the gestures and their relative angularity (see Ex. 6.12).

This rhythmic distinction is preeminent in the first movement, but not in the others. The second movement is a scherzolike chasing among the instruments, which are united in their rhythmic vocabulary, if not in a homophonic ensemble. The third movement is one of overlapping ("lapping" almost literally in this instance) rhythms, the fourth a juxtaposition of streams of steady notes in the three lower instruments against freer, more differentiated rhythms in the other. Here the first violin begins with a single note, accented and *fortissimo,* answered by a unit of two similar notes (see Ex. 6.11). The three lower instruments answer with twenty even eighth notes, articulated only by the subgrouping $4 + 2 + 4 + 2 + 3 + 3 + 2$, or a subdivision of a $(4 + 2)$ + $a + b$ $(3 + 3 + 2)$. As the first violin's lines grow from the single note to twenty notes (each successive phrase is one note longer), the lower

EXAMPLE 6.12. Seeger, String Quartet, first movement, mm. 1–7. © 1941 Merion Music, Inc. Used by Permission of the Publisher.

three instruments' shorten, from the twenty notes of the first long phrase to a unison E halfway through the movement (mm. 57–60), at which point the process reverses, so that the first violin's lines are reduced by one eighth note with each entrance, while the lower three instruments grow by one. The movement ends with a string of twenty even eighth notes in the lower voice and accented *fortissimi*, two notes and then one, in the first violin. Throughout the first half of this movement, the lower three voices move in steady eighth notes, and longer durations occur only at the ends of phrases and at the central E, held for 10½ beats. (In the second half of the movement, the longer durations, on the other hand, come at the beginning of the corresponding phrases.) The first violin's rhythms, however, are unfettered, and use a variety of durations, placed within measures or across barlines, using "irrational" subdivisions of the metrical unit as well as "rational" ones (e.g., five instead of four notes to the half note), and so on. But as with the lower three instruments, at the halfway point of the movement, the rhythms reverse themselves so that the second half is an exact retrograde of the first.

This retrograde arch form, moreover, permeates all aspects of the fourth movement as a whole. As the first violin's lines grow from a single note to twenty, and then diminish back to one, its dynamic levels move from accented *fortissimi* (*ffz*) through a gradual decrescendo to a *pianissimo* at m. 60, the sustained G (the violin's lowest note) that closes the first half. The second half begins *pianissimo* with the phrase of twenty notes; as the first violin's utterances increase in dynamics, they lessen in duration until we reach the punched-out *fortissimi* of the opening measures again in the closing ones. While this is taking place in the first violin, an analogous arch shape unfolds in the lower three voices, beginning with lines of twenty notes, *pianissimo* and muted, the lines then diminishing in length with each phrase but increasing in dynamics (although always muted—compare the second movement of Bartók's Fourth Quartet) to an accented *fortissimo* at the climax of the arch and *ffzp* at its capstone, the sustained E in the lower instruments with the G of the first violin. This process, too, then turns around, so that in the second half, the lines become longer and progressively softer.

The final aspect of this retrograde structure concerns pitch. At m. 60, the capstone of the arch, not only do the dynamics and phrase lengths of the two principal voices reverse themselves, but the melodic contours also form exact retrogrades of those of the first half. The only difference is that the pitches of the second half are a minor second higher than those of the first.

Yet because of the crossings of the simultaneous arch forms—the first violin's progressively longer units become softer while the other three voices' progressively shorter ones become louder, and vice versa, so that one musical element grows as another ebbs—and because of the furious tempo (*allegro possibile*), one hears this movement less as an arch form symmetrical around a central axis (as in Bartók's Fourth and Fifth Quartets) than as a symmetrical binary form, a forward-moving assault in two suggestive gestures. There is no time to contemplate the arch form, and contemplation of its symmetry and its unshakable solidity is precisely the requirement for aesthetic appreciation of a musical arch. The function of Seeger's arch form is not the achievement of a mirror-like symmetry, but rather the duplication of the trajectories of the first half of the movement within a firmly controlled framework, one that increases the potential energy of the music by concentrating and circumscribing its expressive gestures.

The third movement, *andante,* is a truer arch form. The music begins low and soft, builds steadily to a *fff* climax that fills three and a half octaves, then turns around and subsides to the original register and dynamics. (In this way, and in the immediacy of its emotional impact, the movement resembles Samuel Barber's Adagio for Strings—originally the slow movement of his 1936 String Quartet—and the first movement of Bartók's Music for Strings, Percussion, and Celesta, also of 1936.) The novelty of the movement, however, lies in its materials. Each instrument plays continuously, its bow changes "as little audible as possible throughout," according to the score. With each sustained pitch, the dynamics swell slightly, from *ppp* to *piano*. The harmonies are clusters rather than chords, so that one hears texture and relative register rather than pitches. Moreover, the instruments' entrances overlap, so that the beginnings of individual notes are virtually inaudible in the swell and ebb of the dynamics. This movement is a single-mindedly gestural piece, its force emanating from the unbroken continuity of that gesture, the overlapping of smaller, swirling motions within a larger tide.

That tide grows and then fades. Virtually the sole resemblance among movements in this quartet is their singularity of purpose, their making a given gesture without repeating it. The first two movements are forward moving and relatively unclosed. The third movement, as we have seen, grows in dynamics and register and then turns back on itself. The fourth movement combines various crossed musical arches in a binary scheme. Each movement is extremely short—the quartet as a whole takes less than ten minutes in the recording by the Composers Quartet, and only slightly longer in the recording by the Arditti Quartet. This concentration reinforces the gestural directness of each movement, for we have no time to think about what we are hearing, no repetitive sections that lend themselves to contemplation. Moreover, the great dissimilarities among the four movements, their brevity and their concentration, reinforce the reaction that Seeger's composition is something new in the universe of the string quartet, and their gnomic character leaves the listener unsettled at the work's conclusion. There is no particular process from one movement to the next. The movements, played without pause, seem to imply a cohesive series of traditional forms, but that implication is false. The quartet involves both abstraction (the "systems" at work in the last movement) and drama (the first three movements), and insists on experience rather than contemplation or assimilation of that experience. The contradictions among these qualities are not resolved, and Seeger's willingness to leave them simply as they are is perhaps the most modern of the quartet's qualities.

The Post–1945 Quartet in the United States

The postwar American quartet, at least on the East Coast, very much follows in the vein of the Seeger String Quartet.[42] In the treatment of rhythms, the handling of textures, the formal lightness of touch, and especially the conception of the string quartet as an ensemble of four distinct personae, the string quartets of Elliott Carter, Milton Babbitt, George Perle, and others all bear resemblance to Seeger's— granted, more a familial American resemblance than a direct stylistic or aesthetic influence. But within the postwar American group, each composer is quite distinct. Carter's music before World War II had been in the neoclassic Americanist vein, not unlike that of Aaron Copland or Roy Harris. A more individual voice began to emerge in his Piano Sonata (1946) and particularly in the Sonata for Violoncello and Piano of 1948 (see chapters 2 and 5). Carter's music does resemble Babbitt's in that no matter how difficult to play or analyze, it *sounds* wonderfully. But beyond that his music is like no one else's. In fact, each individual piece of Carter's has a striking individuality of sound; for despite certain compositional procedures common from one work to another, Carter likes to invent material specific to each work and designed for its particular performing forces. Close analysis of one Carter work, then, does not necessarily help us to a closer understanding of another Carter work. It is better here to begin with Carter's own discussions of his compositional methods and procedures in the first two string quartets,[43] and then proceed to a consideration of temporality and modernism in these pieces.

Carter has touched on his first two quartets in his articles "Shop Talk by an American Composer" and "The Time Dimension in Music," and in liner and program notes.[44] In the First Quartet he mentions specifically new devices of rhythm and tempo and their effect on form: not only does he use complex polyrhythms, but he also achieves a constant change of pulse by overlapping tempi. In the first movement his four principal themes are each distinguished by different speeds and characters; in the fourth movement, a set of variations, musical ideas continually speed up. The harmonic superstructure is also specific to this quartet. All of Carter's post–1948 music is written in what is sometimes called "free" or "twelve-tone diatonicism," meaning that pitch (or harmonic) structures are specific to the piece in question, that all twelve pitch classes within the octave are available to the composer, and that strict serial procedures (inversion, retrograde, retrograde inversion, the prohibition against close repetition of pitch class) are not in force as the primary compositional techniques. In the case of the First Quartet, Carter uses a "key" four-note chord, which pervades the quartet in various inversions, voicings, and transpositions (not unlike the *Tristan* chord in Wagner's opera).

Equally important as the handling of rhythm and pitch are Carter's textures and forms. He emphasizes the stratification of texture as the four separate instruments gradually, across the work, approach one another more closely. This is one large-scale shaping device at work; another is the noncontiguity of movements and breaks between movements. The First Quartet is in four movements. The first is a fantasia, marked *maestoso,* which the composer describes as a contrapuntal fantasy, the simultaneity of different voices with a plethora of principal and subsidiary themes, essentially through-composed. The second movement is a scherzolike allegro scorrevole. The third is a slow movement, *adagio.* The fourth is the set of variations, of gradually increasing tempi. We thus have the outward shapes of a standard four-movement string quartet, but without the internal structures of the individual movements, an approach not dissimilar to that in Ruth Seeger's quartet. In addition, Carter does not stop his music between movements. Rather, the breaks come in midmovement, during the *allegro scorrevole* and toward the end of the *adagio,* just as the cello has begun the music of the variations. These midmovement pauses are not another manifestation of Carter's predilection for mixing up the "this" and the "that" of his musical material; that predilection is most evident, and most powerful, at the immediate surface level of the music. The effect of these midmovement breaks is rather to disturb temporality: the very breaks emphasize the continuity and malleability of time. Without pauses, Carter's quartet would very much resemble the First Quartet of Schoenberg, at least in its outward mien, and its unbroken continuity would emphasize the work's self-contained insularity, its separate existence in the aural world, a cohesive structure marked off from the rest of the world by clear gestures at the beginning and end. The pauses in midmovement, on the contrary, disturb this separation of "work" and "nonwork," of internal and external time. In the concert hall, the players in the quartet stop playing in midscherzo. They can retune their instruments if necessary. The audience has a chance to resettle itself, to exchange glances or a few words, to unwrap throat lozenges. The quartet members pick up their instruments and continue with exactly the same music from before their pause. Temporal articulation is not necessarily material articulation; and one effect may be that the music has continued unheard during the human intermission.

These breaks and beginning again with the same material are also an aspect of what Carter calls the "dream time" of the quartet.[45] In his 1970 liner notes for the first two string quartets, he writes that

> the general plan [of the First Quartet] was suggested by Jean Cocteau's film *Le Sang d'un poète,* in which the entire dream-like action is framed by an interrupted slow-motion shot of a tall brick chimney in an empty lot being dynamited. Just as the chimney begins to fall apart, the shot is broken off and the entire movie follows, after which the shot of the chimney is resumed at the point it left off, showing its disintegration in mid-air, and closing the film with its collapse on the ground. A similar interrupted continuity is employed in this quartet's starting with a cadenza for cello alone that is continued by the first violin alone at the very end. . . . I interpret Cocteau's idea (and my own) as establishing the difference between external time (measured by the falling chimney, or the cadenza) and internal dream time (the main body of the work)—the dream time lasting but a moment of external time but from the dreamer's point of view, a long stretch.[46]

The modus operandi of the Second String Quartet (1959) also involves the individuation of the instruments and a dramatic scenario (these become the hallmarks of Carter's composing), but realized far more specifically than in the First Quartet. In the Second, each instrument has a particular vocabulary of musical intervals (melodic and harmonic) and rhythms. The characters of the four instruments are indicated in the prefatory note to the score: the first violin is to exhibit the greatest variety of character, but most often plays in a bravura manner; the second violin is regular and often witty; the viola part is predominantly expressive; and the cello's rubato and *accelerando* playing make it sound as if it were trying to draw the other instruments into a temporal world beyond the chronometric.

The forms of the Second Quartet generally resemble the outlines of the First Quartet and even the Cello Sonata. The scheme of the Second Quartet is, again, one of general rapprochement and then reindividuation across the four movements (marked *allegro fantastico, presto scherzando, andante espressivo,* and *allegro*). But these movements are punctuated—connected temporally and materially, separated and held apart, all simultaneously—by a framing introduction and conclusion and by "cadenzas" in which individual instruments confront the others. This is the scheme of the quartet as a whole.

Movement or section	***Leading instrument***
Introduction	All, "companionate"[47]
Allegro fantastico	First violin
Cadenza	Viola
Presto scherzando	Second violin
Cadenza	Cello
Andante espressivo	Viola
Cadenza	First violin
Allegro	Cello (et al.)
Conclusion	All, "companionate"

Carter thus again presents simultaneously (at least) two different structural schemes, one the standard string quartet cycle, the other the dramatic scenario of confrontation and interaction among the four instruments. These ideas of simultaneous and interlocking structural schemes, and (in the First Quartet) temporal circularity, Carter ties directly to the first great generation of twentieth-century modernism, the works of Joyce and Thomas Mann.[48]

It is an interesting analogy. What a structuralist might call the synchronization of temporality is a central concern of much modernist literature. The interfoldings of different temporal progressions, of different chronological eras, of disappearance and rebirth lie at the heart of such different writers as Joyce, Proust, and Faulkner. But it seems to me that Carter is rather disingenuous here, for he ignores the essential aspect of music, that it occurs in chronological time, and that one cannot change that fact (only, perhaps, manipulate it). Carter, of course, knows this fact very well, and all his music speaks directly to it. My assumption is that in his notes on his music, he is endeavoring to bring the relatively uninitiated into the world of his compositions by comparing these to the great masterworks of modernism with which listeners are already acquainted. I am not implying that Carter is trying to ride on Joyce's coattails. But assuming that the self-respecting citizen of the modern artistic world is familiar with Joyce, Proust, Mann, and Cocteau, it makes sense to connect the new (Carter's quartets) with the already known in order to bring the listener into some sort of intelligent contact with the unfamiliar. As a teaching device, this is unexceptionable.

As an aesthetic guide, it is more troublesome. A musical composition is not an artifact. A score or recording, like a novel or painting, is: it exists in space, and to that degree unidirectional chronological flow is irrelevant. But this is not the case for music itself. Although every sophisticated listener listens "backward" as well as in the present, meaning that we carry the musical past of a composition with us as we hear it progress in the present and—to a certain degree—anticipate its future events, we are free to roam at will through a composition only when it is over, when we have reified it in our minds as a past event, the proverbial closed book. Yet even this musical "closure" is not entirely satisfactory, for informed musical response requires that we consider an episode or event not simply in splendid isolation but in the dynamic of a work as a whole, for that dynamic informs every musical event. Such circularity as Carter describes in his Cello Sonata and First Quartet is to my mind an impossibility; in both instances, I think, he has rather provided a framing device. Carter's connecting compositional episodes with Joycean epiphanies or with the recurring archetypes of Joyce, Mann, and others is a closer analogy. But even here one might also prefer to stay with the musical, with the compositional procedures of *Tristan*, of Debussy, of Stravinsky, with the counterexamples of Messiaen and Bartók. Carter's music is in fact modern, especially in its use of pitch and rhythm. In its forms, however, in its essential message to its listeners, in each work as an individuated and meticulously shaped dramatic event, the music is entirely and affirmatively traditional and classicizing. The Carter of the post–World War II years may be as neoclassical as the Carter of the 1930s. It is certainly not in question that the combination of surface modernism and deeper traditionalism has placed his music at the center of the American contemporary scene for more than forty years.

One hundred eighty degrees away from Carter's music is that of George Crumb. With echoes of Debussy, Bartók, and Mahler, Crumb was a new and highly individual voice from the late 1960s, and perhaps the most famous name in contemporary music through the 1970s. He is, in the more obvious and perhaps superficial ways, thoroughly Romantic; but unlike the composers of the so-called neoromantic movement after 1968, or the more meretricious, derivative composers, Crumb never sinks into the *boue de la nostalgie*. His pieces, which work far more effectively in live performance than in recordings because of their dramatic elements (not visual coups de théâtre, but the sight of musicians in almost ritualistic guises), are filled with striking sounds and sonorities, all sorts of "expressive" devices that are at the same time structural and integral, original twists on listeners' expectations and anticipations, and a sense of mysticism (by that I mean a sort of awe at the enduring power of unseen nature, and wonderment at humanity's existential stance, the thinking reed) that matched many of the darker strains in the temper of the 1960s and 1970s in the United States. Crumb's 1970 string quartet *Black Angels* is an example of all this, and an example of a kind of chamber music not seen since *Pierrot lunaire* of 1912—in Crumb's own words a "parable on our troubled world . . . [symbolic of] the essential polarity—God versus Devil," a parable in three movements, which represent a "voyage of the soul."[49] An indication at the beginning of the score reads "in tempore belli, 1970"; while the music reflects nothing specific of the situation in the United States (or Southeast Asia) in that era, it does embody much of the anxiety, the sense of loss, and the very uncertain hope for the more or less distant future then felt by many people.

The work is composed for electric string quartet; the instruments may have contact microphones attached, but Crumb's preference is that they be real electronic string instruments, with built-in pickup microphones. In addition, the four string players are to play maracas, tam-tam (both struck and bowed, at its edge, with a contrabass bow), and "glass harmonica," crystal glasses filled to certain heights with water and then bowed to produce specific pitches. The string players are also called on to speak—in specified rhythms, as if in invocation or religious ceremony—the numbers from one to seven, or the numbers seven and thirteen, in French, German, Russian, Hungarian, Japanese, and Swahili. Finally, the instrumentalists are to approach their instruments in completely unusual ways, beyond the effects produced by the very electrification of the instruments, and beyond the ordinary extended techniques such as the Bartók pizzicato or bowing *col legno*. Two movements call for the violins and viola to be held like viols, with the players bowing up near the pegs, on the "wrong" side of the left hand, as the score says. In one movement (No. 6, "Pavana Lachrymae"), Crumb uses a sort of "Mood Indigo" voicing, the cello playing the highest line and the second violin and viola the lower parts. (In Duke Ellington's 1930 "Mood Indigo," a muted trumpet plays the highest part, muted trombone the middle, and clarinet the lowest. The combination of instruments in unusual registers and voicings gives an almost otherworldly quality to both the Ellington and the Crumb.) Another movement calls for a sort of bottleneck effect, using a glass rod. The movement entitled "Devil-music" calls for increasing the bow pressure to the point that the pitches become noise, and the use of pedal tones to sound the *Dies irae* in a register lower and grislier than the normal. The last movement calls for a very fast tremolo on the strings with two fingers capped with thimbles. Again, these various effects and techniques are much more effective in live performance than on a recording, because of the normal "presence" of a live performance, but even more because one is forced to confront their strangeness in a way that one is not if the sounds are merely coming through speakers in the living room. The special effects are not just extraordinary sounds; the exploitation of the instruments, their use far beyond their normal "limits," becomes programmatic, part of the very work.

That program may be seen in the titles and arrangement of sections and movements, as these are supplied in a quartet's program or in notes with recordings:[50]

BLACK ANGELS

I. DEPARTURE

1. **(Tutti) Threnody I: Night of the Electric Insects** (Vibrant, intense)
2. **(Trio) Sounds of Bones and Flutes** (Delicate and somewhat mechanical)
3. **(Duo) Lost Bells** (Remote, transfigured)
4. **Devil-music [Solo: Cadenza accompagnata]** (In romantic-phantastic style! con bravura)
5. **(Duo) Danse Macabre** (Grotesque, satirical)
   (Duo alternativo: *Dies irae*)[51]

II. ABSENCE

6. **(Trio) Pavana Lachrymae [der Tod und das Mädchen]** (Grave, solemn; like a consort of viols [a fragile echo of an ancient music])
7. **(Tutti) Threnody II: Black Angels!** (Furiously, with great energy)
8. **(Trio) Sarabanda de la Muerte Oscura** (Grave, solemn; like a consort of viols)
9. **(Duo) Lost Bells (Echo)**
   (Duo alternativo: Sounds of Bones and Flutes)

III. RETURN

10. **God-music [Solo: Aria accompagnata]** (Adagio [with profound calm])
11. **(Duo) Ancient Voices**
12. **(Trio) Ancient Voices (Echo)** (Grazioso, flessibile [glissando sempre])
13. **(Tutti) Threnody III: Night of the Electric Insects** (Disembodied, incorporeal)

Thus thirteen continuous sections, asymmetrically grouped into three large movements. (The work as a whole lasts some twenty-one minutes.) The titles of the movements are the stages of the "voyage of the soul" that Crumb has invoked; and although they are the same as the movement titles to Beethoven's *Les adieux* Sonata, Op. 81a, for piano, they have much less—if anything—to do with that work than with the journey in Schoenberg's *Pierrot lunaire*. The difference is that Pierrot's journey was immiscibly intertwined with that of the Poet of the verses, and that the tone of the poem and music veers from light irony to horror and nostalgic sweetness, with many points in between. In Crumb's music, there is no such distancing between the creator and object (Giraud/Schoenberg, Pierrot/Poet, artist/poetry and music) or between the art work and the audience. Crumb's listeners are not to contemplate the journey *Black Angels* represents, but to experience it. Every "representational designator"[52] is in aid of that experience: the titles of the sections and the movements, the instrumental requirements and effects that we have noted, and the original music and the quotations as well. (The "Pavana Lachrymae," as its subtitle suggests, uses the principal melody of Schubert's song "Death and the Maiden." Although the "Sarabanda de la Muerte Oscura" is newly composed, it sounds as if it ought to be a quotation, a ghost returning from the Spanish Renaissance.) All of Crumb's resources are so intensely pointed to this end that the composer Lejaren Hiller has described *Black Angels* as "almost luridly melodramatic."[53]

In addition to the various obvious elements, Crumb has also incorporated into the quartet "secret," not readily audible structures. The bridge between the audible and concealed consists of the arch structure of the musical journey's thirteen sections and the four instrumentalists' reciting the numbers seven and thirteen and counting from one to seven in various languages. The arch structure works in musical connections (Nos. 1, 7, and 13; 2 and 12; 3 and 11; 4 and 10—"Devil-music" and "God-music" respectively—and so on) and in texture (tutti reduced to accompanied solo in No. 4, "Devil-music," back up to tutti in No. 7, "Black Angels!," reduced to accompanied solo again in No. 10, "God-music," and again to tutti in No. 13). This is mapped onto, but not identical to, the three-movement articulation of the piece. In similar fashion, the chanted numbers and the numerology of the arch structure, with its emphasis on 1, 7, and 13, reflect at the surface level a numerology underlying the entire work and signaled in the score (and sometimes in program notes). The numerology revolves entirely around the numbers 7 and 13, in various guises: sections may last 7 or 13 seconds, they may be 7 or 13 measures long, they may contain 7 or 13 notes, and so on. This is of great importance to the composer and to the performers, but it is not audible to an uninformed audience; nor is the same sort of numerology that underlies some works of J. S. Bach, various Renaissance composers, Alban Berg, or any number of composers of mystical or religious bent.

Elliott Carter is one of the leaders of the post–1945 generation of American composers. George Crumb came to the fore some twenty years later. Both are of that group known to music journalism as the academic avant-garde. Unfortunately, too few music critics define which academy they have in mind, or what sort of avant-garde. We can say, I think, that Carter has stood at the forefront of the classicists of his era, writing music that is absolute yet "expressive," its "expressive" elements (such as the conception of the score as a dramatic scenario) forming part of the very structure of each work. The music of Carter and his generation is classicist as well in its general avoidance of programmatic elements in favor of satisfying sounding structures, a reasonably systematic approach to the handling of pitch (and, in some cases, rhythm and meter), and a preference for the traditional performance techniques and the traditional manipulations of texture. Crumb, as we have seen, is often at an opposite extreme from these traditionalist ways of proceeding; an all too facile generalization about his music might be that its structures support the immediate emotional impact of its coloristic and charismatic effects, which are primary. Crumb's voice is very much his own, but he shares with other new composers from the 1960s and 1970s a predilection for new colors and for the loosening of musical structures, and the creation especially of structures that paradoxically are at the same time inherently expressive yet tightly controlled and directed.

The students of Carter, Crumb, and other post–World War II composers are now establishing themselves. It is impossible to characterize this generation at this point. In many ways these composers are their teachers' students, and they follow the paths that were laid out by Carter, Roger Sessions, Arthur Berger, Milton Babbitt, and many others. Although the younger composers considered in our final pages—Joan Tower, Lee Hyla, and others—are highly original, with personal compositional voices, no voice with the newness of John Cage or the authority of Babbitt or Carter has yet come forward. This younger generation is notable for its diversity. We will conclude this study by discussing two examples of the genre by composers born in the 1950s, Steven Mackey and Lee Hyla, and the repertory of one of the most important contemporary ensembles, the Kronos Quartet.

The String Quartet of Steven Mackey (b. 1956) was written in 1983. Although essentially a single long-line structure, it falls into three unequal movements, two of which are further subdivided. The first movement is entitled "An Allegro": the seeming modesty of the indefinite article is really an indication that separates this movement from a standard opening *allegro* of a typical quartet. The second movement is entitled "Two Miniatures," two very brief pieces played with only short pauses between them. The two miniatures are "Hypnogogic Sequence"[54] and "Scherzo." Mackey's finale is made up of four sections, "Quasi Recitative (a third miniature)," "Caricature and Metamorphosis," "An Adagio," and "Epilogue." The first movement, unbroken, lasts between six and seven minutes (6'40" in the recording by the Lydian String Quartet, for whom the piece was written). The "Two Miniatures," together, last about two and a half minutes. The finale, by far the longest of the Quartet's movements, lasts about twelve minutes, but since it is made up of four unequal parts, it does not seem out of proportion; rather, its last three sections appear as the goal to which all that has come before has striven, and the culmination of the quartet as a whole.

The quartet begins diffusely. In his liner notes to the recording, Mackey approvingly cites the description by one member of the Lydian Quartet that the first movement is "a lightning storm—no thunder, just lightning."[55] The movement resembles Babbitt and Webern in its quick-silver, glinting surfaces, the seemingly nervous shifting among ideas and string timbres. The phrasing is unstable, meter and rhythm are largely undefined, motives and figures flit by, and Mackey resorts to an enormous vocabulary of string techniques, hence timbres—bowing on the fingerboard or on the bridge, varying bow pressure, playing harmonics, playing *flautando*, using both right- and left-hand pizzicatos, and so on. In many sections, virtually every measure has character indications (*con fuoco, con bravura, impetuoso, ben articulato, ansioso*). But Mackey's rhythms are not like Babbitt's, and his inchoate melodic figures are not like either Babbitt's or Webern's. Mackey is thinking in long-range terms, setting up and extending a highly unstable first movement, through-composed and varied, that goes on longer than one might expect, toward goals that are not certain, not specifically or inherently implied.

The middle movement, "Two Miniatures," serves the purpose of the traditional slow movement and dance movement. But they are extraordinarily brief here: full thoughts, not truncated, but completely in contrast to the first movement. Mackey's title for the first miniature is very apt; it is quiet, sustained music with occasional flashes of activity, like illusions or visions that may suddenly appear when one is in that state between sleeping and waking. The scherzo, equally characteristic, begins with sustained sounds, like those of the "Hypnogogic Sequence," but the tempo here is faster, the music more metrical; the character of the scherzo is established out of that of the first miniature. The scherzo rounds off the middle movement by subsiding into silence (hypnogogic again), the instrumentalists playing *col legno battuto* (striking the strings with the wood of the bow) and then the three lower players tapping on the bodies of the instruments before a final *pianissimo* pizzicato in the second violin and viola.

The four-part finale reinitiates the various strands of the quartet. The first part is, as Mackey indicates, a third miniature, and it serves as a transition from the second movement to the final movement; at this point the ear begins to weave together the past—the sectional, through-composed, unsettled first movement and the more stable miniatures of the second movement—into the fabric of the immediate present. The "Quasi Recitative" leads directly, without pause, into new music, the "Caricature and Metamorphosis," which recalls the first movement in its activity and quicksilver surface, but which is much more solidly located in meter, rhythms, textures, and ensemble. (That is to say, the string quartet sounds here like an ensemble, a more or less unified group pursuing similar ideas together, unlike the diffused utterances of the first movement.) In addition, this "Caricature and Metamorphosis" is much more audibly direct than any of the music has been up to this point, steadily and geometrically gaining in intensity (through rhythmic activity, dynamics, melodic direction, and so on) to a *fortissimo* passage marked *cataclismico*. This is the first climax of the quartet, resuming the music of the first movement and channeling it, only to explode it. It is followed, unexpectedly at the moment, by an *adagio*.

According to Mackey, this *adagio* "undermines" "the balanced trajectory arching from 'An Allegro' through 'Caricature and Metamorphosis,' " and the section provides "an expressive bulge to the form."[56] One might also hear the *adagio* as the second climax of the quartet, a sort of *Liebestod* in its infinitely long lines following a musical fury, its sustained notes achieving a real timelessness, its texture gradually increasing from solo (second violin) to duet (both violins), trio (with viola), and much later, full quartet. The music of the *adagio* recalls, and seems to absorb, that of the earlier slow movements and sections, to reaffirm these climactically just as the "Metamorphosis" did the faster, unstable music of the first movement. Finally, the *adagio* lasts so long that it takes on much more importance than just an expressive bulge in an otherwise straight line. Its very duration achieves a kind of ecstasy, for, wafting on these high and sustained lines, the listener even forgets the earlier cataclysm. And the power of the *adagio* is increased by its following on the first cataclysmic climax. This *adagio*, to my ears, is the true climax of the quartet.

The climax is followed by a very short epilogue, whose function is not unlike the final pages of *Petrushka, Der Rosenkavalier,* or Ravel's "Scarbo" (from *Gaspard de la nuit,* for piano solo). In all these works, pathos is followed by a light-hearted, impish, or even sardonic conclusion that does not undercut the earlier emotional climax but serves to point it up by contrast. Pathos is prevented from lingering in the ear as bathos, and one is reminded that even the most exquisite movements need not lack humor. So it is with Mackey's epilogue: music has been introduced, explored and developed in both unsystematic and more linear ways, brought to successive climaxes, and now reappears, very close to its original forms. The epilogue rounds off the quartet as the two climaxes have not done, and reinforces its essential internal unity. It is a nice touch, and an example of a musical gesture that changes our perception of a work after the fact, defining it only after its conclusion.

Lee Hyla's Second String Quartet was written in 1985, two years after Mackey's, for the same group, the Lydian Quartet. Also like Mackey's, it is in three interconnected movements; but whereas Mackey's quartet is unified by a single uninterrupted, unfolding line, Hyla's three movements are interconnected in that they share basic materials and a number of motives, much like Bartók's Fourth Quartet. Hyla's work is of unrelenting intensity, realized in part through the concentration of his ideas and in part through his handling of rhythms and texture. He uses few of the extended techniques of Mackey's quartet.

Hyla's quartet is much more melodic than Mackey's. The result is less the sense of anxious instability of Mackey's quartet, more that the music exists in and fully occupies each moment of the present. Intense, unsettling, at times even disturbing, Hyla's music—including *The Dream of Innocent III*, considered in chapter 4—is built in arcs or sections of tension and release. But the sections of release tend to be as intense as those of greater instability. Rarely in Hyla's music does one have the sense that the composer is doing something in order to achieve an effect at a later point, that (for example) dancing, amorphous opening music is a foil for crashes to come. Hyla offers no points where the listener can afford to relax by attending to the (possible) future rather than the concrete present.

Hyla's music reflects not only his composer's knowledge of the canon of Western classical music but also his background (as listener and as keyboard player) in rock and roll, jazz, and original improvisation. This background is not entirely uncommon in Hyla's generation; what is less common is that Hyla still resides in the world of serious composed (i.e., "classical") music, and not in any sort of crossover realm. As a point of reference, Milton Babbitt is a master of the American popular song repertory, but this expertise does not show up to any great degree in his own compositions—one could not deduce from *All Set*, *Partitions* (for solo piano), or one of his string quartets that this is the case. On the other hand, a composer/performer such as Paul Dresher (b. 1951) is as aware of world musics as Hyla, perhaps even more so, and Dresher's performances of his music centrally involve such non-canonic influences, as well as an idea of collective performance (or realization) that is essentially foreign to Western art music before the late twentieth century. Hyla falls somewhere between these two positions. He achieves the intensity and immediacy, the energy, of much rock and jazz, and often through using rock or jazz elements. Yet, without co-opting these elements, he brings them together with an almost Beethovenian compositional ideal (the work of art as free-standing and transcendental; a tight and cohesive structure; a living relationship between design and detail) firmly in line with Western tradition.

A specific example of Hyla's music is the beginning of his Second String Quartet (Ex. 6.13). Like a quartet of Beethoven or Bartók, it is rich with seeds that will flower later, and it is also full of examples of Hyla's general predilections. The first page alone has at least eight examples of techniques or important motives:

1. The first violin melody, which will recur in various guises, and later in the first and third movements in a distinctive duet texture with the cello; this melody passes to the second violin in m. 4.
2. The polyphonic texture, sometimes of varying figures, sometimes of melodies (such as the first and second violins here, the viola later).

EXAMPLE 6.13. Hyla, String Quartet No. 2, first movement, mm. 1–12. © 1985 Lee Hyla.

3. The use of riffs, as important for their rhythmic element as for the melodic (for example, mm. 7 in the second violin, 8–9 in the second violin and cello, 10 in all instruments).

4. The "organic" quality of these riffs, which grow from accompanimental melodies and often connect one section to another (cello riff, coming out of mm. 5–6, developing and repeating through m. 10, continuing into the next section, m. 11).

5. Rock-and-roll rhythms, as in mm. 9–10.
6. The viola's "hovering" melody and its accompaniment, a typical Hyla melody in its combination of sustained, repeated notes and pointed direction, and in its "hovering" quality, which continues through the next page of the score.
7. The sudden contrasts, as in mm. 3–4, 10–11.
8. The violence, or riveting intensity, here indicated by some of the verbal directions.

The second movement of the quartet is marked "nearly motion-less." Over a *tremolo* (F–G or G♯–A) in the cello, the other instruments play single notes, longer and sustained melodies, melodies that pass from one instrument to another or are suddenly doubled in a second instrument, playing harmonics or *sul tasto* (on the fingerboard), with the resulting glassy, distant character, all making music that moves glacially, if at all, and seemingly at a very great but mesmerizing distance. The third movement begins "furiously," like the first movement, with a Bartók pizzicato in the second violin and viola and pseudo-rock-and-roll melodies exchanged between the first violin and cello. This movement is even more intense than the first, which it resembles. It restricts its basic materials even more and emphasizes the wrenching rhythms of the figures. Its contrasting sections maintain textures from the principal sections, especially the idea of mirrored duets, as in Example 6.14. The movement closes the frame opened by the first movement, returning to some of the same material and some of the same manner. But it is not a continuation of that first movement. Here is another aspect of the intensity of Hyla's music: each new movement promises an opportunity for respite, for more relaxation, but such respite never comes. Hyla's pieces tend to be relatively brief, rarely longer than twenty minutes. The emotional intensity and depth of his

EXAMPLE 6.14. Hyla, String Quartet No. 2, third movement, mm. 1–2. © 1985 Lee Hyla.

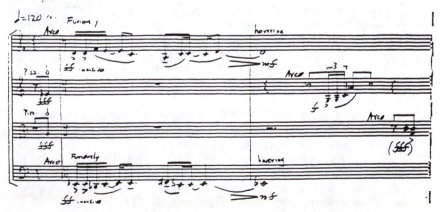

music is difficult to sustain for longer than that, for composer, performers, and the audience as well.

Mackey and Hyla, together or apart, are not the voice of their generation. Such a voice does not exist, or has not yet emerged. Indeed, if such a voice exists at all, it will probably not be found in the realm of the string quartet. This most traditional and rich of chamber music genres stands in an interesting position today, seemingly coming to new life and new popularity, but (perhaps because of that very tradition) still lacking the diversity and versatility of so much other contemporary chamber music. A number of ensembles play a great deal of contemporary music: the Lydian Quartet, for whom Mackey and Hyla wrote their works, the Arditti Quartet, the Composers Quartet, the Colorado and Emerson Quartets, the Juilliard. Most of these groups mix their newer works with the traditional canonic repertory; the Hyla Second Quartet, for example, was premiered on a program that included Beethoven's Op. 59, No. 1. But one particular string quartet has made its career by playing almost solely music of this century, and by attracting both audiences and composers to its concerts and recordings. This is the Kronos Quartet, formed in California in the 1970s and, by the 1980s, probably the most famous "new music" group in the world.

The move that propelled the Kronos to their present position was their beginning to record with Nonesuch/Elektra in 1985. Their first recording with Nonesuch, entitled *Kronos Quartet,* set the pace, with quartets by Peter Sculthorpe, Aulis Sallinen, Philip Glass, and Conlon Nancarrow, and an arrangement of Jimi Hendrix's "Purple Haze." The heterogeneity and even unpredictability of the Kronos repertory are evident from this list: music by an Australian, a Finn, two Americans (the second of whom lives in Mexico and is best known for his works for player piano), and a third American who was a major rock composer and electric guitar virtuoso. None of these names appears in most works about modern chamber music, and none, except for Philip Glass and maybe Jimi Hendrix, is known to an average concertgoer or record buyer. A similar mix, although with more twentieth-century standards, obtains in Kronos's later recordings. *White Man Sleeps* (1987) has a scherzo by Ives, the Bartók Third Quartet, two works by the South African Kevin Volans, *White Man Sleeps #1* and *White Man Sleeps #5,* and four pieces by living Americans, *Pano da Costa* by Jon Jassell, *Morango . . . Almost a Tango* by Thomas Oboe Lee, *Amazing Grace* by Ben Johnston, and an arrangement of Ornette Coleman's "Lonely Woman." (Coleman's original "Lonely Woman" was recorded in 1959 by his quartet of sax, trumpet, bass, and percussion.) The recording *Winter Was Hard* (1989) includes Webern's Six Bagatelles, Op. 9, Samuel Barber's Adagio (the second movement of his String Quartet, Op. 11, usually performed by string orchestra as Adagio for Strings), and works by Aulis Sallinen, Terry Riley, Arvo Pärt, John Zorn, John Lurie, Astor Piazzolla, and Alfred Schnittke—again, names for the most part quite new to contemporary chamber music. Finally, the Kronos has dedicated recordings to single works by Steve Reich (*Different Trains*) and Terry Riley (*Salome Dances for Peace*) and to arrangements of the music of Bill Evans and Thelonious Monk, both jazz composer-pianists.

What is most remarkable about the Kronos repertory is not only its variety but also its gripping immediacy. The Kronos performs some of the most dramatic quartets of the twentieth-century canon: the Webern Bagatelles, the Ives Second, the Bartók Third (but not the Second or the Sixth), the Barber Adagio (an extraordinary performance). The group has recorded only one quartet of Shostakovich (the Eighth) and none by Schoenberg, Berg, Hindemith, Milhaud, or the American generation I have posited as postwar classicists: Babbitt, Perle, and Carter. Likewise, the Kronos's contemporary repertory is equally drawn to the unusual, particularly so-called New Age composers who come out of minimalism (Reich, Riley, et al.) and crossover "downtown" composers whose most obvious attributes are not the classical training of the conservatory, such as John Zorn or John Lurie. (The best title on *Winter Was Hard* is Lurie's "Bella by Barlight.")

In a fairly ill-tempered 1989 piece in *The Village Voice*,[57] Richard Goldstein seems bent on explaining the popularity of the Kronos Quartet. He mentions their trendiness, their synthesis (he uses the word "bricolage"), their attempts at "one-world vibe . . . that betrays this group's origins in the mushfields of California." Yet Goldstein grudgingly gives them their due as well, for he recognizes that much innovation in the history of Western music has resulted from incorporating the exotic into the traditional. The Kronos Quartet is a thoroughly traditional group precisely because it is a string quartet (even given its occasional amplification and occasional addition of other musicians). It remains to be seen whether the quartet becomes the standard-bearer of their generation, and whether its repertory is taken up by other quartets. In the meantime, the popularity of the Kronos ensures concert attendance, both by musicians and by people who have never seen a string quartet of any ilk before. Moreover, these concerts are not just trendy; the programs are coherently planned. (If the Kronos does tend a little heavily to New Age for some tastes, there is always something else on the program to enjoy.) Equally important, the playing is first-rate.

In the most general way, many qualities of the Kronos Quartet are those of modern chamber music in general: experimentation (if often mixed with traditionalism), desire for the immediately and strongly expressive, openness to the exotic, eclecticism. But even the Kronos is too limited a group to represent all twentieth-century chamber music. The Kronos Quartet stands to modern chamber music much as this chapter does to the rest of the book. If the string quartet has been slightly dislodged as the *prima inter pares* of chamber music, the emphasis should be on the word *slightly*. Many of the innovations in other areas of chamber music have infiltrated into the string quartet as well. At the same time, the very history and tradition of the quartet as a phenomenon give its present repertory a weight that other genres and ensembles simply lack. The recently reawakened interest in the string quartet— due much more to the proliferation of new quartets than solely to the example of the Kronos—may be a growing traditionalism, a desire to revitalize the mainstream with the fruits of the present, to take the long view and integrate more fully into historical tradition the works of the present. This is another sort of synthesis, one with which the artists of our century have struggled and worked continuously, only rarely ignoring the question. Just as much modern art has been concerned with the manipulation of time and different conceptions of time, so too has it been concerned with the relationship of music of our day to music from the past. The watchword at the end of the twentieth century seems to be reintegration. Whether that desire continues into the next century as well remains to be seen, heard, and experienced.

Notes

1. Pierre Boulez, *Boulez on Music Today*, trans. Susan Bradshaw and Richard Rodney Bennett (London, 1971), 19 (emphasis original).

2. James McCalla, "Sea-Changes: Boulez's *Improvisations sur Mallarmé*," *Journal of Musicology* 6 (1988): 83–106.

3. See chapter 5 for an example of Stravinsky's "steeping himself" in Beethoven's fugues before writing his Concerto for Two Solo Pianofortes.

4. Arbie Orenstein, *Ravel: Man and Musician* (New York, 1975), 156.

5. In Haydn and Mozart, musical motives and ideas are often heard in a variety of guises at the beginnings of works, and the forms they take later on and in concluding sections may be heard as one option settled among many. Or there may be a great variety of motives and melodies. In the terminology of Leonard B. Meyer, there are many more implications in any one musical gesture than there are resulting realizations, and part of the pleasure of listening to this music is the pleasure of listening to inspired, seemingly unrestricted discourse. With Beethoven, in contrast, the music seems from the beginning to be pointing unidirectionally forward. (This is particularly true of sonata movements.) Part of the enormous visceral excitement of Beethoven comes from this unidirectional pointing, unresolved until (usually) the coda, the very last section, of a movement or work: a goal of extraordinary importance has at last been reached. The change comes in the journey, since the listener must perforce accompany Beethoven in his single-minded drama, intent on its end. There is less time for contemplation in Beethoven, less time for a listener to play with a musical idea. This aspect of Beethoven's music was followed by many of his German-speaking successors—only a few, such as Schubert,

Mendelssohn, and at times Robert Schumann and Liszt, did not—while it was resisted by most of the non-German composers. This unidirectionality is, I think, part of what John Cage meant when he wrote that music had "gone wrong" with Beethoven. It was still strongly in force in the early years of the twentieth century.

6. This had been true of Schoenberg's first published string quartet, the Quartet in D minor, Op. 7, about which Alban Berg wrote in his lecture "Why Is Schoenberg's Music So Difficult to Understand?" Berg's answer to his own question was what I have just pointed up, the constant development of motives and the interpenetration of stable and unstable formal areas.

7. See his essay "Brahms the Progressive," in *Style and Idea,* 398–441.

8. In "Brahms the Progressive," Schoenberg discusses at some length Brahms's String Quartet No. 1 in C Minor, Op. 51, No. 1, in which Brahms arrives at a unison F♯ by m. 21. Schoenberg's quartet does the reverse.

9. Ravel does this, as well, in the first movement of his piano trio (see chapter 5).

10. Schoenberg's first wife temporarily left him for a painter. When she returned to Schoenberg, the painter killed himself.

11. Schoenberg, "Rückblick," in Ursula von Rauchhaupt, ed., *Schoenberg, Berg, Webern: Die Streichquartette, Eine Dokumentation,* translated by Eugene Hartzell, program book with the recordings of the complete string quartets of Schoenberg, Berg, and Webern by the LaSalle Quartet (Deutsche Gramophon 419 994-2, 1971), p. 242 (German original, p. 24).

12. The end of the first movement is an obvious example: the cello moves down from G natural to F♯ as the second violin moves up from E♯ to F♯.

13. Schoenberg, preface to Webern's score (Universal Edition). These pieces were written between 1911 and 1913; this introduction was written for their 1924 publication.

14. This is analogous to hearing a movie or play, even an argument, in an unfamiliar language. What seems to be emotional import, even if the specific emotion may not always be clear, is conveyed by the coloration of the speech.

15. It may also be that performers are unable to reconcile great metrical and temporal freedom with what seem to be overdetermined individual notes—overdetermined in pitch, duration, and timbre. Given such precision at the level of the individual note, one might think, the music at the next level up must also be precise, metronomical. The case ought to be the contrary: given the overloading of each individual note, their grouping into phrases might also be "overloaded," freer, full of Viennese *Schwung.* I owe this apercu to the composer Michael Bushnell.

16. There is a no doubt apocryphal story of Webern's writing out the twelve pitch classes and crossing them off as he used each in a piece. When all twelve had been crossed off, the piece was over.

17. This is also true, to an extent, of his music after 1953 and, to a lesser degree, of his neoclassic music. See chapters 2, 3 (for the *Three Japanese Lyrics* and *Three Songs from William Shakespeare*), 4 (*L'histoire du soldat,* Octet), and 5 (Concerto for Two Solo Pianofortes).

18. When these pieces were transcribed as three of the Four Studies for Orchestra (1914–18, 1928), the titles of the first and third were "Dance" and "Canticle."

19. Compare all this to the first movement of Virgil Thomson's Sonata da Chiesa (1926), the "Chorale" (see chapter 4).

20. Written on Ives's manuscript, transcribed in John Kirkpatrick, comp., "A Temporary Mimeographed Catalogue of the Music Manuscripts and Related Materials of Charles Edward Ives, 1874–1954" ([n.p.]: 1973, 1960), p. 60.

21. In the second movement we hear "Columbia, the Gem of the Ocean," "Hail, Columbia," themes from Tchaikovsky's Sixth Symphony, Brahms's Second, and Beethoven's Ninth, "Marching through Georgia," and "Massa's in de Cold, Cold Ground." In the third movement we hear two traditional hymn tunes, "Nettleton" and "Bethany," and the melody of the Westminster chimes.

22. The composer and literary scholar Lawrence Kramer calls such elements as these titles, or even the tunes quoted in the course of the movements, "representational designators." This is not jargon but a highly useful term. Without Ives's titles, for example, one's hearing of this quartet, from its sections through its movements, and the work as a whole, would be quite different (Kramer, *Music and Poetry: The Nineteenth Century and After* [Berkeley and Los Angeles, 1984]).

23. In his landmark study *Music in the 20th Century* (New York, 1966), 33–41, William W. Austin writes of various composers' escape from the "abyss [of] freedom," taking the term from Stravinsky.

24. Many music reviewers still refer to serialism as a "style." It is not; rather, it is a compositional method. The Schoenberg Fourth Quartet is only one example of the stylistic variety and freedom available to the experienced serial composer, exactly analogous to those available to the tonal composer.

25. See, for example, Heinz-Klaus Metzger's liner notes to the LaSalle Quartet's recording *Die neue Wiener Schule: Die Streichquartette* (DG 2720 029, 1971).

26. Results of new and ongoing research may clarify this, of course. See J. Peter Burkholder, *Charles Ives: The Ideas behind the Music* (New Haven, 1985), and Maynard Solomon, "Charles Ives: Some Questions of Veracity," *Journal of the American Musicological Society* 40 (1987): 443–70.

27. Joseph Kerman, *The Beethoven Quartets* (New York, 1966).

28. Halsey Stevens, *The Life and Music of Béla Bartók*, rev. ed. (London, 1964), 171–73.

29. This device for integrating movements is more commonly associated with post–1945 music. It is found in Elliott Carter's 1948 Sonata for Violoncello and Piano (see chapters 2 and 5) and his Second String Quartet (see below).

30. The timings for the recording by the Tokyo Quartet (DG 2740 235), for example, are 11'32", 8'32", and 9'15".

31. This is the coincidence of Stravinsky's "psychological time" and "ontological time." See his *Poetics*, 39–41, and chapter 2.

32. Schumann, "[Chopin's] Sonata in B-flat Minor, op. 35," in *On Music and Musicians*, ed. Konrad Wolff, trans. Paul Rosenfeld (New York, 1969), 140.

33. I dislike this approach, since one might easily move from what the music is to what it is about, losing the music in the process. But I do submit this as a possible way of hearing the Second Quartet.

34. This is exactly the same device and effect as at the first-movement recapitulation in the Second Quartet.

35. "Night music" ("musiques nocturnes") is the title of one of the movements of Bartók's 1926 piano suite *Out of Doors*. Its characteristic sound includes such devices as static, glassy sonorities; the absence of perceived meter and even of beats; the use of very high registers, or unison melodies played in widely separated registers; and original and unusual coloristic devices, even to the privileging of color over pitches (in tone clusters, for example).

36. The formal analysis in the Boosey and Hawkes pocket score, by the composer György Ligeti, is an excellent summary.

37. There is an interpolation very near the end that Ligeti finds to be an "unexpected and grotesque transformation" of the second theme of the movement, "as if on a barrel-organ" (ibid.). He concludes that its significance "remains a riddle." One may also hear it as funny.

38. There may also be a sort of historical prefiguring at work, in that a listener who has heard the Fourth Quartet may be disposed to anticipate an arch form in the Fifth, and will find the predisposition reinforced on hearing the first movement of the Fifth.

39. See, for instance, Ian MacDonald, *The New Shostakovich* (Boston, 1990), Eric Roseberry, *Ideology, Style, Content, and Thematic Process in the Symphonies, Cello Concertos, and String Quartets of Shostakovich* (New York, 1989), and Richard Taruskin, "Who Was Shostakovich?" *Atlantic Monthly* (February 1995): 62–72.

40. Her name is Ruth Crawford on the score, since she had not yet married the American musicologist Charles Seeger. She is variously called Ruth Crawford and Ruth Crawford Seeger.

41. Schoenberg had developed his "method of composition with twelve tones" less than a decade before in Vienna. By 1930–31, when Schoenberg was living in Berlin, the serial technique had become the medium for a number of great compositions.

42. I specify the American East Coast because the string quartet as a genre was much more central to this school than it was in the similarly "advanced" traditions of Europe—represented by Boulez, Stockhausen, Ligeti, and Berio— or California. Perhaps this fact speaks to the essential conservatism (or classicism) of the East Coast academy.

43. I deal with only the first two (of four) because the Third Quartet to my mind requires a live performance, which makes it unsuitable for discussion here, and because I have not yet been able to hear a live performance of the Fourth Quartet.

44. In *The Writings of Elliott Carter,* ed. Else Stone and Kurt Stone (Bloomington, IN, 1977): "Shop Talk by an American Composer," 199–211; "The Time Dimension in Music," 243–47; "String Quartet No. 2 [Program Note]," 273–74; and "String Quartets No. 1 and No. 2 [Program Notes]," 274–79.

45. Carter, "String Quartets No. 1 and No. 2 [Program Notes]," 276–77.

46. Ibid.

47. Carter's word (ibid., 278).

48. ibid., 277, 275, et passim.

49. George Crumb, liner notes to recording of *Black Angels* by the New York String Quartet (CRI SD 283, 1972).

50. Boldface type indicates titles, roman type the character indications at the head of the movements.

51. The "Duo alternativo," here and in No. 9, is a supporting, obbligato, secondary duo, not alternative music.

52. See note 22 above.

53. Lejaren Hiller, liner notes to *Black Angels* in the recorded anthology *The Avant Garde String Quartet in the USA* (Vox SVBX 5306, 1973).

54. The Oxford English Dictionary (2d edition, 1989) defines *hypnagogic* [sic] as "*Properly* [emphasis original], inducing or leading to sleep; in quots. = that accompanies falling asleep." Although a risky title to use, it does describe the music in the same way as the titles of Elliott Carter's *Night Fantasies* (for solo piano) or Bartók's "musiques nocturnes."

55. Steven Mackey, liner notes (CRI SD 526, 1985).

56. Ibid.

57. "Kronos Quartet: Bow Geste," *Village Voice*, March 21, 1989.

Selected Bibliography

Albera, Philippe. "Matériau et composition: sur trois oeuvres de Luciano Berio." *Canadian University Music Review/Revue de musique des Universités canadiennes* no. 4 (1983), 66–94.

Antokoletz, Elliott. *The Music of Béla Bartók: A Study of Tonality and Progression in Twentieth-Century Music*. Berkeley, 1984.

Armitage, Merle, ed. *Schoenberg*. Westport, CT, 1977. (1st publication 1937.)

Austin, William W. *Music in the 20th Century*. New York, 1966.

Babbitt, Milton. *Words about Music*. Stephen Dembski and Joseph N. Straus, eds. Madison, WI, 1987.

Bacht, Nikolaus. "'L'artisanat furieux' und sein Modell: Vergleichende Analyse von Arnold Schoenberg's *Der kranke Mond* aus *Pierrot lunaire* und Pierre Boulez' *L'artisanat furieux* aus *Le marteau sans maître*." *Die Musikforschung* 54 (Apr.–Jun. 2001), 153–64.

Bailey, Kathryn. "Formal Organization and Structural Imagery in Schoenberg's *Pierrot lunaire*." *Studies in Music* (Canada) 2 (1977), 93–107.

———. *The Twelve-Note Music of Anton Webern: Old Forms in a New Language*. Cambridge, UK, 1990.

———, ed. *Webern Studies*. New York, 1996.

Bailey, Walter B., ed. *The Arnold Schoenberg Companion*. Westport, CT, 1998.

Baron, Carol. "Varèse's Explication of Debussy's *Syrinx* in *Density 21.5* and an Analysis of Varèse's Composition: A Secret Model." *The Music Review* 43, no. 2 (1982), 121–34.

———. "What Motivated Charles Ives's Search for Time Past." *The Musical Quarterly* 78 (1994), 206–19.

Bashford, Christina. "Chamber Music," in Stanley Sadie, ed., *The New Grove Dictionary of Music and Musicians*, 2nd edition. London, 2001, pp. 434–48.

Bayley, Amanda. "Bartók's String Quartet No. 4/III: A New Interpretive Approach." *Music Analysis* 19 (Oct. 2000), 353–82.

Béhague, Gerard. *Heitor Villa-Lobos: The Search for Brazil's Musical Soul*. Austin, TX, 1994.

Bernard, Jonathan W. *Composers of the Twentieth Century*. New Haven, 1987.

———. *The Music of Edgard Varèse*. New Haven, 1987.

———. "Problems of Pitch Structure in Elliott Carter's First and Second String Quartets." *Journal of Music Theory* 37, no. 2 (1993), 231–66.

Berry, Wallace T. "Symmetrical Interval Sets and Derivative Pitch Materials in

Bartók's String Quartet No. 3." *Perspectives of New Music* 18, nos. 1–2 (1979–80), 287–379.

Biringer, Gene. "Musical Metaphors in Schoenberg's *Der kranke Mond*." *In Theory Only* 8 (1985), 3–14.

Bleek, Tobias. "'Entrückung: Text und musikalische Struktur im Schlußsatz von Arnold Schönbergs II. Streichquartett." *Archiv für Musikwissenschaft* 57, no. 4 (2000), 362–88.

Bonis, Ferenc. "Erstes Violinkonzert—erstes Streichquartett: ein Wendepunkt In Béla Bartók's kompositorischer Laufbahn." *Musica* 39, no. 3 (1985), 265–73.

Boretz, Benjamin, and Edward T. Cone, eds. *Perspectives on American Composers.* New York, 1971.

Boulez, Pierre. *Penser la musique aujourd'hui.* Paris, 1963.

Boulez, Pierre, and John Cage. *The Boulez-Cage Correspondence.* Documents collected, edited, and introduced by Jean-Jacques Nattiez. Translated and edited by Robert Samuels. Cambridge, UK, 1993.

Brinkman, Alexander Russell, and Martha R. Mesiti. "Graphic Modeling of Musical Structure." *Computers in Music Research* 3 (Fall 1991), 1–42.

Brinkmann, Reinhold, and Christoph Wolff, eds. *"Music of My Future": The Schoenberg Quartets and Trio.* Cambridge, MA, 2000.

Brinkmann, Reinhold. "What the Sources Tell Us. . . . A Chapter of *Pierrot* Philology." *Journal of the Arnold Schoenberg Institute* 10 (1987), 11–27.

Briscoe, James R., ed. *Debussy in Performance.* New Haven, 1999.

Brody, Elaine. *Paris: The Musical Kaleidoscope, 1870–1925.* New York, 1987.

Brown, Jeanell Wise. *Amy Beach and Her Chamber Music: Biography, Documents, Style.* Metuchen, NJ, 1994.

Buckland, Sidney, and Myriam Chimènes, eds. *Francis Poulenc: Music, Art, and Literature.* Aldershot, 1999.

Burkholder, J. Peter. *All Made of Tunes: Charles Ives and the Uses of Musical Borrowing.* New Haven, 1995.

———, ed. *Charles Ives and His World.* Princeton, 1996.

———. *Charles Ives: The Ideas Behind the Music.* New Haven, 1985.

Burt, Peter. *The Music of Toru Takemitsu.* Cambridge, UK, 2001.

Busch, Regina. "Octaves in Webern's *Bagatelles*." *Tempo* no. 178 (Sept. 1991), 12–15.

Cage, John. *For the Birds: John Cage in Conversation with Daniel Charles.* English version by Richard Gardner. Salem, NH, 1981.

———. *Silence.* Cambridge, MA, 1961.

Carter, Elliott. *The Writings of Elliott Carter.* Compiled, edited, and annotated by Else Stone and Curt Stone. Bloomington and London, 1977.

Chrisman, Richard A. "Anton Webern's *Six Bagatelles* for String Quartet, Op. 9: the Unfolding of Intervallic Successions." *Journal of Music Theory* 23, no. 1 (1979), 81–122.

Cogan, Robert. "Science, Music Values and the Study of Music: Mozart, Tibetan Chant, Boulez." *SONUS* 8, no. 2 (1988), 16–36.

———. "Spectrographic Analysis of Musical Design: Fractals in Bartók's 'Melodia.'" *SONUS* 18, no. 1 (1997), 45–62.

Cohn, Arthur. *The Literature of Chamber Music.* Chapel Hill, NC, 1997.

Cohn, R. "Bartók's Octatonic Strategies: A Motivic Approach." *Journal of the American Musicological Society* 44, no. 2 (1991), 279–97.

Cone, Edward T. "Stravinsky: The Progress of a Method." *Perspectives on Schoenberg and Stravinsky.* Benjamin Boretz and Edward T. Cone, eds. New York, 1972.

Cott, Jonathan. *Stockhausen: Conversations with the Composer.* New York, 1973.

Cowell, Henry, and Sidney Cowell. *Charles Ives and His Music.* London, 1969.

Cross, Charlotte M., and Russell A. Berman, eds. *Schoenberg and Words: The Modernist Years.* New York, 2000.

Dahlhaus, Carl. *Schoenberg and the New Music.* Derrick Puffett and Alfred Clayton, trans. Cambridge, UK, 1987.

Dale, Catherine. "Foreground Motif as a Determinant of Formal and Tonal Structure in the First Movement of Schoenberg's Second String Quartet." *The Music Review* 52, no. 1 (1991), 52–63.

———. "Schoenberg's Concept of Variation Form: A Paradigmatic Analysis of 'Litanei' from the Second String Quartet, Op. 10." *Journal of the Royal Musical Association* 118, no. 1 (1993), 94–120.

Daniel, Keith W. *Francis Poulenc: His Artistic Development and Musical Style.* Ann Arbor, 1982.

Davies, Benjamin K. "Inside Webern's Workshop: A Glimpse of Op. 9 No. 6 in the Making." *Tempo* no. 222 (Oct. 2002), 2–7.

Davis, Peter G. "Hammer and Cycle," *New York* (Nov. 14, 1994), 81–2.

De Dobay, T. R. "The Evolution of Harmonic Style in the Lorca Works of Crumb." *Journal of Music Theory* 28, no. 1 (1984), 89–111.

DeVoto, Mark. "Translator's Remarks to Arnold Schoenberg's 'F-Sharp Minor Quartet': A Technical Analysis." *Journal of the Arnold Schoenberg Institute* 16, no. 1–2 (1993), 293+.

Dibelius, U. "Postmoderne in der Musik." *Neue Zeitschrift für Musik* 150 (Feb. 1989), 8–9.

Dobos, Lora Louis Gingerich. "A Technique for Melodic Motivic Analysis in the Music of Charles Ives." *Music Theory Spectrum* 8 (1986), 75–93.

Dossier de presse de Pierrot lunaire d'Arnold Schoenberg. Geneva, 1985.

Downey, John. "Texture as Psycho-Rhythmics." *Perspectives of New Music* 20, no. 1–2 (1981–2), 640–8.

Drude, Matthias. "'Eine reine Familienangelegenheit?' Entwickelnde Variation und Zwölftontechnik in Schoenbergs 4. Streichquartett Op. 37." *Musica* 48, no. 2 (1994), 78–82.

Dunsby, Jonathan. *Schoenberg, Pierrot lunaire.* Cambridge, UK, 1992.

Edwards, Allen. *Flawed Words and Stubborn Sounds: A Conversation with Elliott Carter.* New York, 1971.

Eimert, Herbert, and Karlheinz Stockhausen, eds. *Anton Webern.* Leo Black and Eric Smith, trans. 2nd rev. ed. Bryn Mawr, 1959.

Everett, William A. *British Piano Trios, Quartets, and Quintets, 1850–1950: A Checklist.* Warren, MI, 2000.

Ewen, David. *Composers of Tomorrow's Music: A Non-Technical Introduction to the Musical Avant-Garde Movement.* New York, 1971.

Faure, Michel. *Musique et société, du Second Empire aux années vingt: Autour de Saint-Saëns, Fauré, Debussy et Ravel.* Paris, 1985.

Fay, Laurel E. *Shostakovich: A Life.* Oxford, UK, 2000.

Feder, Stuart. *Charles Ives, "My Father's Song": A Psychoanalytic Biography*. New Haven, 1992.

Ferguson, Donald Nivison. *Image and Structure in Chamber Music*. Minneapolis, 1964.

Folio, Cynthia Jo. "Analysis and Performance: A Study in *Contrasts*." *Integral* 7 (1993), 1–37.

Forte, Allen. "An Octatonic Essay by Webern: No. 1 of the *Six Bagatelles* for String Quartet, Op. 9." *Music Theory Spectrum* 16, no. 2 (1994), 171–95.

Frisch, Walter. *Brahms and the Principle of Developing Variation*. Berkeley, 1984.

———. *The Early Works of Arnold Schoenberg 1893–1908*. Berkeley, 1993.

———. "Music and Jugendstil." *Critical Inquiry* 17 (1991), 138–61.

———, ed. *Schoenberg and His World*. Princeton, 1999.

Gable, David. "Boulez's Two Cultures: The Post-War European Synthesis and Tradition." *Journal of the American Musicological Society* 43 (1990), 426–56.

Gass, Glenn. "Elliott Carter's Second String Quartet: Aspects of Time and Rhythm." *Indiana Theory Review* 4 (1981).

Gena, Peter, and Jonathan Brent, eds. *A John Cage Reader: In Celebration of His 70th Birthday*. New York, 1982.

Gilbert, Janet Monteith. "Schoenberg's Harmonic Visions: A Study of Text Painting in *Die Kreuze*." *Journal of the Arnold Schoenberg Institute* 8, no. 2 (1984), 116–30.

Gillespie, Don, comp. and ed. *George Crumb: Profile of a Composer*. New York, 1986.

Gillespie, Jeffrey. "Motivic Transformations and Networks in Schoenberg's 'Nacht' from *Pierrot lunaire*." *Integral* 6 (1992), 34–65.

Gillies, Malcolm. *The Bartók Companion*. Portland, OR, 1994.

Glock, William, ed. *Pierre Boulez: A Symposium*. London, 1986.

Griffiths, Paul. *Olivier Messiaen and the Music of Time*. Ithaca, NY, 1985.

Gryc, Stephen M. "Stratification and Synthesis in Mario Davidovsky's *Synchronism No. 6*." *In Theory Only* 4 (1978), 8–39.

Gut, Serge, and Danièle Pistone. *La musique de chambre en France e 1870 à 1918*. Paris, 1978.

Haimo, Ethan, and Paul Johnson. "Isomorphic Partitioning and Schoenberg's Fourth String Quartet." *Journal of Music Theory* 28, no. 1 (1984), 47–72.

———, eds. *Stravinsky Retrospectives*. Lincoln, NE, 1987.

Halbreich, Harry. "Analyse de l'oeuvre." In Edward Lockspeiser, *Claude Debussy: sa vie et sa pensée*. Paris, 1980.

Hamlin, Peter. *"Pierrot lunaire" and the New Sound World of Twentieth-Century Chamber Music*. Ann Arbor, MI, 1994.

Hanninen, D. A. "The Variety of Order Relations in Webern's Music: Studies of Passages from the Quartet Op. 22 and the Variations Op. 30." *Theory and Practice* 20 (1995), 31–56.

Harris, Simon. "Chord-Forms Based on the Whole-Tone Scale in Early Twentieth-Century Music." *The Music Review* 41, no. 1 (1980), 36–51.

Harvey, Jonathan. *The Music of Stockhausen: An Introduction*. Berkeley, 1975.

Harvey, Mark Sumner. "Theomusicology: Western Classical Tradition: Rhythm, Ritual, and Religion: Postmodern (Musical) Agonistes." *Black Sacred Music* 8, no. 1 (1994), 178–201.

Hasty, Christopher. "Composition and Context in Twelve-Note Music of Anton Webern." *Music Analysis* 7, no. 3 (1988), 281–312.

———. "Phrase Formation in Post-Tonal Music." *Journal of Music Theory* 28, no. 2 (1984), 179–86.

Hauer, Christian. "La Citazione di una Canzone Popolare Viennese nel Secondo Quartetto d'Archi Op. 10 di Schoenberg: una Interpretazione Insieme Musicale, Spirituale e Socio-Politica." *Musica/Realtà* 15, no. 46 (1995), 51–70.

Headlam, Dave. *The Music of Alban Berg.* New Haven, 1996.

Heinemann, Stephen John. "Pitch-Class Set Multiplication in Theory and Practice." *Music Theory Spectrum* 20 (Spring 1998), 72–96.

Heyman, Barbara. "Stravinsky and Ragtime." *The Musical Quarterly* 68, no. 4 (1982), 543–62.

Hirota, Yoko. "Past and Present Analytical Perspectives on Bartók's Sonata for Violin and Piano, No. 1 (1922): Intervallic Profiles in the Works of Experimentation." *Acta Musicologica* 69 (Jul.–Dec. 1997), 109–19.

Hisama, Ellie M. *Gendering Musical Modernism: The Music of Ruth Crawford, Marion Bauer, and Miriam Gideon.* Cambridge, UK, 2001.

Hitchcock, H. Wiley. *Ives.* London, 1977.

Hoffman, Michael. "Carter's String Quartet No. 2: An Overview Analysis." *20th Century Music* 6 (Jan. 1999), 11–18.

———. "Pierre Boulez's *Le marteau sans maître*: An Overview Analysis." *20th Century Music* 4, no. 10 (1997), 4–11.

Hofmeyer, Günter. *Kammermusik des 20. Jahrhunderts. 1. Zyklus: Deutsche Kammermusik 1918–1933.* Berlin, 1967.

Hoover, Kathleen O'Donnell, and John Cage. *Virgil Thomson: His Life and Music.* New York, 1959.

Hutcheon, Linda. *A Theory of Parody: The Teachings of Twentieth-Century Art Forms.* New York, 1985.

Imberty, Michel. "How Do We Perceive Atonal Music? Suggestions for a Theoretical Approach." *Contemporary Music Review* 9 (1993), 325–37.

Ives, Charles. *Essays before A Sonata, The Majority, and Other Writings.* Howard Boatwright, ed. New York, 1961.

———. *Memos.* John Kirkpatrick, ed. New York, 1972.

Jameux, Dominique. *Pierre Boulez.* Susan Bradshaw, trans. Cambridge, MA, 1991.

Jarman, Douglas. *The Music of Alban Berg.* Berkeley and Los Angeles, 1979.

Johnson, Julian. *Webern and the Transformation of Nature.* Cambridge, UK, 1999.

Johnson, Marc E. "Charles Ives's (Utopian, Pragmatist, Nostalgic, Progressive, Romantic, Modernist) Yankee Realism." *American Music* 20, no. 2 (Summer 2002), 188–233.

Johnson, Robert Sherlaw. *Messiaen.* Berkeley, 1975.

Jones, D. E. "Text and Music in Luciano Berio's *Circles*." *Ex Tempore* 4, no. 2 (1987–8), 108–14.

Kabbash, P. "Aggregate-Derived Symmetry in Webern's Early Works." *Journal of Music Theory* 28, no. 2 (1984), 226–35.

Kabisch, T. "Oktatonik, Tonalität und Form in der Musik Maurice Ravels." *Musiktheorie* 5, no. 2 (1990), 120–5.

Kárpáti, János. "Alternative Structures in Bartók's *Contrasts*." *Studia Musicologica* 23, no. 1–4 (1981), 201+.

———. *Bartók's Chamber Music*. Stuyvesant, NY, 1994.

———. "Tonal Divergences of Melody and Harmony: A Characteristic Device in Bartók's Musical Language." *Studia Musicologica* 24, no. 3–4 (1982), 373+.

———. "A Typical Jugendstil Composition: Bartók's String Quartet No. 1." *The Hungarian Quarterly* 36 (Spring 1995), 130–40.

Kay, Norman. *Shostakovich*. London, 1971.

Kirkpatrick, John, comp. *A Temporary Mimeographed Catalogue of the Music Manuscripts and Related Materials of Charles Edward Ives 1874–1954*. New Haven, 1973.

Koblyakov, Lev. *Pierre Boulez: A World of Harmony*. London, 1989.

König, W. "Der erste Satz der Lirischen Suite von Alban Berg und seine fast belanglose Stimmung: ein Deutungsversuch." *Nuova Rivista Musicale Italiana* 34 (Oct.–Dec. 2000), 576–8.

Kostelanetz, Richard. *Conversing with Cage*. New York, 1988.

———, ed. *John Cage*. New York, 1970.

———, ed. *Writings about John Cage*. Ann Arbor, 1993.

Koto, Takashi. "Basic Cells and Hybridization in Varèse's *Octandre*." *SONUS* 8, no. 2 (1988), 59–67.

Kozinn, Allan. "Music Review: At a Cultural Crossroads, Yo-Yo Ma Becomes a Spice Trader." *The New York Times* (May 9, 2002), B1, B7.

Kramer, Lawrence. *Music and Poetry: The Nineteenth Century and After*. Berkeley, 1984.

Kreysig, Walter Kurt. "Das BACH-Motive als Grundlage für Symmetriebildungen in Anton Weberns Quartett für Geige, Klarinette, Tenorsaxophon und Klavier op. 22." *Musiktheorie* 4, no. 3 (1989), 247–68.

Lake, William Eastman. "Structural Functions of Segmental Interval–Class 1 Dyads in Schoenberg's Fourth Quartet, First Movement." *In Theory Only* 8, no. 2 (1984), 21–9.

Laki, Peter, ed. *Bartók and His World*. Princeton, 1995.

Lambert, J. P. "Ives's 'Piano-Drum' Chords." *Integral* 3 (1989), 30–3.

Lambert, Philip. *The Music of Charles Ives*. New Haven, 1997.

Lang, Paul Henry, and Nathan Broder, eds. *Contemporary Music in Europe: A Comprehensive Survey*. New York, 1965.

Lendvai, Erno. *Béla Bartók: An Analysis of His Music*. London, 1971.

Lenoir, Y. "Contributions à l'étude de la Sonate pour Violon Solo de Béla Bartók." *Studia Musicologica* 23, no. 1–4 (1981), 209ff.

Leong, Daphne. "Metric Conflict in the First Movement of Bartók's Sonata for Two Pianos and Percussion." *Theory and Practice* 24 (1999), 57–90.

Lerdahl, Fred. "Cognitive Constraints on Compositional Systems." *Contemporary Music Review* 6, no. 2 (1992), 97–121.

Lessem, Alan Philip. *Music and Text in the Works of Arnold Schoenberg: The Critical Years, 1908–1922*. Ann Arbor, 1979.

Lester, Joel. *Analytic Approaches to Twentieth-Century Music*. New York, 1989.

Levin, Gregory. "An Analysis of Movements III and IX from *Le Marteau sans maître* by Pierre Boulez." Ph.D. dissertation, Brandeis University, 1975. University Microfilms UM 75–24, 821.

Lewin, David. "Some Instances of Parallel Voice-Leading in Debussy." *Nineteenth Century Music* 11 (1987) 59–72.

Locke, Derek. "Numerical Aspects of Bartók's String Quartets." *The Musical Times* 128 (June 1987), 322–5.

Lockspeiser, Edward. *Claude Debussy: sa vie et sa pensée*. Paris, 1980.

Loskill, J. "Von Wahnwitz und Todesbein: ein Wiener Komödiantenkabinett In Gelsenkirchen; Schoenbergs *Pierrot lunaire* und H. K. Grubers *Frankenstein*." *Opernwelt* 28, no. 3 (1987), 34–5.

MacDonald, Ian. *The New Shostakovich*. Boston, 1990.

Mack, Dana. "Der französische Pierrot: ein Kapitel aus Schoenbergs Kampf um die moderne Musik." *Österreichische Musikzeitschrift* 44 (Jan. 1989), 25–32.

Mackey, Steven. "Music as an Action Sport." *Current Musicology* no. 67/68 (2002), 269–88.

Maconie, Robin. *The Works of Karlheinz Stockhausen*. London, 1981.

Mahlert, Ulrich. "Die 'göttliche Arabeske' zu Debussys Syrinx." *Archiv für Musikwissenschaft* 43, no. 3 (1986), 18ff.

Maske, Ulrich. *Charles Ives in seiner Kammermusik für drei bis sechs Instrumente*. Regensburg, 1971.

Mason, Colin. "Form in Shostakovich's Quartets." *The Musical Times* 103 (1962), 531.

Mathon, Geneviève. "À propos de *l'Aria* de John Cage." *Revue d'esthétique* no. 28 (1995–6), 137–45.

Mawer, Deborah. *The Cambridge Companion to Ravel*. New York, 2000.

Mead, Andrew. *An Introduction to the Music of Milton Babbitt*. Princeton, 1994.

Messing, Scott. *Neoclassicism in Music: From the Genesis of the Concept through the Schoenberg/Stravinsky Polemic*. Ann Arbor, 1988.

———. "Polemic as History: The Case of Neoclassicism." *The Journal of Musicology* 9, no. 4 (1991), 481–97.

Metzer, David. "The New York Reception of *Pierrot lunaire*: The 1923 Premiere and Its Aftermath." *The Musical Quarterly* 78, no. 4 (1994), 669–99.

Mitchell, Donald. *The Language of Modern Music*. New York, 1963.

Moldenhauer, Hans, and Rosaleen Moldenhauer. *Anton von Webern: A Chronicle of His Life and Work*. New York, 1979.

Morgan, Robert P. *Secret Languages: The Roots of Musical Modernism*. Urbana, IL, 1986.

Morrison, Charles D. "Formal Structure and Functional Qualities in the First Movement of Bartók's Violin Sonata No. 1 (1921)." *Music Analysis* 20, no. 3 (Oct. 2001), 327–45.

———. "Prolongation in the Final Movement of Bartók's String Quartet No. 4." *Music Theory Spectrum* 13, no. 2 (1991), 179–96.

Mosch, Ulrich. "Disziplin und Indisziplin: Zum seriellen Komponieren im 2. Satz des *Marteau sans maître* von Pierre Boulez." *Musikforschung* 43, 39–66.

Mumelter, Martin. "Zu den Violinsonaten von Charles Ives." *Österreichische Musikzeitschrift* 48 (Mar.–Apr. 1993), 147–51.

Newark, Cormac, and Ingrid Wassenaar. "Proust and Music: The Anxiety of Competence." *Cambridge Opera Journal* 9, no. 2 (1997), 163–83.

Nicholls, David. *American Experimental Music, 1890–1940*. Cambridge, UK, 1990.

———, ed. *The Cambridge Companion to John Cage*. Cambridge, UK, 2002.

Nichols, Roger. *Debussy*. London, 1973.

———. *Messiaen*. London, 1975.

Niemiller, Klaus Wolfgang. *John Cage und das Zeitproblem in der Musik des 20. Jahrhunderts*. Regensburg, 1990.

Niemiller, Klaus Wolfgang, Manuel Gervink, and Paul Terse, eds. *Bericht über den Internationale Symposion Charles Ives und die amerikanische Musiktradition bis zur Gegenwart*. Regensburg, 1990.

Nyman, Michael. *Experimental Music: Cage and Beyond*. New York, 1974.

O'Loughlin, Niall. "Shostakovich's String Quartets." *Musical Times* 115 (1974), 744.

Orenstein, Arbie. *Ravel: Man and Musician*. New York, 1975.

———, ed. *A Ravel Reader: Correspondence, Articles, Interviews*. New York, 1990.

Osmond-Smith, David. *Berio*. Oxford, 1991.

Ouellette, Fernand. *Edgard Varèse*. Derek Coltman, trans. New York, 1968.

Paccione, P. "Chromatic Completion: Its Significance in Tonal and Atonal Contexts." *College Music Symposium* 28 (1988), 90–2.

Parks, Richard S. *The Music of Claude Debussy*. New Haven, 1989.

Pasler, Jann, ed. *Confronting Stravinsky: Man, Musician, and Modernist*. Berkeley, 1986.

Patterson, David W. *John Cage: Music, Philosophy, and Intention, 1933–1950*. New York, 2002.

Pearsall, E. R. "Harmonic Progressions and Prolongation in Post-Tonal Music." *Music Analysis* 10, no. 3 (1991), 350–4.

Perconti, E. S. "Three Keyboard Pieces by Barbara Kolb." *Women of Note Quarterly* 4, no. 2 (1996), 20–6.

Perle, George. "The Secret Program of the *Lyric Suite*." *The Musical Times* 118 (1977), 629–32, 709–13, 809+.

Perlis, Vivian. *Charles Ives Remembered: An Oral History*. New Haven, 1974.

Perloff, Marjorie, and Charles Junkerman, eds. *John Cage: Composed in America*. Chicago, 1994.

Perry, Rosalie Sandra. *Charles Ives and the American Mind*. Kent, OH, 1974.

Petersen, Peter. "Rhythmik und Metrik in Bartóks Sonate für zwei Klaviere und Schlagzeug und die Kritik des jungen Stockhausen an Bartók." *Musiktheorie* 9, no. 1 (1994), 39–48.

Pople, Anthony, ed. *The Cambridge Companion to Berg*. Cambridge, UK, 1997.

———. "Messiaen: Quatuor pour la fin du temps." *Music and Letters* 82 (Feb. 2001) 143–45.

Porter, Andrew. "Musical Events: Testimony." *The New Yorker* 58 (May 24, 1982), 106–14.

Poulin, Pamela L. "Three Styles in One: Poulenc's Chamber Works for Wind Instruments." *The Music Review* 50, 271–80.

Pritchett, James. *The Music of John Cage*. Cambridge, UK, 1993.

Rauchhaupt, Ursula von, editor. *Schoenberg, Berg, Webern: Die Streichquartette der Wiener Schule, Eine Dokumentation*. Munich, 1971.

Reiner, T. "A Chameleon Called Musical Time: Some Observations about Time and Musical Time." *Context* no. 5 (Winter 1993), 19–20.

Revers. Peter. "Sprachcharakter und Zeitgestalt: Aspekte der Gattung Streichquartett." *Österreichische Musikzeitschrift* 51, no. 4 (1996), 231–42.

Revill, David. *The Roaring Silence: John Cage, A Life*. New York, 1992.

Roeder, John Barlow. "Interacting Pulse Streams in Schoenberg's Atonal Polyphony." *Music Theory Spectrum* 16, no. 2 (1994), 231–49.

Roseberry, Eric. *Ideology, Style, Content, and Thematic Process in the Symphonies, Cello Concertos, and String Quartets of Shostakovich.* New York, 1989.

Rosen, Charles. *Arnold Schoenberg.* New York, 1975.

———. *Sonata Forms.* New York, 1980.

Ross, Alex. "Musical Events: Journey's End." *The New Yorker* (May 27, 2002), 122–3.

Rossiter, Frank R. *Charles Ives and His America.* New York, 1975.

Santa, Matthew S. "Defining Modular Transformations." *Music Theory Spectrum* 21 (Fall 1999), 200–29.

Savage, Roger W. H. *Structure and Sorcery: The Aesthetics of Post-War Serial Compositions and Indeterminacy.* New York, 1987.

Schiff, David. *The Music of Elliott Carter.* New York, 1983.

Schmidt, Carl B. *The Music of Francis Poulenc: A Catalogue.* Oxford, 1995.

Schmidt, Doerte. "The Practical Problems of the Composer: Der schwierige Weg Vom Auftrag zur Uraufführung von Elliott Carters Zweitem Streichquartett." *Die Musikforschung* 48, no. 4 (1994), 400.

Schoenberg, Arnold. *Style and Idea.* Leo Stein, ed. Leo Black, trans. New York, 1975.

———. *Theory of Harmony.* Roy E. Carter, trans. Berkeley, 1978.

Schreiner, Martin. "Expansion as Design in the Fantasia of Elliott Carter's String Quartet No. 1." *SONUS* 12, no. 2 (1992), 11–26.

Seiber, Matyas. *The String Quartets of Béla Bartók.* London, 1945.

Shawn, Allen. *Arnold Schoenberg's Journey.* New York, 2001.

Shostakovich, Dmitri. *Testimony: The Memoirs of Dmitri Shostakovich.* Solomon Volkov, ed. Antonina W. Bouis, trans. New York, 1979.

Shultis, Christopher. *Silencing the Sounded Self: John Cage and the American Experimental Tradition.* Boston, 1998.

Simms, Bryan R. *The Atonal Music of Arnold Schoenberg, 1908–1923.* Oxford, 2000.

———. *Music of the Twentieth Century: Style and Structure.* New York, 1986.

———. "The Society for Private Performances: Resources and Documents in Schoenberg's Legacy." *Journal of the Arnold Schoenberg Institute* 3, no. 2 (1979), 126–49.

Solomon, Maynard. "Charles Ives: Some Questions of Veracity." *Journal of the American Musicological Society* 40 (1987), 443–70.

Spitz, Ellen Handler. "*Ancient Voices of Children*: A Psychoanalytic Interpretation." *Current Musicology* 40 (1985), 7–21.

Stacey, Peter F. *Boulez and the Modern Concept.* Lincoln, NE, 1987.

Starr, Larry. *A Union of Diversities: Style in the Music of Charles Ives.* New York, 1992.

Stein, Leonard, ed. *From Pierrot to Marteau: An International Conference and Concert Celebrating the Tenth Anniversary of the Arnold Schoenberg Institute, University of Southern California School of Music, March 14–16, 1987.* Los Angeles, 1987.

Sterne, Colin C. "Pythagoras and Pierrot: An Approach to Schoenberg's Use of Numerology in the Construction of *Pierrot lunaire*." *Perspectives of New Music* 21 (1982/3), 506–34.

Stevens, Halsey. *The Life and Music of Béla Bartók.* Rev. ed. London, 1964.

Stockhausen, Karlheinz. *Stockhausen on Music: Lectures and Interviews.* Robin Maconie, comp. London, 1989.

Straus, Joseph N. "The 'Anxiety of Influence' in Twentieth-Century Music." *The Journal of Musicology* 9, no. 4 (1991), 430–47.

———. *The Music of Ruth Crawford Seeger*. Cambridge, UK, 1995.

———. "The Myth of Serial 'Tyranny' in the 1950s and 1960s." *The Musical Quarterly* LXXXIII (Fall 1999), 301–43.

———. *Remaking the Past: Musical Modernism and the Influence of the Tonal Tradition*. Cambridge, MA, 1990.

———. *Stravinsky's Late Music*. New York, 2001.

Stravinsky, Igor. *An Autobiography*. New York, 1962.

———. *Poetics of Music in the Form of Six Lessons*. Cambridge, MA, 1970.

Stuckenschmidt, H. H. *Twentieth Century Music*. Richard Deveson, trans. New York, 1969.

Suchoff, Benjamin. *Béla Bartók: Life and Work*. Lanham, MD, 2001.

Swift, Richard G. *Tonal Relations in Schoenberg's Verklärte Nacht*. Berkeley, 1990.

Taruskin, Richard. *Stravinsky and the Russian Traditions: A Biography of the Works Through Mavra*. Berkeley and Los Angeles, 1996.

———. "Who Was Shostakovich?" *The Atlantic Monthly* 275 (Feb. 1995), 62–72.

Tenney, J., and L. Polansky. "Temporal Gestalt Perception in Music." *Journal of Music Theory* 24, no. 2 (1980), 231–5. (On Debussy's *Syrinx*.)

Thomas, Jennifer Swinger. "The Use of Color in Three Chamber Works of the Twentieth Century." *Indiana Theory Review* 4, no. 3 (1981), 24–40.

Thomson, Virgil. *American Music Since 1910*. New York, 1971.

———. *A Virgil Thomson Reader*. New York, 1981.

Tick, Judith. *Ruth Crawford Seeger: A Composer's Search for American Music*. New York, 1997.

Tingley, George Peter. "Metric Modulation and Elliott Carter's First String Quartet." *Indiana Theory Review* 4, no. 3 (1981), 3–11.

Tomkins, Calvin. *The Bride and the Bachelors: Five Masters of the Avant Garde*. New York, 1968.

Toop, Richard. *György Ligeti*. London, 1999.

Unverricht, Hubert. *Kammermusik im 20. Jahrhundert: zum Bedeutungswandel der Begriff*. Munich, 1983.

Van den Toorn, Pieter. *The Music of Igor Stravinsky*. New Haven, 1983.

Walsh, Stephen. *Bartók Chamber Music*. London, 1982.

———. *Stravinsky: A Creative Spring: Russia and France, 1882–1934*. New York, 1999.

Watkins, Glenn. *Pyramids at the Louvre: Music, Culture, and Collage from Stravinsky to the Postmodernists*. Cambridge, MA, 1994.

Wellesz, Egon. *Arnold Schoenberg*. London, 1921.

Welsh, John Patrick. "John Cage's 'Trio' from *Amores* (1943): A Study of Rhythmic Structure and Density." *Ex Tempore* 4, no. 2 (1987–8), 80–92.

Wentzel, Wayne Clifford. "Dynamic and Attack Associations in Boulez's *Le marteau sans maître*." *Perspectives of New Music* 29, no. 1 (1991), 142–70.

White, Eric Walter. *Stravinsky: The Composer and His Works*. 2nd ed. Berkeley, 1979.

Whittall, Arnold. *Schoenberg Chamber Music*. Seattle, 1972.

Wilson, Paul. "Function and Pitch Hierarchy in Movement II of Bartók's Fifth Quartet." *Theory and Practice* 14–15 (1989–90), 179–86.

———. *The Music of Béla Bartók*. New Haven, 1992.

Winham, Godfrey Charles. "Schoenberg's Fourth Quartet: Vertical Order of the Opening." *Theory and Practice* 17 (1992), 59–65.

Winick, Steven David. "Symmetry and Pitch-Duration Associations in Boulez' *Le marteau sans maître.*" *Perspectives of New Music* 24, no. 2 (1986), 280–321.

Wright, Simon. *Villa-Lobos.* Oxford, 1992.

Youens, Susan. "Excavating an Allegory: The Texts of *Pierrot Lunaire.*" *Journal of the Arnold Schoenberg Institute* 8 (1984), 95–115.

Zur, Menachem. "Tonal Ambiguities as a Constructive Force in the Language of Stravinsky." *The Musical Quarterly* 68, no. 4 (1982), 516–26.

Index